INDIANA

SCIENCE

Fusion

fusion [FYOO • zhuhn] a combination of two or more things that releases energy

This **Interactive Student Edition** belongs to

_____

Teacher/Room

_____

HOLT McDOUGAL

 HOUGHTON MIFFLIN HARCOURT

Consulting Authors

Michael A. DiSpezio

Global Educator
North Falmouth, Massachusetts

Michael DiSpezio is a renaissance educator who moved from the research laboratory of a Nobel Prize winner to the K–12 science classroom. He has authored or co-authored numerous textbooks and written more than 25 trade books. For nearly a decade he worked with the JASON Project, under the auspices of the National Geographic Society, where he designed curriculum, wrote lessons, and hosted dozens of studio and location broadcasts. Over the past two decades, he has developed supplementary material for organizations and shows that include PBS *Scientific American Frontiers, Discover* magazine, and the Discovery Channel. He has extended his reach outside the United States and into topics of crucial importance today. To all his projects, he brings his extensive background in science and his expertise in classroom teaching at the elementary, middle, and high school levels.

Marjorie Frank

Science Writer and Content-Area Reading Specialist
Brooklyn, New York

An educator and linguist by training, a writer and poet by nature, Marjorie Frank has authored and designed a generation of instructional materials in all subject areas, including past HMH Science programs. Her other credits include authoring science issues of an award-winning children's magazine; writing game-based digital assessments in math, reading, and language arts; and serving as instructional designer and co-author of pioneering school-to-work software for Classroom Inc., a nonprofit organization dedicated to improving reading and math skills for middle and high school learners. She wrote lyrics and music for *SCIENCE SONGS*, which was an American Library Association nominee for notable recording. In addition, she has served on the adjunct faculty of Hunter, Manhattan, and Brooklyn Colleges, teaching courses in science methods, literacy, and writing.

Acknowledgments for Covers

Front cover: *light echo* NASA/ESA/Hubble Heritage Team (STScI/AURA); *ice cave* ©Tyler Stableford/Stone/Getty Images; *fly* ©Gary Meszaros/ Photo Researchers, Inc.; *bat hitting ball* ©Tetra Images/Corbis; test tubes ©PHOTOTAKE Inc./Alamy.

Back cover: *lasers* ©U. Bellhsuser/ScienceFoto/Getty Images; *water ripples* ©L. Clarke/Corbis; *snowboarder* ©Jonathan Nourok/Photographer's Choice/Getty Images; *Ferris wheel* ©Geoffrey George/Flickr/Getty Images.

Printed in the U.S.A.

ISBN 978-0-547-43849-8

7 8 9 10 0877 20 19 18 17 16 15 14 13

4500415461   CDEFG

Michael R. Heithaus

Director, School of Environment and Society
Associate Professor, Department of Biological Sciences
Florida International University
North Miami, Florida

Mike Heithaus joined the Florida International University Biology Department in 2003. He has served as Director of the Marine Sciences Program and is now Director of the School of Environment and Society, which brings together the natural and social sciences and humanities to develop solutions to today's environmental challenges. While earning his doctorate, he began the research that grew into the Shark Bay Ecosystem Project in Western Australia, with which he still works. Back in the U.S., he served as a Research Fellow with National Geographic, using remote imaging in his research and hosting a 13-part *Crittercam* television series on the National Geographic Channel. His current research centers on predator-prey interactions among vertebrates, such as tiger sharks, dolphins, dugongs, sea turtles, and cormorants.

Donna M. Ogle

Professor of Reading and Language
National-Louis University
Chicago, Illinois

Creator of the well-known KWL strategy, Donna Ogle has directed many staff development projects translating theory and research into school practice in middle and secondary schools throughout the United States. She is a past president of the International Reading Association and has served as a consultant on literacy projects worldwide. Her extensive international experience includes coordinating the Reading and Writing for Critical Thinking Project in Eastern Europe, developing an integrated curriculum for a USAID Afghan Education Project, and speaking and consulting on projects in several Latin American countries and in Asia. Her books include *Coming Together as Readers; Reading Comprehension: Strategies for Independent Learners; All Children Read;* and *Literacy for a Democratic Society.*

Program Advisors/Reviewers

PROGRAM ADVISORS

Rose Pringle, Ph.D.
Associate Professor
School of Teaching and Learning
College of Education
University of Florida
Gainesville, FL

Carolyn Staudt, M.Ed.
Curriculum Designer for Technology
KidSolve, Inc./The Concord Consortium
Concord, MA

CONTENT REVIEWERS

Paul D. Asimow, Ph.D.
Associate Professor of Geology and Geochemistry
Division of Geological and Planetary Sciences
California Institute of Technology
Pasadena, CA

Nigel S. Atkin son, Ph.D.
Professor of Neurobiology
Section of Neurobiology
The University of Texas at Austin
Austin, TX

Laura K. Baumgartner, Ph.D.
Postdoctoral Researcher
Pace Laboratory
Molecular, Cellular, and Developmental Biology
University of Colorado
Boulder, CO

Sonal Blumenthal, Ph.D.
Science Education Consultant
Austin, TX

Monica E. Cardella, Ph.D.
Assistant Professor
School of Engineering Education
Purdue University
West Lafayette, IN

Eileen Cashman, Ph.D.
Professor
Department of Environmental Resources Engineering
Humboldt State University
Arcata, CA

Shanna R. Daly, Ph.D.
Research Fellow and Lecturer
College of Engineering and the Design Science Program
University of Michigan
Ann Arbor, MI

Program Advisors/Reviewers *(continued)*

Elizabeth A. De Stasio, Ph.D.
Raymond H. Herzog Professor of Science
Professor of Biology
Department of Biology
Lawrence University
Appleton, WI

Heidi A. Diefes-Dux, Ph.D.
Associate Professor
School of Engineering Education
Purdue University
West Lafayette, IN

Julia R. Greer, Ph.D.
Assistant Professor of Materials Science and Mechanical Engineering
Division of Engineering and Applied Science
California Institute of Technology
Pasadena, CA

John E. Hoover, Ph.D.
Professor
Department of Biology
Millersville University
Millersville, PA

Charles W. Johnson, Ph.D.
Chairman, Division of Natural Sciences, Mathematics, and Physical Education
Associate Professor of Physics
South Georgia College
Douglas, GA

Ping H. Johnson, Ph.D.
Associate Professor
Department of Health, Physical Education, and Sport Science
Kennesaw State University
Kennesaw, GA

Tatiana A. Krivosheev, Ph.D.
Associate Professor of Physics
Department of Natural Sciences
Clayton State University
Morrow, GA

Louise McCullough, M.D., Ph.D.
Associate Professor of Neurology and Neuroscience
Director of Stroke Research and Education
University of Connecticut Health Center & The Stroke Center at Hartford Hospital
Farmington, CT

Mark Moldwin, Ph.D.
Professor of Space Sciences
Department of Atmospheric, Oceanic, and Space Sciences
University of Michigan
Ann Arbor, MI

Hilary Clement Olson, Ph.D.
Research Scientist Associate V
Institute for Geophysics,
Jackson School of Geosciences
The University of Texas at Austin
Austin, TX

Russell S. Patrick, Ph.D.
Professor of Physics
Department of Biology, Chemistry, and Physics
Southern Polytechnic State University
Marietta, GA

James L. Pazun, Ph.D.
Professor and Chairman
Chemistry and Physics
Pfeiffer University
Misenheimer, NC

L. Jeanne Perry, Ph.D.
Director (Retired)
Protein Expression Technology Center
Institute for Genomics and Proteomics
University of California, Los Angeles
Los Angeles, CA

Senay Purzer, Ph.D.
Assistant Professor
School of Engineering Education
Purdue University
West Lafayette, IN

Kenneth H. Rubin, Ph.D.
Professor
Department of Geology and Geophysics
University of Hawaii
Honolulu, HI

Michael J. Ryan, Ph.D.
Clark Hubbs Regents Professor in Zoology
Section of Integrative Biology
The University of Texas at Austin
Austin, TX

Brandon E. Schwab, Ph.D.
Associate Professor
Department of Geology
Humboldt State University
Arcata, CA

Miles R. Silman, Ph.D.
Associate Professor
Department of Biology
Wake Forest University
Winston-Salem, NC

Marllin L. Simon, Ph.D.
Associate Professor
Department of Physics
Auburn University
Auburn, AL

Kristin Walker, Ph.D.
Assistant Professor of Physics
Department of Chemistry and Physics
Pfeiffer University
Misenheimer, NC

Matt A. Wood, Ph.D.
Professor
Department of Physics and Space Sciences
Florida Institute of Technology
Melbourne, FL

Adam D. Woods, Ph.D.
Associate Professor
Department of Geological Sciences
California State University, Fullerton
Fullerton, CA

Contents in Brief

I can't see wind, but I can see how it moves a kite through the air!

I've never seen gold in its natural form before!

© Houghton Mifflin Harcourt Publishing Company • Image Credits: (t) ©Martin Bennett/Alamy; (b) ©Dan Suzio/Photo Researchers, Inc.

Contents

A thermal photograph can show the different heat levels in a volcano. This is Mount St. Helens.

Unit test date: _____

Luster is a physical property of metal that can make it beautiful and, therefore, valuable.

Assignments:

_____

_____

_____

_____

_____

_____

Contents *(continued)*

I wonder how hot air balloons rise in the atmosphere.

Unit test date: _____

Mountains can affect the climate of an area.

Assignments:

_____
_____
_____
_____
_____
_____
_____
_____
_____
_____

Contents *(continued)*

It's easy to see that people are having an impact on the environment.

Assignments:

_____
_____
_____
_____
_____
_____
_____
_____
_____
_____

This blue frog uses hemoglobin in its red blood cells to get oxygen from air. Human beings do the same thing!

Contents (continued)

Unit test date: _____

During fertilization, male sperm fight to enter the female egg. It's a race to the finish line!

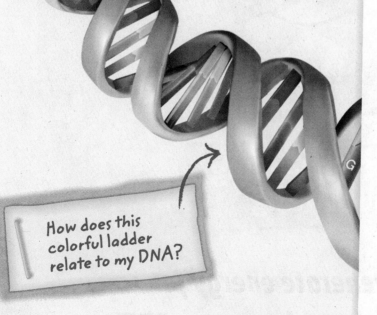

How does this colorful ladder relate to my DNA?

Assignments:
_____
_____
_____
_____
_____
_____
_____
_____
_____
_____
_____

Power up with Science Fusion!

Your program fuses...

Online Virtual Experiences

Inquiry-Based Labs and Activities

Active Reading and Writing

...to generate energy for today's science learner — *you.*

Active Reading and Writing

Be an active reader and make this book your own!

You can answer questions, ask questions, create graphs, make notes, write your own ideas, and highlight information right in your book.

By the end of the school year, your book will become a record of the knowledge and skills you learned in science.

Inquiry-Based Labs and Activities

ScienceFusion includes lots of exciting hands-on inquiry labs and activities, each one designed to bring science skills and concepts to life and get you involved.

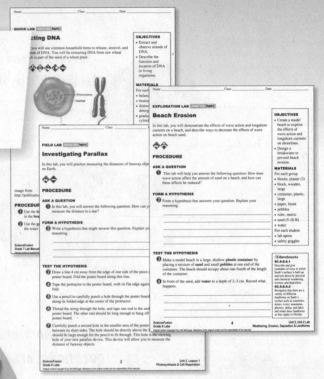

By asking questions, testing your ideas, organizing and analyzing data, drawing conclusions, and sharing what you learn...

You are the scientist!

Online Virtual Experiences

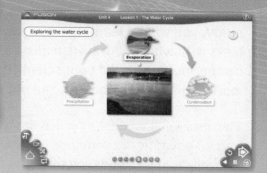

Explore cool labs, activities, interactive lessons, and videos in the virtual world—where science comes alive and you make it happen.

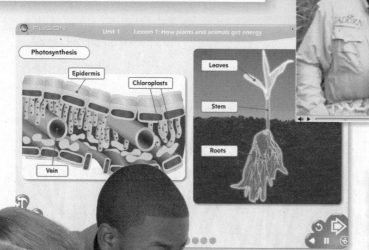

See your science lessons from a completely different point of view—a digital point of view.

Science Fusion!
is a new source
of energy...
just for YOU!

Indiana Standards

An Overview and What It Means to You

This book and this class are structured around the Indiana Academic Standards for Science. As you read, experiment, and study, you will be learning what you need to know to take the tests with which educators measure your progress. You will also be continuing to build your scientific literacy, which makes you a more skillful person both in and out of school.

The tests you'll take are intended to measure how well you learned scientific facts and procedures, and how well you can apply them to situations you might find in the real world. What you remember long after the tests, called enduring understandings, will help you see, measure, interpret, and evaluate many more situations you encounter in life.

The Indiana Academic Standards for Science describe major themes and overarching concepts in science. The standards appear throughout your book. Look for them on the opening pages of each Unit and Lesson.

The next few pages address several questions, including:

- What are the standards underlying the instruction?
- Where is each standard found in this book?
- What makes the standards relevant to you now?
- What kinds of questions will you be asked on the tests?

Notice the **Essential Question** on the Lesson opener. This question is a hint to the enduring understanding you may take away from this lesson, long after you've studied it and passed a test and perhaps forgotten some of the details.

Find the **Core Standards** for the unit on the Unit opener.

Find the **standards** for each lesson on the Lesson opener.

Nature of Science

Students gain scientific knowledge by observing the natural and constructed world, performing and evaluating investigations and communicating their findings. These principles should guide student work and be integrated into the curriculum along with the content standards on a daily basis.

What It Means to You

If you suddenly found yourself somewhere that you had never been before, you would probably look around yourself with curiosity. You would compare what you saw, heard, smelled, and felt to what you knew about other places. You might experiment a little and then draw some conclusions. Then you would be able to describe your surroundings to someone else. You would be thinking like a scientist.

A scientist taking a water sample

Standards

NOS 8.1 Make predictions and develop testable questions based on research and prior knowledge.
Where to Check It Out Unit 1, Lesson 3

NOS 8.2 Plan and carry out investigations as a class, in small groups or independently often over a period of several class lessons.
Where to Check It Out Unit 1, Lesson 3

NOS 8.3 Collect quantitative data with appropriate tools or technologies and use appropriate units to label numerical data.
Where to Check It Out Unit 1, Lessons 1, 3, & 4

NOS 8.4 Incorporate variables that can be changed, measured or controlled.
Where to Check It Out Unit 1, Lesson 3

NOS 8.5 Use the principles of accuracy and precision when making measurement.
Where to Check It Out Look It Up! Reference Section; Unit 1, Lesson 3

NOS 8.6 Test predictions with multiple trials.
Where to Check It Out Unit 1, Lesson 3

NOS 8.7 Keep accurate records in a notebook during investigations.
Where to Check It Out Unit 1, Lesson 3

NOS 8.8 Analyze data, using appropriate mathematical manipulation as required, and use it to identify patterns and make inferences based on these patterns.
Where to Check It Out Unit 1, Lessons 3 & 4; Units 1, 3, 6, 7, & 8, Think Science

NOS 8.9 Evaluate possible causes for differing results (valid data).
Where to Check It Out Unit 1, Lesson 3

NO 8.10 Compare the results of an experiment with the prediction.
Where to Check It Out Unit 1, Lessons 1 & 3

NOS 8.11 Communicate findings using graphs, charts, maps and models through oral and written reports.
Where to Check It Out Unit 1, Lesson 4; Unit 6, Think Science

Sample Question Circle the correct answer.

1 Scientists use different tools to investigate how and why things happen. Some examples of tools that can be used to gather data are: a graduated cylinder, a measuring cup, and a graduated beaker. Which unit might be used for data obtained using ALL of these tools?

A. meter

B. kilogram

C. milliliter

D. grams per liter

The Design Process

As citizens of the constructed world, students will participate in the design process. Students will learn to use materials and tools safely and employ the basic principles of the engineering design process in order to find solutions to problems.

What It Means to You

You are thinking like a scientist when you plan and carry out investigations to solve a problem or answer a question. For example, you use the proper tools and materials in a safe way. And you gather and analyze data and report your findings to the rest of the class.

This chair is designed to be portable.

Standards

DP 8.1 Identify a need or problem to be solved.
Where to Check It Out Units 1, 3, 4, 6, & 7 Citizen Science; The Design Process

DP 8.2 Brainstorm potential solutions.
Where to Check It Out Units 3 & 6 Citizen Science; The Design Process

DP 8.3 Document the design throughout the entire design process so that it can be replicated in a portfolio/notebook with drawings including labels.
Where to Check It Out Unit 6 Citizen Science; The Design Process

DP 8.4 Select a solution to the need or problem.
Where to Check It Out Unit 7 Citizen Science; The Design Process

DP 8.5 Select the most appropriate materials to develop a solution that will meet the need.
Where to Check It Out Units 1 & 4 Citizen Science; The Design Process

DP 8.6 Create the solution through a prototype.
Where to Check It Out Unit 3 Citizen Science; The Design Process

DP 8.7 Test and evaluate how well the solution meets the goal.
Where to Check It Out Unit 4 Citizen Science; The Design Process

DP 8.8 Evaluate and test the design using measurement.
Where to Check It Out Unit 4 Citizen Science; The Design Process

DP 8.9 Present evidence using mathematical representations (graphs, data tables).
Where to Check It Out The Design Process

DP 8.10 Communicate the solution including evidence using mathematical representations (graphs, data tables), drawings or prototypes.
Where to Check It Out Units 4 & 7 Citizen Science; The Design Process

DP 8.11 Redesign to improve the solution based on how well the solution meets the need.
Where to Check It Out Unit 4 Citizen Science; The Design Process

Sample Question

2 While organizing supplies in his science classroom, Dion finds rope, yarn, and sewing thread. All three of these materials can be used to tie or bind things.

Explain a circumstance in which Dion would use rope, but not yarn or sewing thread.

_____

_____

_____

Dion also finds many types of paper, including graph paper, toilet tissue, and poster board.

Select the type of paper that would be most appropriate for drawing a model of the classroom and explain your reasoning.

_____

_____

_____

Dion finds many measuring devices in the room, including thermometers, tape measures, balances, graduated cylinders, metersticks, and spring scales.

Which measuring device(s) can be used for measuring the volume

of a liquid? _____

Which measuring device(s) can be used for measuring mass?

_____

Dion designs and builds a sturdy wooden box to store a fragile piece of laboratory equipment. Explain the kinds of measurements Dion should take to make sure the box meets the storage needs.

Indiana Standards (continued)

Physical Science

Core Standard

Describe how atomic structure determines chemical properties and how atoms and molecules interact.

What It Means to You

All matter is made up of particular arrangements of atoms. The structure of an atom determines how that atom interacts with its environment, and what sorts of arrangements the atom makes with other atoms. The organization of atoms in matter determines the chemical properties of substances, such as reactivity with water and flammability.

Oil and vinegar separating

Standards

8.1.1 Explain that all matter is composed of particular arrangements of atoms of approximately one hundred elements.
Where to Check It Out Unit 2, Lessons 3 & 5

8.1.2 Understand that elements are organized on the periodic table based on atomic number.
Where to Check It Out Unit 2, Lesson 5

8.1.3 Explain how the arrangement of atoms and molecules determines chemical properties of substances.
Where to Check It Out Unit 2, Lesson 6

8.1.4 Describe the structure of an atom and relate the arrangement of electrons to how that atom interacts with other atoms.
Where to Check It Out Unit 4, Lessons 4 & 6

8.1.5 Explain that atoms join together to form molecules and compounds and illustrate with diagrams the relationship between atoms and compounds and/or molecules.
Where to Check It Out Unit 2, Lessons 3 & 6

8.1.6 Explain that elements and compounds have characteristic properties such as density, boiling points and melting points that remain unchanged regardless of the sample size.
Where to Check It Out Unit 2, Lessons 1 & 3

8.1.7 Explain that chemical changes occur when substances react and form one or more different products, whose physical and chemical properties are different from those of the reactants.
Where to Check It Out Unit 2, Lessons 2 & 6

8.1.8 Demonstrate that in a chemical change, the total numbers of each kind of atom in the product are the same as in the reactants and that the total mass of the reacting system is conserved.
Where to Check It Out Unit 2, Lessons 2 & 6

Sample Question Circle the correct answer.

3 Which phrase BEST describes the periodic table?

A. an arrangement of approximately 100 elements organized in groups and families

B. approximately 100 elements classified as metals, nonmetals, and compounds

C. an arrangement of all elements that are metals

D. approximately 100 elements arranged in order of increasing mass

Earth Science

Core Standards

Explain how the sun's energy heats the air, land, and water driving the processes that result in wind, ocean currents, and the water cycle.

Describe how human activities have changed the land, water, and atmosphere.

What It Means to You

The Earth is our home, and the sun is our main source of energy. Energy from the sun drives most of the processes that we see every day. For example, energy from the sun drives weather systems, ocean currents, and the water cycle. While we will not run out of solar energy any time soon, the same cannot be said of other resources. We need to reduce the rate at which we use Earth's resources, and recycle or reuse resources whenever possible. We also need to reduce the pollution that can result from the use of Earth's resources.

Standards

8.2.1 Recognize and demonstrate how the sun's energy drives convection in the atmosphere and in bodies of water, which results in ocean currents and weather patterns.
Where to Check It Out Unit 3, Lessons 1, 2, 3, 4, & 5; Unit 4, Lessons 1, 3, & 5

8.2.2 Describe and model how water moves through the earth's crust, atmosphere, and oceans in a cyclic way, as liquid, vapor, and solid.
Where to Check It Out Unit 3, Lesson 1; Unit 4, Lessons 1, 2, 3, & 5

8.2.3 Describe the characteristics of ocean currents and identify their effects on weather patterns.
Where to Check It Out Unit 3, Lessons 1, & 5; Unit 4, Lessons 3 & 5

8.2.4 Describe the physical and chemical composition of the atmosphere at different elevations.
Where to Check It Out Unit 3, Lessons 1 & 2

8.2.5 Describe the conditions that cause Indiana weather and weather-related events such as tornadoes, lake effect snow, blizzards, thunderstorms, and flooding.
Where to Check It Out Unit 4, Lessons 2, 3, 4, & 6

8.2.6 Identify, explain, and discuss some effects human activities have on the biosphere, such as air, soil, light, noise and water pollution.
Where to Check It Out Unit 5, Lessons 2, 3, 4, & 5

8.2.7 Recognize that some of Earth's resources are finite and describe how recycling, reducing consumption and the development of alternatives can reduce the rate of their depletion.
Where to Check It Out Unit 5, Lessons 1 & 5

8.2.8 Explain that human activities, beginning with the earliest herding and agricultural activities, have drastically changed the environment and have affected the capacity of the environment to support native species. Explain current efforts to reduce and eliminate these impacts and encourage sustainability.
Where to Check It Out Unit 5, Lessons 2, 3, 4, & 5

Sample Question Circle the correct answer.

4 Humans can cause different types of pollution. When fertilizers and pesticides make their way into water systems, which type of pollution has taken place?

A. air

B. biological

C. chemical

D. thermal

Indiana Standards *(continued)*

Life Science

Core Standards

Understand the predictability of characteristics being passed from parents to offspring.

Explain how a particular environment selects for traits that increase the likelihood of survival and reproduction by individuals bearing those traits.

What It Means to You

All living things have DNA. Each parent passes half of his or her DNA to his or her offspring. This is why children and their parents share certain traits. Life on our planet depends on living things reproducing. Successful reproduction depends on how well organisms can adapt to changing environmental conditions. Scientists have succeeded in manipulating the DNA of some plants, such as corn, to yield varieties with more calories and better resistance to environmental conditions, such as disease.

Standards

8.3.1 Explain that reproduction is essential for the continuation of every species and is the mechanism by which all organisms transmit genetic information.
Where to Check It Out Unit 6, Lesson 1; Unit 7, Lessons 1, 3

8.3.2 Compare and contrast the transmission of genetic information in sexual and asexual reproduction.
Where to Check It Out Unit 7, Lesson 3

8.3.3 Explain that genetic information is transmitted from parents to offspring mostly by chromosomes.
Where to Check It Out Unit 7, Lessons 1, 2, 3 & 4

8.3.4 Understand the relationship between deoxyribonucleic acid (DNA), genes, and chromosomes.
Where to Check It Out Unit 7, Lessons 1, & 4; Unit 8, Lesson 1

8.3.5 Identify and describe the difference between inherited traits and physical and behavioral traits that are acquired or learned.
Where to Check It Out Unit 6, Lesson 1; Unit 7, Lesson 4

8.3.6 Observe anatomical structures of a variety of organisms and describe their similarities and differences. Use the data collected to organize the organisms into groups and predict their relatedness.
Where to Check It Out Unit 6, Lessons 2 & 3

8.3.7 Recognize and explain that small genetic differences between parents and offspring can accumulate in successive generations so that descendants may be different from their ancestors.
Where to Check It Out Unit 6, Lesson 1

8.3.8 Examine traits of individuals within a population of organisms that may give them an advantage in survival and reproduction in a given environment or when the environment changes.
Where to Check It Out Unit 6, Lesson 1

8.3.9 Describe the effect of environmental changes on populations of organisms when their adaptive characteristics put them at a disadvantage for survival. Describe how extinction of a species can ultimately result.
Where to Check It Out Unit 6, Lesson 1

8.3.10 Recognize and describe how new varieties of organisms have come about from selective breeding.
Where to Check It Out Unit 6, Lesson 1; Unit 8, Lesson 2

Sample Question Circle the correct answer.

5 Dylan is listing the molecules that make up DNA. Which of these substances is a NUCLEOTIDE BASE in DNA?

A. adenine

C. sugar

B. phosphate

D. uracil

Science, Technology and Engineering

 Core Standard

Identify the appropriate materials to be used to solve a problem based on their specific properties and characteristics.

What It Means to You

In engineering, it is important to construct objects using the right materials. For example, the frame of a car has to be strong enough to carry people and cargo safely but light enough to be energy saving. When you understand the specific properties and characteristics of materials, and how different materials can be combined, you can select the proper materials to use for constructing different objects.

Standards

8.4.1 Understand how the strength of attractive forces between particles in a material helps to explain many physical properties of the material, such as why different materials exist as gases, liquids or solids at a given temperature.
Where to Check It Out Unit 2, Focus on Engineering

8.4.2 Rank the strength of attractions between the particles of room-temperature materials.
Where to Check It Out Unit 2, Focus on Engineering

8.4.3 Investigate the properties (mechanical, chemical, electrical, thermal, magnetic, and optical) of natural and engineered materials.
Where to Check It Out Unit 2, Focus on Engineering

Sample Question Circle the correct answer.

6 Engineers define tensile strength as the maximum force a material can withstand without tearing. Which of the following laboratory procedures would test tensile strength?

A. A rubber tire rotates against a rough surface until the rubber reaches a certain temperature.

B. A giant presser pushes the water from wood pulp to make paper.

C. Copper is melted in a superheated boiler and pulled into a thin wire.

D. Two robotic arms holding a silk thread pull in opposite directions until the thread breaks.

Nature of Science

Nature of Science

Students gain scientific knowledge by observing the natural and constructed world, performing and evaluating investigations and communicating their findings. These principles should guide student work and be integrated into the curriculum along with the content standards on a daily basis.

Skier testing
aerodynamic properties
in a wind tunnel

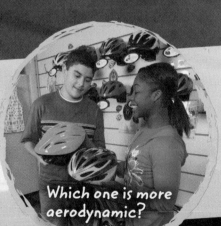

Which one is more
aerodynamic?

What do you think?

Scientists perform tests and experiments to answer questions, increase our knowledge, and improve the products we use. How can you apply scientific thought in your everyday activities?

Indiana Standards

CITIZEN SCIENCE
Weather Myths

People pass on lots of stories about how to predict the weather. Around the country, Groundhog Day is thought to predict when winter will end. The story says that if a groundhog does not see its shadow, and leaves its hole, winter will end in six weeks. The tradition has no basis in scientific fact. But does science support other weather myths?

1 Think About It

Many people believe that the number of times a cricket chirps in a given time period is a way to determine the temperature. Why might this be a believable weather myth?

_____

_____

_____

Count the number of chirps in 14 seconds, then add 40 to get the temperature in degrees Fahrenheit.

② Ask A Question

How can people test whether this is accurate?

As a class, design a plan for testing whether cricket chirps can accurately determine the temperature. Remember that crickets do not chirp all day long.

Things to Consider

☐ Is the temperature the same where your thermometer and cricket are located?

☐ Have you collected enough data and performed enough trials?

③ Apply Your Knowledge

A Determine what materials you will need to carry out your class plan.

_____

_____

_____

_____

B Describe the procedure you will use to run your experiment. What will you specifically do to ensure your data lead to reliable results?

_____

_____

_____

_____

_____

_____

_____

_____

C Carry out your plan to test the cricket chirp theory. Record your data and results in a notebook. Analyze your results and write your conclusion below.

_____

_____

_____

_____

_____

_____

_____

_____

Take It Home

Research other weather myths, especially any that are unique to your area. Do they have any basis in science? Share your findings with your class.

What Is Science?

Any chef will tell you, cooking is a lot like science. Today, there are a growing number of chefs using scientific knowledge to take traditional foods and recipes in new directions. Here, the chef is using super-cold liquid nitrogen to give a new meaning to the term "Hard-boiled egg."

ESSENTIAL QUESTION

What are the characteristics of science?

By the end of this lesson, you should be able to distinguish what characterizes science and scientific explanations, and differentiate between science and pseudoscience.

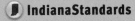

IndianaStandards

NOS 8.3 Collect quantitative data with appropriate tools or technologies and use appropriate units to label numerical data.

NOS 8.10 Compare the results of an experiment with the prediction.

Engage Your Brain

1 Predict Check T or F to show whether you think each statement is true or false.

T   F

☐ ☐ Science is the study of the natural world.

☐ ☐ Scientific explanations should be logical and testable.

☐ ☐ The methods of science can be used in other fields.

☐ ☐ Scientific explanations do not change.

☐ ☐ Creativity does not play a role in science.

2 Compose In this lamp, heating of the liquid at the bottom causes the wax globs in it to rise and fall in interesting patterns. What is a scientific question you could ask about this lamp? What is a non-scientific question you could ask about this lamp?

_____

_____

_____

_____

_____

Active Reading

3 Synthesize You can often define an unknown word if you know the meaning of its word parts. Use the word parts and sentence below to make an educated guess about the meaning of the word *pseudoscience*.

Word part	Meaning
pseudo-	false; pretending to be
science	the systematic study of the natural world

Example Sentence
Their belief that space aliens visited the Earth in ancient times is based on <u>pseudoscience</u> and faulty logic.

pseudoscience:

_____

_____

_____

Vocabulary Terms

- science
- empirical evidence
- pseudoscience

4 Apply As you learn the definition of each vocabulary term in this lesson, create your own definition or sketch to help you remember the meaning of the term.

Character Witness

What characterizes science?

Many people think of science as simply a collection of facts. **Science** is the systematic study of natural events and conditions. Scientific subjects can be anything in the living or nonliving world. In general, all scientific subjects can be broken down into three areas—life science, Earth science, and physical science.

Life science, or biology, is the study of living things. Life scientists may study anything from how plants produce food to how animals interact in the wild. Earth science, or geology, is the study of the surface and interior of Earth. An Earth scientist may study how rocks form or what past events produced the volcano you see in the photo. Physical science includes the subjects of physics and chemistry. Physicists and chemists study nonliving matter and energy. They may study the forces that hold matter together or the ways electromagnetic waves travel through space.

Of course, the three areas contain much more than this. Indeed, the subjects of science can seem practically limitless. As you will see, however, they all share some common characteristics and methods.

Community Consensus

One aspect that really sets the study of science apart from other pursuits is its need for openness and review. Whatever information one scientist collects, others must be able to see and comment upon.

The need for openness is important, because scientific ideas must be testable and reproducible. This means that if one scientist arrives at an explanation based on something he or she observed, that scientist must make the data available to other scientists. This allows others the chance to comment upon the results. For example, a scientist may claim that her evidence shows the volcano will erupt in five days. If the scientist declines to describe what that evidence is or how she collected it, why should anyone else think the claim is accurate?

 **Active Reading**

5 Identify As you read, underline three areas of science.

Visualize It!

6 Predict What kinds of evidence might the scientists in the photo be collecting about the volcano?

_____

_____

7 Explain How might the study of volcanoes affect the people who live near them?

_____

_____

_____

Use of Empirical Evidence

If scientific evidence must be open to all, it needs to be the kind of evidence all can observe. It must be something measurable and not just one person's opinion or guess. Evidence in science must be evidence that can be gained by the senses or empirical evidence. **Empirical evidence** includes observations and measurements. It includes all the data that people gather and test to support and evaluate scientific explanations.

For example, a scientist studying a volcano would visit the volcano to get empirical evidence. The scientist might use specialized tools to make observations and take measurements. Many tools help scientists collect more accurate evidence. Tools often make collecting data safer. For example, few scientists would want to go to the top of the volcano and look down into it. Mounting a thermal camera on an airplane allows scientists to get an aerial shot of the volcano's mouth. Not only does the shot show the detail they want, but also it's a lot safer.

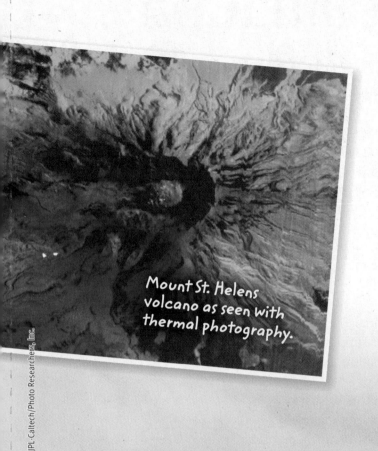

Mount St. Helens volcano as seen with thermal photography.

Scientists use special thermal cameras to take photographs that show the temperature regions of volcanoes.

"Give me an explanation..."

What is a scientific explanation?

Empirical evidence is the basis for scientific explanations. A scientific explanation provides a description of how a process in nature occurs. Scientific explanations are based on observations and data. Beliefs or opinions that are not based on explanations that can be tested are not scientific.

Scientists may begin developing an explanation by gathering all the empirical evidence they have. This could be the observations and measurements they have made or those from other scientists. Then they think logically about how all of this evidence fits together. The explanation they propose must fit all the available evidence.

Often, other scientists will then further evaluate the explanation by testing it for themselves. The additional observations and tests may provide data that further support the explanation. If the results do not support the explanation, the explanation is rejected or modified and retested.

Consider a scientific explanation for how metal rusts. Rust is a compound of oxygen and a metal, usually iron. Oxygen makes up one-fifth of the air we breathe. Therefore, rust may form when oxygen in the air combines with metal. We observe that most rusted metals have also been exposed to large amounts of water. We also observe that the rate of rusting increases if the water contains salt, as it does near oceans. A scientist would propose that water causes metal to rust and that salt increases the rate of rusting. How might you test this statement?

Active Reading

8 Apply As you read, underline the characteristics of a scientific explanation.

How is a scientific explanation evaluated?

So, how would you evaluate the explanation of why some metals rust? Look at the explanation below and start to consider what you know.

First, look at your empirical evidence. Think of all the evidence you could gather to support the statement. A few examples are there for you. Think carefully about what you notice when you look at rusty metal.

Second, consider if the explanation is logical. Does it contradict anything you know or other evidence you have seen?

Third, think of other tests you could do to support your ideas. Could you think of a test that might contradict the explanation?

Last, evaluate the explanation. Do you think it has stood up to the tests? Do you think the tests have addressed what they were supposed to?

> **The Scientific Explanation:**
> Many metals that rust contain iron that reacts with water and oxygen.

The Evidence

9 Identify What evidence do you have about when some metal objects rust?

- I've seen bridges, cars, and many metal objects exposed to the outdoors rust
- I left several garden tools outside that rusted

The Logic

Second, consider if the explanation is consistent with other evidence you have seen. Think about if all metals rust in the same way.

Inquiry

10 Infer Describe how well your explanation fits all of the evidence you have, with all that you know.

- Some metals, like aluminum, don't rust
- Older metals rust more than newer ones

The Tests

Next, think of other tests you could do that would support the explanation.

11 Predict How might you test the conditions under which different metals rust?

- Expose different metals to the same conditions and see if they rust
- Could put metals in regular water and saltwater and note the rate of rusting

The Conclusion

Only after gathering evidence, thinking logically, and doing additional testing do you evaluate the scientific explanation.

12 Evaluate Does this empirical evidence support your explanation? Explain your answer.

Common Habits

What is involved in scientific work?

Even though science and the people who study it are very diverse, scientists have several characteristics in common. Scientists are curious, creative, and careful observers. They are also logical, skeptical, and objective.

You do not have to be a scientist to have these characteristics. When you use these habits of mind, you are thinking like a scientist!

13 Apply Which of the characteristics above do you use most often?

_____

_____

_____

Rachel Carson's careful observations led to laws banning the pesticide DDT.

Careful Observation

Scientists observe with their senses as well as with scientific tools. All observations contribute to the understanding of a subject.

For example, ecologist Rachel Carson spent her entire life observing the natural world around her. She studied the oceans and wrote books and articles about them. She spent years researching and documenting the effects of pesticides, like DDT, on the environment. Her book, *Silent Spring*, drew the world's attention to the problem.

Curiosity

Scientists are curious about the world around them and about the things they observe. Most scientific discoveries are the result of someone asking why or how something happens.

For example, Rachel Carson was curious about all of nature. This curiosity drove her to identify the connections in it. It allowed her to understand how one part affects another.

14 List Name two things you are curious about.

_____

_____

Creativity

Being creative means to be original. Creative people think for themselves and always try to see other ways things might be.

In science, creativity is used when scientists apply their imaginations to come up with new solutions. For example, prairie fires can start suddenly and cause destruction. Instead of trying to prevent them, some scientists often start them under controlled conditions to minimize the damage.

15 Identify Name an activity you do in which you are creative.

_____

_____

19 Apply Research shows that interaction with animals can benefit humans. In the discussion of dolphin therapy to the right, fill in the blanks with the appropriate characteristics scientists are showing.

Scientists saw how well people responded to animals and imagined _____ that these interactions might be helpful in some types of therapy.

Scientists were _____ about whether dolphins could be used as therapy animals.

Early studies showed that dolphin therapy has helped to improve certain conditions in humans. But scientists must be _____. They must not draw conclusions too quickly.

They need to conduct more tests and make _____ to determine the effects of dolphin therapy.

When they have more data, they will assess it _____ before drawing a conclusion.

They will consider all the evidence _____ before making decisions about the advantages and disadvantages of dolphin therapy.

Logic

Thinking logically involves reasoning through information and making conclusions supported by the evidence. Logical thinking is an important tool for the scientist.

For example, toothpaste helps to prevent tooth decay. Some mouthwash also helps to prevent tooth decay. It is logical to think that if the two products are used together they might work even better. This logical conclusion should then be tested.

16 Infer What is another career that relies on logic?

_____

Skepticism

Being skeptical means that you don't accept everything you hear or read immediately. You ask questions before deciding whether you will accept information as factual. Scientists are skeptical of drawing conclusions too quickly. Instead, they repeat observations and experiments, and they review and try to replicate the work of others.

17 Conclude Why should you be skeptical of some advertisements?

_____

_____

Objectivity

Being objective requires that you set aside your personal feelings, moods, and beliefs while you evaluate something. Science requires unbiased observations, experiments, and evaluations. Scientists want their tests to support their ideas. Scientists must be careful not to let this hope influence what they see.

18 Explain Describe a time when it was difficult to be objective.

_____

_____

_____

"Space Aliens built the Pyramids"

How is pseudoscience similar to and different from science?

People have marveled at the pyramids for thousands of years. Even today, scientists still question how ancient people could have built such awesome structures. Some have given a possible explanation for this—the pyramids were built by an advanced race of beings from outer space. Because it is unclear how ancient people could have built the pyramids, supporters of this idea think it provides one possible answer.

Some people will claim to have scientific evidence to support an explanation when in fact they do not. **Pseudoscience** is a belief or practice that is based on incorrectly applied scientific methods. Pseudoscience can seem like real science, but pseudoscientific ideas are based on faulty logic and are supported by claims that can't be tested.

Similarities

Pseudoscience is like science in that it often involves topics related to the natural world. People who believe in pseudoscience have explanations that can sound logical. Like science, pseudoscience uses technical language or scientific-sounding terms. Both science and pseudoscience claim to be based on empirical evidence.

Differences

The biggest difference between science and pseudoscience is that pseudoscience does not use accepted scientific methods. The evidence that supports pseudoscience may be very vague or lack any measurements. Some pseudoscientific claims lack the ability to be tested at all. Other pseudoscientific beliefs are supported only by personal experiences. Unlike scientists, pseudoscientists might claim that results not proven false must be true. This is faulty logic. Scientists must offer evidence for their conclusions. Pseudoscience asks skeptics to prove it false. In the case of the pyramids, pseudoscientists claim the pyramids' complexity is proof of their alien origin. To disprove the claim, you must prove aliens did not visit Earth 5,000 years ago. This is almost impossible to do.

Active Reading **20 Identify** Name two traits of pseudoscience.

_____

_____

Science vs. Pseudoscience

Science	Pseudoscience
Based on logic	Not based on logic or logic is exaggerated
Has testable explanations	Explanations generally not testable
Relies on empirical evidence	Empirical evidence is not available; personal opinions often are used as empirical evidence
Results can be reproduced by others	Results cannot be reproduced by others
Explanations that are not proven false continue to be tested	Explanations that are not proven false are assumed to be true
Explanations are modified by new evidence	Explanations do not change with new evidence

22 Analyze Someone tells you they've heard of a powder that, if worn in a pouch around the neck, will cure a cold. This person claims that the powder has cured everyone with a cold who has worn it. How do you explain to this person that, despite the positive results, this is a pseudoscientific claim?

_____

_____

_____

_____

21 Explain Would it be possible for something to initially be regarded as pseudoscience and then later be supported by science? Explain your answer.

_____

_____

_____

_____

Even today, researchers don't know how ancient people hauled the large stones needed to build the pyramids. Does this prove that aliens did it?

Think Outside the Book

23 Evaluate A popular hoax on the Internet warned of the dangers of the chemical dihydrogen monoxide. The supposed opponents claimed the chemical could cause death if inhaled and severe burns if touched. Do some research to find out what this chemical is. How are the claims made about it like the claims made by pseudoscientists?

Visual Summary

To complete this summary, fill in the blanks with the correct word or phrase. Then use the key below to check your answers. You can use this page to review the main concepts of the lesson.

What Is Science?

Science is the systematic study of natural events and conditions.

24 Explanations in science must be testable and have_____ of other scientists.

25 The _____ collected in scientific investigations is often in the form of measurements.

Scientists may study very different things, but they share many common traits.

26 Scientists use empirical evidence, logical thinking, and tests to_____ a scientific explanation.

27 Scientists are _____ about the subjects they study.

Science and pseudoscience both deal with the natural world, but pseudoscience only deceptively appears to be science.

28 Many claims of pseudoscience are not refutable because they can't be _____

Answers: 24 consensus; 25 empirical evidence; 26 evaluate; 27 curious; 28 tested

29 **Hypothesize** How might the characteristics of a scientist be displayed in a person of your age?

Lesson Review

Vocabulary

Fill in the blank with the term that best completes the following sentences.

1 _____ is the systematic study of the natural world.

2 _____ is often mistakenly regarded as being based on science.

3 _____ _____ is the name for the observations and data on which a scientific explanation can be based.

Key Concepts

4 Describe What are two things that characterize the practice of science?

_____

_____

_____

5 Sequence What are the three steps scientists take to evaluate a scientific explanation?

_____

_____

_____

_____

6 Describe What are six traits of a good scientific observer?

_____

_____

_____

_____

_____

7 Justify Why is it good for scientists to be skeptical?

_____

_____

_____

_____

Critical Thinking

Use the table below to answer the following questions.

Characteristic	Science	Pseudoscience
Concerns the natural world		
Explanations can sound logical		
Results can always be tested by others		
Explanations can be proven false		
Allows personal opinions to be used as evidence		

8 Assess Place an "x" in the appropriate box if the characteristic could describe science, pseudoscience, or both. What might this tell you about the relationship between science and pseudoscience?

_____

_____

_____

_____

_____

9 Judge Good scientists use their imagination. What do you think is the difference between being imaginative in doing science and doing pseudoscience?

_____

_____

_____

_____

_____

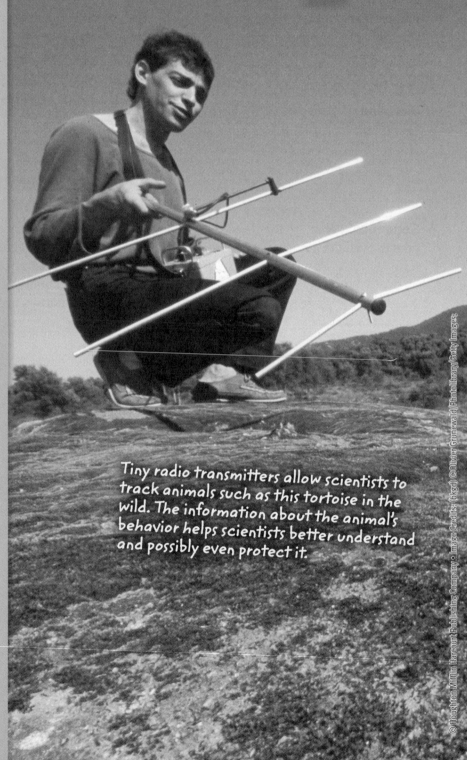

Scientific Knowledge

ESSENTIAL QUESTION

How do scientists develop explanations?

By the end of this lesson, you should be able to analyze how scientists chose their methods, develop explanations, and identify support for a theory.

Tiny radio transmitters allow scientists to track animals such as this tortoise in the wild. The information about the animal's behavior helps scientists better understand and possibly even protect it.

Engage Your Brain

1 Describe Fill in the blank with the word or phrase that you think correctly completes the following sentences.

Scientists can study in the field or in the _____.

A good scientific theory is often_____ when new evidence is found but is rarely completely rejected.

The results of a scientific investigation either support or do not support a claim; they do not offer conclusive _____

2 Hypothesize Describe how you might study the butterfly coming out of the cocoon. What actions would you take? What tools would you use? What might you want to avoid doing?

_____

_____

_____

_____

_____

_____

 Active Reading

3 Apply Many scientific words such as *method* have everyday meanings. Use context clues to write your own definition for the meaning of the word *method*.

Example Sentence
Gloria felt there was only one <u>method</u> for cooking spaghetti.

_____

_____

Vocabulary

4 Identify As you read, place a question mark next to any words that you don't understand. When you finish reading the lesson, go back and review the words that you marked. If the information is still confusing, consult a classmate or a teacher.

Method
Acting

How do scientists choose their methods?

Active Reading

5. Identify As you read, underline examples of tools used in scientific investigations.

Scientists plan investigations to address a specific problem or question. The goal is to come up with a scientific explanation. Each problem or question is unique and so requires a unique method and the proper tools.

You wouldn't lock yourself in a closet to study the birds in your neighborhood. You wouldn't use a microscope to measure the force propelling a model rocket. Science also has methods and tools to study different kinds of problems. Learning to be a scientist is learning how to use these methods and tools properly.

Visualize It!

6 Infer Scientists have all kinds of tools available to them. They select them based on what they study. Can you tell where or how scientist might use the tools in each of the two photos?

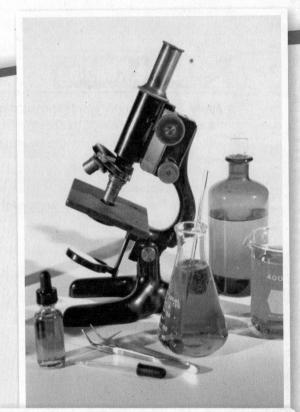

A
_____
_____
_____
_____

B
_____
_____
_____
_____

By the Tools Available

Scientists did not know about cells before there was a microscope. No one had seen the moons of the planet Jupiter before there was the telescope. Severe weather tracking and prediction reached a new level of sophistication with the invention of doppler radar. Scientists need their tools.

Scientists, however, know that they can't always have the tools they may need. Some might be too expensive. Others simply may not exist. So, scientists also need to be creative in the ways they use their tools. For example, astronomers study the light from a star to get an idea of its chemical makeup. Similarly, geologists study what Earth's interior is like by looking at seismograph readings during an earthquake. Tools are only useful if the scientist using them can interpret the data they provide. This skill is a large part of the education of a scientist.

By the Subject Under Study

Generally, scientific investigations fall into two types: experiments and fieldwork. Experiments involve scientists controlling different variables during an investigation. Experiments usually are done under very precise and controlled conditions in a laboratory. Physicists and chemists generally do a lot of experiments.

In contrast, scientists doing fieldwork make observations of what is around them. They watch and observe and try to make sense of what they see. Instead of controlling variables, they try to determine what variables are at work and how they relate to each other. A large part of doing fieldwork is often coming to understand the variables that exist. Biologists and geologists generally do a lot of fieldwork. Sometimes, a scientist will do fieldwork and then take a specimen back to a laboratory to do more testing.

Visualize It!

7 Identify For each photo, identify some tools a scientist might use to study the subject of the photo. Use examples from the photos on the other page for suggestions.

A
_____
_____
_____
_____

B
_____
_____
_____
_____

Well, Prove It!

How do scientific theories become accepted?

In science, a theory is not the same as an educated guess. A theory is not an explanation for a single fact. A scientific *theory* is a system of ideas that explains many related observations and is supported by a large body of evidence acquired through scientific investigation. Scientific theories may be modified but are rarely rejected.

Being Supported by Evidence

About 65 million years ago, dinosaurs and many other organisms suddenly became extinct. Scientists have offered many explanations for why this happened, from widespread disease to sudden climate change.

In the 1970s, Walter and Luis Alvarez found a thin layer of iridium-rich clay at various places on Earth. These layers dated to 65 million years ago, the same time as the mass extinction. Iridium is a rare element on Earth but is found in large amounts in meteorites. The Alvarezes proposed that perhaps Earth had been struck by a large meteorite at that time. They proposed that this massive impact was what caused the dinosaurs' extinction.

In the 1990s, evidence of a crater of the right size, type, and age was found near the city of Chicxulub (CHIK-shuh-loob) in Mexico. With this evidence, most scientists agreed that a meteorite impact did play a role in the extinction of the dinosaurs.

This rock specimen was collected from the Chicxulub crater. Scientists used samples like this to determine when the meteorite struck Earth. The map shows the location of the crater.

Incorporating New Evidence

Many scientists were skeptical that a single meteorite impact could result in a mass extinction. Further research was needed.

Evidence was found of major volcanic eruptions in India occurring at the end of the dinosaur age. Volcanic ash in the atmosphere can block sunlight and contribute to global cooling. Thus, many scientists thought that volcanoes were the main cause of the mass extinction, and a volcanic-eruption explanation was put forth. But further research showed that these volcanoes had been erupting for about 500,000 years before the Chicxulub impact without having a massive effect on the global environment.

For years scientists studied the evidence using tools and technology from many different fields. Recently, scientists around the world have come to agree that the Chicxulub impact was most likely the trigger that caused tidal waves, earthquakes, landslides, and blasts of dust that, together with the volcanic ash that was already present, darkened the skies. This led to global cooling and reduced plant life, which killed the dinosaurs. With the evidence unified into a well-supported explanation, the meteorite impact explanation for dinosaur extinction could now be called a theory.

The Chicxulub meteorite was about 6 mi (10 km) in diameter. It formed a crater about 3300 ft (1000 m) deep and 110 mi (180 km) wide. The meteorite's impact triggered waves thousands of feet high and darkened the skies with dust.

The modern site for the Chicxulub crater is found buried under limestone in the Yucatan peninsula of Mexico. Finding the crater was evidence in support of the meteorite impact theory.

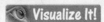

Chicxulub Crater

Visualize It!

10 Infer Why would the Chicxulub crater be covered up now?

_____

_____

How can you know who's right?

The most reliable scientific information is found in professional science journals. These contain articles written and reviewed by other scientists. The reason the information is reliable is simple. It has been checked and rechecked by experts in the same area of science as the journal articles. The downside to reading scientific journals is that they are not easy to understand. They contain many words that nonscientists may not recognize.

You should be very cautious of accepting scientific explanations from advertisers or anyone trying to sell you something. They can be more concerned with getting you to buy their products than with teaching you science.

When you read anything, or assess any scientific claim, you need to ask yourself if it makes sense logically. You should always think critically. When presented with a claim, ask yourself whether the results support it. Do the results agree with what you know about the world? Remember, scientists do not claim to prove anything. Scientists attempt to provide an explanation that agrees with the results of observation and testing.

11 Identify As you read, underline an example of what you need to be aware of when reading a scientific explanation.

12 Appraise Conduct library or Internet research to investigate the scientific claims below. Check the appropriate box according to whether you find the theory is supported or not supported by scientific evidence.

The impact of a large meteorite caused the extinction of the dinosaurs.	☐ Results support ☐ Results fail to support Why? _____ _____
Tests have shown that water exists on Mars and the moon.	☐ Results support ☐ Results fail to support Why? _____ _____
The moon is made of blue cheese.	☐ Results support ☐ Results fail to support Why? _____ _____

A Theory for the Birds

Dinosaurs Take Flight

The fossil *archaeopteryx*, shown to the right, gave the first solid evidence linking dinosaurs to modern birds. Although it had wings and feathers and may even have been able to fly, it seems to be more dinosaur than bird. It had jaws with teeth, three-fingered claws, and a tail.

Gone But Not Forgotten

Not all dinosaurs of the past were large, like the ones we see reconstructed in museums. Some were small. *Archaeopteryx* was about as big as a medium-sized dog.

Family Resemblance?

Pigeons are thought to be one modern bird that closely resembles its ancient counterpart. Few scientists today debate the dinosaur origins of birds. They do, however, debate how it may have occurred.

Extend

Inquiry

13 Determine Do the fossil remains appear to support or fail to support the idea that today's birds are the descendants of dinosaurs?

14 Relate How might the theory of dinosaurs' relation to birds be modified?

15 Infer Recent DNA evidence shows that dinosaurs and birds are genetically closer than either are to alligators. What does this say about the strength of the theory that birds and dinosaurs are related?

Visual Summary

To complete this summary, fill in the blanks with the correct word or phrase. Then use the key below to check your answers. You can use this page to review the main concepts of the lesson.

Scientific Knowledge

Scientists in different fields use different methods to develop scientific explanations.

16 What might a scientist be doing with the tools shown below?

_____

Good scientific theories are supported by a lot of evidence.

17 A good scientific theory is often _____ with new evidence but is rarely discarded.

18 Scientists don't claim to _____ the theory. They just claim that the results _____ it.

Answers: 16 lab work/experimenting; 17 modified; 18 prove; support

19 **Integrate** Why do you think scientists claim to offer only supporting evidence for a theory and not proof?

Lesson Review

Vocabulary

Fill in the blank with the term that best completes the following sentence.

1 An explantion in science that has a lot of evidence to back it up is a scientific

_____

2 Scientists never say a theory is proven or not. They only say if the evidence

_____ or _____ it.

Key Concepts

3 List What are two types of scientific investigations?

_____

_____

4 Infer You've been assigned to observe the habits of the birds living in your neighborhood. What tools might you take along?

_____

_____

_____

5 Describe What kinds of tools might you use in a laboratory?

_____

_____

6 Judge Any time a scientific theory is challenged, it means it's not a good theory. Do you agree with this statement? Explain.

_____

_____

_____

_____

7 Discriminate Why would you be cautious of scientific information you hear from advertisers?

_____

_____

Critical Thinking

Use the photo below to answer the following questions.

8 Relate What type of investigation would a scientist studying this sinkhole use? What tools might be used to study it?

_____

_____

_____

9 Apply What are some questions a scientist might want to find out about this sinkhole?

_____

_____

_____

_____

10 Assess Do you think it's wise for scientists not to accept a theory immediately, even if the theory has a lot of evidence to support it?

_____

_____

_____

_____

Scientific Investigations

ESSENTIAL QUESTION

How do scientists discover things?

By the end of this lesson, you should be able to summarize the processes and characteristics of different kinds of scientific investigations.

Indiana Standards

NOS 8.1 Make predictions and develop testable questions based on research and prior knowledge.

NOS 8.2 Plan and carry out investigations as a class, in small groups or independently often over a period of several class lessons.

NOS 8.3 Collect quantitative data with appropriate tools or technologies and use appropriate units to label numerical data.

NOS 8.4 Incorporate variables that can be changed, measured or controlled.

NOS 8.5 Use the principles of accuracy and precision when making measurements.

NOS 8.6 Test predictions with multiple trials.

NOS 8.7 Keep accurate records during investigations.

NOS 8.8 Analyze data, using appropriate mathematical manipulation as required, and use it to identify patterns and make inferences based on these patterns.

NOS 8.9 Evaluate possible causes for differing results (valid data).

NOS 8.10 Compare the results of an experiment with the prediction.

This scientist is studying DNA, the molecule of life!

Engage Your Brain

1 Discriminate Circle the word or phrase that best completes the following sentences.

A *hypothesis / dependent variable* is a possible explanation of a scientific problem.

Scientists conduct controlled experiments because this method enables them to test the effects of a single *variable / theory*.

Graphing of results is most often done as part of *writing hypotheses / analyzing data*.

Making observations *in the field / in laboratories* allows a scientist to collect data about wildlife in their natural environments.

2 Explain Draw a picture of what you think a scientific investigation might look like. Write a caption to go with your picture.

Active Reading

3 Synthesize Many English words have their roots in other languages. Use the Latin words below to make an educated guess about the meaning of the words *experiment* and *observation*.

Latin word	Meaning
experiri	to try
observare	to watch

Example sentence:
Shaun's favorite <u>experiment</u> involved pouring vinegar onto baking soda.

Experiment:

_____

_____

Example sentence:
Telescopes are used to make <u>observations</u>.

Observation:

_____

_____

Vocabulary Terms

- experiment
- observation
- hypothesis
- independent variable
- dependent variable
- data

4 Apply As you learn the definition of each vocabulary term in this lesson, write a sentence that includes the term to help you remember it.

Testing, Testing, 1, 2, 3

What are some parts that make up scientific investigations?

An **experiment** is an organized procedure to study something under controlled conditions. Scientists often investigate the natural world through experiments. But scientists must learn about many things through observation. **Observation** is the process of obtaining information by using the senses. The term can also refer to the information obtained by using the senses. Scientific investigations may also involve the use of models, which are representations of an object or system.

Elements of Investigations

Hypothesis

A **hypothesis** (hy•PAHTH•eh•sys) is a testable idea or explanation that leads to scientific investigation. A scientist may think of a hypothesis after making observations or after reading findings from other scientists' investigations.

Hypotheses must be carefully constructed so they can be tested in a practical and meaningful way. For example, suppose you find a bone fossil, and you form the hypothesis that it came from a dinosaur that lived 200 million years ago. You might test your hypothesis by comparing the fossil to other fossils that have been found and by analyzing the fossil to determine its age.

If an investigation does not support a hypothesis, it is still useful. The information from the investigation can help scientists form a better hypothesis. Scientists may go through many cycles of testing and analysis before they arrive at a hypothesis that is supported.

Active Reading **5 Explain** Why should hypotheses be testable?

_____

_____

_____

This young plant is growing in a hostile environment.

Visualize It!

6 Infer Write a hypothesis offering a possible explanation of what will happen to the plant above.

_____

_____

_____

Independent and Dependent Variables

A variable is any factor that can change in a scientific investigation. An **independent variable** is the factor that is deliberately manipulated. A **dependent variable** changes as a result of manipulation of one or more independent variables.

Imagine that you want to test the hypothesis that increasing the heat under a pot of water will cause the water to boil faster. You fill three pots with the same amount of water, then heat them until the water boils. The independent variable is the amount of heat. The dependent variable is the time it takes for the water to boil. You measure this variable for all three pots to determine whether your hypothesis is supported.

If possible, a controlled experiment should have just one independent variable. Scientists try to keep other variables constant, or unchanged, so they do not affect the results. For example, in the experiment described above, both pots should be made of the same material because some materials change temperature more easily than others.

Observations and Data

Data are information gathered by observation or experimentation that can be used in calculating or reasoning. This information may be anything that a scientist perceives through the senses or detects through instruments.

In an investigation, everything a scientist observes must be recorded. The setup and procedures need to be recorded. By carefully recording this information, scientists make sure they will not forget anything.

Scientists analyze data to determine the relationship between the independent and dependent variables in an investigation. Then they draw conclusions about whether the data support the investigation's hypothesis.

---

7 Apply Suppose you want to test the hypothesis that plants grow taller when they receive more sunlight. Identify an independent variable and a dependent variable for this investigation.

_____

_____

_____

_____

_____

You may have thought that the plant at the left will die. But as this photograph shows, plants can get enough nutrients to thrive under similar conditions.

Many Methods

What are some scientific methods?

Conducting experiments and other scientific investigations is not like following a cookbook recipe. Scientists do not always use the same steps in every investigation or use steps in the same order. They may even repeat some of the steps. The following graphic shows one path that a scientist might follow while conducting an experiment.

👁 Visualize It!

8 Diagram Using a highlighter, trace the path a scientist might follow if the data from an experiment did not support the hypothesis.

Defining a Problem

After making observations or reading scientific reports, a scientist might be curious about some unexplained aspect of a topic. A scientific problem is a specific question that a scientist wants to answer. The problem must be well-defined, or precisely stated, so that it can be investigated.

Planning an Investigation

A scientific investigation must be carefully planned so that it tests a hypothesis in a meaningful way. Scientists need to decide whether an investigation should be done in the field or in a laboratory. They must also determine what equipment and technology are required and how materials for the investigation will be obtained.

Forming a Hypothesis and Making Predictions

When scientists form a hypothesis, they are making an educated guess about a problem. A hypothesis must be tested to see if it is true. Before testing a hypothesis, scientists usually make predictions about what will happen in an investigation.

Identifying Variables

The independent variable of an experiment is identified in the hypothesis. But scientists need to decide how the independent variable will change. They also must identify other variables that will be controlled. In addition, scientists must determine how they will measure the results of the experiment. The dependent variable often can be measured in more than one way. For example, if the dependent variable is fish health, scientists could measure size, weight, or number of offspring.

Collecting and Organizing Data

The data collected in an investigation must be recorded and properly organized so that they can be analyzed. Data such as measurements and numbers are often organized into tables, spreadsheets, or graphs.

Interpreting Data and Analyzing Information

After they finish collecting data, scientists must analyze this information. Their analysis will help them draw conclusions about the results. Scientists may have different interpretations of the same data because they analyze it using different methods.

Drawing and Defending Conclusions

Scientists conclude whether the results of their investigation support the hypothesis. If the hypothesis is not supported, scientists may think about the problem some more and try to come up with a new hypothesis to test. Or they may repeat an experiment to see if any mistakes were made. When they publish the results of their investigation, scientists must be prepared to defend their conclusions if they are challenged by other scientists.

Life Lessons

Do these birds learn their songs from older birds? Or is their singing genetic?

How are scientific methods used?

Scientific methods are used in physical, life, and earth sciences. Which methods are used depends on the type of investigation that is to be conducted.

Different Situations Require Different Methods

Scientists choose the setting for an investigation very carefully. Some problems are suited for field investigations. For example, many life scientists work in the field in order to study living things in their natural habitat. Many geologists begin in the field, collecting rocks and samples. But, those same geologists might then study their samples in a laboratory, where conditions can be controlled.

Sometimes scientists study things that are very large, very small, or that occur over a very long period of time. In these cases, scientists can use models in their investigations. A scientific model is a representation of an object or a process that allows scientists to study something in detail. Scientists can conduct experiments and make observations using models.

Think Outside the Book Inquiry

9 Describe Do research to learn about a new hypothesis that has replaced an older explanation of something in the natural world. Describe the process that led to this change in thinking.

When finches were first isolated, they didn't sing like wild finches. But later generations of isolated finches sang just like wild birds.

10 Identify As you read, underline the scientific methods used in the study.

Scientific Methods Are Used in Life Science

Life scientists use scientific methods to study how traits are passed from parents to offspring.

One team of scientists recently studied birds called zebra finches. Zebra finches learn songs by imitating the singing of older relatives. But the scientists thought that genes might play a role in how the birds learn their songs.

To test this hypothesis, they isolated a group of young zebra finches from older birds. When these young birds grew up, they sang differently than wild finches did. Then, the scientists placed another group of young males in with the isolated finches. The younger finches imitated the songs of the older ones, but the songs were slightly different. As the scientists continued to add new groups of young finches in with the isolated ones, each new group started to sing more like wild finches. The scientists concluded that genes influence the way zebra finches learn how to sing.

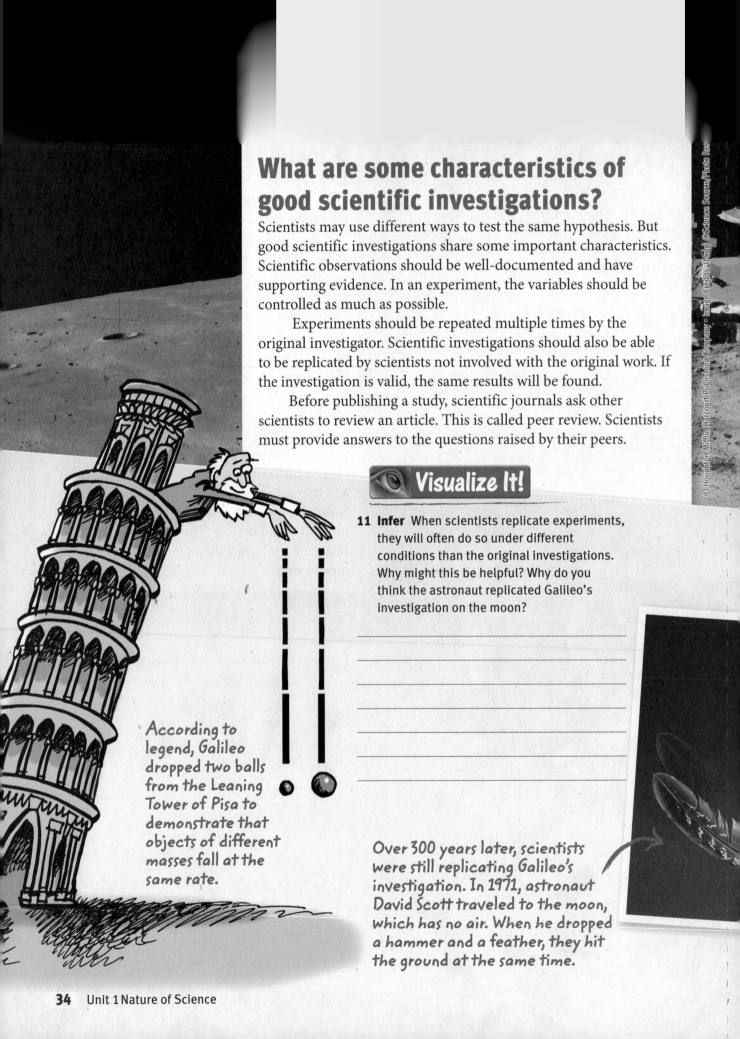

What are some characteristics of good scientific investigations?

Scientists may use different ways to test the same hypothesis. But good scientific investigations share some important characteristics. Scientific observations should be well-documented and have supporting evidence. In an experiment, the variables should be controlled as much as possible.

Experiments should be repeated multiple times by the original investigator. Scientific investigations should also be able to be replicated by scientists not involved with the original work. If the investigation is valid, the same results will be found.

Before publishing a study, scientific journals ask other scientists to review an article. This is called peer review. Scientists must provide answers to the questions raised by their peers.

Visualize It!

11 Infer When scientists replicate experiments, they will often do so under different conditions than the original investigations. Why might this be helpful? Why do you think the astronaut replicated Galileo's investigation on the moon?

_____

_____

_____

_____

_____

_____

According to legend, Galileo dropped two balls from the Leaning Tower of Pisa to demonstrate that objects of different masses fall at the same rate.

Over 300 years later, scientists were still replicating Galileo's investigation. In 1971, astronaut David Scott traveled to the moon, which has no air. When he dropped a hammer and a feather, they hit the ground at the same time.

How can you evaluate the quality of scientific information?

Scientific information is available on the Internet, on television, and in magazines. Some sources are more trustworthy than others. The most reliable scientific information is published in scientific journals. However, these articles are often difficult to understand. Sometimes, summaries of these articles are published for the public.

Many scientists write books for the general public. These publications are trustworthy if the scientist is writing about his field of study. Reliable books may also be written by people who aren't scientists but who are knowledgeable about a particular field.

Usually, the most reliable Internet sources are government or academic webpages. Commercial webpages are often unreliable because they are trying to sell something.

12 Apply Find two sources of information about the same scientific investigation. Then, fill out the chart below to explain why you think each source is trustworthy or untrustworthy.

What is this investigation about? _____

_____

Source	Trustworthy? Why or why not?

Think Outside the Book

13 Design Suppose that you are conducting a field experiment with plants. You are testing the hypothesis that plants grow faster when mulch covers the soil. Plan how you would conduct the experiment. Then plan how you would repeat it.

Visual Summary

To complete this summary, fill in the blanks with the correct word or phrase. Then, use the key below to check your answers. You can use this page to review the main concepts of the lesson.

Scientific investigations include experiments, fieldwork, surveys, and models.

14 A type of investigation that allows scientists to control variables is a(n)

_____

15 Scientific experiments test relationships between _____ and _____ variables.

16 A scientific hypothesis must be

_____

There is no single correct way to conduct a scientific investigation.
Some methods include making and testing hypotheses, collecting data, analyzing data, and drawing conclusions.

17 A(n) _____ is either supported or unsupported by the results of an investigation.

18 The results of an investigation are the

_____

Reliable scientific information comes from investigations with reproducible results.
Sources of reliable scientific information include scientific journals and government web sites.

19 An investigation that has been done by more than one scientist with similar findings has been _____

20 The most reliable scientific information is published in _____

Answers: 14 experiment; 15 independent, dependent; 16 testable 17 hypothesis; 18 data; 19 replicated; 20 scientific journals

21 Apply Choose an organism that you can observe in its environment. Write a hypothesis that you could test about this organism.

Lesson Review

Vocabulary

Fill in the blank with the term that best completes the following sentences.

1 A scientific _____ is a proposed explanation that can be tested.

2 A(n) _____ is the factor that is deliberately changed in an experiment.

3 The information gathered in an investigation is called _____

4 A(n) _____ should have only one independent variable.

5 _____ can be made in the field or in the laboratory.

Key Concepts

6 Infer What kinds of scientific investigations involve making observations?

_____

_____

7 Apply In an experiment, which variable changes in response to the manipulation of another variable?

_____

8 Explain When might a scientist use a model?

_____

_____

_____

_____

9 Compare How are repetition and replication alike and different?

_____

_____

_____

_____

_____

Critical Thinking

Use the table below to answer the following questions.

Plant	Amount of Water Given	Amount of Fertilizer Given	Height
1	10 mL	none	6 cm
2	20 mL	5 g	8 cm
3	30 mL	10 g	7 cm
4	40 mL	15 g	12 cm

10 Evaluate The table above shows the data collected during an experiment about plant height. Based on the data collected, is this a controlled experiment? Why or why not?

_____

_____

_____

_____

_____

_____

11 Describe How would you experiment to find out how much water this plant type needs for optimal growth?

_____

_____

_____

12 Recommend Write a checklist with at least three entries for how you can evaluate whether scientific information is reliable.

_____

_____

_____

_____

_____

Indiana Standards
NOS 8.8 Analyze data, using appropriate mathematical manipulation as required, and use it to identify patterns and make inferences based on these patterns.

Supporting Hypotheses

Scientists repeat investigations whenever possible to test the validity of hypotheses. A hypothesis is more strongly supported when more than one investigation gives similar results. But sometimes investigations with similar hypotheses give different results. When this happens, it is important that scientists ask questions to help them judge whether the differences in the results are insignificant or meaningful.

Tutorial

Two groups of students worked together to test a hypothesis. Each group collected four samples of seawater and four samples of drinking water to test. Their hypothesis and the measurements that the students made are shown below. The two groups shared their data and asked the following questions as they evaluated their results.

Conductivity Report

Background: Seawater contains dissolved salts in the form of positive and negative ions. These ions may allow seawater to conduct electric current. Conductivity is a measure of how well a material conducts an electric current.

Hypothesis: The conductivity of seawater is higher than the conductivity of drinking water.

Average Conductivity in Siemens per Meter

	Group 1 Values (S/m)	Group 2 Values (S/m)
Seawater	3.97	4.82
Drinking water	0.005	0.0045

Are the results of the two investigations similar or different? The average conductivity of seawater measured by each group was different.

Do the different results still support the original hypothesis? Even though the groups had different results for seawater conductivity, both groups' results supported the hypothesis that the conductivity of seawater is higher than that of drinking water.

What additional investigations would help to explain the groups' results? The students designed a second investigation in which they would bring all of their samples to the same temperature and then repeat their measurements.

What could account for differences in the results? Students examined the following factors:
- type of equipment
- procedure
- conditions
- materials used

One student did more research and learned that temperature affects conductivity. The students realized that the two groups had made conductivity measurements of seawater samples at different temperatures.

You Try It!

A class was divided into two groups and instructed to investigate the conductivity of rock salt (NaCl) and of quartz (SiO$_2$). The hypothesis and supporting data collected by the groups are shown below.

Hypothesis: The conductivity of a solid substance increases when the substance is placed in water.

Results of Conductivity Tests

	Group A			Group B		
	NaCl	SiO$_2$	H$_2$O	NaCl	SiO$_2$	H$_2$O
Conductivity (solid)	No	No	—	No	No	—
Conductivity (in water)	Yes	Yes	No	Yes	No	No

1 Evaluating Data Compare the results of the two groups.

_____

_____

_____

_____

_____

_____

2 Judging Results Based on the results, what would each group conclude about whether their original hypothesis is supported? Explain your reasoning.

_____

_____

_____

_____

_____

_____

3 Evaluating Methods When the students examined their procedures, they found that Group A used a single beaker for both solids, and Group B used a different beaker of water for each solid and for the H$_2$O. How might this difference in methods explain the difference in their results?

_____

_____

_____

_____

_____

_____

_____

_____

Take It Home

With an adult, find a book or article about experiments in cold fusion. Were the results reproduced? Did they support the original hypothesis? Write a paragraph about your findings.

Representing Data

ESSENTIAL QUESTION

How do scientists show the results of investigations?

By the end of this lesson, you should be able to use tables, graphs, and models to display and analyze scientific data.

Indiana Standards

NOS 8.3 Collect quantitative data with appropriate tools or technologies and use appropriate units to label numerical data.

NOS 8.8 Analyze data, using appropriate mathematical manipulation as required, and use it to identify patterns and make inferences based on these patterns.

NOS 8.11 Communicate findings using graphs, charts, maps and models through written reports.

This clay tablet, which dates back to 2400 BCE, displays accounting records written in cuneiform script. Cuneiform is a picture-writing system that uses symbols. Today the tablet is located in the Louvre, in Paris, France.

Engage Your Brain

1 Evaluate Check T or F to show whether you think each statement is true or false.

T F

☐ ☐ A graph should always have a title describing what the graph is about.

☐ ☐ The factor that is manipulated in an experiment is usually plotted on the vertical axis of a graph.

☐ ☐ A model can be used to represent something that is too small to see with the naked eye.

2 Assemble Write a word or phrase beginning with each letter of the word MODEL that is an example or use of a model. Think of a model as anything that represents something else.

M _____

O _____

D _____

E _____

L _____

Active Reading

3 Apply Use context clues to write your own definition for the words *independent* and *dependent*.

Example sentence
After <u>independent</u> studies, the two scientists reached very different conclusions.

independent:

_____

_____

Example sentence
The cost of the service is <u>dependent</u> on its availability.

dependent:

_____

_____

Vocabulary Terms

- independent variable
- dependent variable
- model

4 Apply As you learn the definition of each vocabulary term in this lesson, create your own definition or sketch to help you remember the meaning of the term.

Modeling Data with Graphs

How do scientists make sense of data?

There are many different kinds of scientific investigations conducted in science, all of which involve the collection of data. *Data* are the facts, figures, and other evidence scientists gather when they conduct an investigation.

Scientists Organize the Data

Scientists use data tables to organize and record the data that they collect. By creating a data table, they can record their observations and measurements in an orderly way.

Data tables often have two columns. One column lists the **independent variable**. This is the variable that is deliberately manipulated in an investigation. The other column lists the **dependent variable**. This is the variable that changes as a result of the manipulation of the independent variable. When creating a data table, any units of measurement, such as seconds or degrees, should be included in the table's column headings and not in the individual cells.

The data table below shows the high temperatures for certain days and the number of cold drinks sold at a concession stand on those days.

Drink Sales

High temperature (°F)	Number of cold drinks sold
25	43
40	55
58	60
70	72
81	70

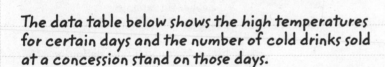 **Visualize It!**

5 Apply Name the independent variable and the dependent variable in the data table. Explain your answer.

_____

_____

_____

_____

_____

© Houghton Mifflin Harcourt Publishing Company • Image Credits: (bkgd) ©David Madison/Photographer's Choice/Getty Images; ©Burazin/Photographer's Choice/Getty Images

Scientists Graph and Analyze the Data

Scientists often analyze data for patterns or trends by constructing graphs of the data. The type of graph they construct depends upon the data they collected and what they want to show.

A *scatter plot* is a graph with points plotted to show a possible relationship between two sets of data. A scatter plot has a horizontal *x*-axis and a vertical *y*-axis. The *x*-axis usually represents the independent variable in the data table. The *y*-axis usually represents the dependent variable.

To show the general relationship between the two variables in the graph, a "line of best fit" is often used. A line of best fit is a line that is drawn to "fit," or come close to, most of the data points.

The graphs below show steps used to construct a scatter plot of the drink sales data at the left.

6 Identify Which axis of a graph usually represents the independent variable?

_____

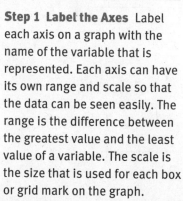 Visualize It!

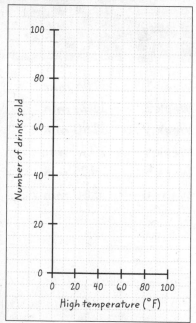

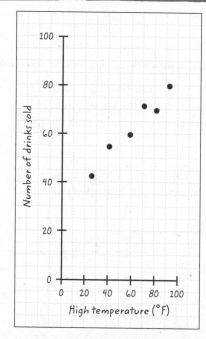

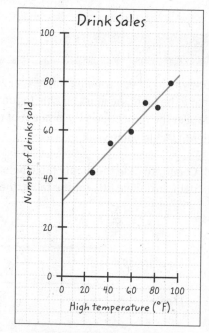

Step 1 Label the Axes Label each axis on a graph with the name of the variable that is represented. Each axis can have its own range and scale so that the data can be seen easily. The range is the difference between the greatest value and the least value of a variable. The scale is the size that is used for each box or grid mark on the graph.

Step 2 Plot the Data Points Plot the data from the table as data points on the graph.

7 Analyze Do you see a trend in these data? Explain.

_____

_____

_____

_____

Step 3 Draw a Line of Best Fit Draw a line that comes close to most of the data points. The line shows the pattern described by the data. It also shows how the data differ from the pattern.

More Graphing!

What do graphs show?

Different types of graphs are used to show different types of information about data. On the previous pages, you read about scatter plots. Other graphs include bar graphs and circle graphs. A *bar graph* is used to display and compare data in a number of separate, or distinct, categories. Data about the number of inches it rained each month can be displayed in a bar graph. A *circle graph* is used when you are showing how each group of data relates to all of the data. Data about the number of boys and girls in your class can be displayed in a circle graph.

Active Reading **8 List** Name three different types of graphs.

_____

_____

_____

Visualize It!

Dwayne has been training for several weeks for cross-country tryouts. To make the team, he must be able to run 1 mile in less than 8 minutes. The data at the right shows the amount of time in minutes that it took Dwayne to run a mile each week.

Week 1	11.95 min
Week 2	11.25 min
Week 3	11.40 min
Week 4	10.10 min
Week 5	9.25 min
Week 6	8.60 min

9 Complete Use the empty table below to organize Dwayne's running data. Include a title for the table, the column heads, and all of the data.

Title

Headings

Data

© Houghton Mifflin Harcourt Publishing Company • Image Credits: ©Daniel Schoenen/age fotostock

Visualize It!

Use the steps below to construct a graph of Dwayne's running data. The horizontal and vertical axes have been drawn for you.

Step 1
Label each axis with the name of the variable that is represented.

Step 2
Find the range for each axis. For the running data, the range of the independent variable is 6 weeks. Thus, the *x*-axis must cover at least 6 weeks.

Step 3
Decide the scale for each axis. For the running data, use a scale of 1 week for each grid mark on the *x*-axis.

Step 4
Graph the points by putting a dot on the graph for each pair of data in the data table.

Step 5
Title the graph. A good title tells a reader what the graph is all about.

10 Graph Use the steps at the left to construct a scatter plot of the running data given.

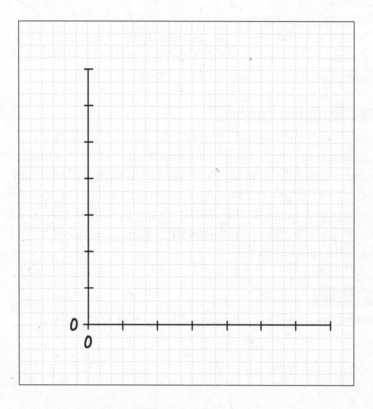

11 Assess Explain how you could use the graph to predict whether Dwayne will run 1 mile in less than 8 minutes.

_____

_____

_____

_____

_____

_____

_____

_____

_____

_____

_____

_____

_____

Throw Me a Curve!

What kinds of patterns can be shown using graphs?

When you graph data, you can identify what the pattern, or *trend*, of the data is. A trend shows the relationship between the two variables studied in the experiment. Graphs make it easy to tell if something is increasing, decreasing, or staying the same.

Linear Relationships

A line can sometimes be used to show the trend of data on a graph. A graph in which the relationship between the independent variable and dependent variable can be shown with a straight line is called a *linear graph*. A straight line shows that the rate of change of the dependent variable with respect to the independent variable is constant. In other words, y always increases or decreases by the same value in relation to x.

Visualize It!

12 Interpret Use the graph to determine the mass of 7 cm^3 of water.

_____

_____

_____

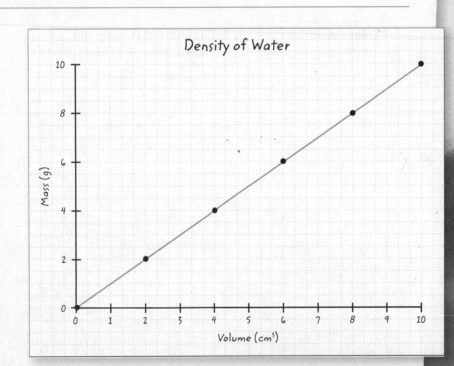

The density of water is an example of a linear relationship.

Nonlinear Relationships

Sometimes, the graph of the relationship between the independent variable and dependent variable studied is not a straight line but a smooth curve. Any graph in which the relationship between the variables cannot be shown with a straight line is called a *nonlinear graph*.

Graphs allow scientists to determine the relationship between variables. In a direct relationship, the value of one variable increases as the value of the other variable increases. In contrast, an inverse relationship is one in which the value of one variable decreases as the other increases. The graph of a direct relationship is an upward sloping line. The graph of an inverse relationship is a downward sloping line.

Active Reading **13 Apply** Describe the difference between linear and nonlinear relationships on a graph.

_____

_____

_____

_____

_____

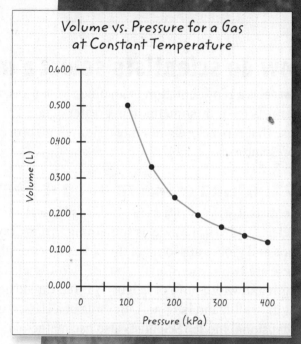

Both of these graphs show nonlinear relationships.

Visualize It!

14 Infer Describe the relationship shown in the graph of Suzi's Surf Shop Sales. Then use the graph to find the approximate sales of the surf shop in 2007.

_____

_____

_____

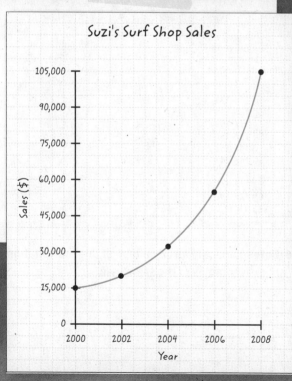

The Perfect Model

How do scientists select a model?

A **model** is a representation of an object or a process that allows scientists to study something in greater detail. The best models are those that most closely resemble the system, process, or object they represent.

By the Kind of Information It Shows

Scientists use many different kinds of physical and mathematical models. A physical model is something that is drawn or built. Maps and globes are some of the oldest types of physical models. These are two-dimensional models. Two-dimensional models have length and width but not height. A three-dimensional model has length, width, and height. A diorama of a classroom is a three-dimensional model. Scientists also use mathematical models to represent how the natural world functions. With mathematical models, you can predict the results of changes in a system. A computer simulation is one type of mathematical model.

📖 **Active Reading**

15 Apply As you read, underline some examples of models.

Visualize It!

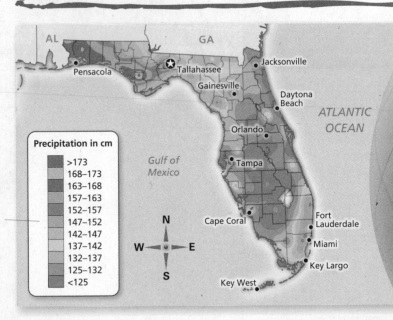

Precipitation in cm

	>173
	168–173
	163–168
	157–163
	152–157
	147–152
	142–147
	137–142
	132–137
	125–132
	<125

AL

GA

Pensacola

Tallahassee

Jacksonville

Gainesville

Daytona Beach

ATLANTIC OCEAN

Orlando

Gulf of Mexico

Tampa

Cape Coral

Fort Lauderdale

Miami

Key Largo

Key West

N
W E
S

16 Defend Identify an advantage of this precipitation map over tables of the same data.

_____

_____

_____

By How It Can Be Used

A two-dimensional floor plan of a building would give you a good idea of the building's layout. You could add furniture to the floor plan to see how you would use the space, but you would not be able to determine anything about the height of the furniture in the room. A three-dimensional model would allow you to see the walls and windows, and get a better feeling for how objects fit in the room. A computerized simulation of the building could enable you to see what it would be like to move through the building.

Similar models could be made of a molecule such as DNA. A two-dimensional drawing of the molecule would show the atoms that make up the molecule and how those atoms are arranged. A three-dimensional model would enable you to study the molecule from different angles. A simulation would enable you to see how the molecule functions. Today, many processes in science can be modeled in great detail. The information needed from the model determines the type of model that is used.

Think Outside the Book Inquiry

19 Criticize Many advertisements feature models. Find an example of a nonhuman model in a magazine. Write a critique of the model. Consider the following questions: "How useful is the model? What has been left out or exaggerated? How could the model be improved?"

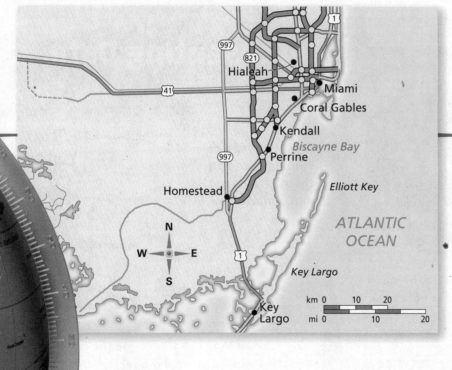

18 Predict Scale is the relationship between the dimensions of a model and the dimensions of the real object. How could the scale on this map be helpful when taking a trip?

_____

_____

_____

_____

_____

Inquiry

17 Infer What are two advantages of the globe over the precipitation map of Florida for understanding characteristics of Florida? What are two advantages of the map over the globe?

_____

_____

_____

Visual Summary

To complete this summary, circle the correct word. Then use the key below to check your answers. You can use this page to review the main concepts of the lesson.

A graph in which the relationship between the independent and dependent variable can be shown with a straight line is a linear graph.

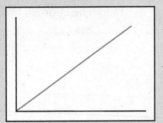

20 The dependent / independent variable is usually found on the x-axis of a graph.

A graph in which the relationship between the variables cannot be shown with a straight line is called a nonlinear graph.

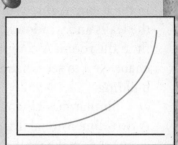

21 If the rate of change of the dependent variable with respect to the independent variable is not constant, then the relationship between the variables is linear / nonlinear.

Representing Data

A scientific model is a representation of an object or system.

22 A globe is an example of a mathematical / physical model.

23 An equation is an example of a mathematical / physical model.

Scientists select models based on their advantages and limitations.

24 A road map is a two-dimensional / three-dimensional model.

25 Conclude You and a friend each decide to build the same model airplane. After the airplanes are built, you decide to conduct an investigation to determine which airplane can glide through the air the longest. Outline a plan to conduct your investigation.

© Houghton Mifflin Harcourt Publishing Company • Image Credits: (b) ©Cartesia/Photodisc/Getty Images

Lesson Review

Vocabulary

Fill in the blank with the term that best completes the following sentences.

1 The _____ variable in an investigation is the variable that is deliberately manipulated.

2 The _____ variable in an investigation is the variable that changes in response to changes in the investigation.

3 A(n) _____ can be a physical or mathematical representation of an object or a process.

Key Concepts

4 Identify Alfonso is conducting an experiment to determine whether temperature affects how fast earthworms move. What are the independent and dependent variables in his experiment?

_____

_____

_____

_____

5 Apply When creating a graph, why is an appropriate title for a graph important?

_____

_____

_____

6 Provide Give an example of a model used in science that is larger than the real object and an example of a model that is smaller than the real object.

_____

_____

_____

_____

Critical Thinking

Use this graph to answer the following questions.

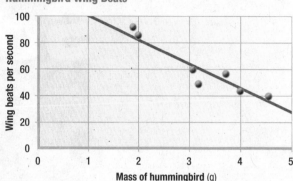

Hummingbird Wing Beats

7 Interpret In this graph, what are the independent and dependent variables?

_____

_____

_____

8 Describe Explain a trend or pattern you observe in the graph.

_____

_____

_____

_____

_____

9 Analyze Both a globe and a flat world map can model features of Earth. Give an example of when you would use each of these models.

_____

_____

_____

_____

_____

Science and Society

ESSENTIAL QUESTION

How do science and society work together?

By the end of this lesson, you should be able to describe the impact that science has had on society and society has had on science, especially in regard to political, social, and economic concerns and decisions.

Science and society work hand in hand. For example, when society requires high-security measures, science answers with iris scanners, such as this one. An iris scanner uses unique patterns in a person's eye to identify the person.

RECYCLABLE

RECYCLABLE PACKAGING

Engage Your Brain

1 Discriminate Circle the word that best completes the following sentences.

Few / Most parts of our lives today have been influenced by science.

Political, economic, and social decision-making is *often / never* based on scientific information.

All / Many important scientific discoveries have been made within the past 100 years.

2 Relate You may have seen the icon above on recycling containers. Write your impression of how the recycling icon might symbolize the effects of science on society.

_____

_____

_____

_____

_____

_____

_____

Active Reading

3 Synthesize Many English words have their roots in other languages. The word science comes from the Latin word *scientia*, which means *knowledge*. Use the word *scientist* or *scientific* in a sentence.

_____

_____

_____

_____

_____

Vocabulary

4 Apply In this lesson, you'll learn about *society*, *economics*, and *politics* in relation to science. As you learn about each term in this lesson, create your own explanation or sketch to remind you what each term refers to.

In what areas does science help us make decisions?

Science has led to lifesaving discoveries and has taught us to protect our resources, too. Science also helps people make decisions that affect us all. For example, scientists can gather data about the health of our environment. Then, decision-makers use this data to make rules and laws.

Water-quality rules and laws depend on science. Over 150 years ago, doctor John Snow found that bacteria in polluted water could make people sick with cholera, a deadly disease. The polluted water was not safe to drink! Now, decision-makers use science to decide how much bacteria and other substances can be found in water before it is unsafe to drink.

Active Reading

5 Diagram As you read, complete the graphic organizer below about science and decisions.

Science affects decisions made

In Communities

Community governments make decisions about a local area. For example, they make sure the water in their area follows water-quality rules and laws. Water supplies are tested often. If levels of bacteria are too high, your community leaders may decide to warn you to boil water before drinking it.

In States

State governments make decisions that affect the whole state or many parts of the state. For example, state agencies test water used by more than one community. They may decide to close a beach if they find levels of bacteria that scientists say are harmful. They also may make rules against fishing if fish show high levels of dangerous substances.

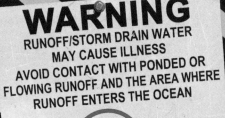

WARNING
RUNOFF/STORM DRAIN WATER MAY CAUSE ILLNESS
AVOID CONTACT WITH PONDED OR FLOWING RUNOFF AND THE AREA WHERE RUNOFF ENTERS THE OCEAN

AVISO
CORRIENTE DE AGUA/AGUA DEL DRENAJE DE TORMENTA PUEDE CAUSAR ENFERMEDADES
EVITE CONTACTO CON AGUA DE DESAGÜE QUE ESTE ESTANCADA O CORRIENDO Y EL AREA DONDE DESEMBOCA AL OCEANO

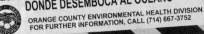

ORANGE COUNTY ENVIRONMENTAL HEALTH DIVISION
FOR FURTHER INFORMATION, CALL (714) 667-3752

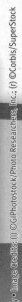

everywhere!

Throughout the Nation

Some decisions affect the whole country. The United States government created the Environmental Protection Agency (EPA) in 1970. The EPA sets rules and laws for water quality for the entire country. These laws are often based on science. The EPA may make rules about how industries can use our country's water. For example, there are rules about whether waste materials can be dumped into lakes and rivers. The rules help us keep our water safe.

Taking water samples for scientific testing

6 Explain How does science help us protect our nation's resources?

_____

_____

_____

At the International Level

Some decisions affect more than one country. Oceans, rivers, and other bodies of water often affect more than one country. For example, the Great Lakes touch both the United States and Canada. Any action taken by one country could affect the other in matters of health and environmental policy. So, nations also need to adhere to agreed-upon rules for the proper use of shared water resources. Science gives a country's representatives the data they need to talk about and make decisions about important matters like these.

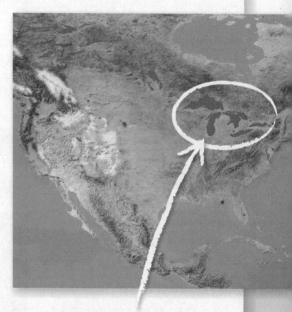

The Great Lakes are bordered by Canada to the north and the United States to the south.

7 Describe How might a nation be affected if another nation did not follow agreed-upon water rules?

_____

_____

_____

_____

High Goals

How can science and politics affect each other?

Scientific investigations have led to new technologies that have improved human lives. How do scientists decide what to investigate? The direction of science is influenced by many things, such as political, societal, and economic concerns. Science, in turn, affects politics, society, and the economy.

The Space Race is an example of how science and politics affect each other. In 1957, the former Soviet Union sent the first satellite into orbit. American leaders wanted to show that we could excel in space exploration, too.

Government Sets a Goal

The Space Race was not only a scientific rivalry. It was part of a bigger political contest between nations. Politics and government leaders sometimes set a direction or goal for science. In 1961, U.S. president John F. Kennedy announced the goal that the United States would put an American on the moon within the decade. Kennedy made it clear the country would give all the resources it could to this task. Without such political drive, scientists would not have had the funding and other resources to take on space exploration.

Active Reading

8 Apply As you read, underline events that influenced the path of science.

The Space Race: A Decade of Science

Americans responded to the Space Race with supreme scientific effort and enormous funding.

9 Predict How do you think you would have reacted to President Kennedy's call to Americans to support the Space Race?

_____

_____

_____

_____

In 1961, President Kennedy announced the goal of putting a person safely on the moon. Scientists got to work on the goal!

Science Meets the Goal

Researchers from all fields of science worked on the challenges of space flight. Many scientists worked on how to support human life in space. For example, they dehydrated food to ensure an adequate supply for astronauts. They also learned how to communicate from thousands of miles away. When *Apollo 11* landed on the moon in 1969, it was a win for both the nation and science. The work of the scientists and engineers had put two Americans on the moon.

The United States landed on the moon because government and politics made the work of scientists possible. But was the Space Race worth our effort and money? Some people say we should have focused on problems here on Earth. Other people say the Space Race led to other discoveries that improved the lives of everyone. For example, the Space Race taught us ways to preserve food. As a result, we can get more nourishment to people all over the world.

10 List Use the table below to list some pros and cons of using resources for the Space Race.

Pros	Cons

11 Devise If you were an astronaut in space, what would you want to explore to help society?

_____

_____

_____

1969: An American on the moon!

Where do we go from here?

Big Help!

How do science, society, and economics interact?

Politics are not the only drivers of science. Societal needs and economics influence science, too. If society sees no value in certain research, scientists may not get funding for the research. Also, people may not buy or use new technologies when they are made.

Society Has a Need

One example of societal needs driving science happens when there are outbreaks of diseases, such as polio, AIDS, or the H1N1 influenza. Polio, AIDS, and H1N1 are diseases caused by viruses. These diseases can cause suffering and even death. Society needs solutions when diseases threaten the health of the nation and world. So, society turns to science.

Active Reading

12 Identify What is an example of a societal need that science can address? _____

13 Apply Influenza, also called the flu, is a viral infection. In addition to getting vaccinated, what are some ways that you can avoid influenza?

_____
_____
_____
_____
_____

One way to stop the spread of disease is to limit exposure of sick people to healthy people. This airport scanner allows airport employees to see if passengers have fevers, a sign of illness.

Science Addresses the Need

Scientists find many ways to meet the needs of society. Societal needs may lead some scientists to prioritize research such as vaccine development. Vaccines prevent people from getting viral diseases. After an outbreak of polio in the early 1950s, Jonas Salk pioneered the first successful polio vaccine. This vaccine was given as a shot. Later, Albert Sabin developed another polio vaccine that was taken by mouth. Scientists continue to explore and learn new things. Sometimes, new scientific knowledge improves upon or challenges existing knowledge.

Science and Economics Affect Each Other

Preventing disease is just one example of how science benefits society. But science can be expensive. Priorities for how to spend money on science must be set. Science, in turn, affects the economy. Lifesaving improvements allow people to live longer, which changes how much money we make over our lifetimes. Making more money allows us to spend more. And spending more puts money back into the economy.

Think Outside the Book · Inquiry

14 Investigate In 1900, the three leading causes of death in the United States were all infectious diseases. In 2000, none of the three leading causes were infectious diseases. Do research to find out the current leading causes of death. Then, make a poster describing prevention methods that you and your family can use.

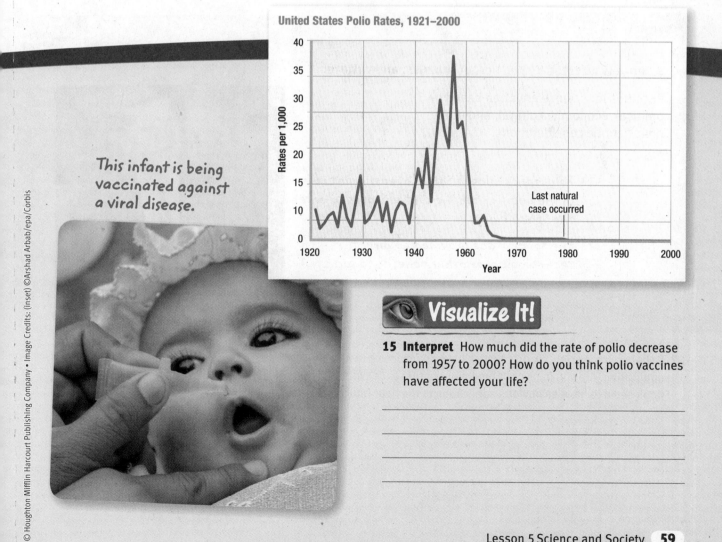

This infant is being vaccinated against a viral disease.

United States Polio Rates, 1921–2000

Last natural case occurred

Visualize It!

15 Interpret How much did the rate of polio decrease from 1957 to 2000? How do you think polio vaccines have affected your life?

_____

_____

_____

_____

Visual Summary

To complete this summary, check the box that indicates true or false. Then, use the key below to check your answers. You can use this page to review the main concepts of the lesson.

Science and Society

Science helps society.

Scientific advancements improve our quality of life.

T	F	
☐	☐	**16** The discovery that diseases can be spread in water led to water quality regulation.
☐	☐	**17** Scientific findings can be used to conserve Earth's natural resources.

Society promotes science.

Societal needs are some of the issues addressed by science.

T	F	
☐	☐	**18** Science sets its own goals without influence from society.
☐	☐	**19** Society, economics, and politics drive the direction of science.

Science is affected by politics, economics, and culture.

Priorities for science are often based on political, economic, cultural, and other nonscientific considerations.

T	F	
☐	☐	**20** Political considerations played a great role in the decision for the United States to enter the Space Race.
☐	☐	**21** The Space Race provided no direct technological or other benefits to society.

Answers: 16 T; 17 T; 18 F; 19 T; 20 T; 21 F

22 Debate Some scientific discoveries have no obvious practical application. Are you in favor of funding scientific endeavors that don't seem to have an obvious application in the near future?

Lesson Review

Vocabulary

Draw a line to connect the following terms to how they affect science.

1 economics

2 politics

3 society

A leaders may promote certain scientific research

B events, such as disease outbreak, prioritize scientific research

C funding is not available for all potential research

Key Concepts

4 **Discriminate** What was Jonas Salk's scientific contribution to society?

A He developed a cure for polio.

B He convinced Americans to support the Space Race.

C He developed a vaccine to prevent polio.

D He demonstrated that a disease could be spread in water.

5 **List** Science helps policy-makers decide which laws and rules to make. At what levels does science affect policies?

_____

_____

_____

6 **Determine** Give an example of how politics can affect science.

_____

_____

_____

_____

_____

Critical Thinking

The table below shows the sources of power for the people in the city of Riverview. Use this table to answer the following questions.

Power Sources for City of Riverview		
Source	**Percent from Source**	**Type**
Coal burning	20%	Nonrenewable resource
Hydroelectric power	70%	Renewable resource
Wind power	10%	Renewable resource

7 **Apply** What is the main source of power in Riverview?

_____

8 **Conclude** Ten years ago, the only power source in Riverview came from coal burning. Why might the people of Riverview have wanted to change their power source?

_____

_____

_____

_____

_____

9 **Infer** What role did science play in this change?

_____

_____

_____

_____

_____

My Notes

Unit 1 Summary

Representing Data **is critical for** → Scientific Investigations

Representing Data → What is Science?

Scientific Investigations → What is Science?

Scientific Knowledge → What is Science?

Science and Society → What is Science?

Scientific Knowledge **impacts the relationship between** → Science and Society

1 Interpret Science is the systematic study of natural events and conditions. Explain how the Graphic Organizer above illustrates this definition.

_____

_____

_____

_____

2 Relate How can scientific knowledge impact a decision about treating a disease outbreak?

_____

_____

_____

_____

3 Explain Why is empirical evidence used to support scientific explanations?

_____

_____

_____

_____

_____

_____

4 Apply Why is it important to organize scientific data?

_____

_____

_____

_____

_____

Name _____

Multiple Choice

1 Scientists use objective measurements and logical reasoning to classify both living and nonliving things. Among the nonliving things they classify are stars. The table below shows one way scientists classify stars.

Color	Surface temperature (K)	Mass compared with our Sun	Brightness compared with our Sun
blue	over 10,000	at least 2.1 times	at least 25 times brighter
yellow/white	6,000 to 10,000	slightly larger	at least 1.5 times brighter
yellow	5,200 to 6,000	about the same	about the same
orange	3,900 to 5,200	less than 0.8 times	about half the brightness
red	under 3,900	less than 0.3 times	very faint

What NEW information would cause scientists to reevaluate this method of classifying stars?

A. The discovery of a red star that has about twice the mass of the sun.

B. The discovery of a blue star that has twenty times the mass of the sun.

C. The discovery of a yellow/white star that has a surface temperature of 8,625 K.

D. The discovery of a star that has about half the mass of the sun and gives off an orange light.

2 Julio investigates the effect of varying amounts of sunlight on the rate of plant growth. He experiments by exposing seedlings to different amounts of sunlight each day. Julio carefully measures the length of each plant each day and records the amount of growth in his notebook. When each seedling reaches 20 cm in height, he records the time and removes the seedling from the investigation. Why is careful MEASUREMENT so important to the validity of the data in this investigation?

A. The rate of growth is unrelated to the amount of sunlight.

B. The rate of growth determines the amount of water he gives each plant.

C. Each plant has to reach 20 cm and no more because the time and height calculate the rate. Sunlight is the controlled variable.

D. It is important because the amount of sunlight depends on the amount of time the plant grows.

3 Several medications for the cure of a common illness have been tested under different conditions. All of the medications are being manufactured by different companies. The advertisers all claim that their medication is the best and most reliable. Which of the medications do you think is MOST LIKELY the most reliable?

A. Medicine A because it was tested by the manufacturer on mice.

B. Medicine B because it was derived from a long-used folk remedy.

C. Medicine C because it was tested by different scientists several times with the same results.

D. Medicine D because it was derived from a medication that is used frequently to treat a similar disease.

4 Scientists are not certain what signals cause manatees to begin migrating, although manatees seem to sense when cold weather is coming. By tracking manatees, scientists have found evidence that manatees travel hundreds of miles during their seasonal migration. The map below shows the migratory range of the manatee.

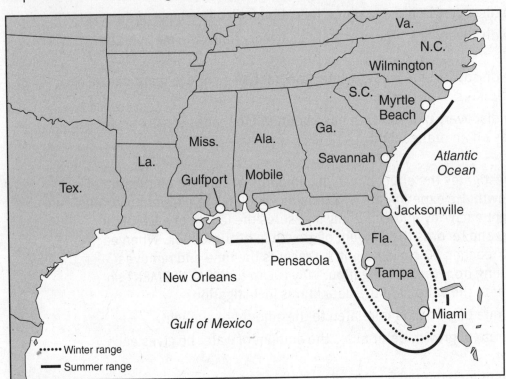

According to the map, which are the FARTHEST points in the Atlantic Ocean and Gulf of Mexico where manatees commonly migrate?

A. Wilmington, North Carolina, and Mobile, Alabama

B. Savannah, Georgia, and Tampa, Florida

C. Pensacola, Florida, and Jacksonville, Florida

D. Miami, Florida, and Mobile, Alabama

5 Marissa is conducting an experiment in which she is testing a substance she believes will turn green when put into different acid solutions. In several repetitions of the investigation, she finds that sometimes the substance turns green, but other times it turns red. How should she change her procedure when she tests a revised hypothesis?

A. She should only test the substance once.

B. She should record only the color that she expects.

C. She should test a different substance as a control.

D. She should keep careful records of the pH of each acid solution.

6 The graph below shows the number of people who visited doctors because of influenza-like illnesses over a two-year period.

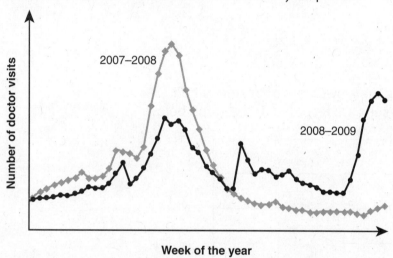

What can you conclude from this graph?

A. Influenza-like illnesses follow a steady pattern throughout the year.

B. The number of influenza-like illnesses will decrease for 2009–2010.

C. People who got medical care in both years generally reported feeling better than if they had not gotten treatment.

D. The number of people who developed influenza-like illnesses did not peak at the same time in 2008–2009 as it did in 2007–2008.

7 The school physician performed an experiment to investigate the effects of aerobic exercise on high school freshmen. He examined 25 student volunteers, and then had each student perform aerobic exercises, such as jogging, swimming, and bicycling. The doctor recorded the students' pulse rates before each activity, during each activity, and after each activity. Which is the DEPENDENT VARIABLE in this experiment?

A. the exercises

B. the pulse rates

C. the volunteers

D. the physician

Constructed Response

8 Make a prediction about how an increased use of solar energy may affect the use of other energy sources, such as oil. Then explain your reasoning.

_____

_____

_____

State ONE way that solar energy technology may benefit the environment.

_____

_____

Extended Response

9 Scientists are studying the growth rate of bacteria at different temperatures. Their results are recorded in the graph below.

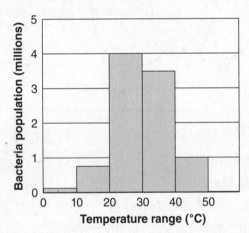

Based on these data, what temperature range is ideal for bacteria growth?

_____

Do warmer termperatures always cause faster bacteria growth? Explain.

_____

Can these bacteria survive freezing temperatures? Explain.

_____

The scientists have left out information on the table that is important to understand the data as a RATE of growth. What information is missing?

_____

UNIT 2
Matter

© Houghton Mifflin Harcourt Publishing Company • Image Credits: (bkgrd) ©Osman Orsal/Reuters/Corbis; (br)

At room temperature, gold is a solid. But at very high temperatures, solid gold becomes a liquid that flows.

What do you think?

Gold is a shiny metal that can be used to make jewelry. Water is a clear liquid that makes up over half of the human body. Though gold and water have different properties, they are both made of matter. What is matter?

Unit 2
Matter

Matter Up Close

Matter is anything that has mass and takes up space. Even the smallest things on Earth are made up of matter!

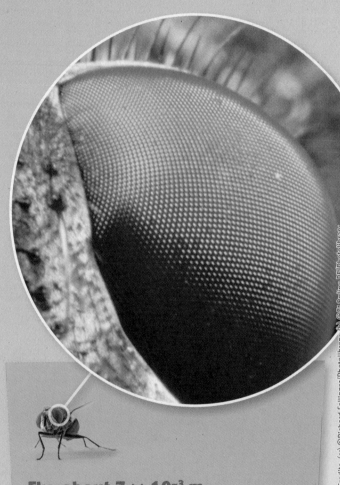

Fly, about 7×10^{-3} m
The eye of a fly has been magnified so that you can see more detail. Magnification allows us to see things we cannot see with the human eye alone.

Grain of salt, about 5×10^{-4} m

This seasoning and preservative can be harvested from seawater.

Table salt

Rhinovirus, about 3×10^{-8} m

Watch out for this virus—it causes the common cold.

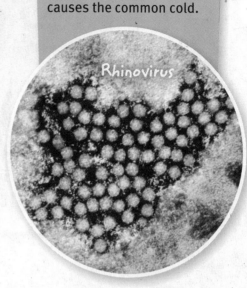

Rhinovirus

Helium atom, about 3×10^{-11} m

Atoms are so small that they cannot be viewed with traditional light microscopes. Often, they are represented by models such as this one.

Object	Width
Grain of salt	5×10^{-4} m (or 0.0005 m)
Rhinovirus	3×10^{-8} m (or 0.00000003 m)
Helium atom	3×10^{-11} m (or 0.00000000003 m)

 **Size Is Relative**

By looking at ratios of sizes, you can compare the relative sizes of objects. How many times greater is the size of a grain of salt than a rhinovirus particle? You can write a ratio to find the answer.

$$\frac{\text{grain of salt}}{\text{rhinovirus}} = \frac{0.0005 \text{ m}}{0.00000003 \text{ m}} \approx 20{,}000$$

A grain of salt is about 20,000 times the size of a rhinovirus.

A Determine how many times greater a rhinovirus is than a helium atom.

B Measure the width of one of your textbooks to the nearest millimeter. How many helium atoms could you line up across the book?

Properties of Matter

ESSENTIAL QUESTION

What are physical and chemical properties of matter?

By the end of this lesson, you should be able to classify and compare substances based on their physical and chemical properties.

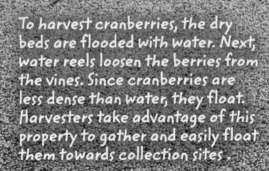

To harvest cranberries, the dry beds are flooded with water. Next, water reels loosen the berries from the vines. Since cranberries are less dense than water, they float. Harvesters take advantage of this property to gather and easily float them towards collection sites.

Indiana Standards

8.1.6 Explain that elements and compounds have characteristic properties such as density, boiling points and melting points, that remain unchanged regardless of sample size.

Engage Your Brain

1 Predict Check T or F to show whether you think each statement is true or false.

T F

☐ ☐ Liquid water freezes at the same temperature at which ice melts: 0 °C.

☐ ☐ A bowling ball weighs less than a Styrofoam ball of the same size.

☐ ☐ An object with a density greater than the density of water will float in water.

☐ ☐ Solubility is the ability of one substance to dissolve in another.

2 Describe If you were asked to describe an orange to someone who had never seen an orange, what would you tell the person?

_____

_____

_____

_____

_____

Active Reading

3 Synthesize Many English words have their roots in other languages. The root of the word *solubility* is the Latin word *solvere,* which means "to loosen." Make an educated guess about the meaning of the word *solubility*.

_____

_____

_____

Vocabulary Terms

- physical property
- chemical property

4 Apply As you learn the definition of each vocabulary term in this lesson, create your own definition or sketch to help you remember the meaning of the term.

Physical Education

What are physical properties of matter?

What words would you use to describe a table? A chair? A piece of cloth? You would probably say something about the shape, color, and size of each object. Next, you might consider whether the object is hard or soft, smooth or rough. Normally, when describing an object, you identify what it is about that object that you can observe without changing its identity.

They Are Used to Describe a Substance

A characteristic of a substance that can be observed and measured without changing the identity of the substance is called a **physical property**. Gold is one metal prized for its physical properties. Gold can be bent and shaped easily and has a lasting shine. Both properties make it an excellent metal for making coins and jewelry.

All of your senses can be used to detect physical properties. Color, shape, size, and texture are a few of the physical properties you encounter. Think of how you would describe an object to a friend. Most likely, your description would be a list of the object's physical properties.

Active Reading **5 Describe** Does observing a physical property of a substance change the identity of the substance? Explain.

_____

_____

_____

_____

Gold is a highly sought-after metal for making jewelry. Gold is dense, soft, and shiny, and it is resistant to tarnishing. Gold is often mixed with other metals to make it stronger.

© Houghton Mifflin Harcourt Publishing Company • Image Credits: ©Lester Lefkowitz/Stone/Getty Images

In this factory, gold is being purified by the process of smelting. This process uses pressure, high heat, and chemicals to remove impurities from the gold.

They Can Be Observed without Changing the Identity of a Substance

The physical properties of an object can be observed with the senses. Some properties can be measured, too. For example, you can look at a table to observe its relative size. Or, you can measure its length, width, and height by using a tool like a measuring tape. When you observe a physical property, you do not change the substance's identity. The material that makes up the table keeps its identity.

Imagine that you conducted an experiment to measure the temperature at which water boils. This temperature, called the boiling point, is a physical property. You placed a beaker of water over a heating source and measured the increase in water temperature using a thermometer. Once the water reached its boiling point, some of the water had become a gas. In this experiment, the water had to change to a gas before you could record the boiling point of water. However, the water did not change in identity. It is water whether it is a solid, liquid, or gas.

Visualize It!

6 Observe Describe the physical properties of objects you see in this photo.

_____

_____

_____

_____

Think Outside the Book

7 Apply Describe a common object by naming its properties. Trade your mystery-object description with a classmate's and try to guess what object he or she has described.

Common Physical Properties

On these two pages, you can read about some common physical properties. The physical properties of a substance often describe how the substance can be useful.

Electrical conductivity

Electrical conductivity is a measure of how well an electric current can move through a substance.

Density

Density is a measure of the amount of mass in a given amount of volume.

8 Explain The photo above shows oil and vinegar in a pitcher. The top layer is the oil. Describe the density of the vinegar compared to the density of the oil.

_____

_____

_____

Thermal conductivity

Thermal conductivity is the rate at which a substance transfers heat.

Solubility

Solubility is the ability of a substance to dissolve in another substance. This powdered drink mix is dissolving in water. When fully dissolved, the particles of the drink mix will be spread throughout the water.

9 Predict If you let all of the liquid evaporate out of the pitcher, would you be able to see the solid particles of the drink mix? Explain.

_____

_____

_____

Malleability

Malleability (mal·ee·uh·BIL·i·tee) is the ability of a substance to be rolled or pounded into various shapes. Aluminum has the property of malleability.

10 Identify Name something made of aluminum and explain why malleability is a useful property.

_____

_____

_____

Luster

Many metals often have a shine, or luster, that makes them prized by decorators.

Some metals exert a magnetic attraction. Magnetic attraction can act at a distance.

Magnetic attraction

Melting point

The melting point of a substance is the temperature at which it changes from a solid to a liquid.

Boiling water beneath the surface of Earth powers this geyser.

Boiling point

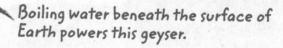

Inquiry

11 Infer Compare what happens when a geyser erupts to what happens when a tea kettle whistles.

_____

_____

_____

_____

What are chemical properties of matter?

Active Reading **12 Identify** As you read, underline the definition of a chemical property.

Physical properties are not the only properties that describe matter. A **chemical property** describes a substance's ability to change into a new substance with different properties. Common chemical properties include flammability and reactivity with substances such as oxygen, water, and acids.

They Describe How a Substance Changes

Can you think of a chemical property for the metal iron? When left outdoors in wet weather, iron rusts. The ability to rust is a chemical property of iron. The metal silver does not rust, but eventually a darker substance, called tarnish, forms on its surface. You may have noticed a layer of tarnish on some silver spoons or jewelry. Rusting and tarnishing are chemical properties because the metal changes. After rusting or tarnishing, a portion of the metal is no longer the metal but a different substance.

13 Predict Why do automobiles rust more easily in wet climates than drier climates?

_____

_____

_____

_____

Iron can form rust, turning a once shiny car into a crumbling relic.

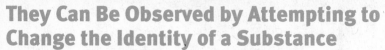

They Can Be Observed by Attempting to Change the Identity of a Substance

One way to identify a chemical property is to observe the changes that a substance undergoes. Wood for a campfire has the chemical property of flammability—the ability to burn. When wood burns, new substances are formed: water, carbon dioxide, and ash. These new substances have different properties than the wood had. Reactivity is another chemical property that can be identified by observing changes. Reactivity is the ability of a substance to interact with another substance and form one or more new substances.

You can also observe a chemical property of a substance by attempting to change the substance, even if no change occurs. For example, you can observe that gold is nonflammable by attempting to burn it. A chemical property of gold is that it is nonflammable.

Reactivity is a chemical property. Vinegar and baking soda react to make a salt, water, and carbon dioxide gas.

Flammability, or the ability of a substance to burn, is a chemical property. For example, the wood building in the photo is flammable, and the suits that help keep the firefighters safe are flame resistant.

Property Boundaries

What is the difference between physical and chemical properties?

A physical property can always be observed without changing the identity of a substance. The mass of a log can be observed without changing the log. A chemical property, however, is observed by attempting to change the identity of a substance. To witness a log's flammability, you must try to set the log on fire.

A substance always has physical and chemical properties. For example, a log is flammable even when it's not burning.

Active Reading **14 Compare** Describe the difference between a physical property and a chemical property.

_____

_____

_____

Visualize It!

Bending an iron nail will change its shape but not its identity.

An iron nail can react with oxygen in the air to form iron oxide, or rust.

15 Distinguish What type of property is being shown by each nail?

_____

_____

16 Predict Check the correct box to show whether each property of an iron nail is a physical or a chemical property.

Malleable	☐ Physical
	☐ Chemical
Reacts with oxygen	☐ Physical
	☐ Chemical
Magnetic	☐ Physical
	☐ Chemical
Nonflammable	☐ Physical
	☐ Chemical

At the Scene

FORENSIC SCIENCE

The collection and study of physical evidence in a criminal investigation is known as *forensic science*. Forensic scientists are experts in observing the physical and chemical properties of evidence at crime scenes.

Arson Investigation

A forensic scientist can gently heat ashes from an arson scene to help determine what chemicals were used to start the fire. If detectives know how the fire began, then they might be able to determine who is responsible for the crime.

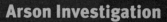

Studying Paint

Flecks of paint left on a tree where a car hit it can be examined with a special microscope. How the paint absorbs light can reveal what chemicals were used in the paint. This information could help authorities determine what kind of vehicle a criminal suspect drove.

Fiber Analysis

Magnified fibers, like those shown above, can provide clues, too. An acrylic fiber might be material from a boat cover or a rug. Or, polyester could have come from a suspect's shirt.

Extend

Inquiry

17 Identify List physical and chemical properties used to identify evidence at a crime scene.

18 Predict When examining evidence, why might investigators want to be more careful examining chemical properties than physical properties?

19 Evaluate By examining the physical and chemical properties of evidence at a crime scene, investigators can often be more certain about what a suspicious substance is not than about what it is. Why do you think this is the case?

How can physical and chemical properties identify a substance?

Properties unique to a substance are its *characteristic properties*. Characteristic properties can be physical properties, such as density, or chemical properties, such as flammability. Characteristic properties stay the same regardless of the amount of a sample. They can help identify a substance.

Iron pyrite is one of several minerals having a color similar to that of gold. Miners can find iron pyrite near deposits of gold, and sometimes mistake it for gold. Color and location, however, are about the only properties iron pyrite shares with gold. The two substances have quite different characteristic properties.

For example, gold flattens when hit with a hammer, but iron pyrite shatters. When rubbed on a ceramic plate, gold leaves a yellow streak, but iron pyrite leaves a greenish black one. Gold keeps its shine even if beneath the sea for years, but iron pyrite turns green if exposed to water.

An easy way for miners to tell iron pyrite and gold apart is by using the property of density. Miners collect gold by sifting through dirt in pans. Because of its high density, gold stays in the pan while dirt and most other substances wash over the side as the miner swirls the contents in the pan. Since gold has a density almost four times that of iron pyrite, distinguishing gold from iron pyrite should be an easy task for the experienced miner.

To find the density of a substance, use the following formula, where *D* is density, *m* is mass, and *V* is volume:

$$D = \frac{m}{V}$$

20 Infer Check the box to show which would tell you for sure if you had a sample of real gold.

	Yes	No
Color of your sample.	☐	☐
What happens when you strike your sample with a hammer.	☐	☐
The location where your sample was found.	☐	☐

In pan mining, as the contents in the pan are swirled, less dense substances are washed away.

Do the Math

Sample Problem

A sample of gold has a mass of 579 g. The volume of the sample is 30 cm³. What is the density of the gold sample?

Identify

A. What do you know?

mass = 579 g, volume = 30 cm³

B. What do you want to find? Density

Plan

C. Write the formula: $D = \dfrac{m}{V}$

D. Substitute the given values into the formula:

$D = \dfrac{579 \text{ g}}{30 \text{ cm}^3}$

Solve

E. Divide: $\dfrac{579 \text{ g}}{30 \text{ cm}^3} = 19.3 \text{ g/cm}^3$

F. Check that your units agree:

The given units are grams and cubic centimeters, and the measure found is density. Therefore, the units should be g/cm³. The units agree.

Answer: 19.3 g/cm³

You Try It

21 Calculate A student finds an object with a mass of 64.54 g and a volume of 14 cm³. Find the density of the object. Is the object gold?

Identify

A. What do you know?

B. What do you want to find?

Plan

C. Write the formula:

D. Substitute the given values into the formula:

Solve

E. Divide:

F. Check that your units agree:

Answer:

Is the object gold?	Yes	No
	☐	☐

Gold

Iron pyrite

Visual Summary

To complete this summary, circle the correct word. Then use the key below to check your answers. You can use this page to review the main concepts of the lesson.

Physical and Chemical Properties

A physical property is a property that can be observed or measured without changing the identity of the substance.

22 Solubility / Flammability is a physical property.

23 The melting point of a substance is the temperature at which the substance changes from a solid to a gas / liquid.

A chemical property is a property that describes a substance's ability to form new substances.

24 Reactivity with water / Magnetism is a chemical property.

25 Flammability is the ability of a substance to transfer heat / burn.

The properties that are most useful in identifying a substance are its characteristic properties. Characteristic properties can be physical properties or chemical properties.

26 The characteristic properties of a substance do / do not depend on the size of the sample.

Answers: 22 Solubility; 23 liquid; 24 Reactivity with water; 25 burn; 26 do not

27 **Synthesize** You have two solid substances that look the same. What measurements would you take and which tests would you perform to determine whether they actually are the same?

Lesson Review

Vocabulary

Fill in the blanks with the term that best completes the following sentences.

1 Flammability is an example of a _____ property.

2 Electrical conductivity is an example of a _____ property.

Key Concepts

3 Identify What are three physical properties of aluminum foil?

_____

_____

_____

4 Describe What effect does observing a substance's physical properties have on the substance?

_____

_____

_____

_____

5 Explain Describe how a physical property, such as mass or texture, can change without causing a change in the substance.

_____

_____

_____

_____

_____

6 Justify Must new substances be formed when you observe a chemical property? Explain.

_____

_____

_____

_____

_____

Critical Thinking

Use this table to answer the following question.

Element	Melting Point (°C)	Boiling Point (°C)
Bromine	–7.2	59
Chlorine	–100	–35
Iodine	110	180

7 Infer You are given samples of the substances shown in the table. The samples are labeled A, B, and C. At room temperature, sample A is a solid, sample B is a liquid, and sample C is a gas. What are the identities of samples A, B, and C? (Hint: Room temperature is about 20 °C.)

_____

_____

_____

8 Conclude The density of gold is 19.3 g/cm^3. The density of iron pyrite is 5.0 g/cm^3. If a nugget of iron pyrite and a nugget of gold each have a mass of 50 g, what can you conclude about the volume of each nugget?

_____

_____

_____

_____

9 Predict Suppose you need to build a raft to cross a fast-moving river. Describe the physical and chemical properties of the raft that would be important to ensure your safety.

_____

_____

_____

_____

_____

_____

Focus on ENGINEERING

Materials Matter

Indiana Standards

8.4.1 Understand how the strength of attractive forces between particles in a material helps to explain many physical properties of the material, such as why different materials exist as gases, liquids or solids at a given temperature.

8.4.2 Rank the strength of attractions between the particles of room-temperature materials.

8.4.3 Investigate the properties (mechanical, chemical, electrical, thermal, magnetic, and optical) of natural and engineered materials.

What makes a material useful for a certain application?

If you were designing a new type of cell phone, would you choose to make the phone out of glass? Probably not. Glass is heavy and brittle. A phone must be lightweight yet durable. And the materials that make up the phone might need to have a certain shape or withstand certain temperatures. Materials scientists must consider these factors when they are developing new types of materials.

Visualize It!

1 Compare Place a 1, 2, or 3 in each circle to rank the attraction, from greatest to least, between particles in the three states of matter at room temperature.

What a Steel!
The Empire State Building in New York contains 60,000 tons of steel! Steel is a metal mixture made up mostly of iron. Like other solids, steel is a rigid material. Steel is very strong and resistant to chemical changes due to weathering.

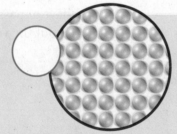

The particles that make up a **solid** are locked into place by strong attractive forces between the particles.

Argon: An Invisible Insulator
Argon is an invisible gas and a good thermal insulator. These properties make it useful for updating windows like these to be more energy efficient. Argon is placed between two panes of glass. The argon atoms move apart to fill the space between the panes.

The higher kinetic energy of particles in a **gas** overcomes the attractive forces between particles.

Keep Your Cool!

A mixture of antifreeze and water helps keep a car's engine cool. This liquid has a low freezing point and a high boiling point. The particles that make up the liquid slide past one another. As a result, the antifreeze mixture can move through hoses to reach different parts of the engine.

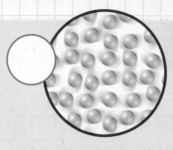

Attractive forces between the particles in a **liquid** allow the particles to slide past one another.

Shape Shifters

This computer screen is a liquid crystal display, or LCD. Liquid crystal particles move like a liquid. However, the particles can be ordered like those of a solid. When liquid crystals interact with an electric current, their optical properties change. Some computer hard drives contain seals that contain ferrofluids. Ferrofluids can flow like a liquid. However, their particles become ordered in the presence of a magnetic field.

Review

2 Compare At room temperature, how does the attraction between particles in a liquid compare to the attraction between particles in a solid?

_____

_____

3 Explain You are reviewing prototypes of a lightweight insulated mug. Each prototype is made of two solid layers with a different insulating material in between. What properties of the insulator should you consider during your review of the prototypes?

_____

_____

4 Extend Solid foams are engineering materials that have special properties. Research a solid foam and describe its physical properties and uses by doing one of the following:
- make a brochure
- create a web page
- write a short essay

How does nature inspire engineering?

Scientists who design materials or products for engineering applications often turn to nature for inspiration. For example, a scientist trying to create a material that harnesses solar energy might study how plants use the sun's energy for photosynthesis. The practice of modeling engineered materials after natural ones is called biomimicry. These materials mimic, or behave like, biological processes or living things.

Shark Attack

This magnified image of shark skin shows that its surface contains grooved, diamond-shaped scales. These scales reduce the shark's drag through the water. They also limit the growth of bacteria. Scientists have designed a synthetic material that has a similar texture. This fabric has been used in underwater apparel such as the swimsuit at the right.

5 Apply How could the antimicrobial properties of this fabric be applied to a product or process?

_____

_____

_____

_____

_____

Dogfish shark

A Clever Cane

Bats locate their prey by a process called echolocation. In echolocation, bats emit sound waves that reflect off objects and bounce back toward the bat. The timing of the reflected waves gives the bat information about the location and size of nearby objects. This process inspired the development of a cane that assists visually-impaired people. An electronic device on the cane emits sound waves and records the timing of the reflected waves.

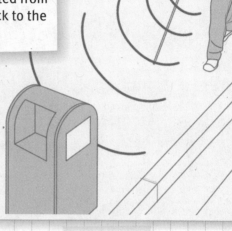

6 Infer At the right, draw the sound waves that would be reflected from the mailbox back to the cane.

Visualize It!

7 Design Consider the mechanical properties of the silk threads of a spider web. Then, draw a sketch of a material or product that is inspired by the silk. Label your drawing to explain the product's use.

Review

8 Apply Define *biomimicry* in your own words.

_____

_____

_____

9 Apply Lotus leaves have a special surface that repels water. How could this physical property be useful in an engineering application?

_____

_____

_____

10 Extend Work with a partner to identify an engineering problem that is being actively researched. Brainstorm solutions that are inspired by biological processes or living things. Share your designs by doing one of the following:

- make a poster
- create a computer presentation

Physical and Chemical Changes

ESSENTIAL QUESTION

What are physical and chemical changes of matter?

By the end of this lesson, you should be able to distinguish between physical and chemical changes of matter.

Rusty beams are all that remain of these large boats. The rust is the result of an interaction of the iron beams with water and air.

Indiana Standards

8.1.7 Explain that chemical changes occur when substances react and form one or more different products, whose physical and chemical properties are different from those of the reactants.

8.1.8 Demonstrate that in a chemical change, the total numbers of each kind of atom in the product are the same as in the reactants and that the total mass of the reacting system is conserved.

Engage Your Brain

1 Predict Check T or F to show whether you think each statement is true or false.

T	F	
☐	☐	When an ice cube melts, it is still water.
☐	☐	Matter is lost when a candle is burned.
☐	☐	When your body digests food, the food is changed into new substances.

2 Describe Write a word or phrase beginning with each letter of the word CHANGE that describes changes you have observed in everyday objects.

C _____

H _____

A _____

N _____

G _____

E _____

Active Reading

3 Apply Use context clues to write your own definitions for the words *interact* and *indicate*.

Example sentence
As the two substances <u>interact</u>, gas bubbles are given off.

interact:

_____

_____

_____

Example sentence
A color change may <u>indicate</u> that a chemical change has taken place.

indicate:

_____

_____

_____

Vocabulary Terms

- physical change
- chemical change
- law of conservation of mass

4 Apply As you learn the definition of each vocabulary term in this lesson, create your own definition or sketch to help you remember the meaning of the term.

Change of Appearance

What are physical changes of matter?

A physical property of matter is any property that can be observed or measured without changing the chemical identity of the substance. A **physical change** is a change that affects one or more physical properties of a substance. Physical changes occur when a substance changes from one form to another. However, the chemical identity of the substance remains the same.

Changes in Observable Properties

The appearance, shape, or size of a substance may be altered during a physical change. For example, the process of turning wool into a sweater requires that the wool undergo physical changes. Wool is sheared from the sheep. The wool is then cleaned, and the wool fibers are separated from one another. Shearing and separating the fibers are physical changes that change the shape, volume, and texture of the wool.

Active Reading

5 Explain What happens to a substance during a physical change?

Physical Changes Turn Wool into a Sweater

A Wool is sheared from the sheep. The raw wool is then cleaned and placed into a machine that separates the wool fibers from one another.

B The wool fibers are spun into yarn. Again, the shape and volume of the wool change. The fibers are twisted so that they are packed more closely together and are intertwined with one another.

C The yarn is dyed. The dye changes the color of the wool, but it does not change the wool into another substance. This type of color change is a physical change.

Changes That Do Not Alter the Chemical Identity of the Substance

During the process of turning wool into a sweater, many physical changes occur in the wool. However, the wool does not change into some other substance as a result of these changes. Therefore, physical changes do not change the chemical identity of a substance.

Another example of a physical change happens when you fill an ice cube tray with water and place it inside a freezer. If the water gets cold enough, it will freeze to form ice cubes. Freezing water does not change its chemical makeup. In fact, you could melt the ice cube and have liquid water again! Changes of state, and all physical changes, do not change the chemical makeup of the substance.

6 Identify The list below gives several examples of physical changes. Write your own examples of physical changes on the blank lines.

Examples of Physical Changes
Stretching a rubber band
Dissolving sugar in water
Cutting your hair
Melting butter
Bending a paper clip
Crushing an aluminum can

_____

_____

_____

D Knitting the yarn into a sweater also does not change the wool into another substance. A wool sweater is still wool, even though it no longer resembles the wool on the sheep.

Visualize It!

7 Analyze How does the yarn in the sweater differ from the wool on the sheep?

_____

_____

_____

Change from

What are chemical changes of matter?

Think about what happens to the burning logs in a campfire. They start out dry, rough, and dense. After flames surround them, the logs emerge as black and powdery ashes. The campfire releases a lot of heat and smoke in the process. Something has obviously happened, something more than simply a change of appearance. The wood has stopped being wood. It has undergone a chemical change.

Changes in Substance Identity

A **chemical change** occurs when one or more substances change into entirely new substances with different properties. For example, in the campfire, the dry, dense wood became the powdery ashes—new substances with different properties. When a cake is baked, the liquid cake batter becomes the solid, spongy treat. Whenever a new substance is formed, a chemical change has occurred.

Be aware that chemical *changes* are not exactly the same as chemical *properties*. Burning is a chemical change; flammability is a chemical property. The chemical properties of a substance describe which chemical changes can or cannot happen to that substance. Chemical changes are the *processes* by which substances actually change into new substances. You can learn about a substance's chemical properties by watching the chemical changes that substance undergoes.

Visualize It!

8 Identify Use the boxes provided to identify the wood, ashes, and flames involved in the chemical change. Then write a caption describing the chemical changes you see in the photo.

_____

_____

_____

_____

the inside

A _____

B _____

C _____

Changes to the Chemical Makeup of a Substance

In a chemical change, a substance's identity changes because its chemical makeup changes. This happens as the particles and chemical bonds that make up the substance get rearranged. For example, when iron rusts, molecules of oxygen from the air combine with iron atoms to form a new compound. Rust is not iron or oxygen. It is a new substance made up of oxygen and iron joined together.

Because chemical changes involve changes in the arrangements of particles, they are often influenced by temperature. At higher temperatures, the particles in a substance have more average kinetic energy. They move around a lot more freely and so rearrange more easily. Therefore, at higher temperatures, chemical reactions often happen more quickly. Think of baking a cake. The higher the temperature of the oven, the less time the cake will need to bake because the faster the chemical reactions occur.

Active Reading **9 Explain** How do higher temperatures influence a chemical change?

_____

_____

_____

Think Outside the Book (Inquiry)

10 Infer Think of ways you control temperature to influence chemical changes during a typical day. (Hint: Cooking, Art class)

Look for the signs

How can you tell a chemical change has happened?

Physical changes and chemical changes are different. Chemical changes result in new substances, while physical changes do not. However, it may not be obvious that any new substances have formed during a chemical change. Here are some signs that a chemical change may have occurred. If you observe two or more of these signs during a change, you likely are observing a chemical change.

Active Reading **11 Compare** How are physical and chemical changes different?

_____

_____

_____

_____

Production of an Odor

Some chemical changes produce odors. The chemical change that occurs when an egg is rotting, for example, produces the smell of sulfur. Milk that has soured also has an unpleasant smell—because bacteria have formed new substances in the milk. And if you've gone outdoors after a thunderstorm, you've probably noticed a distinct smell. This odor is an indication that lightning has caused a chemical change in the air.

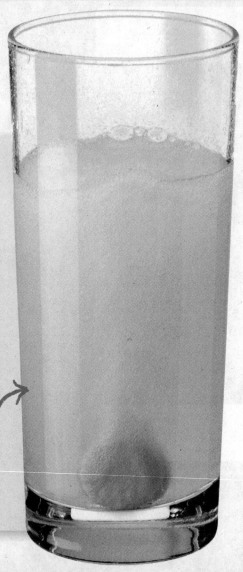

Production of a Gas

Chemical changes often cause fizzing or foaming. For example, a chemical change is involved when an antacid tablet is dropped into a glass of water. As the tablet makes contact with the water and begins to react with it, bubbles of gas appear. One of the new substances that is formed is carbon dioxide gas, which forms the bubbles that you see.

It is important to note that some physical changes, such as boiling, can also produce gas bubbles. Therefore, the only way to know for sure whether a chemical change has taken place is to identify new substances.

Bubbles form when an antacid tablet reacts with water. The bubbles contain a new, gaseous substance, which signals that a chemical change has happened.

© Houghton Mifflin Harcourt Publishing Company • Image Credits: ©PhotoSpin, Inc/Alamy

Formation of a Precipitate

Chemical changes may result in products in different physical states. Liquids sometimes combine to form a solid called a *precipitate*. For example, colorless potassium iodide and lead nitrate combine to form the bright yellow precipitate lead iodide, as shown below.

Bright yellow lead iodide precipitates from the clear solution.

Change in Color

A change in color is often an indication of a chemical change. For example, when gray iron rusts, the product that forms is brown.

Change in Energy

Chemical changes can cause energy to change from one form into another. For example, in a burning candle, the chemical energy stored in the candle converts to heat and light energy.

A change in temperature is often a sign of a chemical change. The change need not always be as dramatic as the one in the photo, however.

The reaction of powdered aluminum with a metal oxide releases so much heat that it is often used to weld metals together. Here it is being used to test the heat-resistant properties of steel.

12 Infer List the observations you might make as you witness each of the changes below. Then classify each change as a physical change or a chemical change.

Change	Signs/observations	Type of change
Boiling water		
Baking a cake		
Burning wood		
Painting a door		

Conservation is the Law

What is the law of conservation of mass?

If you freeze 5 mL of water and then let the ice melt, you have 5 mL of water again. You can freeze and melt the water as much as you like. The mass of water will not change.

This does not always seem true for chemical changes. The ashes remaining after a fire contain much less mass than the logs that produced them. Mass seems to vanish. In other chemical changes, such as those that cause the growth of plants, mass seems to appear out of nowhere. This puzzled scientists for years. Where did the mass go? Where did it come from?

In the 1770s, the French chemist Antoine Lavoisier (an•TWAHN luh•VWAH•zee•ay) studied chemical changes in which substances seemed to lose or gain mass. He showed that the mass was most often lost to or gained from gases in the air. Lavoisier demonstrated this transformation of mass by observing chemical changes in sealed glass bulbs. This was the first demonstration of the *law of conservation of mass*. The **law of conservation of mass** states that in ordinary chemical and physical changes, mass is not created or destroyed but is only transformed into different substances.

The examples at the right will help you understand how the law works in both physical and chemical changes. In the top example, the second robot may have a different shape than the first, but it clearly has the same parts. In the second example, vinegar and baking soda undergo a chemical change. Mix the baking soda with the vinegar in the flask, and mass seems to vanish. Yet the balloon shows that what really happens is the production of a gas—carbon dioxide gas.

Active Reading 13 **Identify** What is the law of conservation of mass?

_____

_____

_____

The water may freeze or the ice may melt, but the amount of matter in this glass will stay the same.

Conservation of Mass in Physical Changes

When the long gray piece is moved from its arms to its waist, the toy robot gets a new look. It's still a toy robot—its parts are just rearranged. Most physical changes are reversible. All physical changes follow the law of conservation of mass.

Before **After**

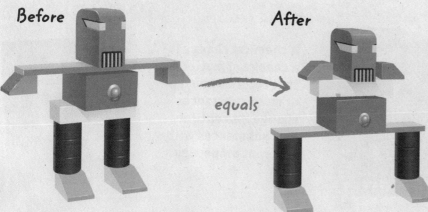

equals

👁 Visualize It!

14 Describe How is the physical change in the robot reversible, and how can you tell that the change follows the law of conservation of mass?

_____
_____
_____
_____
_____

Conservation of Mass in Chemical Changes

When vinegar and baking soda are combined, they undergo a chemical change. The balloon at the right is inflated with carbon dioxide gas that was produced as a result of the change. The mass of the starting materials is the same as the mass of the products. Without the balloon to catch it, however, the gas would seem to disappear.

Before **After**

vinegar

baking soda

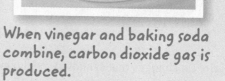

equals

When vinegar and baking soda combine, carbon dioxide gas is produced.

👁 Visualize It!

15 Infer What would you observe about the mass in the flask if you did not put the balloon on top? Why?

_____
_____

Visual Summary

To complete this summary, circle the correct word or phrase. Then use the key below to check your answers. You can use this page to review the main concepts of the lesson.

How Matter Changes

A physical change is a change of matter from one form to another without a change in the identity of the substance.

16 Burning / Dyeing wool is an example of a physical change.

A chemical change is a change of matter that occurs when one or more substances change into entirely new substances with different properties.

17 The formation of a precipitate signals a physical / chemical change.

Chemical changes often cause the production of an odor, fizzing or foaming, the formation of a precipitate, or changes in color or temperature.

18 This physical / chemical change results in the formation of new substances.

The law of conservation of mass states that mass cannot be created or destroyed in ordinary chemical and physical changes.

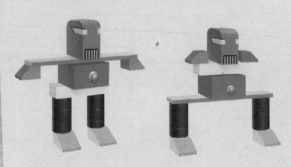

19 The mass of the toy on the right is the same as / different from the mass of the toy on the left.

Answers: 16 Dyeing; 17 chemical; 18 chemical; 19 the same as

20 Explain Do changes that cannot be easily reversed, such as burning, observe the law of conservation of mass? Explain.

Lesson Review

Vocabulary

In your own words, define the following terms.

1 physical change

_____

_____

2 chemical change

_____

_____

3 law of conservation of mass

_____

_____

Key Concepts

4 Identify Give an example of a physical change and an example of a chemical change.

_____

_____

_____

_____

5 Compare How is a chemical change different from a physical change?

_____

_____

_____

6 Apply Suppose a log's mass is 5 kg. After burning, the mass of the ash is 1 kg. Explain what may have happened to the other 4 kg.

_____

_____

_____

_____

Critical Thinking

Use this photo to answer the following question.

7 Analyze As the bright sun shines upon the water, the water slowly disappears. The same sunlight gives energy to the surrounding plants to convert water and carbon dioxide into sugar and oxygen gas. Which change is physical and which is chemical?

_____

_____

_____

8 Compare Relate the statement "You can't get something for nothing" to the law of the conservation of mass.

_____

_____

_____

_____

9 Infer Sharpening a pencil leaves behind pencil shavings. Is sharpening a pencil a physical change or a chemical change? Explain.

_____

_____

_____

_____

Pure Substances and Mixtures

ESSENTIAL QUESTION

How do pure substances and mixtures compare?

By the end of this lesson, you should be able to distinguish between pure substances and mixtures.

Seawater is a unique mixture that contains many dissolved substances. One such substance, called calcium carbonate, is used by these stony coral to build their hard skeletons.

Indiana Standards

8.1.1 Explain that all matter is composed of particular arrangements of atoms of approximately one hundred elements.

8.1.5 Explain that atoms join together to form molecules and compounds and illustrate with diagrams the relationship between atoms and compounds and/or molecules.

8.1.6 Explain that elements and compounds have characteristic properties such as density, boiling points and melting points that remain unchanged regardless of the sample size.

Engage Your Brain

1 Predict Check T or F to show whether you think each statement is true or false.

T	F	
☐	☐	Atoms combine in different ways to make up all the substances you encounter every day.
☐	☐	Saltwater can be separated into salt and water.
☐	☐	A mixture of soil has the same chemical composition throughout.

2 Apply Think of a substance that does not dissolve in water. Draw a sketch below that shows what happens when this substance is added to water.

 Active Reading

3 Synthesize Many English words have their roots in other languages. Use the Greek words below to make an educated guess about the meanings of the words *homogeneous* and *heterogeneous*.

Greek word	Meaning
genus	type
homos	same
heteros	different

Example sentence
Saltwater is <u>homogeneous</u> throughout.

homogeneous:

_____

_____

Example sentence
A <u>heterogeneous</u> mixture of rocks varies from handful to handful.

heterogeneous:

_____

_____

Vocabulary Terms

- atom
- element
- compound
- mixture
- pure substance
- heterogeneous
- homogeneous

4 Identify This list contains the key terms you'll learn in this lesson. As you read, circle the defnition of each term.

A Great Combination

How can matter be classified?

What kinds of food could you make with the ingredients shown below? You could eat slices of tomato as a snack. Or, you could combine tomato slices with lettuce to make a salad. Combine more ingredients, such as bread and cheese, and you have a sandwich. Just as these meals are made up of simpler foods, matter is made up of basic "ingredients" known as *atoms*. **Atoms** are the smallest unit of an element that maintains the properties of that element. Atoms, like the foods shown here, can be combined in different ways to produce different substances.

The substances you encounter every day can be classified into one of the three major classes of matter: *elements, compounds,* and *mixtures.* Atoms are the basic building blocks for all three types of matter. Elements, compounds, and mixtures differ in the way that atoms are combined.

Active Reading **5 Compare** What do elements, compounds, and mixtures have in common?

_____

_____

Think Outside the Book **Inquiry**

6 Predict If you have ever baked a cake or bread, you know that the ingredients that combine to make it taste different from the baked food. Why do you think that is?

Just as these ingredients combine to make a tasty sandwich, atoms are the basic "ingredients" that make up matter.

Matter Can Be Classified into Elements, Compounds, and Mixtures

You can think of atoms as the building blocks of matter. Like these toy blocks, atoms can be connected in different ways. The models below show how atoms make up elements and compounds. Elements and compounds, in turn, make up mixtures.

 An atom is like a building block of matter.

 An **element** is made up of one or more of the same kind of atom chemically combined.

Oxygen

 A **compound** is made up of different kinds of atoms chemically combined. Compounds have different properties from the elements that make them up.

Water

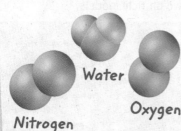 A **mixture** contains a variety of elements and compounds that are not chemically combined with each other.

Water

Nitrogen   Oxygen

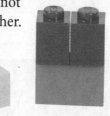 

Visualize It!

7 Analyze Why are the spheres representing nitrogen and oxygen different colors?

_____

_____

_____

_____

Pure Genius

What are pure substances?

Elements and compounds are **pure substances**. A pure substance is a substance that has definite physical and chemical properties such as appearance, melting point, and reactivity. No matter the amount of a pure substance you have, it will always have the same properties. This is because pure substances are made up of one type of particle.

Pure Substances Are Made Up of One Type of Particle

Copper, like all elements, is a pure substance. Take a look at the element copper, shown below. The atoms that make up copper are all the same. No matter where in the world you find pure copper, it will always have the same properties.

Compounds are also pure substances. Consider water, shown on the next page. Two different kinds of atoms make up each chemically combined particle, or *molecule*. Every water molecule is identical. Each molecule is made up of exactly two hydrogen atoms and one oxygen atom. Because water is a pure substance, we can define certain properties of water. For example, at standard pressure, water always freezes at 0 °C and boils at 100 °C.

Visualize It!

8 Identify Fill in the blanks to label the two particle models.

Ⓐ Copper _____

9 Explain Copper is an element. How do these images of copper illustrate this?

_____

_____

_____

_____

Pure Substances Cannot Be Formed or Broken Down by Physical Changes

Physical changes such as melting, freezing, cutting, or smashing do not change the identity of pure substances. For example, if you cut copper pipe into short pieces, the material is still copper. And if you freeze liquid water, the particles that make up the ice remain the same: two hydrogen atoms combined with one oxygen atom.

The chemical bonds that hold atoms together cannot be broken easily. To break or form chemical bonds, a chemical change is required. For example, when an electric current is passed through water, a chemical change takes place. The atoms that make up the compound break apart into two elements: hydrogen and oxygen. When a pure substance undergoes a chemical change, it is no longer that same substance. A chemical change changes the identity of the substance. Individual atoms cannot be broken down into smaller parts by normal physical or chemical changes.

Active Reading **11 Identify** What happens when a pure substance undergoes a chemical change?

_____

_____

_____

_____

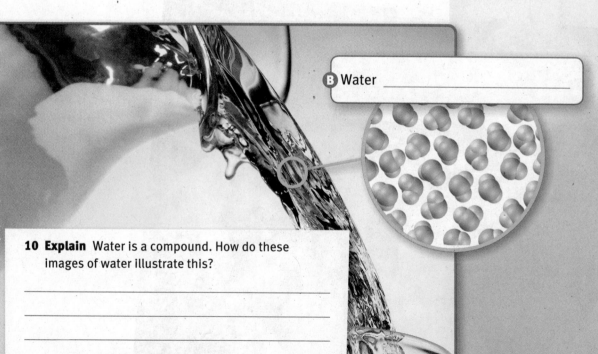

B Water _____

10 Explain Water is a compound. How do these images of water illustrate this?

_____

_____

_____

_____

Classified Information

How can elements be classified?

Active Reading

12 Identify As you read, underline the ways in which elements are organized on the periodic table.

Differences in physical and chemical properties allow us to classify elements. By knowing the category to which an element belongs, you can predict some of its properties. Elements are broadly classified as metals, nonmetals, or metalloids. Most metals are shiny, conduct heat and electricity well, and can be shaped into thin sheets and wires. Nonmetals are not shiny and do not conduct heat or electricity well. Metalloids have some properties of both metals and nonmetals.

There are over 100 elements known to exist. Each element has a place in an arrangement called the periodic table of the elements. The periodic table is a useful tool that can help you to identify elements that have similar properties. Metals, nonmetals, and metalloids occupy different regions in the periodic table. Metals start at the left and make up most of the elements in the periodic table. Nonmetals are at the right and are often shaded with a color different from that of the metals. Not surprisingly, the metalloids lie between the metals and nonmetals. In many instances, you can even predict which elements combine with others to form compounds based on their positions in the periodic table.

Aluminum, like many metals, can be formed into a thin foil.

Charcoal, made mostly of carbon atoms, is brittle and dull like many other nonmetals.

How can compounds be classified?

You are surrounded by compounds. Compounds make up the food you eat, the school supplies you use, and the clothes you wear—even you! There are so many compounds that it would be very difficult to list or describe them all. Fortunately, these compounds can be grouped into a few basic categories by their properties.

13 Classify Read about some of the ways in which compounds can be classified. Then fill in the blanks to complete the photo captions.

By Their pH

Compounds can be classified as acidic, basic, or neutral by measuring a special value known as *pH*. Acids have a pH value below 7. Vinegar contains acetic acid, which gives a sharp, sour taste to salad dressings. Bases, on the other hand, have pH values greater than 7. Baking soda is an example of a basic compound. Bases have a slippery feel and a bitter taste. Neutral compounds, such as pure water and table salt, have a pH value of 7. Water and salt are formed when an acid and a base react. A type of paper called litmus paper can be used to test whether a compound is an acid or a base. Blue litmus paper turns red in the presence of an acid. Red litmus paper turns blue in the presence of a base. Although some foods are acidic or basic, you should NEVER taste, smell, or touch a chemical to classify them. Many acids and bases can damage your body or clothing.

Baking soda is an example of a(n) _____

As Organic or Inorganic

You may have heard of organically-grown foods. But in chemistry, the word *organic* refers to compounds that contain carbon and hydrogen. Organic compounds are found in most foods. They can also be found in synthetic goods. For example, gasoline contains a number of organic compounds, such as octane and heptane.

The compounds that make up plastic are _____ because they contain carbon.

By Their Role in the Body

Organic compounds that are made by living things are called biochemicals. Biochemicals are divided into four categories: carbohydrates, lipids, proteins, and nucleic acids. *Carbohydrates* are used as a source of energy and include sugars, starches, and fiber. *Lipids* are biochemicals that store excess energy in the body and make up cell membranes. Lipids include fats, oils, and waxes. *Proteins* are one of the most abundant types of compounds in your body. They regulate chemical activities of the body and build and repair body structures. *Nucleic acids* such as DNA and RNA contain genetic information and help the body build proteins.

Your body gets _____ such as sugars, starches, and fiber, from many of the foods you eat.

Mix and Match

What are mixtures?

Imagine that you roll out some dough, add tomato sauce, and sprinkle some cheese on top. Then you add green peppers, mushrooms, and pepperoni. What have you just made? A pizza, of course! But that's not all. You have also created a mixture.

A mixture is a combination of two or more substances that are combined physically but not chemically. When two or more materials are put together, they form a mixture if they do not change chemically to form a new substance. For example, cheese and tomato sauce do not react when they are combined to make a pizza. They keep their original identities and properties. So, a pizza is a mixture.

Mixtures Are Made Up of More Than One Type of Particle

Unlike elements and compounds, mixtures are not pure substances. Mixtures contain more than one type of substance. Each substance in a mixture has the same chemical makeup it had before the mixture formed.

Unlike pure substances, mixtures do not have definite properties. Granite from different parts of the world could contain different minerals in different ratios. Pizzas made by different people could have different toppings. Mixtures do not have defined properties because they do not have a defined chemical makeup.

Visualize It!

14 Describe This student is going to make and separate a mixture of sand and salt. Complete these captions to describe what is taking place in each photo.

Ⓐ Sand and salt are poured into a single beaker. The result is a mixture because

_____

_____

_____

Mixtures Can Be Separated by Physical Changes

You don't like mushrooms on your pizza? Just pick them off. This change is a physical change of the mixture because the identities of the substances do not change. But not all mixtures are as easy to separate as a pizza. You cannot just pick salt out of a salt water mixture. One way to separate the salt from the water is to heat the mixture until the water evaporates. The salt is left behind. Other ways to separate mixtures are shown at the right and below.

A magnet can separate a mixture of aluminum nails and iron nails.

Active Reading **15 Devise** How could you separate a mixture of rocks and sand?

_____

_____

_____

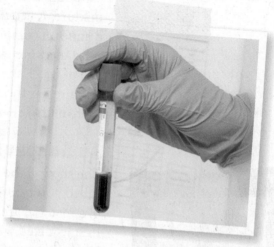

A machine called a centrifuge separates mixtures by the densities of the components. It can be used to separate the different parts of blood.

B When water is added to the sand-salt mixture,

_____

_____

_____

C When the liquid is poured through a filter,

_____

_____

_____

D The remaining salt water is heated until

_____

_____

_____

A Simple Solution

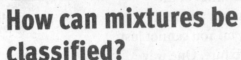

A snow globe contains a suspension.

How can mixtures be classified?

It is clear that something is a mixture when you can see the different substances in it. For example, if you scoop up a handful of soil, it might contain dirt, rocks, leaves, and even insects. Exactly what you see depends on what part of the soil is scooped. Such a mixture is called a heterogeneous (het•uhr•uh•JEE•nee•uhs) mixture. A **heterogeneous** mixture is one that does not have a uniform composition. In other types of mixtures, the substances are evenly spread throughout. If you add sugar to a cup of water, the sugar dissolves. Each part of the sugar-water mixture has the same sweet taste. This is called a **homogeneous** (hoh•muh•JEE•nee•uhs) mixture.

As Suspensions

The snow globe (above) contains a type of heterogeneous mixture called a *suspension*. Suspensions are mixtures in which the particles of a material are spread throughout a liquid or gas but are too large to stay mixed without being stirred or shaken. If a suspension is allowed to sit, the particles will settle out.

As Solutions

Tea is a solution.

Tea is an example of a type of homogeneous mixture known as a *solution*. In a solution, one substance is dissolved in another substance. When you make tea, some of the compounds inside the tea leaves dissolve in the hot water. These compounds give your tea its unique color and taste. Many familiar solutions are liquids. However, solutions may also be gases or solids. Air is an example of a gaseous solution. Alloys, such as brass and steel, are solid solutions in which substances are dissolved in metals.

As Colloids

Gelatin is a colloid.

Colloids are a third type of mixture that falls somewhere between suspensions and solutions. As in a suspension, the particles in a colloid are spread throughout a liquid or gas. Unlike the particles in a suspension, colloid particles are small and do not settle out quickly. Milk and gelatin are colloids. Colloids look homogeneous, but we consider them to be heterogeneous.

17 Summarize Complete the graphic organizer below by filling in the blanks with terms from this lesson. Then add definitions or sketches of each term inside the appropriate box.

Classifying Matter

Matter
Definition:

Matter is anything that has mass and takes up space. Matter is made up of building blocks called atoms.

Pure Substances
Definition:

Sketch:

Elements
Sketch:

Definition:

Sketch:

Homogeneous
Definition:

Suspensions
Sketch:

Colloids
Definition:

Definition:

Visual Summary

To complete this summary, circle the correct word or phrase. Then use the key below to check your answers. You can use this page to review the main concepts of the lesson.

Pure substances are made up of a single type of particle and cannot be formed or broken down by physical changes.

18 Water is a pure substance / mixture.

19 Water is a(n) element / compound.

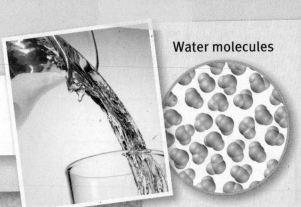

Water molecules

Pure Substances and Mixtures

Mixtures are made up of more than one type of particle and can be separated into their component parts by physical changes.

20 Saltwater and sand can be separated with a magnet / filter.

21 Saltwater is a homogeneous / heterogeneous mixture.

Answers: 18 pure substance; 19 compound; 20 filter; 21 homogeneous

22 **Predict** Why do you think that the particles of a suspension settle out but the particles of a colloid do not?

Lesson Review

Vocabulary

Fill in the blanks with the term that best completes the following sentences.

1 The basic building blocks of matter are called

_____

2 A(n) _____ is a substance that is made up of a single kind of atom.

3 Elements and compounds are two types of

_____

4 A(n) _____ is a combination of substances that are combined physically but not chemically.

Key Concepts

5 Identify What kind of mixture is a solution? A suspension? A colloid?

_____
_____
_____
_____

6 Apply Fish give off the compound ammonia, which has a pH above 7. To which class of compounds does ammonia belong?

_____
_____

7 Compare Fill in the following table with properties of elements and compounds.

How are elements and compounds similar?	How are elements and compounds different?

Use this drawing to answer the following question.

8 Identify What type of mixture is this salad dressing?

_____

Critical Thinking

9 Explain Could a mixture be made up of only elements and no compounds? Explain.

_____
_____
_____
_____

10 Synthesize Describe a procedure to separate a mixture of sugar, black pepper, and pebbles.

_____
_____
_____
_____
_____
_____
_____
_____
_____

Shirley Ann Jackson

PHYSICIST AND EDUCATOR

How can you make contributions to many areas of science all at once? One way is to promote the study of science by others. This is precisely what physicist Dr. Shirley Ann Jackson does as the president of Rensselaer Polytechnic Institute in Troy, New York.

Earlier in her career, she was a research scientist, investigating the electrical and optical properties of matter. Engineers used her research to help develop products for the telecommunications industry. She later became a professor of physics at Rutgers University in New Jersey.

In 1995, President Bill Clinton appointed Dr. Jackson to chair the U.S. Nuclear Regulatory Commission (NRC). The NRC is responsible for promoting the safe use of nuclear energy. At the NRC, Dr. Jackson used her knowledge of how the particles that make up matter interact and can generate energy. She also used her leadership skills. She helped to start the International Nuclear Regulators Association. This group made it easier for officials from many nations to discuss issues of nuclear safety.

Dr. Jackson's interest in science started when she observed bees in her backyard. She is still studying the world around her, making careful observations, and taking actions based on what she learns. These steps for learning were the foundation for all her later contributions to science. As a student, Dr. Jackson learned the same things about matter and energy that you are learning.

Nuclear power plant

Language Arts Connection

Research how nuclear energy is generated, what it can be used for, and what concerns surround it. Write a summary report to the government outlining the risks and benefits of using nuclear energy.

JOB BOARD

Chemical Technician

What You'll Do: Help chemists and chemical engineers in laboratory tests, observe solids, liquids, and gases for research or development of new products. You might handle hazardous chemicals or toxic materials.

Where You Might Work: Mostly indoors in laboratories or manufacturing plants, but may do some research outdoors.

Education: An associate's degree in applied science or science-related technology, specialized technical training, or a bachelor's degree in chemistry, biology, or forensic science is needed.

Other Job Requirements: You need to follow written steps of procedures and to accurately record measurements and observations. You need to understand the proper handling of hazardous materials.

Chef

What You'll Do: Prepare, season, and cook food, keep a clean kitchen, supervise kitchen staff, and buy supplies and equipment.

Where You Might Work: Restaurants, hotels, the military, schools, and in your own kitchen as a private caterer.

Education: Many chefs gain on-the-job training without formal culinary school training. However, you can also learn cooking skills at culinary institutes and earn a two-year or four-year degree.

Other Job Requirements: Your job will require you to be on your feet for many hours and lift heavy equipment and boxes of food.

PEOPLE IN SCIENCE NEWS

Andy Goldsworthy

Changing Matter Is Art

Andy Goldsworthy is interested in how matter changes over time. He is inspired by the changes that occur in nature. As a sculptor, he uses materials found in nature, like snow, ice, twigs, and leaves. Many of his sculptures do not last for very long, but these materials show the changing state of matter. For example, for one of his art projects, he made 13 large snowballs in the winter and placed them in cold storage. In the middle of summer, he placed the snowballs around London. It took five days for the snowballs to melt. During that time they were reminders of a wider world of nature. Movement, change, light, growth, and decay are factors that affect his pieces. Because his work is constantly changing, Goldsworthy takes photographs of his sculptures.

The Atom

ESSENTIAL QUESTION

What makes up an atom?

By the end of this lesson, you should be able to describe the atomic theory by identifying atoms and the parts that make them up.

When you examine this painting closely, you can see that it is made up of tiny dots of paint. These dots of paints—and all matter—are made up of even smaller particles called atoms.

© Houghton Mifflin Harcourt Publishing Company • Image Credits: (bkgd) ©The London Art Archive/Alamy; (inset) ©The London Art Archive/Alamy

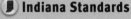

Indiana Standards

8.1.1 Explain that all matter is composed of particular arrangements of atoms of approximately one hundred elements.

8.1.4 Describe the structure of an atom and relate the arrangement of electrons to how that atom interacts with other atoms.

Engage Your Brain

1 Predict Check T or F to show whether you think each statement is true or false.

T	F	
☐	☐	Atoms can be seen with an ordinary light microscope.
☐	☐	Atoms have mass.
☐	☐	Different substances are made up of different types of atoms.

2 Predict Imagine that you could shrink down to the size of an atom. Draw what you think an atom would look like if you could see it.

Active Reading

3 Synthesize Many English words have their roots in other languages. Use the Greek word below to make an educated guess about the meaning of the word *atom*.

Greek word	Meaning
atomos	unable to be divided

Example sentence
A single grain of salt contains billions of <u>atoms</u>.

atom:

_____

_____

Vocabulary Terms

- atom
- proton
- neutron
- nucleus
- electron
- electron cloud
- atomic number
- mass number

4 Apply As you learn the definition of each vocabulary term in this lesson, create your own definition or sketch to help you remember the meaning of the term.

As a Matter of Fact...

What is matter made of?

Imagine that you cut a piece of paper in half. Then, you cut each half in half again. Could you keep cutting the pieces in half forever? Around 440 BCE, a Greek philosopher named Democritus (di•MAHK•ri•tuhz) thought that you would eventually end up with a particle that could not be cut. He called this particle *atomos*, a Greek word meaning "not able to be divided." Aristotle (AR•ih•staht•uhl), another Greek philosopher, disagreed with Democritus's ideas. Aristotle did not believe that such a particle could make up the variety of substances found in nature. Instead, he thought that all matter was infinitely divisible. To him and many others, the idea of atoms did not make much sense. How could something exist that you couldn't see?

Within the past 200 years, scientists have come to agree that matter is made up of small particles. We use Democritus's term, *atom*, to describe these particles. The illustrations below show how ideas about the atom have changed over time.

Active Reading **5 Describe** Who was Democritus?

_____

_____

_____

Development of the Atomic Theory

Observe how models of the atom have changed over time.

1803

John Dalton proposed that all substances are made of small particles, called atoms, that cannot be divided.

1897

J. J. Thomson performed experiments that detected smaller particles within the atom. He believed that these particles were mixed throughout the atom.

© Houghton Mifflin Harcourt Publishing Company

What are atoms?

An **atom** is the smallest particle into which an element can be divided and still be the same substance. In 1808, a British chemist named John Dalton published an atomic theory. Dalton's theory stated that all atoms of a particular element are identical, but are different from atoms of all other elements. Every atom of silver, for example, is the same as every other atom of silver, but different from an atom of iron. Dalton's atomic theory also assumed that atoms could not be divided into anything simpler. Scientists later discovered that this was not exactly true. They found that atoms are made of even smaller particles, called subatomic particles. As new information was discovered about atoms, scientists revised Dalton's atomic theory.

Like the tiny grains of sand that form huge beaches, tiny atoms combine to form all of the matter around us. Atoms are so small that they cannot be seen with an ordinary microscope. Only powerful instruments can produce images of atoms. How small are atoms? Think about a penny. A penny contains about 2×10^{22}, or 20,000,000,000,000,000,000,000 atoms of copper and zinc. That's over 3,000 billion times more atoms than there are people on Earth!

A big, sandy beach is made up of very small grains of sand.

These grains of sand are made up of billions of atoms.

1932

Today

In the early 1900s, experiments by scientists such as Ernest Rutherford and James Chadwick revealed the nature of the dense center of the atom.

© Houghton Mifflin Harcourt Publishing Company • Image Credits: (t) ©SuperStock RF/SuperStock; (inset) ©Michael Szoenyi/Photo Researchers, Inc.

Visualize It! (Inquiry)

6 Analyze Today's model of the atom looks different from the models that came before it. Why do you think ideas about the structure of the atom have changed over time?

_____

_____

_____

_____

Up and Atom!

What are the parts of an atom?

As tiny as an atom is, it is made up of even smaller particles. These particles are *protons, neutrons,* and *electrons.* This model of an atom shows where these particles are found within the atom. The particles in this model are not shown in their correct proportions. If they were, the protons and neutrons would be too small to see.

The Nucleus: Protons and Neutrons

Positively-charged particles within the atom are called **protons**. The mass of a proton is about 1.7×10^{-24} g. This number can also be written as 0.00000000000000000000000017 g. Because the masses of particles in the atom are so small, scientists made a new unit for them: the unified atomic mass unit (u). Each proton has a mass of about 1 u. The relative charge of a single proton is often denoted as 1+.

Neutrons are particles having no electric charge and about the same mass as a proton, 1 u. Atoms usually have as many or more neutrons as they do protons.

Together, protons and neutrons form the **nucleus** of the atom, located at the atom's center. As you can see in this model of a beryllium atom, this nucleus contains four protons and five neutrons. Because each proton has a 1+ charge, the overall charge of this nucleus is 4+. (Remember, neutrons have no electrical charge.) The volume of the nucleus is very small compared to the rest of the atom. But protons and neutrons are the most massive particles in an atom, so the nucleus is very dense. If it were possible to have a nucleus the volume of a grape, that nucleus would have a mass greater than 9 million metric tons!

Proton

Neutron

Nucleus

The Electron Cloud

The negatively-charged particles in the atom are called **electrons**. Electrons move around the nucleus very quickly. Scientists have found that it is not possible to determine their exact positions with certainty. This is why we picture the electrons as being in an **electron cloud** around the nucleus.

Compared with protons and neutrons, electrons are very small in mass. It takes more than 1,800 electrons to equal the mass of 1 proton. The mass of an electron is so small that it is usually thought of as almost 0 u.

The charge of a single electron is represented as 1–. The charges of protons and electrons are opposite but equal. The number of protons in an atom equals the number of electrons. So the atom has a net, or overall, charge of 0. For example, this beryllium atom contains four electrons. The combined charge of the electrons is 4–. But, remember that the charge of the nucleus is 4+.

$$(4+) + (4-) = 0$$

The net charge of the atom is 0.

An atom can lose or gain electrons. When this happens, we refer to the atom as an *ion*. Ions do not have a net charge of 0.

8 Summarize Complete the following table with information about the parts of the atom.

Part of the atom	Location in the atom	Electrical charge	Relative mass
Proton			Slightly less massive than a neutron
	Nucleus		
		1–	

Take a Number!

How can we describe atoms?

Think of all the substances you see and touch every day. Are all of these substances the same? No. The substances that make up this book are quite different from the substances in the air you're breathing. If all atoms are composed of the same particles, how can there be so many different types of substances? Different combinations of protons, neutrons, and electrons produce atoms with different properties. The number of each kind of particle within an atom determines its unique properties. In turn, these different atoms combine to form the different substances all around us.

By Atomic Number

The number of protons distinguishes the atoms of one element from the atoms of another. For example, every hydrogen atom contains one proton. And every carbon atom has exactly six protons in its nucleus.

The number of protons in the nucleus of an atom is the **atomic number** of that atom. Hydrogen has an atomic number of 1 because its atoms contain just one proton. Carbon has an atomic number of 6.

Active Reading **9 Compare** How are two atoms of the same element alike?

_____

_____

_____

_____

By Mass Number

While the atoms of a certain element always have the same number of protons, they may not always have the same number of neutrons. For example, all chlorine atoms have 17 protons. But some chlorine atoms have 18 neutrons, while other chlorine atoms have 20 neutrons. These two types of chlorine atoms are called isotopes. *Isotopes* are atoms of the same element that have a different number of neutrons. Some elements have many isotopes, while other elements have just a few.

The total number of protons and neutrons in an atom's nucleus is its **mass number.** Different isotopes of chlorine have different mass numbers. What is the mass number of a chlorine atom that contains 18 neutrons?

$$17 + 18 = 35$$

The mass number of this atom is 35.

---

11 Calculate Use this model of a helium atom to find its atomic number and mass number.

→ Helium

Atomic number: ☐

Mass number: ☐

The helium in these balloons is less massive than the nitrogen in the air so the balloons float.

© Houghton Mifflin Harcourt Publishing Company • Image Credits: ©Yana Paskova/Getty Images

10 Apply Conduct research about how scientists can use certain isotopes in fields such as medicine or Earth science. Choose one useful isotope and create a brochure that describes its properties and uses.

Visual Summary

To complete this summary, check the box that indicates true or false. Then use the key below to check your answers. You can use this page to review the main concepts of the lesson.

Atomic theory states that matter is made up of very small particles known as atoms.

	T	F	
12	☐	☐	Each grain of sand on this beach is made up of many atoms.
13	☐	☐	Atoms can be seen with a hand lens.

The Atom

Atoms contain a positively-charged nucleus surrounded by a negatively-charged electron cloud.

	T	F	
14	☐	☐	The nucleus of an atom contains protons and electrons.

Model of a helium atom

Atoms can be characterized by their atomic number and their mass number.

	T	F	
15	☐	☐	The atomic number of helium is 2.
16	☐	☐	The mass number of this helium atom is 2.

Answers: 12 T; 13 F; 14 F; 15 T; 16 F

17 Explain Is there any particle of matter that is smaller than an atom? Explain.

Lesson Review

Vocabulary

Circle the term that best completes the following sentences.

1 An *atom / electron* is the smallest particle of an element that has the properties of that element.

2 Electrons are found in the *electron cloud / nucleus* of the atom.

3 *Neutrons / Protons* have a positive charge.

4 The number of protons in an atom is the same as its *atomic number / mass number*.

Key Concepts

Complete the table below with the properties of a neutral sodium atom.

Properties of a Sodium Atom	
Number of protons	11
Number of neutrons	12
5 Apply Number of electrons	
6 Apply Atomic number	
7 Apply Mass number	
8 Apply Net charge	

9 Compare Compare the charges and masses of protons, neutrons, and electrons.

_____

_____

_____

_____

_____

Use this image to answer the following questions.

10 Analyze How many protons are in the nucleus of this atom?

_____

11 Analyze What is the mass number of this atom?

_____

Critical Thinking

12 Apply You can see the cells that make up your body with a light microscope. Do cells contain atoms? Explain.

_____

_____

_____

_____

_____

13 Explain If atoms are made up of smaller parts such as electrons, why are atoms considered the smallest particles of an element?

_____

_____

_____

_____

_____

The Periodic Table

ESSENTIAL QUESTION

How are elements arranged on the periodic table?

By the end of this lesson, you should be able to describe the relationship between the arrangement of elements on the periodic table and the properties of those elements.

> In this market, similar foods are arranged in groups. Can you identify some of the properties each group shares?

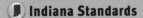

Indiana Standards

8.1.1 Explain that all matter is composed of particular arrangements of atoms of approximately one hundred elements.

8.1.2 Understand that elements are organized on the periodic table based on atomic numbers.

Engage Your Brain

1 Describe Write a word or phrase beginning with each letter of the word GOLD that describes the properties of these gold coins.

G _____

O _____

L _____

D _____

2 Describe As you will learn in this lesson, elements are arranged by their properties on the periodic table. What other objects are often arranged by their properties?

_____

_____

_____

_____

_____

_____

Active Reading

3 Apply Many scientific words, such as *table*, also have everyday meanings. Use context clues to write your own definition for each meaning of the word *table*.

Example sentence
The books are on the <u>table</u>.

table:

_____

_____

Example sentence
A data <u>table</u> is a useful way to organize information.

table:

_____

_____

Vocabulary Terms

- periodic table
- chemical symbol
- average atomic mass
- metal
- nonmetal
- metalloid
- group
- period

4 Apply As you learn the definition of each vocabulary term in this lesson, create your own definition or sketch to help you remember the meaning of the term.

Get Organized!

What are elements?

People have long sought to find the basic substances of matter. It was once believed that fire, wind, earth, and water, in various combinations, made up all objects. By the 1860s, however, scientists considered there to be at least 60 different basic substances, or elements. They saw that many of these elements shared certain physical and chemical properties and began classifying them. Knowing what you know about the properties of matter, try classifying the elements below.

Bismuth

Sulfur

Chlorine

👁 Visualize It!

5 Identify Observe the appearance of these six elements. Create two or three categories that group the elements by similar properties. Below each element, write the name of the category in which the element belongs.

Mercury

Copper

Bromine

How are the elements organized?

Around this time, a Russian chemist named Dmitri Mendeleev (dih•MEE•tree men•duh•LAY•uhf) began thinking about how he could organize the elements based on their properties. To help him decide how to arrange the elements, Mendeleev made a set of element cards. Each card listed the mass of an atom of each element as well as some of the element's properties. Mendeleev arranged the cards in various ways, looking for a pattern to emerge. When he arranged the element cards in order of increasing atomic mass, the properties of those elements occurred in a *periodic,* or regularly repeating, pattern. For this reason, Mendeleev's arrangement of the elements became known as the **periodic table.** Mendeleev used the periodic pattern in his table to predict elements that had not yet been discovered.

In the early 1900s, British scientist Henry Moseley showed how Mendeleev's periodic table could be rearranged. After determining the numbers of protons in the atoms of the elements, he arranged the elements on the table in order of increasing number of protons, or *atomic number.* Moseley's new arrangement of the elements corrected some of the flaws in Mendeleev's table.

The periodic table is a useful tool to scientists because it makes clear many patterns among the elements' properties. The periodic table is like a map or a calendar of the elements.

Active Reading

6 Explain How did Henry Moseley revise Mendeleev's periodic table?

_____

_____

_____

_____

_____

7 Apply What are you doing this week? Fill in the calendar with activities or plans you have for this week and next. Do any events occur periodically? Explain.

_____

_____

_____

What does the periodic table have in common with a calendar? They both show a periodic pattern. On a calendar, the days of the week repeat in the same order every 7 days.

Sunday	Monday	Tuesday	Wednesday	Thursday	Friday	Saturday

The Periodic Table of Elements

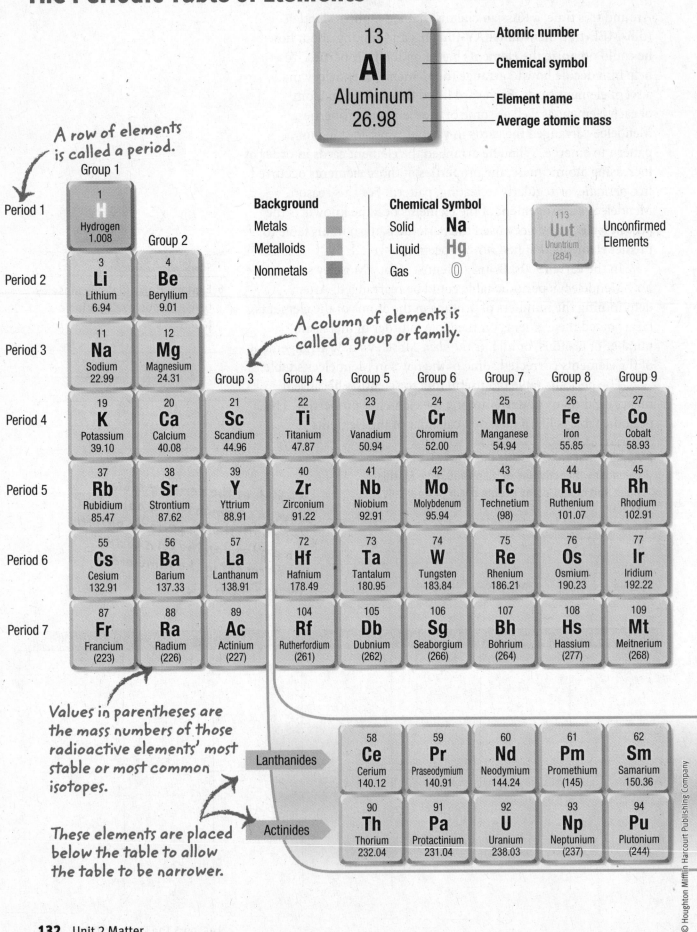

13
Al
Aluminum
26.98

— Atomic number
— Chemical symbol
— Element name
— Average atomic mass

A row of elements is called a period.

Group 1

Period 1 — 1 **H** Hydrogen 1.008

Group 2

Period 2 — 3 **Li** Lithium 6.94 | 4 **Be** Beryllium 9.01

Background

Metals
Metalloids
Nonmetals

Chemical Symbol

Solid **Na**
Liquid **Hg**
Gas Ⓞ

113 **Uut** Ununtrium (284) — Unconfirmed Elements

A column of elements is called a group or family.

Period 3 — 11 **Na** Sodium 22.99 | 12 **Mg** Magnesium 24.31

| Group 3 | Group 4 | Group 5 | Group 6 | Group 7 | Group 8 | Group 9 |

Period 4 — 19 **K** Potassium 39.10 | 20 **Ca** Calcium 40.08 | 21 **Sc** Scandium 44.96 | 22 **Ti** Titanium 47.87 | 23 **V** Vanadium 50.94 | 24 **Cr** Chromium 52.00 | 25 **Mn** Manganese 54.94 | 26 **Fe** Iron 55.85 | 27 **Co** Cobalt 58.93

Period 5 — 37 **Rb** Rubidium 85.47 | 38 **Sr** Strontium 87.62 | 39 **Y** Yttrium 88.91 | 40 **Zr** Zirconium 91.22 | 41 **Nb** Niobium 92.91 | 42 **Mo** Molybdenum 95.94 | 43 **Tc** Technetium (98) | 44 **Ru** Ruthenium 101.07 | 45 **Rh** Rhodium 102.91

Period 6 — 55 **Cs** Cesium 132.91 | 56 **Ba** Barium 137.33 | 57 **La** Lanthanum 138.91 | 72 **Hf** Hafnium 178.49 | 73 **Ta** Tantalum 180.95 | 74 **W** Tungsten 183.84 | 75 **Re** Rhenium 186.21 | 76 **Os** Osmium 190.23 | 77 **Ir** Iridium 192.22

Period 7 — 87 **Fr** Francium (223) | 88 **Ra** Radium (226) | 89 **Ac** Actinium (227) | 104 **Rf** Rutherfordium (261) | 105 **Db** Dubnium (262) | 106 **Sg** Seaborgium (266) | 107 **Bh** Bohrium (264) | 108 **Hs** Hassium (277) | 109 **Mt** Meitnerium (268)

Values in parentheses are the mass numbers of those radioactive elements' most stable or most common isotopes.

Lanthanides — 58 **Ce** Cerium 140.12 | 59 **Pr** Praseodymium 140.91 | 60 **Nd** Neodymium 144.24 | 61 **Pm** Promethium (145) | 62 **Sm** Samarium 150.36

These elements are placed below the table to allow the table to be narrower.

Actinides — 90 **Th** Thorium 232.04 | 91 **Pa** Protactinium 231.04 | 92 **U** Uranium 238.03 | 93 **Np** Neptunium (237) | 94 **Pu** Plutonium (244)

8 Analyze According to the periodic table, how many elements are a liquid at room temperature?

_____

9 Analyze According to the periodic table, how many elements are metalloids?

_____

The zigzag line separates metals from nonmetals.

Group 18

| 2 |
| **He** |
| Helium |
| 4.003 |

Group 13	Group 14	Group 15	Group 16	Group 17	
5 **B** Boron 10.81	6 **C** Carbon 12.01	7 **N** Nitrogen 14.01	8 **O** Oxygen 16.00	9 **F** Fluorine 19.00	10 **Ne** Neon 20.18
13 **Al** Aluminum 26.98	14 **Si** Silicon 28.09	15 **P** Phosphorus 30.97	16 **S** Sulfur 32.07	17 **Cl** Chlorine 35.45	18 **Ar** Argon 39.95

Group 10	Group 11	Group 12						
28 **Ni** Nickel 58.69	29 **Cu** Copper 63.55	30 **Zn** Zinc 65.41	31 **Ga** Gallium 69.72	32 **Ge** Germanium 72.64	33 **As** Arsenic 74.92	34 **Se** Selenium 78.96	35 **Br** Bromine 79.90	36 **Kr** Krypton 83.80
46 **Pd** Palladium 106.42	47 **Ag** Silver 107.87	48 **Cd** Cadmium 112.41	49 **In** Indium 114.82	50 **Sn** Tin 118.71	51 **Sb** Antimony 121.76	52 **Te** Tellurium 127.6	53 **I** Iodine 126.9	54 **Xe** Xenon 131.29
78 **Pt** Platinum 195.08	79 **Au** Gold 196.97	80 **Hg** Mercury 200.59	81 **Tl** Thallium 204.38	82 **Pb** Lead 207.2	83 **Bi** Bismuth 208.98	84 **Po** Polonium (209)	85 **At** Astatine (210)	86 **Rn** Radon (222)
110 **Ds** Darmstadtium (271)	111 **Rg** Roentgenium (272)	112 **Cn** Copernicium (285)	113 **Uut** Ununtrium (284)	114 **Uuq** Ununquadium (289)	115 **Uup** Ununpentium (288)	116 **Uuh** Ununhexium (292)		118 **Uuo** Ununoctium (294)

63 **Eu** Europium 151.96	64 **Gd** Gadolinium 157.25	65 **Tb** Terbium 158.93	66 **Dy** Dysprosium 162.5	67 **Ho** Holmium 164.93	68 **Er** Erbium 167.26	69 **Tm** Thulium 168.93	70 **Yb** Ytterbium 173.04	71 **Lu** Lutetium 174.97
95 **Am** Americium (243)	96 **Cm** Curium (247)	97 **Bk** Berkelium (247)	98 **Cf** Californium (251)	99 **Es** Einsteinium (252)	100 **Fm** Fermium (257)	101 **Md** Mendelevium (258)	102 **No** Nobelium (259)	103 **Lr** Lawrencium (262)

Ma**K**ing Arrangements

What information is contained in each square on the periodic table?

The periodic table is not simply a list of element names. The table contains useful information about each of the elements. The periodic table is usually shown as a grid of squares. Each square contains an element's chemical name, atomic number, chemical symbol, and average atomic mass.

Atomic Number

The number at the top of the square is the atomic number. The atomic number is the number of protons in the nucleus of an atom of that element. All atoms of an element have the same atomic number. For example, every aluminum atom has 13 protons in its nucleus. So the atomic number of aluminum is 13.

Chemical Symbol

The **chemical symbol** is an abbreviation for the element's name. The first letter is always capitalized. Any other letter is always lowercase. For most elements, the chemical symbol is a one- or two-letter symbol. However, some elements have temporary three-letter symbols. These elements will receive a permanent one- or two-letter symbol once it has been reviewed by an international committee of scientists.

13

Al

Aluminum

26.98

Chemical Name

The names of the elements come from many sources. Some elements, such as mendelevium, are named after scientists. Others, such as californium, are named after places.

Average Atomic Mass

All atoms of a given element contain the same number of protons. But the number of neutrons in those atoms can vary. So different atoms of an element can have different masses. The **average atomic mass** of an atom is the weighted average of the masses of all the naturally occurring isotopes of that element. A weighted average accounts for the percentages of each isotope. The unit for atomic mass is u.

Active Reading

10 Apply What is the average atomic mass of aluminum?

_____

_____

How are the elements arranged on the periodic table?

Have you ever noticed how items in a grocery store are arranged? Each aisle contains a different kind of product. Within an aisle, similar products are grouped together on shelves. Because the items are arranged in categories, it is easy to find your favorite brand of cereal. Similarly, the elements are arranged in a certain order on the periodic table. If you understand how the periodic table is organized, you can easily find and compare elements.

Metals, Nonmetals, and Metalloids Are Found in Three Distinct Regions

Elements on the periodic table can be classified into three major categories: metals, nonmetals, and metalloids. The zigzag line on the periodic table can help you identify where these three classes of elements are located. Except for hydrogen, the elements to the left of the zigzag line are metals. **Metals** are elements that are shiny and conduct heat and electricity well. Most metals are solid at room temperature. Many metals are *malleable,* or able to be formed into different shapes. Some metals are *ductile,* meaning that they can be made into wires. The elements to the right of the zigzag line are nonmetals. **Nonmetals** are poor conductors of heat and electricity. Nonmetals are often dull and brittle. Metalloids border the zigzag line on the periodic table. **Metalloids** are elements that have some properties of metals and some properties of nonmetals. Some metalloids are used to make semiconductor chips in computers.

11 Identify Fill in the blanks below with the word *metal, nonmetal,* or *metalloid.*

Iron is a good conductor of thermal energy.

Silicon has some properties of metals and some properties of nonmetals. Silicon is used in solar panels.

Graphite is brittle, meaning that it breaks easily. Graphite is made of carbon.

Elements in Each Column Have Similar Properties

The periodic table groups elements with similar properties together. Each vertical column of elements (from top to bottom) on the periodic table is called a **group**. Elements in the same group often have similar physical and chemical properties. For this reason, a group is sometimes called a *family*.

The properties of elements in a group are similar because the atoms of these elements have the same number of *valence electrons*. Valence electrons are found in the outermost portion of the electron cloud of an atom. Because they are far from the the attractive force of the nucleus, valence electrons are able to participate in chemical bonding. The number of valence electrons helps determine what kind of chemical reactions the atom can undergo. For example, all of the atoms of elements in Group 1 have a single valence electron. These elements are very reactive. The atoms of elements in Group 18 have a full set of valence electrons. The elements in Group 18 are all unreactive gases.

Active Reading 12 **Explain** Why do elements within a group have similar chemical properties?

_____

_____

_____

Just as this family is made up of members that have similar characteristics, families in the periodic table are made up of elements that have similar properties.

Groups of Elements Have Similar Properties

Observe the similarities of elements found in Group 1 and in Group 18.

Alkali metals, found in Group 1, share the property of reactivity with water.

Sodium has 1 valence electron.

Potassium has 1 valence electron.

Elements in Each Row Follow Periodic Trends

Each horizontal row of elements (from left to right) on the periodic table is called a **period**. The physical and chemical properties of elements change in predictable ways from one end of the period to the other. For example, within any given period on the periodic table, atomic size decreases as you move from left to right. The densities of elements also follow a pattern. Within a period, elements at the left and right sides of the table are the least dense, and the elements in the middle are the most dense. The element osmium has the highest known density, and it is located at the center of the table. Chemists cannot predict the exact size or density of an atom of elements based on that of another. However, these trends are a valuable tool in predicting the properties of different substances.

Elements Are Arranged in Order of Increasing Atomic Number

As you move from left to right within a period, the atomic number of each element increases by one. Once you've reached the end of the period, the pattern resumes on the next period. You might have noticed that two rows of elements are set apart from the rest of the periodic table. These rows, the lanthanides and actinides, are placed below the table to allow it to be narrower. These elements are also arranged in order of increasing atomic number.

© Houghton Mifflin Harcourt Publishing Company • Image Credits: (l) ©Charles D. Winters/Photo Researchers, Inc.; (r) ©Charles D. Winters/Photo Researchers, Inc.

Think Outside the Book Inquiry

13 Apply Imagine that you have just discovered a new element. Explain where this element would appear on the periodic table and why. Describe the element's properties and propose a chemical symbol and name for the element.

Noble gases, found in Group 18, glow brightly when an electric current is passed through them.

Neon has 8 valence electrons.

Xenon has 8 valence electrons.

14 Analyze List three other elements that have 1 valence electron. (Hint: Refer to the periodic table.)

_____

_____

15 Analyze List three other elements that have 8 valence electrons. (Hint: Refer to the periodic table.)

_____

_____

_____

Visual Summary

To complete this summary, fill in the blanks with the correct word or phrase. Then use the key below to check your answers. You can use this page to review the main concepts of the lesson.

The periodic table arranges elements in columns and rows.

16 Elements in the same _____ have similar properties.

17 Rows on the periodic table are known as _____

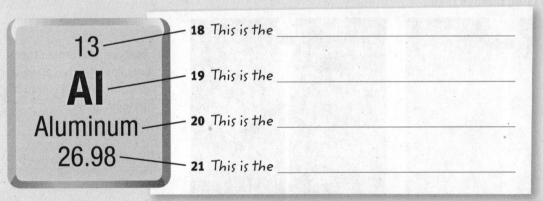

1 H																	2 He
3 Li	4 Be											5 B	6 C	7 N	8 O	9 F	10 Ne
11 Na	12 Mg											13 Al	14 Si	15 P	16 S	17 Cl	18 Ar
19 K	20 Ca	21 Sc	22 Ti	23 V	24 Cr	25 Mn	26 Fe	27 Co	28 Ni	29 Cu	30 Zn	31 Ga	32 Ge	33 As	34 Se	35 Br	36 Kr
37 Rb	38 Sr	39 Y	40 Zr	41 Nb	42 Mo	43 Tc	44 Ru	45 Rh	46 Pd	47 Ag	48 Cd	49 In	50 Sn	51 Sb	52 Te	53 I	54 Xe
55 Cs	56 Ba	57 La	72 Hf	73 Ta	74 W	75 Re	76 Os	77 Ir	78 Pt	79 Au	80 Hg	81 Tl	82 Pb	83 Bi	84 Po	85 At	86 Rn
87 Fr	88 Ra	89 Ac	104 Rf	105 Db	106 Sg	107 Bh	108 Hs	109 Mt	110 Ds	111 Rg	112 Cn	113 Uut	114 Uuq	115 Uup	116 Uuh		118

Lanthanides	58 Ce	59 Pr	60 Nd	61 Pm	62 Sm	63 Eu	64 Gd	65 Tb	66 Dy	67 Ho	68 Er	69 Tm	70 Yb	71 Lu
Actinides	90 Th	91 Pa	92 U	93 Np	94 Pu	95 Am	96 Cm	97 Bk	98 Cf	99 Es	100 Fm	101 Md	102 No	103 Lr

The **Periodic** Table

The periodic table contains information about each element.

13

Al

Aluminum

26.98

18 This is the _____

19 This is the _____

20 This is the _____

21 This is the _____

22 **Describe** Some elements are highly unstable and break apart within seconds, making them difficult to study. How can the periodic table help scientists infer the properties of these elements?

Lesson Review

Vocabulary

Draw a line to connect the following terms to their definitions.

1 metal

2 nonmetal

3 metalloid

A an element that has properties of both metals and nonmetals

B an element that is shiny and that conducts heat and electricity well

C an element that conducts heat and electricity poorly

Key Concepts

4 Identify Elements in the same _____ on the periodic table have the same number of valence electrons.

5 Identify Properties of elements within a _____ on the periodic table change in a predictable way from one side of the table to the other.

6 Describe What is the purpose of the zigzag line on the periodic table?

_____

_____

_____

7 Apply Thorium (Th) has an average atomic mass of 232.0 and an atomic number of 90. In the space below, draw a square from the periodic table to represent thorium.

Critical Thinking

Use this graphic to answer the following questions.

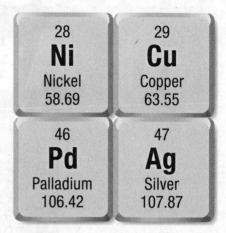

28	29
Ni	**Cu**
Nickel	Copper
58.69	63.55

46	47
Pd	**Ag**
Palladium	Silver
106.42	107.87

8 Infer What can you infer about copper and silver based on their position relative to each other?

_____

_____

_____

9 Apply How does the nucleus of a copper atom compare to the nucleus of a nickel atom?

_____

_____

_____

10 Explain Explain how chemists can state with certainty that no one will discover an element that would appear on the periodic table between sulfur (S) and chlorine (Cl).

_____

_____

_____

_____

_____

_____

_____

Interactions of Atoms

ESSENTIAL QUESTION

How do atoms interact?

By the end of this lesson, you should be able to describe chemical bonding with balanced chemical equations and atomic models.

Indiana Standards

8.1.3 Explain how the arrangement of atoms and molecules determines chemical properties of substances.

8.1.4 Describe the structure of an atom and relate the arrangement of electrons to how that atom interacts with other atoms.

8.1.5 Explain that atoms join together to form molecules and compounds and illustrate with diagrams the relationship between atoms and compounds and/or molecules.

8.1.7 Explain that chemical changes occur when substances react and form one or more different products, whose physical and chemical properties are different from those of the reactants.

8.1.8 Demonstrate that in a chemical change, the total numbers of each kind of atom in the product are the same as in the reactants and that the total mass of the reacting system is conserved.

What makes this firefly larva glow? Light energy is released when a chemical reaction takes place inside the insect's body.

1 Describe Sometimes, scientists can represent the same type of information in different ways. Convert these examples by filling in the blank boxes below.

Equation using symbols	Equation described with words
$3 + 15 = 18$	
	Force equals mass times acceleration

Active Reading

3 Apply Many scientific words, such as *product*, also have everyday meanings. Use context clues to write your own definition for each meaning of the word *product*.

Example sentence
This cleaning <u>product</u> is sold in grocery stores.

product:

_____

_____

_____

Example sentence
Oxygen is a <u>product</u> of the chemical reaction.

product:

_____

_____

_____

2 Predict Atoms can join together to form different substances. In the space below, draw a sketch that depicts atoms joined together. After you read this lesson, revise your sketch as needed.

Vocabulary Terms

- chemical bond
- molecule
- chemical equation
- chemical formula
- reactant
- product
- valence electron

4 Apply As you learn the definition of each vocabulary term in this lesson, create your own definition or sketch to help you remember the meaning of the term.

Breaking Up and Making Up

Chemical changes cause leaves to change color during fall.

What happens to atoms during a chemical change?

Did you know that the changing colors of leaves during fall is the result of a chemical change? As warm daylight hours become shorter, the pigment that produces green color in leaves breaks down chemically. The yellow and orange pigments do not.

In a chemical change, atoms that make up a substance are not created or destroyed. The atoms themselves do not change either. Yet the result of a chemical change is a new substance with completely different chemical properties. So what exactly happens during a chemical change?

Chemical Bonds Are Formed or Broken

The atoms that make up a substance are joined together by chemical bonds. A **chemical bond** is an interaction that holds two atoms together. During chemical changes, chemical bonds are formed and broken. The result is different combinations of atoms joined by chemical bonds. When the atoms in a substance are rearranged, the identity of that substance is changed. It no longer has the same chemical properties.

A **molecule** is a distinct group of atoms held together by chemical bonds. The models below show how chemical bonds between atoms in molecules of hydrogen and chlorine break and form to produce two molecules of hydrogen chloride. Each of these molecules is made up of two atoms. Other molecules, like DNA, can contain billions of atoms!

 **Visualize It!**

5 Identify Draw a line to connect the atoms on the left to the corresponding atoms in the hydrogen chloride molecules on the right.

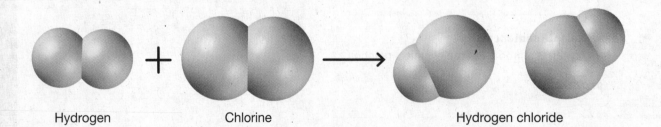

Hydrogen   Chlorine   Hydrogen chloride

The bonds joining the atoms in these molecules must break before the atoms can be rearranged.

Each molecule of hydrogen chloride forms when a bond is made between a hydrogen atom and a chlorine atom.

© Houghton Mifflin Harcourt Publishing Company • Image Credits: ©Dorling Kindersley/Getty Images

How are chemical changes described?

You can describe what happens to a substance during a chemical change, or *reaction*, by recording your observations. But how would you describe what happens to the atoms? You cannot see them. One way to represent the reaction is with a chemical equation. A **chemical equation** uses symbols to represent the various substances that interact during a reaction. The chemical equation below describes the interaction between carbon and oxygen gas to form carbon dioxide.

Active Reading

6 Explain As you read, underline the sentence that describes the purpose of a subscript in a chemical formula.

Chemical Formulas Represent the Substances Involved in a Chemical Change

In a chemical equation, each substance is represented by a chemical formula. A **chemical formula** is a shorthand way of describing a substance's chemical makeup using symbols and numbers. Consider the chemical formula CO_2. The letters C and O represent the elements carbon and oxygen. The small 2 in the formula is a subscript. A *subscript* is a number written below and to the right of a chemical symbol in a formula. The subscript tells you how many atoms of the element are present. If a symbol has no subscript, only one atom of that element is present. The chemical formula CO_2 tells you that one carbon dioxide molecule is made of one atom of carbon (C) and two atoms of oxygen (O).

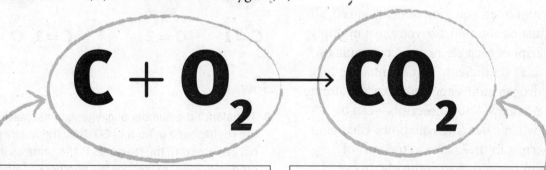

Reactants Appear on the Left

The starting materials in a chemical reaction are called **reactants**. The chemical formulas of the reactants are written to the left of the arrow, also called a *yields sign*. The reactants shown here are separated by a plus sign.

7 Apply Name the reactant(s) in this chemical equation.

_____

_____

Products Appear on the Right

The substances formed in a reaction are called **products**. The chemical formulas of the products are written to the right of the yields sign. If more than one product is formed, each product is separated by a plus sign.

8 Apply Name the product(s) in this chemical equation.

_____

_____

A Balancing Act

How do chemical equations show the law of conservation of mass?

The law of conservation of mass states that matter is neither created nor destroyed in ordinary physical and chemical changes. This law means that a chemical equation must show the same numbers and kinds of atoms on both sides of the arrow. When writing a chemical equation, you must be sure that the reactants and products contain the same number of atoms of each element. This is called balancing the equation.

To balance an equation, you can use coefficients. A *coefficient* is a number that is placed in front of a chemical symbol or formula. For example, $3H_2O$ represents three water molecules. The number 3 is the coefficient. For an equation to be balanced, all atoms must be counted. So, you must multiply the subscript of each element in a formula by the formula's coefficient. $3H_2O$ contains a total of six hydrogen atoms and three oxygen atoms. Only coefficients—not subscripts—can be changed when balancing equations. Changing the subscripts in the chemical formula of a compound would change the identity of that compound.

Active Reading **9 Compare** What is the difference between a coefficient and a subscript?

_____

_____

_____

_____

_____

_____

Do the Math **Sample Problem**

Follow these steps to write a balanced chemical equation.

Identify

A Count the atoms of each element in the reactants and in the products. You can see that there are more oxygen atoms in the reactants than in the product.

$$C \quad + \quad O_2 \quad \longrightarrow \quad CO$$

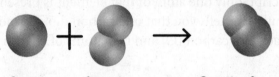

$$C = 1 \qquad O = 2 \qquad\qquad C = 1 \quad O = 1$$

Solve

B To balance the number of oxygen atoms, place the coefficient 2 in front of CO. Now the number of oxygen atoms in the reactants is the same as in the products. Then, to balance the number of carbon atoms, place the coefficient 2 in front of C. Finally, be sure to double-check your work!

$$2C \quad + \quad O_2 \quad \longrightarrow \quad 2CO$$

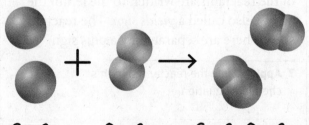

$$C = 2 \qquad O = 2 \qquad\qquad C = 2 \quad O = 2$$

Do the Math You Try It

10 Calculate Fill in the blanks below to balance this chemical equation. Sketch the products and reactants to show that the number of each type of atom is the same.

Identify

A Count the atoms of each element in the reactants and product in the unbalanced equation.

H_2 + O_2 ⟶ H_2O

H = _____ O = _____   H = _____ O = _____

Solve

B To balance the number of each type of atom, place coefficients in front of the appropriate chemical formulas. Sketch the products and reactants, showing the correct number of molecules of each.

_____ H_2 + _____ O_2 _____ H_2O

+ ⟶

H = _____ O = _____   H = _____ O = _____

Think Outside the Book Inquiry

11 Apply Research hydrogen-powered vehicles. Create a poster that describes the advantages and disadvantages of vehicles that use hydrogen as a fuel. Be sure to include a balanced chemical equation to represent the use of hydrogen fuel.

Hydrogen and oxygen react to form water, shown here as a cloud of steam, and energy. The energy released helps to propel this space shuttle.

Let's Get Together!

How is chemical bonding modeled?

Because atoms are too small to see, scientists often study models of atoms. The diagrams below show three different models of the same sodium atom. The model on the left shows an atom that looks like a solid pink sphere. This kind of model does not contain many details about the atom, but it is a simple representation that is useful when many atoms are being represented at once. The atom model in the center shows a nucleus and its surrounding electron cloud. This model is helpful in showing the general location of the parts of the atom. The model on the right is called a *Bohr model*, named after the physicist Niels Bohr (NEELS•BOHR). In this model, electrons are shown as dots arranged in rings around the nucleus. This model does not show the true arrangement of the particles in the atom. However, the Bohr model is useful for predicting how and why atoms bond.

Visualize It!

Three models of a sodium atom

This is a simple model of a sodium atom.

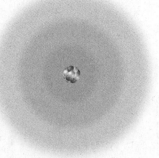

This atom model shows the location of the nucleus and the electron cloud.

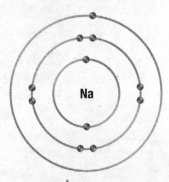

This Bohr model of a sodium atom shows which electrons are available to form chemical bonds.

Sodium chloride

12 Infer Sodium atoms can bond with chlorine atoms to form a rigid network of atoms known as sodium chloride, or table salt. In the sodium chloride model at the left, why do you think that simple atom models were used to represent sodium (pink) and chlorine (green)?

_____

_____

_____

_____

Bohr Models Show the Arrangement of Electrons into Energy Levels

Electrons in an atom are arranged in energy levels. In a Bohr model, energy levels are represented by rings around the nucleus. The first, innermost energy level can hold up to two electrons. The second energy level can hold up to eight electrons. Some atoms have more energy levels beyond these. The energy levels are "filled" with electrons starting with the first energy level. Most atoms form bonds using only the electrons in their outermost energy level. The electrons in the outermost energy level are called **valence electrons**.

The number of electrons in each energy level depends on the identity of the atom. For example, a lithium atom has three electrons. Two electrons fill the first energy level. The second energy level contains the third electron. For lithium, the second energy level is the outermost. So a lithium atom contains one valence electron.

The single valence electron in a lithium atom plays an important role in the lithium-ion batteries found in many electronic devices.

 **13 Describe** What is the maximum number of electrons that the first energy level of an atom can hold? _____

Visualize It!

Drawing a Bohr Model of Fluorine

A fluorine atom has nine electrons. How do you draw a Bohr model of a fluorine atom?

Step 1

The first energy level is closest to the nucleus and can hold up to two electrons. Fluorine has nine electrons, so there are seven electrons left to draw.

Step 2

Electrons begin filling the second energy level only after the first energy level is full. The second energy level can hold up to eight electrons, often shown as four pairs. The first four electrons are shown as being spaced equally apart around the ring.

Step 3

14 Apply Complete the fluorine atom sketch at the right by adding the remaining three electrons to the correct energy level.

15 Interpret How many valence electrons does a fluorine atom have? _____

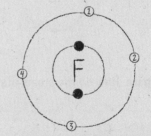

Bohr Models Show Which Electrons Participate in Chemical Bonding

Imagine that atoms join together like the pieces of a puzzle. Not all puzzle pieces fit together. Similarly, not all atoms join together to form new substances. But you can predict which atoms will form bonds by using Bohr models.

When an energy level of an atom contains the maximum number of electrons, the energy level is full. An atom with a full outermost energy level is stable and usually does not form bonds. Atoms that have a full outermost energy level, such as helium, are not reactive. However, an atom can form bonds if its outermost energy is not full. Atoms form bonds by gaining, losing, or sharing their valence electrons with other atoms in order to achieve a full outermost energy level.

Visualize It!

16 Apply Place a check mark next to the models of atoms that have a full outermost energy level.

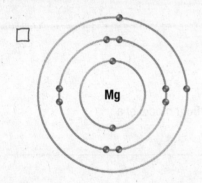

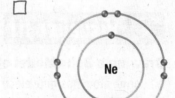

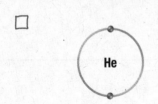

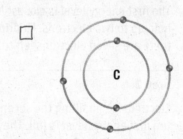

17 Compare How do the atoms that you marked differ?

_____
_____
_____
_____
_____

18 Apply Are the atoms that you marked likely to participate in chemical bonding? Explain.

_____
_____
_____
_____
_____
_____

Sharing electrons

Some atoms, such as carbon and hydrogen, can form bonds by sharing electrons. The product of this reaction is methane, CH_4.

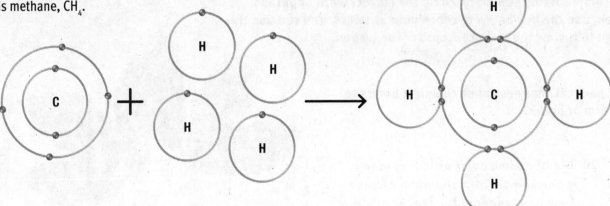

This carbon atom has 4 valence electrons.

These hydrogen atoms each have 1 valence electron.

By sharing electrons, each atom achieves a full outermost energy level.

Transferring electrons

Atoms like sodium and fluorine form bonds by gaining or losing electrons. Sodium and fluorine combine to form sodium fluoride.

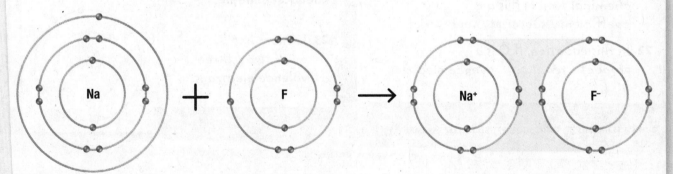

This sodium atom has 1 valence electron.

This fluorine atom has 7 valence electrons.

When sodium transfers an electron to fluorine, both outermost energy levels are full.

19 **Synthesize** Sodium fluoride is a compound that is added to some toothpastes to prevent cavities. In the reactants above, draw an arrow to show the transfer of a valence electron from sodium to fluorine when they bond to form sodium fluoride.

Visual Summary

To complete this summary, circle the correct word or phrase. Then, use the key below to check your answers. You can use this page to review the main concepts of the lesson.

Chemical changes cause chemical bonds to form or break.

20 The changing color of leaves in fall is an example of a chemical change. New substances in the leaves contain new atoms / bonds / electrons.

Interactions of Atoms

Balanced chemical equations describe chemical changes.

$$2H_2 + O_2 \longrightarrow 2H_2O$$

21 The small 2 that follows the chemical symbol H is a coefficient / subscript / superscript.

22 In this equation, H_2O is a product / reactant / valence electron.

Bohr models are used to predict chemical bonding.

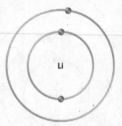

23 Lithium has one / two / three valence electrons.

Answers: 20 bonds; 21 subscript; 22 product; 23 one

24 **Explain** How can a Bohr model be used to predict whether an atom is likely to undergo a chemical reaction?

Lesson Review

Vocabulary

Fill in the blanks with the term that best completes the following sentences.

1 An interaction that holds two atoms together is a(n) _____

2 A(n) _____ is a group of atoms held together by chemical bonds.

Key Concepts

3 Apply Place coefficients in the blanks to balance this equation.

____ CH_4 + ____ O_2 ⟶ ____ CO_2 + ____ H_2O

4 Identify List the reactant(s) and product(s) in this chemical equation.

_____

_____

_____

5 Analyze Compared to other types of models, what are the advantages of a Bohr model?

_____

_____

_____

Critical Thinking

6 Analyze Sodium is a highly reactive metal. Chlorine is a green, toxic gas. The two elements react to form table salt. Does this mean that table salt is not safe to eat? Explain.

_____

_____

_____

_____

_____

_____

Use this image to answer the following questions.

7 Apply A beryllium atom has 4 electrons. What does a Bohr model of beryllium look like? Complete the model above by drawing dots in the appropriate rings.

8 Analyze A beryllium atom can form bonds with other atoms by losing electrons. How many electrons does beryllium lose? Explain.

_____

_____

_____

_____

_____

_____

9 Synthesize When heated, magnesium carbonate ($MgCO_3$) breaks down to form magnesium oxide (MgO) and carbon dioxide (CO_2). Explain how one substance can react to form two new substances while still observing the law of conservation of mass.

_____

_____

_____

_____

My Notes

Unit 2 **Summary**

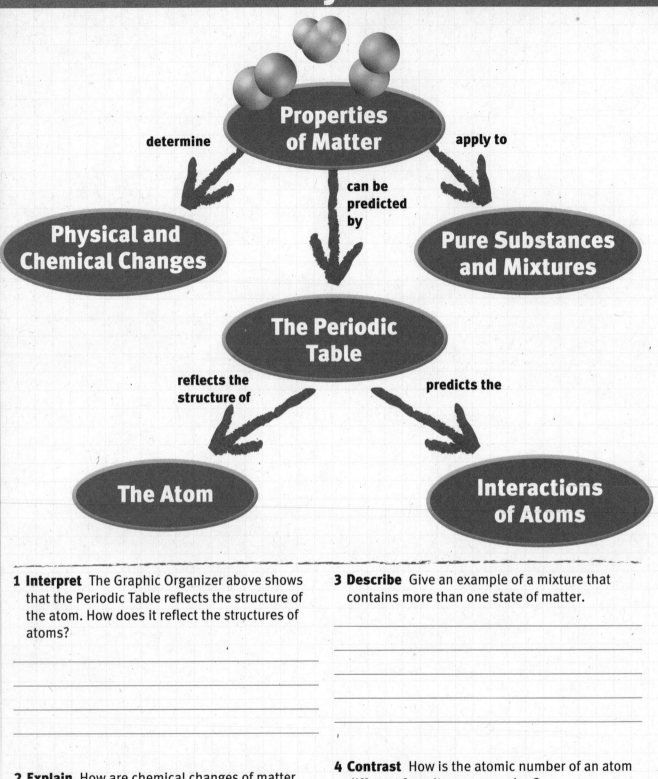

Properties of Matter

determine →

Physical and Chemical Changes

apply to →

Pure Substances and Mixtures

can be predicted by ↓

The Periodic Table

reflects the structure of ↓

The Atom

predicts the ↓

Interactions of Atoms

1 Interpret The Graphic Organizer above shows that the Periodic Table reflects the structure of the atom. How does it reflect the structures of atoms?

_____

_____

_____

_____

2 Explain How are chemical changes of matter related to the organization of the periodic table?

_____

_____

_____

3 Describe Give an example of a mixture that contains more than one state of matter.

_____

_____

_____

_____

_____

4 Contrast How is the atomic number of an atom different from its mass number?

_____

_____

_____

_____

Multiple Choice

1 A physical property can be observed or measured without changing the identity of a substance. Some physical properties depend on the size of the sample, and some are present no matter the size of the sample. Which choice describes a PHYSICAL PROPERTY that remains unchanged no matter the size of the sample?

   A. whether or not a metal will rust

   B. the mass of a certain type of plastic

   C. the way the substance reacts with water

   D. the density of aluminum

2 Which phrase BEST describes the periodic table?

   A. an arrangement of approximately 100 elements organized in groups and families

   B. approximately 100 elements classified as metals, nonmetals, and compounds

   C. an arrangement of all elements that are metals

   D. approximately 100 elements arranged in order of increasing mass

3 Engineers define tensile strength as the maximum force a material can withstand without tearing. Which of the following laboratory procedures would test tensile strength?

   A. A rubber tire rotates against a rough surface until the rubber reaches a certain temperature.

   B. A giant presser pushes the water from wood pulp to make paper.

   C. Copper is melted in a superheated boiler and pulled into a thin wire.

   D. Two robotic arms holding a silk thread pull in opposite directions until the thread breaks.

4 Which electrons in a Bohr model are MOST LIKELY to be involved in chemical reactions?

   A. any electron shown in the model

   B. the valence, or outer, electrons

   C. electrons that are closest to the nucleus

   D. the valence, or inner, electrons

5 Trini adds 10 g of baking soda to 100 g of vinegar. The mixture begins to bubble. When the bubbling stops, Trini finds the mass of the mixture. She determines that the mixture's mass is 105 g. Why has the mass CHANGED?

A. A gas has formed and left the mixture.

B. Vinegar evaporated during the experiment.

C. Baking soda loses mass when it reacts with vinegar.

D. Mass was destroyed when vinegar reacted with baking soda.

6 When carbon, oxygen, and hydrogen undergo a chemical change, one of many different compounds forms. Fructose, or fruit sugar, is one possible compound formed. Which statement BEST describes the properties of fructose?

A. They are similar to the properties of carbon.

B. They are similar to the properties of oxygen.

C. They are similar to the properties of hydrogen.

D. They are different from the properties of all the elements fructose contains.

7 Reactants are the substances that go into a chemical reaction. Products are the result of the reaction. Both reactants and products are substances.

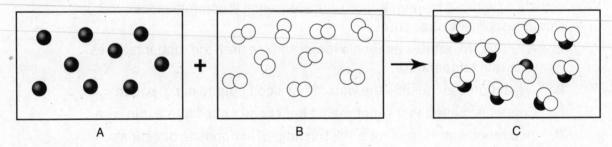

What TYPE OF SUBSTANCE is reactant B?

A. a nucleus

B. a mixture

C. an element

D. a compound

8 At what temperature are the attractive forces among water particles the greatest?

   A. below 0 °C, when water is a solid

   B. between 0 °C and 100 °C, when water is a liquid

   C. at 100 °C, when water is boiling

   D. above 100 °C, when water is a gas

9 Look at the materials in the illustration below.

  Air in balloon   Water   Orange juice   Plate

At room temperature, in which of these materials is the average attractive force among particles the greatest?

   A. air in balloon

   B. water

   C. orange juice

   D. plate

10 When carbon in charcoal reacts with oxygen in the air, the primary product is carbon dioxide, as shown in the following chemical equation:

$$C + O_2 \rightarrow CO_2$$

Which of the following is TRUE of this process?

   A. The product has more carbon and oxygen atoms than the reactants.

   B. Chemical properties of the product differ from those of the reactants.

   C. Carbon dioxide is the reactant in this process.

   D. The product has fewer carbon and oxygen atoms than the reactants.

11 A magnet was placed near a pile that contained both iron and sulfur. The magnet was moved gradually closer to the pile. As it neared the pile, the magnet started attracting small pieces of iron from the pile.

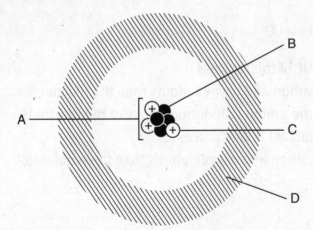

How would the results change if the size of the pile were TWICE the size of this pile?

A. The magnet would no longer remove iron from the pile.

B. The magnet would still remove iron, but not sulfur, from the pile.

C. The magnet would begin removing sulfur only from the pile.

D. The magnet would now remove both iron and sulfur.

12 Every atom has a nucleus and an electron cloud. The diagram below shows a model of an atom.

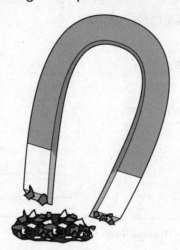

Which label points to the ELECTRON CLOUD?

A. A

B. B

C. C

D. D

13 Atoms are a basic building block of certain types of matter. Atoms make up the elements that combine to form compounds, which make up much of what we use every day. Which of these substances is NOT made out of atoms?

A. oxygen

B. protons

C. trees

D. carbon dioxide

14 Janet is studying the element nitrogen. She wants to identify the element with an atomic number one greater than the atomic number of nitrogen.

Part of the Periodic Table

							18 VIIA
		13 IIIA	14 IVA	15 VA	16 VIA	17 VIIA	2 **He** Helium 4.002602
		5 **B** Boron 10.811	6 **C** Carbon 12.011	7 **N** Nitrogen 14.0067	8 **O** Oxygen 15.9994	9 **F** Fluorine 18.998403	10 **Ne** Neon 20.1797
11 IB	12 IIB	13 **Al** Aluminum 26.981539	14 **Si** Silicon 28.0855	15 **P** Phosphorus 30.973762	16 **S** Sulfur 32.066	17 **Cl** Chlorine 35.4527	18 **Ar** Argon 39.948
29 **Cu** Copper 63.546	30 **Zn** Zinc 65.39	31 **Ga** Gallium 69.723	32 **Ge** Germanium 72.61	33 **As** Arsenic 74.92159	34 **Se** Selenium 78.96	35 **Br** Bromine 79.904	36 **Kr** Krypton 83.8
47 **Ag** Silver 107.8682	48 **Cd** Cadmium 112.411	49 **In** Indium 114.818	50 **Sn** Tin 118.71	51 **Sb** Antimony 121.760	52 **Te** Tellurium 127.6	53 **I** Iodine 126.90447	54 **Xe** Xenon 131.29
79 **Au** Gold 196.96654	80 **Hg** Mercury 200.59	81 **Tl** Thallium 204.3833	82 **Pb** Lead 207.2	83 **Bi** Bismuth 208.98039	84 **Po** Polonium 208.9824	85 **At** Astatine 209.9871	86 **Rn** Radon 222.0176
111 **Rg** Roentgenium 272	112 **Uub** Ununbium 277	113 **Uut** Ununtrium 284	114 **Uuq** Ununquadium 289	115 **Uup** Ununpentium 288	116 **Uuh** Ununhexium 292	117 **Uus** Ununseptium n/a	118 **Uuo** Ununoctium 294

Which element should Janet identify?

A. boron (B)

B. carbon (C)

C. oxygen (O)

D. phosphorous (P)

Constructed Response

15 Explain how an atom is related to an element.

_____

How do the properties of an atom compare to the properties of the related element?

_____

Extended Response

16 Sulfur and oxygen react to form sulfur dioxide according to this chemical equation.

$$S + O_2 \rightarrow SO_2$$

Which substance is both an element and a molecule?

_____

Explain how you know this substance is both an element and a molecule.

_____

_____

Which substance is both a compound and a molecule?

_____

Explain how you know this substance is both a compound and a molecule.

_____

_____

Which substance is an element but not a molecule?

_____

Explain how you know this substance is an element but not a molecule.

_____

_____

Energy in the Earth System

Core Standard

Explain how the sun's energy heats the air, land, and water driving the processes that result in wind, ocean currents, and the water cycle.

Waves break on the reef crest, which protects the lagoon and shoreline behind it from the energy of the waves.

Organisms of the reef crest can stand up to high-energy waves.

What do you think?

Large amounts of energy can be transferred from one place to another through winds and waves. Sometimes, winds and waves can be destructive. How do we protect ourselves from powerful winds and waves?

Energy in the Earth System

Indiana Standards

As citizens of the constructed world, students will participate in the design process. Students will learn to use materials and tools safely and employ the basic principles of the engineering design process in order to find solutions to problems.

DP 8.1 Identify a need or problem to be solved.

DP 8.2 Brainstorm potential solutions.

DP 8.6 Create the solution through a prototype.

CITIZEN SCIENCE

Clearing the Air

There are more vehicles on the roads every day. Some of the gases from vehicle exhausts react with sunlight to form ozone. There are days when there is so much ozone in the air, it becomes a health hazard. Those days are especially difficult for people who have asthma or other similar conditions. What can you do to reduce gas emissions?

1 Think About It

A How do you get to school every day?

_____

_____

_____

B How many of the students in your class come to school in a car?

_____

Gas emissions are high during rush hour traffic.

Ride a bicycle to school.

② Ask a Question

How can you reduce the number of vehicles students take to get to school for one day each month?

With your teacher and classmates, brainstorm different ways in which you can reduce the number of vehicles students use to come to school.

Check off the points below as you use them to design your plan.

☐ How far do students live from the school?

☐ What kinds of transportation do students have available to them?

③ Make a Plan

A Write down all of the different ways you can reduce the number of vehicles that bring students to school.

_____
_____
_____
_____
_____
_____
_____

B Create a short presentation for your principal about how the whole school could become involved. Write down the points of your presentation in the space below.

_____
_____
_____
_____
_____
_____
_____
_____
_____

C In the space below, design a sign-up sheet for your classmates to choose how they will come to school on the designated day.

Take It Home

Give your presentation to the adults at home. Then, have them brainstorm ways they, too, can reduce gas emissions every day.

Earth's Spheres

ESSENTIAL QUESTION

What are the parts of the Earth system?

By the end of this lesson, you should be able to describe Earth's spheres and provide examples of interactions between the spheres.

Emperor penguins spend time on land, and need to breathe in oxygen from the air.

These penguins also swim and hold their breath for about 18 min as they hunt for fish. What do you have in common with these penguins?

Indiana Standards

8.2.1 Recognize and demonstrate how the sun's energy drives convection in the atmosphere and in bodies of water, which results in ocean currents and weather patterns.

8.2.2 Describe and model how water moves through the earth's crust, atmosphere, and oceans in a cyclic way, as liquid, vapor, and solid.

8.2.3 Describe the characteristics of ocean currents and identify their effects on weather patterns.

8.2.4 Describe the physical and chemical composition of the atmosphere at different elevations.

Engage Your Brain

1 Predict Check T or F to show whether you think each statement is true or false.

T	F	
☐	☐	Earth is made up completely of solid rocks.
☐	☐	Animals live only on land.
☐	☐	Water in rivers often flows into the ocean.
☐	☐	Air in the atmosphere can move all over the world.

2 Analyze Think about your daily activities and list some of the ways in which you interact with Earth.

_____

_____

_____

_____

_____

_____

Active Reading

3 Synthesize You can often define an unknown word if you know the meaning of its word parts. Use the word parts and sentence below to make an educated guess about the meaning of the word *geosphere*.

Word part	Meaning
geo-	earth
-sphere	ball

Example sentence:
Water flows across the surface of the geosphere.

geosphere:

_____

_____

_____

Vocabulary Terms

- Earth system
- geosphere
- hydrosphere
- cryosphere
- atmosphere
- biosphere

4 Apply As you learn the definition of each vocabulary term in this lesson, create your own notecards to help you remember the meaning of the term.

What on Earth?

What is the Earth system?

A system is a group of related objects or parts that work together to form a whole. From the center of the planet to the outer edge of the atmosphere, Earth is a system. The **Earth system** is all of the matter, energy, and processes within Earth's boundary. Earth is a complex system made up of many smaller systems. The Earth system is made of nonliving things, such as rocks, air, and water. It also contains living things, such as trees, animals, and people. Matter and energy continuously cycle through the smaller systems that make up the Earth system. The Earth system can be divided into five main parts—the geosphere (JEE•oh•sfir), the hydrosphere (HY•druh•sfir), the cryosphere (KRY•uh•sfir), the atmosphere, and the biosphere.

Visualize It!

5 Identify Fill in the boxes under each of the three labels that have lines. List an example of that sphere. Write whether that example is a living thing or a nonliving thing.

atmosphere

cryosphere
_____
_____

geosphere

biosphere
_____
_____

hydrosphere
_____,
_____

What is the geosphere?

Active Reading 6 **Identify** As you read, underline what each of the three different compositional layers of the geosphere is made up of.

The **geosphere** is the mostly solid, rocky part of Earth. It extends from the center of Earth to the surface of Earth. The geosphere is divided into three layers based on chemical composition: the crust, the mantle, and the core.

The crust is the thin, outermost layer of the geosphere. The crust is divided into plates that move slowly over Earth's surface. The crust beneath the oceans is called oceanic crust, and is only 5 to 10 km thick. The continents are made of continental crust, and ranges in thickness from about 15 to 70 km. Continental crust is thickest beneath mountain ranges. The crust is made mostly of silicate minerals.

The mantle lies just below the crust. A small layer of the solid mantle, right below the crust, is just soft enough to flow. Movements in this layer move the plates of the crust. The mantle is about 2,900 km thick. It is made of silicate minerals that are more dense than those in the crust are.

The central part of Earth is the core, which has a radius of 3,400 km. It is made of iron and nickel and is very dense.

Crust
The crust is the thin, solid outermost layer of Earth. It is made mostly of silicates.

Mantle
The mantle is the hot layer of rock between Earth's crust and core. The mantle is more dense than Earth's crust is.

Core
The core is Earth's center. The core is about twice as dense as the mantle is.

7 **Summarize** Fill in the table below, with the characteristics of each of the geosphere's compositional layers.

Compositional layer	Thickness	Relative density

Got Water?

What is the hydrosphere?

The **hydrosphere** is the part of Earth that is liquid water. Ninety-seven percent of all of the water on Earth is the saltwater found in the oceans. Oceans cover 71% of Earth's surface. The hydrosphere also includes the water in lakes, rivers, and marshes. Clouds and rain are also parts of the hydrosphere. Even water that is underground is part of the hydrosphere.

The water on Earth is constantly moving. It moves through the ocean in currents, because of wind and differences in the density of ocean waters. Water also moves from Earth's surface to the air by evaporation. It falls back to Earth as rain. It flows in rivers and through rocks under the ground. It even moves into and out of living things.

Active Reading

8 Identify What are two things through which water moves?

_____

_____

Visualize It!

9 Identify Write whether the example of water in each photo is part of the hydrosphere or the cryosphere.

A

Water vapor condenses forming clouds.

Water flows over Earth's surface.

B

What is the cryosphere?

Earth's **cryosphere** is made up of all of the frozen water on Earth. Therefore, all of the snow, ice, sea ice, glaciers, ice shelves, icebergs, and frozen ground are a part of the cryosphere. Most of the frozen water on Earth is found in the ice caps in Antarctica and in the Arctic. However, snow and glaciers are found in the mountains and at high latitudes all over the world. The amount of frozen water in most of these areas often changes with the seasons. These changes, in turn, play an important role in Earth's climate and in the survival of many species.

10 Compare Fill in the Venn diagram to compare and contrast the hydrosphere and the cryosphere.

Hydrosphere   Both   Cryosphere

Ships can get stuck in ice-covered seas.

C

D

Water moves in ocean currents across huge distances.

What a Gas!

What is the atmosphere?

The **atmosphere** is a mixture of mostly invisible gases that surrounds Earth. The atmosphere extends outward about 500 to 600 km from the surface of Earth. But most of the gases lie within 8 to 50 km of Earth's surface. The main gases that make up the atmosphere are nitrogen and oxygen. About 78% of the atmosphere is nitrogen. Oxygen makes up 21% of the atmosphere. The remaining 1% is made of many other gases, including argon, carbon dioxide, and water vapor.

The atmosphere contains the air we breathe. The atmosphere also traps some of the energy from the sun's rays. This energy helps keep Earth warm enough for living things to survive, and multiply. Uneven warming by the sun gives rise to winds and air currents that move large amounts of air around the world.

Parts of the atmosphere absorb and reflect harmful ultra-violet (UV) rays from the sun, protecting Earth and its living things. Other parts of the atmosphere cause space debris to burn up before reaching Earth's surface and causing harm. Have you ever seen the tail of a meteor across the sky? Then you have seen a meteoroid burning up as it moves through the atmosphere!

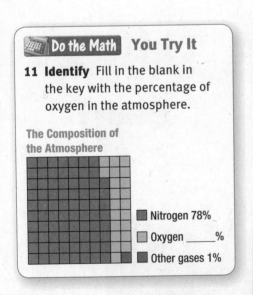

Do the Math   You Try It

11 Identify Fill in the blank in the key with the percentage of oxygen in the atmosphere.

The Composition of the Atmosphere

- ■ Nitrogen 78%
- □ Oxygen _____%
- ■ Other gases 1%

The atmosphere is a very thin layer around Earth. It is made up of a mixture of gases.

Think Outside the Book

12 Apply Design a magazine ad for the atmosphere to show what it does for Earth.

What is the biosphere?

The **biosphere** is made up of living things and the areas of Earth where they are found. The rocks, soil, oceans, lakes, rivers, and lower atmosphere all support life. Organisms have even been found deep in Earth's crust and high in clouds. But no matter where they live, all organisms need certain factors to survive.

Many organisms need oxygen or carbon dioxide to carry out life processes. Liquid water is also important for most living things. Many organisms also need moderate temperatures. You will not find a polar bear living in a desert because it is too hot for the polar bear. However, some organisms do live in extreme environments, such as in ice at the poles and at volcanic vents on the sea floor.

A stable source of energy is also important for life. For example, plants and algae use the energy from sunlight to make their food. Other organisms get their energy by eating these plants or algae.

Active Reading

13 Identify What factors are needed for life?

_____

_____

© Houghton Mifflin Harcourt Publishing Company • Image Credits: (bkgd) ©Blaine Harrington III/Corbis; (sloth) ©Gaertner/Alamy; (crabs) ©OAR/National Undersea Research Program (NURP), Texas A&M Univ.

Visualize It! (Inquiry)

14 Predict What would happen if the biosphere in this picture stopped interacting with the atmosphere?

_____

_____

_____

_____

_____

_____

These crabs and clams live on the deep ocean floor where it is pitch dark. They rely on special bacteria for their food. Why are these bacteria special? They eat crude oil.

The hair on the sloth looks green because it has algae in it. The green color helps the sloth hide from predators. This is very useful because the sloth moves very, very slowly.

What's the Matter?

How do Earth's spheres interact?

Earth's spheres interact as matter and energy change and cycle between the five different spheres. A result of these interactions is that they make life on Earth possible. Remember that the Earth system includes all of the matter, energy, and processes within Earth's boundary.

If matter or energy never changed from one form to another, life on Earth would not be possible. Imagine what would happen if there were no more rain and all of the freshwater drained into the oceans. Most of the life on land would quickly die. But how do these different spheres interact? An example of an interaction is when water cycles between land, ocean, air, and living things. To move between these different spheres, water absorbs, releases, and transports energy all over the world in its different forms.

Visualize It!

15 Analyze Fill in the boxes below each photo with the names of at least two spheres that are interacting in that photo.

Rain provides water for living things.

A

The deer carcass is being decomposed by many kinds of organisms.

B

Matter Can Be Exchanged Between Spheres

Earth's spheres interact as matter moves between spheres. For example, the atmosphere interacts with the hydrosphere or cryosphere when rain or snow falls from the air. The opposite also happens as water from the hydrosphere and cryosphere moves into the atmosphere.

Sometimes, matter moves through different spheres. For example, some bacteria in the biosphere remove nitrogen gas from the atmosphere. These bacteria then release a different form of nitrogen into the soil, or geosphere. Plants in the biosphere use this nitrogen to grow. When the plant dies and decays, the nitrogen is released in different forms. One of these forms returns to the atmosphere.

Active Reading **16 Identify** What is the relationship between Earth's spheres and matter?

Energy Can Be Exchanged Between Spheres

Earth's spheres also interact as energy moves between them. For example, plants use solar energy to make their food. Some of this energy is passed on to animals that eat plants. Some of the energy is released into the atmosphere as heat as the animals move around. Some of the energy is released into the geosphere when organisms die and decay. In this case, energy entered the biosphere and moved into the atmosphere and geosphere.

Energy also moves back and forth between spheres. For example, solar energy reflected by Earth's surface warms up the atmosphere, creating winds. Winds create waves and surface ocean currents that travel across the world's oceans. When warm winds and ocean currents reach colder areas, thermal energy moves into the colder air, warming it up. In this case, the energy has cycled between the atmosphere and the hydrosphere.

Icebergs melt in the sun.

D

Waves break in shallow areas.

C

Visual Summary

To complete this summary, fill in the box below each photo with the name of the sphere being shown in the photo. Then use the key below to check your answers. You can use this page to review the main concepts of the lesson.

17 _____

Earth's Spheres

18 _____

21 _____

20 _____

19 _____

Answers: 17 geosphere; 18 biosphere;
19 cryosphere; 20 hydrosphere; 21 atmosphere

22 Synthesize Diagram an interaction between any two of Earth's spheres.

Lesson Review

Vocabulary

Circle the term that best completes each of the following sentences.

1 The ice caps in the Antarctic and the Arctic are a part of the *geosphere/cryosphere/biosphere*.

2 Most of the water on Earth can be found in the *biosphere/hydrosphere/geosphere*.

3 The *hydrosphere/geosphere/atmosphere* protects organisms that live on Earth by blocking out harmful UV rays from the sun.

Key Concepts

Location	Sphere
4 Identify Forms a thin layer of gases around Earth	
5 Identify Extends from Earth's core to Earth's crust	
6 Identify Extends from inside Earth's crust to the lower atmosphere	

7 Describe What does the Earth system include?

_____

_____

8 Analyze Which spheres are interacting when a volcano erupts and releases gases into the air?

_____

_____

9 Identify What are the two most common gases in the atmosphere?

_____

10 Describe How do Earth's spheres interact?

_____

_____

Critical Thinking

Use this graph to answer the following question.

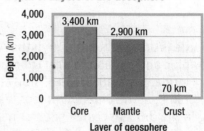

Depth of Layers of the Geosphere

11 Analyze What is the diameter of the geosphere?

_____

12 Identify Name two ways in which the Earth system relies on energy from the sun?

_____

_____

_____

_____

_____

13 Analyze How does the biosphere rely on the other spheres for survival?

_____

_____

_____

14 Infer Where is most of the liquid water on Earth, and what would have to be done so that humans could drink it?

_____

_____

_____

_____

Evan B. Forde
OCEANOGRAPHER

Pillow lava on the ocean floor, seen from *Alvin*

Evan B. Forde is an oceanographer at the Atlantic Oceanographic and Meteorological Laboratory in Miami, Florida. His main areas of study have included looking at the different processes occurring in the U.S. east coast submarine canyons. To study these canyons, Evan became the first African American to participate in research dives in underwater submersibles—machines that can take a human being under water safely—such as *Alvin*. He is currently studying how conditions in the atmosphere relate to the formation of hurricanes.

Evan graduated with degrees in Geology and Marine Geology and Geophysics from Columbia University in New York City. Along with his scientific research, he is committed to science education. He has developed and taught courses on Tropical Meteorology at the University of Miami. Keeping younger students in mind, he created an oceanography course for middle-school students through the Miami-Dade Public Libraries. Evan speaks often to students about oceanography and the sciences, and is involved with many community youth projects.

Social Studies Connection

Mendocino Canyons
Monterey Canyon — San Francisco
Sur Canyon — CALIFORNIA
Hueneme Canyon — Los Angeles
Santa Monica Canyon
Redondo Canyon — San Diego
Scripps Canyon
La Jolla Canyon

BAJA CALIFORNIA

PACIFIC OCEAN

MEXICO

N W E S

San Lucas Canyon

Research the Monterey Submarine Canyon shown on the map. Find out its size and if it is still considered one of the largest canyons off the Pacific Coast. Research the kind of organisms that can live there.

Evan B. Forde

JOB BOARD

Wind Turbine Technician

What You'll Do: Operate and maintain wind turbine units, including doing repairs and preventative maintenance.

Where You Might Work: You will need to travel often to the different wind farms that have wind turbines. Some technicians may have the chance to travel to wind farms in different countries to complete repairs on wind turbines.

Education: Typically, technicians will graduate from a wind energy program. Technicians should have a solid understanding of math, meteorology, computer, and problem solving skills.

Other Job Requirements: To do these tasks, you will need to climb wind towers as high as 125 meters, so it is helpful if you do not have a fear of heights.

Environmental Engineering Technician

What You'll Do: Help environmental engineers and scientists prevent, control, and get rid of environmental hazards. Inspect, test, decontaminate, and operate equipment used to control and help fix environmental pollution.

Where You Might Work: Offices, laboratories, or industrial plants. Most technicians have to complete field work, so they do spend time working outdoors in all types of weather.

Education: You will need an associate's degree in environmental engineering technology, environmental technology, or hazardous materials information systems technology.

Wind turbine

The Atmosphere

© Houghton Mifflin Harcourt Publishing Company • Image Credits: ©NASA

ESSENTIAL QUESTION

What is the atmosphere?

By the end of this lesson, you should be able to describe the composition and structure of the atmosphere and explain how the atmosphere protects life and insulates Earth.

The atmosphere is a very thin layer compared to the whole Earth. However, it is essential for life on our planet.

Indiana Standards

8.2.1 Recognize and demonstrate how the sun's energy drives convection in the atmosphere and in bodies of water, which results in ocean currents and weather patterns.

8.2.4 Describe the physical and chemical composition of the atmosphere at different elevations.

Engage Your Brain

1 Predict Check T or F to show whether you think each statement is true or false.

T	F	
☐	☐	Oxygen is in the air we breathe.
☐	☐	Pressure is not a property of air.
☐	☐	The air around you is part of the atmosphere.
☐	☐	As you climb up a mountain, the temperature usually gets warmer.

2 Explain Does the air in this balloon have mass? Why or why not?

_____

_____

_____

_____

Active Reading

3 Synthesize Many English words have their roots in other languages. Use the ancient Greek words below to make an educated guess about the meanings of the words *atmosphere* and *mesosphere*.

Greek word	Meaning
atmos	vapor
mesos	middle
sphaira	ball

Vocabulary Terms

- atmosphere
- air pressure
- thermosphere
- mesosphere
- stratosphere
- troposphere
- ozone layer
- greenhouse effect

4 Apply As you learn the definition of each vocabulary term in this lesson, create your own definition or sketch to help you remember the meaning of the term.

atmosphere:

_____

_____

mesosphere:

_____

_____

Up and Away!

What is Earth's atmosphere?

The mixture of gases that surrounds Earth is the **atmosphere**. This mixture is most often referred to as air. The atmosphere has many important functions. It protects you from the sun's damaging rays and also helps to maintain the right temperature range for life on Earth. For example, the temperature range on Earth allows us to have an abundant amount of liquid water. Many of the components of the atmosphere are essential for life, such as the oxygen you breathe.

A Mixture of Gases and Small Particles

As shown below, the atmosphere is made mostly of nitrogen gas (78%) and oxygen gas (21%). The other 1% is other gases. The atmosphere also contains small particles such as dust, volcanic ash, sea salt, and smoke. There are even small pieces of skin, bacteria, and pollen floating in the atmosphere!

Water is also found in the atmosphere. Liquid water, as water droplets, and solid water, as snow and ice crystals, are found in clouds. But most water in the atmosphere exists as an invisible gas called water vapor. Under certain conditions, water vapor can change into solid or liquid water. Then, snow or rain might fall from the sky.

Visualize It!

5 Identify Fill in the missing percentage for oxygen.

Nitrogen is the most abundant gas in the atmosphere.

Oxygen is the second most abundant gas in the atmosphere.

The remaining 1% of the atmosphere is made up of argon, carbon dioxide, water vapor, and other gases.

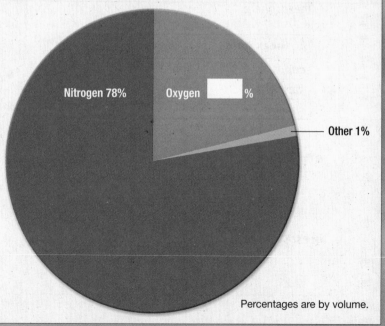

Composition of the Atmosphere

Nitrogen 78%

Oxygen ___ %

Other 1%

Percentages are by volume.

How do pressure and temperature change in the atmosphere?

The atmosphere is held around Earth by gravity. Gravity pulls gas molecules in the atmosphere toward Earth's surface, causing air pressure. **Air pressure** is the measure of the force with which air molecules push on an area of a surface. At sea level, air pressure is over 1 lb for every square centimeter of your body. That is like carrying a 1-liter bottle of water on the tip of your finger!

However, air pressure is not the same throughout the atmosphere. Although there are many gas molecules that surround you on Earth, there are fewer and fewer gas molecules in the air as you move away from Earth's surface. So, as altitude increases, air pressure decreases.

As altitude increases, air temperature also changes. These changes are mainly due to the way solar energy is absorbed in the atmosphere. Some parts of the atmosphere are warmer because they contain a high percentage of gases that absorb solar energy. Other parts of the atmosphere contain less of these gases and are cooler.

Active Reading

6 Identify As you read, underline what happens to temperature and to pressure as altitude increases.

Inquiry

7 Explain Why does a mountain climber need an oxygen supply at very high altitudes, even though the air still contains 21% oxygen?

_____

_____

_____

At high altitudes such as the top of Mount Everest, air pressure and temperature are lower than they are at sea level.

Look Way

What are the layers of the atmosphere?

Earth's atmosphere is divided into four layers, based on temperature and other properties. As shown at the right, these layers are the troposphere (TROH•puh•sfir), stratosphere (STRAT•uh•sfir), mesosphere (MEZ•uh•sfir), and thermosphere (THER•muh•sfir). Although these names sound complicated, they give you clues about the layers' features. *Tropo-* means "turning" or "change," and the troposphere is the layer where gases turn and mix. *Strato-* means "layer," and the stratosphere is where gases are layered and do not mix very much. *Meso-* means "middle," and the mesosphere is the middle layer. Finally, *thermo-* means "heat," and the thermosphere is the layer where temperatures are highest.

Think Outside the Book

8 Describe Research the part of the thermosphere called the ionosphere. Describe what the aurora borealis is.

The aurora borealis occurs in the thermosphere.

Thermosphere

The **thermosphere** is the uppermost layer of the atmosphere. The temperature increases as altitude increases because gases in the thermosphere absorb high-energy solar radiation. Temperatures in the thermosphere can be 1,500 °C or higher. However, the thermosphere feels cold. The density of particles in the thermosphere is very low. Too few gas particles collide with your body to transfer heat energy to your skin.

Mesosphere

The **mesosphere** is between the thermosphere and stratosphere. In this layer, the temperature decreases as altitude increases. Temperatures can be as low as –120 °C at the top of the mesosphere. Meteoroids begin to burn up in the mesosphere.

Stratosphere

The **stratosphere** is between the mesosphere and troposphere. In this layer, temperatures generally increase as altitude increases. Ozone in the stratosphere absorbs ultraviolet radiation from the sun, which warms the air. An ozone molecule is made of three atoms of oxygen. Gases in the stratosphere are layered and do not mix very much.

Troposphere

The **troposphere** is the lowest layer of the atmosphere. Although temperatures near Earth's surface vary greatly, generally, temperature decreases as altitude increases. This layer contains almost 80% of the atmosphere's total mass, making it the densest layer. Almost all of Earth's carbon dioxide, water vapor, clouds, air pollution, weather, and life forms are in the troposphere.

© Houghton Mifflin Harcourt Publishing Company • Image Credits: ©John Warden/Stone/Getty Images

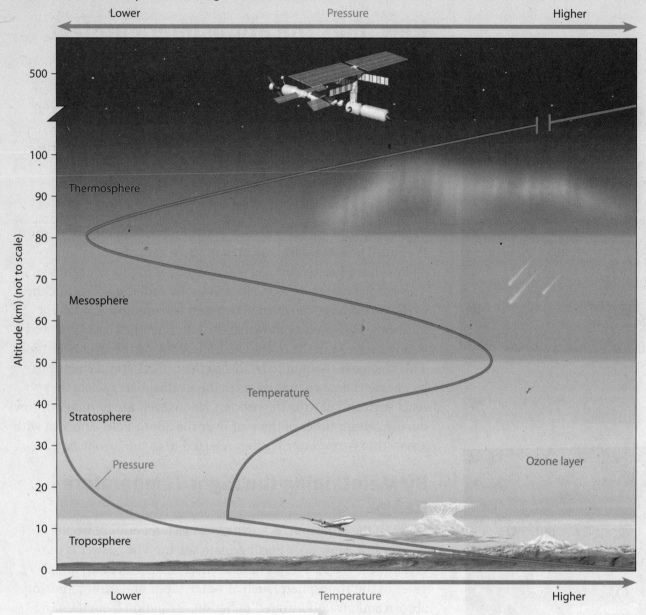

Visualize It!

In the graph, the green line shows pressure change with altitude.
The red line shows temperature change with altitude.

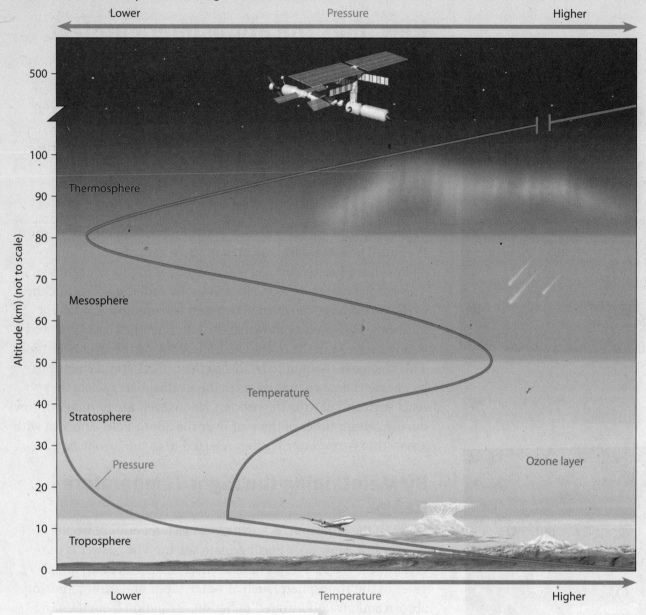

Lower   Pressure   Higher

Altitude (km) (not to scale)

500

100

90 — Thermosphere

80

70

60 — Mesosphere

50

40

30 — Stratosphere

Temperature

20

Pressure   Ozone layer

10

Troposphere

0

Lower   Temperature   Higher

The layers of the atmosphere are
defined by changes in temperature.

9 Analyze Using the graph and
descriptions provided, indicate
if air pressure and temperature
increase or decrease with
increased altitude in each layer
of the atmosphere. One answer
has been provided for you.

Layer	Air pressure	Temperature
Thermosphere	decreases	
Mesosphere		
Stratosphere		
Troposphere		

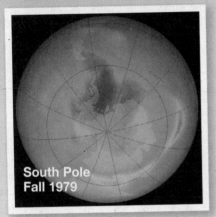
South Pole
Fall 1979

Less ozone   More ozone

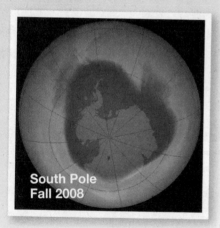
South Pole
Fall 2008

10 Compare How did the ozone layer over the South Pole change between 1979 and 2008?

_____

_____

How does the atmosphere protect life on Earth?

The atmosphere surrounds and protects Earth. The atmosphere provides the air we breathe. It also protects Earth from harmful solar radiation and from space debris that enters the Earth system. In addition, the atmosphere controls the temperature on Earth.

By Absorbing or Reflecting Harmful Radiation

Earth's atmosphere reflects or absorbs most of the radiation from the sun. The **ozone layer** is an area in the stratosphere, 15 km to 40 km above Earth's surface, where ozone is highly concentrated. The ozone layer absorbs most of the solar radiation. The thickness of the ozone layer can change between seasons and at different locations. However, as shown at the left, scientists have observed a steady decrease in the overall volume of the ozone layer over time. This change is thought to be due to the use of certain chemicals by people. These chemicals enter the stratosphere, where they react with and destroy the ozone. Ozone levels are particularly low during certain times of the year over the South Pole. The area with a very thin ozone layer is often referred to as the "ozone hole."

By Maintaining the Right Temperature Range

Without the atmosphere, Earth's average temperature would be very low. How does Earth remain warm? The answer is the greenhouse effect. The **greenhouse effect** is the process by which gases in the atmosphere, such as water vapor and carbon dioxide, absorb and give off infrared radiation. Radiation from the sun warms Earth's surface, and Earth's surface gives off infrared radiation. Greenhouse gases in the atmosphere absorb some of this infrared radiation and then reradiate it. Some of this energy is absorbed again by Earth's surface, while some energy goes out into space. Because greenhouse gases keep energy in the Earth system longer, Earth's average surface temperature is kept at around 15°C (59°F). In time, all the energy ends up back in outer space.

🔎 **Active Reading** **11 List** Name two examples of greenhouse gases.

_____

_____

the Sun ...

The Greenhouse Effect

Greenhouse gas molecules absorb and emit infrared radiation.

Atmosphere without Greenhouse Gases	Atmosphere with Greenhouse Gases
Without greenhouse gases in Earth's atmosphere, radiation from Earth's surface is lost directly to space. **Average Temperature: -18°C**	With greenhouse gases in Earth's atmosphere, radiation from Earth's surface is lost to space more slowly, which makes Earth's surface warmer. **Average Temperature: 15°C**

═══ sunlight   ═══ infrared radiation

The atmosphere is much thinner than shown here.

12 Illustrate Draw your own version of how greenhouse gases keep Earth warm.

Visual Summary

To complete this summary, fill in the blanks with the correct word or phrase. Then, use the key below to check your answers. You can use this page to review the main concepts of the lesson.

Both air pressure and temperature change within the atmosphere.

13 As altitude increases, air pressure

_____

The atmosphere protects Earth from harmful radiation and helps to maintain a temperature range that supports life.

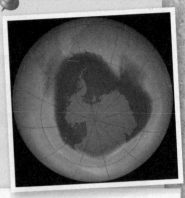

14 Earth is protected from harmful solar radiation by the

_____

The Atmosphere

The atmosphere is divided into four layers, according to temperature and other properties.

15 The four layers of the atmosphere are the

_____

_____

_____

_____

16 **Hypothesize** What do you think Earth's surface would be like if Earth did not have an atmosphere?

Lesson Review

Vocabulary

Fill in the blanks with the terms that best complete the following sentences.

1 The _____ is a mixture of gases that surrounds Earth.

2 The measure of the force with which air molecules push on a surface is called _____ .

3 The _____ is the process by which gases in the atmosphere absorb and reradiate heat.

Key Concepts

4 List Name three gases in the atmosphere.

_____

5 Identify What layer of the atmosphere contains the ozone layer?

_____

6 Identify What layer of the atmosphere contains almost 80% of the atmosphere's total mass?

_____

7 Describe How and why does air pressure change with altitude in the atmosphere?

_____

_____

_____

8 Explain What is the name of the uppermost layer of the atmosphere? Why does it feel cold there, even though the temperature can be very high?

_____

_____

_____

_____

Critical Thinking

9 Hypothesize What would happen to life on Earth if the ozone layer was not present?

_____

_____

_____

10 Criticize A friend says that temperature increases as altitude increases because you're moving closer to the sun. Is this true? Explain.

_____

_____

_____

11 Predict Why would increased levels of greenhouse gases contribute to higher temperatures on Earth?

_____

_____

_____

Use this graph to answer the following questions.

Changes in Temperature with Altitude

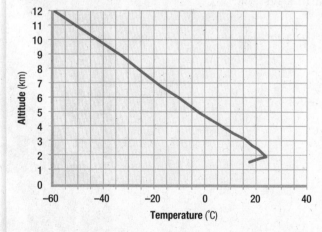

Source: National Weather Service. Data taken at Riverton, Wyoming, 2001

12 Analyze The top of Mount Everest is at about 8,850 m. What would the approximate air temperature be at that altitude? _____

13 Analyze What is the total temperature change between 3 km and 7 km above Earth's surface? _____

Energy Transfer

ESSENTIAL QUESTION

How does energy move through Earth's system?

By the end of this lesson, you should be able to summarize the three mechanisms by which energy is transferred through Earth's system.

Ice absorbs energy from the sun. This can cause ice to melt—even these icicles in Antarctica.

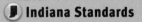 **Indiana Standards**

8.2.1 Recognize and demonstrate how the sun's energy drives convection in the atmosphere and in bodies of water, which results in ocean currents and weather patterns.

Engage Your Brain

1 Describe Fill in the blank with the word or phrase that you think correctly completes the following sentences.

An example of something hot is

_____

An example of something cold is

_____

The sun provides us with

_____

A thermometer is used to measure

_____

2 Explain If you placed your hands around this mug of hot chocolate, what would happen to the temperature of your hands? Why do you think this would happen?

_____

_____

_____

_____

_____

Active Reading

3 Apply Many scientific words, such as *heat*, are used to convey different meanings. Use context clues to write your own definition for each meaning of the word *heat*.

The student won the first <u>heat</u> of the race.

heat:

_____

_____

The man wondered if his rent included <u>heat</u>.

heat:

_____

_____

Energy in the form of <u>heat</u> was transferred from the hot pan to the cold counter.

heat:

_____

_____

Vocabulary Terms

- temperature
- thermal energy
- thermal expansion
- heat
- radiation
- convection
- conduction

4 Identify This list contains the vocabulary terms you'll learn in this lesson. As you read, circle the definition of each term.

Hot and Cold

How are energy and temperature related?

All matter is made up of moving particles, such as atoms or molecules. When particles are in motion, they have kinetic energy. Because particles move at different speeds, each has a different amount of kinetic energy.

Temperature (TEMM•per•uh•choor) is a measure of the average kinetic energy of particles. The faster a particle moves, the more kinetic energy it has. As shown below, the more kinetic energy the particles of an object have, the higher the temperature of the object. Temperature does not depend on the number of particles. A teapot holds more tea than a cup. If the particles of tea in both containers have the same average kinetic energy, the tea in both containers is at the same temperature.

Thermal energy is the total kinetic energy of particles. A teapot full of tea at a high temperature has more thermal energy than a teapot full of tea at a lower temperature. Thermal energy also depends on the number of particles. The more particles there are in an object, the greater the object's thermal energy. The tea in a teapot and a cup may be at the same temperature, but the tea in the pot has more thermal energy because there is more of it.

Visualize It!

5 Analyze Which container holds particles with the higher average kinetic energy?

_____

_____

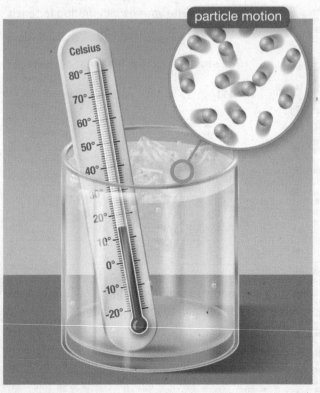

What is thermal expansion?

When the temperature of a substance increases, the substance's particles have more kinetic energy. Therefore, the particles move faster and move apart. As the space between the particles increases, the substance expands. The increase in volume that results from an increase in temperature is called **thermal expansion**. Most substances on Earth expand when they become warmer and contract when they become cooler. Water is an exception. Cold water expands as it gets colder and then freezes to form ice.

Thermal expansion causes a change in the density of a substance. *Density* is the mass per unit volume of a substance. When a substance expands, its mass stays the same but its volume increases. As a result, density decreases. Differences in density that are caused by thermal expansion can cause movement of matter. For example, air inside a hot-air balloon is warmed, as shown below. The air expands as its particles move faster and farther apart. As the air expands, it becomes less dense than the air outside the balloon. The less-dense air inside the balloon is forced upward by the colder, denser air outside the balloon. This same principle affects air movement in the atmosphere, water movement in the oceans, and rock movement in the geosphere.

7 Apply Why would an increase in the temperature of the oceans contribute to a rise in sea level?

_____

_____

_____

6 Predict What might happen to the hot-air balloon if the air inside it cooled down?

_____

_____

When the air in this balloon becomes hotter, it becomes less dense than the surrounding air. So, the balloon goes up, up, and away!

Getting Warm

What is heat?

You might think of the word *heat* when you imagine something that feels hot. But heat also has to do with things that feel cold. In fact, heat is what causes objects to feel hot or cold. You may often use the word *heat* to mean different things. However, in this lesson, the word *heat* has only one meaning. **Heat** is the energy that is transferred between objects that are at different temperatures.

Energy Transferred Between Objects

When objects that have different temperatures come into contact, energy will be transferred between them until both objects reach the same temperature. The direction of this energy transfer is always from the object with the higher temperature to the object with the lower temperature. When you touch something cold, energy is transferred from your body to that object. When you touch something hot, like the pan shown below, energy is transferred from that object to your body.

Active Reading

8 Identify As you read, underline the direction of energy transfer between objects that are at different temperatures.

Visualize It!

9 Predict Draw an arrow to show the direction in which energy is transferred between the pan and the oven mitts.

This pan is being removed from the oven and is very hot.

Why can the temperatures of land, air, and water differ?

When the same amount of energy is being transferred, some materials will get warmer or cooler at a faster rate than other materials. Suppose you are walking along a beach on a sunny day. You may notice that the land feels warmer than the air and the water, even though they are all exposed to the same amount of energy from the sun. This is because the land warms up at a faster rate than the water and air do.

Specific Heat

The different rates at which materials become warmer or cooler are due to a property called *specific heat*. A substance that has a high specific heat requires a lot of energy to show an increase in temperature. A substance with a lower specific heat requires less energy to show the same increase in temperature. Water has a higher specific heat than land. So, water warms up more slowly than land does. Water also cools down more slowly than land does.

10 **Predict** Air has a lower specific heat than water. Once the sun goes down, will the air or the water cool off faster? Why?

_____

_____

_____

The temperatures of land, water, and air may differ—even when they are exposed to the same amount of energy from the sun.

Heat

How is energy transferred by radiation?

On a summer day, you can feel warmth from the sun on your skin. But how did that energy reach you from the sun? The sun transfers energy to Earth by radiation. **Radiation** is the transfer of energy as electromagnetic (ee•LEK•troh•mag•NEH•tik) waves. Radiation can transfer energy between objects that are not in direct contact with each other. Many objects other than the sun also radiate energy as light and heat. These include a hot burner on a stove and a campfire, shown below.

Electromagnetic Waves

Energy from the sun is called *electromagnetic radiation*. This energy travels in waves. You are probably familiar with one form of radiation called *visible light*. You can see the visible light that comes from the sun. Electromagnetic radiation includes other forms of energy, which you cannot see. Most of the warmth that you feel from the sun is infrared radiation. This energy has a longer wavelength and lower energy than visible light. Higher-energy radiation includes x-rays and ultraviolet light.

Visualize It!

11 Analyze Write a caption for the campfire photo on the right. Make sure the caption relates the image to radiation.

_____

_____

_____

Energy from this hot burner is being transferred by radiation.

© Houghton Mifflin Harcourt Publishing Company • Image Credits: (br) ©Creatas/age fotostock

Energy from the sun is transferred through space.

Where does radiation occur on Earth?

We live almost 150 million km from the sun. Yet almost all of the energy on Earth is transmitted from the sun by radiation. The sun is the major source of energy for processes at Earth's surface. Receiving that energy is absolutely vital for life on Earth. The electromagnetic waves from the sun also provide energy that drives the water cycle.

When solar radiation reaches Earth, some of the energy is reflected and scattered by Earth's atmosphere. But much of the energy passes through Earth's atmosphere and reaches Earth's surface. Some of the energy that Earth receives from the sun is absorbed by the atmosphere, geosphere, and hydrosphere. Then, the energy is changed into thermal energy. This thermal energy may be reradiated into the Earth system or into space. Much of the energy is transferred through Earth's systems by the two other ways—convection and conduction.

Think Outside the Book

13 Apply Research ultraviolet radiation from the sun and its role in causing sunburns.

12 Summarize Give two examples of what happens when energy from the sun reaches Earth.

_____

_____

_____

_____

Heating Up

How is energy transferred by convection?

Have you ever watched a pot of boiling water, such as the one below? If so, you have seen convection. **Convection** (kun•VECK•shuhn) is the transfer of energy due to the movement of matter. As water warms up at the bottom of the pot, some of the hot water rises. At the same time, cooler water from other parts of the pot sink and replace the rising water. This water is then warmed and the cycle continues.

Convection Currents

Convection involves the movement of matter due to differences in density. Convection occurs because most matter becomes less dense when it gets warmer. When most matter becomes warmer, it undergoes thermal expansion and a decrease in density. This less-dense matter is forced upward by the surrounding colder, denser matter that is sinking. As the hot matter rises, it cools and becomes more dense. This causes it to sink back down. This cycling of matter is called a *convection current*. Convection most often occurs in fluids, such as water and air. But convection can also happen in solids.

wax

energy sources

convection current

© Houghton Mifflin Harcourt Publishing Company

Visualize It! Inquiry

14 Apply How is convection related to the rise and fall of wax in lava lamps?

_____

_____

_____

_____

Where does convection occur on Earth?

If Earth's surface is warmer than the air, energy will be transferred from the ground to the air. As the air becomes warmer, it becomes less dense. This air is pushed upward and out of the way by cooler, denser air that is sinking. As the warm air rises, it cools and becomes denser and begins to sink back toward Earth's surface. This cycle moves energy through the atmosphere.

Convection currents also occur in the ocean because of differences in the density of ocean water. More dense water sinks to the ocean floor, and less dense water moves toward the surface. The density of ocean water is influenced by temperature and the amount of salt in the water. Cold water is denser than warmer water. Water that contains a lot of salt is more dense than less-salty water.

Energy produced deep inside Earth heats rock in the mantle. The heated rock becomes less dense and is pushed up toward Earth's surface by the cooler, denser surrounding rock. Once cooled near the surface, the rock sinks. These convection currents transfer energy from Earth's core toward Earth's surface. These currents also cause the movement of tectonic plates.

Active Reading **15 Name** What are three of Earth's spheres in which energy is transferred by convection?

_____

Visualize It!

16 Apply Draw the convection current that could occur in the body of water in this image.

Convection currents occur throughout the Earth system.

Ouch!

How is energy transferred by conduction?

Have you ever touched an ice cube and wondered why it feels cold? An ice cube has only a small amount of energy, compared to your hand. Energy is transferred to the ice cube from your hand through the process of conduction. **Conduction** (kun•DUHK•shuhn) is the transfer of energy from one object to another object through direct contact.

Direct Contact

Remember that the atoms or molecules in a substance are constantly moving. Even a solid block of ice has particles in constant motion. When objects at different temperatures touch, their particles interact. Conduction involves the faster-moving particles of the warmer object transferring energy to the slower-moving particles in the cooler object. The greater the difference in energy of the particles, the faster the transfer of energy by conduction occurs.

Active Reading **17 Apply** Name two examples of conduction that you experience every day.

_____

_____

_____

_____

These desert sands would feel hot because of conduction.

Where does conduction occur on Earth?

Energy can be transferred between the geosphere and the atmosphere by conduction. When cooler air molecules come into direct contact with the warm ground, energy is passed to the air by conduction. Conduction between the ground and the air happens only within a few centimeters of Earth's surface.

Conduction also happens between particles of air and particles of water. For example, if air transfers enough energy to liquid water, the water may evaporate. If water vapor transfers energy to the air, the kinetic energy of the water decreases. As a result, the water vapor may condense to form liquid water droplets.

Inside Earth, energy transfers between rock particles by conduction. However, rock is a poor conductor of heat, so this process happens very slowly.

 **Visualize It!**

18 Compare Does conduction also occur in a city like the one shown below? Explain.

_____

_____

_____

_____

_____

19 Summarize Complete the following spider map by describing the three types of energy transfer. One answer has been started for you.

Radiation
Transfer of energy as
_____
_____

_____
_____
_____

Types of Energy Transfer

_____
_____
_____

Visual Summary

To complete this summary, fill in the blanks with the correct word or phrase. Then, use the key below to check your answers. You can use this page to review the main concepts of the lesson.

Heat is the energy that is transferred between objects that are at different temperatures.

20 The particles in a hot pan have _____ kinetic energy than the particles in a cool oven mitt.

Energy Transfer

Energy can be transferred in different ways.

21 The three ways that energy can be transferred are labeled in the image as

A: _____

B: _____

C: _____

Answers: 20 more; 21 A: radiation, B: conduction, C: convection

22 **Apply** What type of energy transfer is responsible for making you feel cold when you are swimming in cool water? Explain your answer.

Lesson Review

Vocabulary

In your own words, define the following terms.

1 radiation

_____

_____

2 convection

_____

_____

3 conduction

_____

_____

Key Concepts

4 Compare What is the difference between temperature, thermal energy, and heat?

_____

_____

_____

_____

5 Describe What is happening to a substance undergoing thermal expansion?

_____

_____

_____

6 Explain What is the main source of energy for most processes at Earth's surface?

_____

_____

7 Summarize What happens when two objects at different temperatures touch? Name one place where it occurs in Earth's system.

_____

_____

_____

8 Identify What is an example of convection in Earth's system?

_____

_____

Critical Thinking

9 Apply Why can metal utensils get too hot to touch when you are cooking with them?

_____

_____

_____

10 Predict You are doing an experiment outside on a sunny day. You find the temperature of some sand is 28°C. You also find the temperature of some water is 25°C. Explain the difference in temperatures.

_____

_____

_____

_____

_____

Use this image to answer the following questions.

11 Analyze Name one example of where energy transfer by radiation is occurring.

_____

12 Analyze Name one example of where energy transfer by conduction is occurring.

_____

13 Analyze Name one example of where energy transfer by convection is occurring.

_____

Wind in the Atmosphere

ESSENTIAL QUESTION

What is wind?

By the end of this lesson, you should be able to explain how energy provided by the sun causes atmospheric movement, called wind.

Although you cannot see wind, you can see how it affects things like these kites.

Indiana Standards

8.2.1 Recognize and demonstrate how the sun's energy drives convection in the atmosphere and in bodies of water, which results in ocean currents and weather patterns.

Engage Your Brain

1 Predict Check T or F to show whether you think each statement is true or false.

T	F	
☐	☐	The atmosphere is often referred to as air.
☐	☐	Wind does not have direction.
☐	☐	During the day, there is often a wind blowing toward shore from the ocean or a large lake.
☐	☐	Cold air rises and warm air sinks.

2 Explain if you opened the valve on this bicycle tire, what would happen to the air inside of the tire? Why do you think that would happen?

_____

_____

_____

Active Reading

3 Synthesize You can often define an unknown phrase if you know the meaning of its word parts. Use the word parts below to make an educated guess about the meanings of the phrases *local wind* and *global wind*.

Word part	Meaning
wind	movement of air due to differences in air pressure
local	involving a particular area
global	involving the entire Earth

Vocabulary Terms

- wind
- Coriolis effect
- global wind
- jet stream
- local wind

4 Identify This list contains the vocabulary terms you'll learn in this lesson. As you read, circle the definition of each term.

local wind:

_____

_____

global wind:

_____

_____

What causes wind?

The next time you feel the wind blowing, you can thank the sun! The sun does not warm the whole surface of the Earth in a uniform manner. This uneven heating causes the air above Earth's surface to be at different temperatures. Cold air is more dense than warmer air is. Colder, denser air sinks. When denser air sinks, it places greater pressure on the surface of Earth than warmer, less-dense air does. This results in areas of higher air pressure. Air moves from areas of higher pressure toward areas of lower pressure. The movement of air caused by differences in air pressure is called **wind**. The greater the differences in air pressure, the faster the air moves.

Areas of High and Low Pressure

Cold, dense air at the poles creates areas of high pressure at the poles. Warm, less-dense air at the equator forms an area of lower pressure. This pressure gradient results in global movement of air. However, instead of moving in one circle between the equator and the poles, air moves in smaller circular patterns called *convection cells*, shown below. As air moves from the equator, it cools and becomes more dense. At about 30°N and 30°S latitudes, a high-pressure belt results from the sinking of air. Near the poles, cold air warms as it moves away from the poles. At around 60°N and 60°S latitudes, a low-pressure belt forms as the warmed air is pushed upward.

Visualize It!

5 Identify In the white oval area on the map, draw the convection cell that was left out. Use a pencil to indicate warm air and a pen to indicate cool air.

The warming and cooling of air produces pressure belts every 30° of latitude.

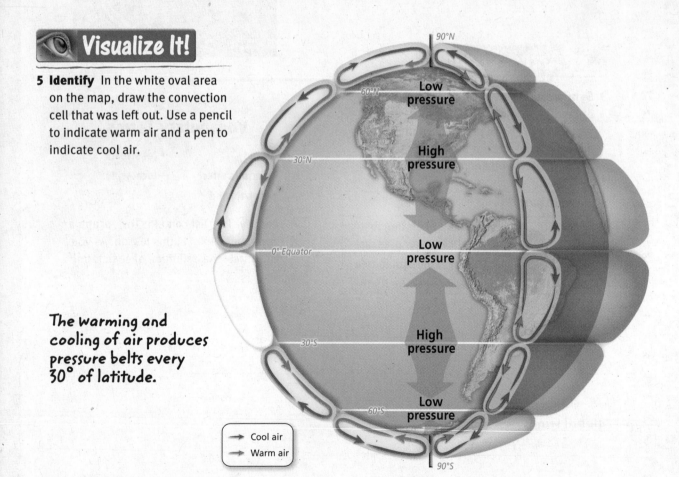

90°N

60°N — Low pressure

30°N — High pressure

0° Equator — Low pressure

30°S — High pressure

60°S — Low pressure

90°S

→ Cool air
→ Warm air

How does Earth's rotation affect wind?

Pressure differences cause air to move between the equator and the poles. If Earth was not rotating, winds would blow in a straight line. However, winds are deflected, or curved, due to Earth's rotation, as shown below. The apparent curving of the path of a moving object from an otherwise straight path due to Earth's rotation is called the **Coriolis effect** (kawr•ee•OH•lis ih•FEKT). This effect is most noticeable over long distances.

Because each point on Earth makes one complete rotation every day, points closer to the equator must travel farther and, therefore, faster than points closer to the poles do. When air moves from the equator toward the North Pole, it maintains its initial speed and direction. If the air travels far enough north, it will have traveled farther east than a point on the ground beneath it. As a result, the air appears to follow a curved path toward the east. Air moving from the North Pole to the equator appears to curve to the west because the air moves east more slowly than a point on the ground beneath it does. Therefore, in the Northern Hemisphere, air moving to the north curves to the east and air moving to the south curves to the west.

Active Reading

6 Identify As you read, underline how air movement in the Northern Hemisphere is influenced by the Coriolis effect.

Visualize It!

7 Label In the white ovals on the map, draw the direction and path of the winds that would occur at those locations on Earth.

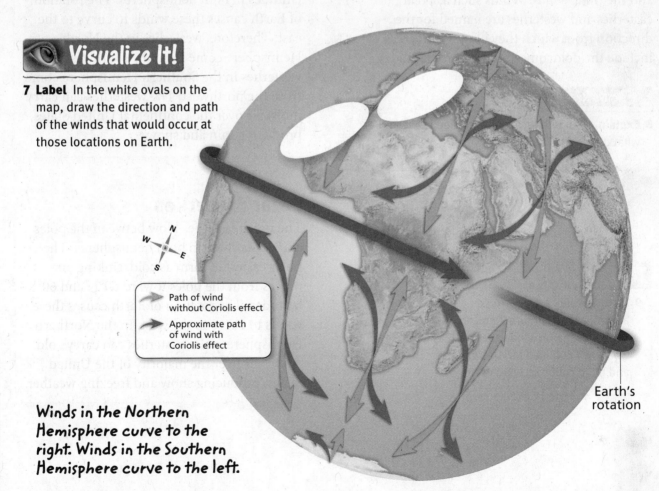

Path of wind without Coriolis effect

Approximate path of wind with Coriolis effect

Earth's rotation

Winds in the Northern Hemisphere curve to the right. Winds in the Southern Hemisphere curve to the left.

Blowin' Around

What are examples of global winds?

Recall that air travels in circular patterns called convection cells that cover approximately 30° of latitude. Pressure belts at every 30° of latitude and the Coriolis effect produce patterns of calm areas and wind systems. These wind systems occur at or near Earth's surface and are called **global winds**. As shown at the right, the major global wind systems are the *polar easterlies* (EE•ster•leez), the *westerlies* (WES•ter•leez), and the *trade winds*. Winds such as polar easterlies and westerlies are named for the direction from which they blow. Calm areas include the doldrums and the horse latitudes.

Active Reading

8 Explain If something is being carried by westerlies, what direction is it moving toward?

Think Outside the Book Inquiry

9 Model Winds are described according to their direction and speed. Research wind vanes and what they are used for. Design and build your own wind vane.

Trade Winds

The trade winds blow between 30° latitude and the equator in both hemispheres. The rotation of Earth causes the trade winds to curve to the west. Therefore, trade winds in the Northern Hemisphere come from the northeast, and trade winds in the Southern Hemisphere come from the southeast. These winds became known as the trade winds because sailors relied on them to sail from Europe to the Americas.

Westerlies

The westerlies blow between 30° and 60° latitudes in both hemispheres. The rotation of Earth causes these winds to curve to the east. Therefore, westerlies in the Northern Hemisphere come from the southwest, and westerlies in the Southern Hemisphere come from the northwest. The westerlies can carry moist air over the continental United States, producing rain and snow.

Polar Easterlies

The polar easterlies blow between the poles and 60° latitude in both hemispheres. The polar easterlies form as cold, sinking air moves from the poles toward 60°N and 60°S latitudes. The rotation of Earth causes these winds to curve to the west. In the Northern Hemisphere, polar easterlies can carry cold Arctic air over the majority of the United States, producing snow and freezing weather.

10 Identify Label the polar easterlies, the westerlies, and the trade winds in the white boxes on the map.

The major global wind systems

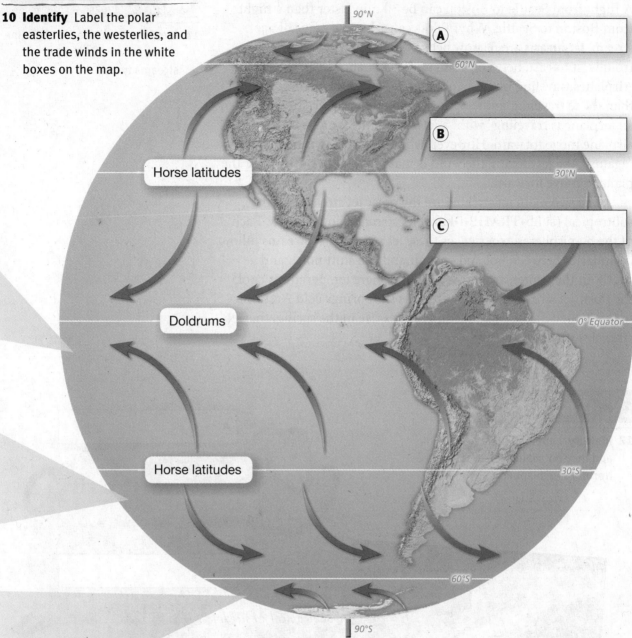

Horse latitudes

Doldrums

Horse latitudes

The Doldrums and Horse Latitudes

The trade winds of both hemispheres meet in a calm area around the equator called the *doldrums* (DOHL•druhmz). Very little wind blows in the doldrums because the warm, less-dense air results in an area of low pressure. The name doldrums means "dull" or "sluggish." At about 30° latitude in both hemispheres, air stops moving and sinks. This forms calm areas called the *horse latitudes*. This name was given to these areas when sailing ships carried horses from Europe to the Americas. When ships were stalled in these areas, horses were sometimes thrown overboard to save water.

The Jet Streams

A flight from Seattle to Boston can be 30 min faster than a flight from Boston to Seattle. Why? Pilots can take advantage of a jet stream. **Jet streams** are narrow belts of high-speed winds that blow from west to east, between 7 km and 16 km above Earth's surface. Airplanes traveling in the same direction as a jet stream go faster than those traveling in the opposite direction of a jet stream. When an airplane is traveling "with" a jet stream, the wind is helping the airplane move forward. However, when an airplane is traveling "against" the jet stream, the wind is making it more difficult for the plane to move forward.

The two main jet streams are the polar jet stream and the subtropical (suhb•TRAHP•i•kuhl) jet stream, shown below. Each of the hemispheres experiences these jet streams. Jet streams follow boundaries between hot and cold air and can shift north and south. In the winter, as Northern Hemisphere temperatures cool, the polar jet stream moves south. This shift brings cold Arctic air to the United States. When temperatures rise in the spring, this jet stream shifts to the north.

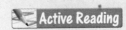 **Active Reading**

11 Identify As you read, underline the direction that the jet streams travel.

Visualize It!

12 Identify Label the polar jet stream and the subtropical jet stream in the Northern Hemisphere.

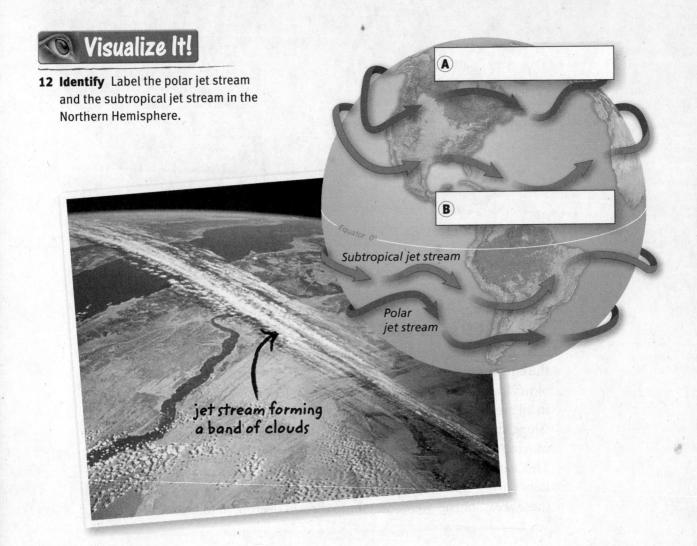

jet stream forming a band of clouds

A

B

Equator 0°

Subtropical jet stream

Polar jet stream

Desert Trades

How does some of the Sahara end up in the Americas? Global winds carry it.

Trade Wind Carriers
Trade winds can carry Saharan dust across the Atlantic Ocean to Florida and the Caribbean.

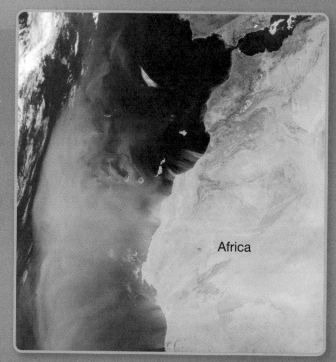

Africa

Florida Meets the Sahara
This hazy skyline in Miami is the result of a dust storm. Where did the dust come from? It all started in the Sahara.

The Sahara
The Sahara is the world's largest hot desert. Sand and dust storms that produce skies like this are very common in this desert.

Extend

Inquiry

13 Explain Look at a map and explain how trade winds carry dust from the Sahara to the Caribbean.

14 Relate Investigate the winds that blow in your community. Where do they usually come from? Identify the wind system that could be involved.

15 Apply Investigate how winds played a role in distributing radioactive waste that was released after an explosion at the Chernobyl Nuclear Power Plant in Ukraine. Present your findings as a map illustration or in a poster.

Feelin' Breezy

What are examples of local winds?

Local geographic features, such as a body of water or a mountain, can produce temperature and pressure differences that cause local winds. Unlike global winds, **local winds** are the movement of air over short distances. They can blow from any direction, depending on the features of the area.

Sea and Land Breezes

Have you ever felt a cool breeze coming off the ocean or a lake? If so, you were experiencing a sea breeze. Large bodies of water take longer to warm up than land does. During the day, air above land becomes warmer than air above water. The colder, denser air over water flows toward the land and pushes the warm air on the land upward. While water takes longer to warm than land does, land cools faster than water does. At night, cooler air on land causes a higher-pressure zone over the land. So, a wind blows from the land toward the water. This type of local wind is called a land breeze.

Active Reading

16 Identify As you read, underline two examples of geographic features that contribute to the formation of local winds.

Visualize It!

17 Analyze Label the areas of high pressure and low pressure.

sea breeze

Ⓑ _____ pressure

Ⓐ _____ pressure

land breeze

Ⓓ _____ pressure

Ⓒ _____ pressure

Valley and Mountain Breezes

Areas that have mountains and valleys experience local winds called mountain and valley breezes. During the day, the sun warms the air along the mountain slopes faster than the air in the valleys. This uneven heating results in areas of lower pressure near the mountain tops. This pressure difference causes a valley breeze, which flows from the valley up the slopes of the mountains. Many birds float on valley breezes to conserve energy. At nightfall, the air along the mountain slopes cools and moves down into the valley. This local wind is called a mountain breeze.

Visualize It!

18 Analyze Label the areas of high pressure and low pressure.

valley breeze

B _____ pressure

A _____ pressure

mountain breeze

D _____ pressure

C. _____ pressure

Visual Summary

To complete this summary, circle the correct word or phrases.
Then use the key below to check your answers. You can use this
page to review the main concepts of the lesson.

Wind is the move-
ment of air from
areas of higher
pressure to
areas of lower
pressure.

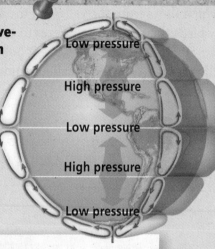

Low pressure

High pressure

Low pressure

High pressure

Low pressure

19 Cool air sinks, causing an area of
high / low air pressure.

Global wind systems occur on Earth.

20 High-speed wind between 7 km and
16 km above Earth's surface is a
jet stream / mountain breeze.

Wind in the Atmosphere

Geographic features can produce local winds.

21 During the day, an area of high / low air pressure forms
over water and a sea / land breeze occurs.

22 Explain Would there be winds if the air above Earth's surface was the same temperature
everywhere? Explain your answer.

Lesson Review

Vocabulary

Fill in the blanks with the term that best completes the following sentences.

1 Another term for air movement caused by differences in air pressure is

_____

2 Pilots often take advantage of the _____ , which are high-speed winds between 7 km and 16 km above Earth's surface.

3 The apparent curving of winds due to Earth's rotation is the _____

Key Concepts

4 Explain How does the sun cause wind?

_____
_____
_____

5 Predict If Earth did not rotate, what would happen to the global winds? Why?

_____
_____
_____

6 Explain How do convection cells in Earth's atmosphere cause high- and low-pressure belts?

_____
_____
_____
_____

7 Describe What factors contribute to global winds? Identify areas where winds are weak.

_____
_____
_____
_____

8 Identify Name a latitude where each of the following occurs: polar easterlies, westerlies, and trade winds.

_____
_____

Critical Thinking

9 Predict How would local winds be affected if water and land absorbed and released heat at the same rate? Explain your answer.

_____
_____
_____

10 Compare How is a land breeze similar to a sea breeze? How do they differ?

_____
_____
_____
_____

Use this image to answer the following questions.

11 Analyze What type of local wind would you experience if you were standing in the valley? Explain your answer.

_____
_____

12 Infer Would the local wind change if it was nighttime? Explain.

_____
_____
_____

Indiana Standards

NOS 8.8 Analyze data, using appropriate mathematical manipulation as required, and use it to identify patterns and make inferences based on these patterns.

Evaluating Claims

Scentific methods teach us how to evaluate ideas or claims to find out if they are credible, and if our explanations are reliable and logical. We can apply critical thinking to all matters in life—even to things like deciding what detergent to buy or what to eat.

Ever since the 1930s, the legend of the Loch Ness monster living in their deep lake had become part of everyday life for the people of Inverness, Scotland. But there has been much controversy over whether or not the Loch Ness monster really exists. Who do we believe? In this case, using scientific thinking to evaluate the credibility of the claim can help.

Tutorial

Consider the evidence surrounding the Loch Ness monster claim—does the creature exist or not? How will you evaluate the evidence to come to a conclusion? Follow the steps below to shape your argument.

1 What were the methods used to collect the data? Think critically and find out why an explanation or claim has been accepted by looking at the experiments, data, and methods used to support the idea.

2 Has the data presented been tested with further observations? Think about whether the evidence supports the explanation or claim. Sometimes, facts are used to support a claim even though they cannot be retested or reproduced.

3 Is there any evidence that contradicts the explanation or claim? Is there a reasonable alternative explanation? It is important to know whether any evidence casts doubt on the explanation or claim.

Huge monster found in Scotland! Could it be a surviving dinosaur?

This is a famous photograph from 1934, showing the Loch Ness Monster. In 1994, the actual fraudster reported the "monster" as being only 14 inches tall and created by fastening an artificial head to a toy submarine.

You Try It!

Evaluating whether or not scientific evidence supports a claim can be useful in science and in everyday life. Read the brochure below, and assess the validity of the claims as you answer the questions that follow.

Geo-Vento Energy

Let Us Install Wind Turbines at Your School

The use of wind turbines to generate electrical energy at your school will:

Save nonrenewable resources!

Save money!

Say "goodbye" to electric bills!

Geo-Vento offers the following proof:

- A school in Cape Cod, MA, generates all of its electrical energy from wind turbines. This school no longer pays any electric bills.

- It is a well-established theory that wind is an excellent energy source throughout the United States. No more electric bills for anyone!

1 Evaluating Methods Evaluate the claims made in the brochure. What evidence in the brochure supports these claims?

_____

_____

_____

_____

2 Determining Factual Accuracy Is the evidence in the brochure related to the claims that are made? Explain your answer.

_____

_____

_____

3 Communicating Results Can you think of evidence that might disprove the claims that are made? Share your answer with your classmates and record their ideas.

_____

_____

_____

_____

4 Evaluating Theories Do you think the theory offered as proof is scientific? Why might this statement not be widely accepted?

_____

_____

_____

_____

5 Forming Alternative Hypotheses Write a claim that is a reasonable alternative to one of the claims made in the brochure. Consider and list the evidence you need to back it up.

_____

_____

_____

_____

_____

Take It Home

With an adult, find a newspaper or magazine that appears to make scientific claims about a product. Carefully evaluate the claims and determine whether you think they are valid. Bring the ad to class and be prepared to share your evaluation.

Ocean Currents

ESSENTIAL QUESTION

How does water move in the ocean?

By the end of this lesson, you should be able to describe the movement of ocean water, explain what factors influence this movement, and explain why ocean circulation is important in the Earth system.

This iceberg off the coast of Newfoundland broke off an Arctic ice sheet and drifted south on ocean surface currents.

© Houghton Mifflin Harcourt Publishing Company • Image Credits: ©Thomas Kitchin & Victoria Hurst/First Light/Getty Images

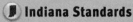 **Indiana Standards**

8.2.1 Recognize and demonstrate how the sun's energy drives convection in the atmosphere and in bodies of water, which results in ocean currents and weather patterns.

8.2.3 Describe the characteristics of ocean currents and identify their effects on weather patterns.

Engage Your Brain

1 Predict Check T or F to show whether you think each statement is true or false.

T	F	
☐	☐	Ocean currents are always cold.
☐	☐	Continents affect the directions of currents.
☐	☐	Currents only flow near the surface of the ocean.
☐	☐	Wind affects currents.
☐	☐	The sun affects currents near the surface of the ocean.

2 Analyze What can you learn about ocean currents from this image?

_____

_____

_____

_____

This image shows sea ice caught in ocean currents.

Active Reading

3 Synthesize You can often define an unknown word if you know the meaning of its word parts. Use the word parts and sentence below to make an educated guess about the meaning of the word *upwelling*.

Word part	Meaning
up-	from beneath the ground or water
well	to rise

Example Sentence
In areas where <u>upwelling</u> occurs, plankton feed on nutrients from deep in the ocean.

upwelling: _____

_____

Vocabulary Terms

- ocean current
- surface current
- Coriolis effect
- deep current
- convection current
- upwelling

4 Apply As you learn the definition of each vocabulary term in this lesson, create your own definition or sketch to help you remember the meaning of the term.

Going with the Flow

What are ocean currents?

The oceans contain streamlike movements of water called **ocean currents**. Ocean currents that occur at or near the surface of the ocean, caused by wind, are called **surface currents**. Most surface currents reach depths of about 100 m, but some go deeper. Surface currents also reach lengths of several thousand kilometers and can stretch across oceans. An example of a surface current is the Gulf Stream. The Gulf Stream is one of the strongest surface currents on Earth. The Gulf Stream transports, or moves, more water each year than is transported by all the rivers in the world combined.

Infrared cameras on satellites provide images that show differences in temperature. Scientists add color to the images afterward to highlight the different temperatures, as shown below.

What affects surface currents?

Surface currents are affected by three factors: continental deflections, the Coriolis effect, and global winds. These factors keep surface currents flowing in distinct patterns around Earth.

Active Reading

5 Identify As you read, underline three factors that affect surface currents.

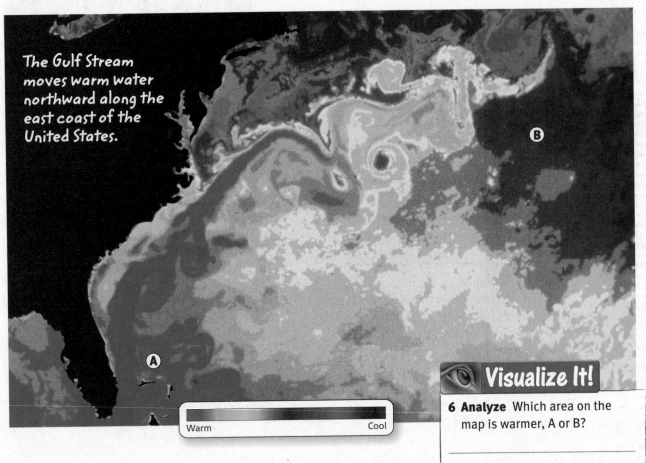

The Gulf Stream moves warm water northward along the east coast of the United States.

A

B

Warm   Cool

Visualize It!

6 Analyze Which area on the map is warmer, A or B?

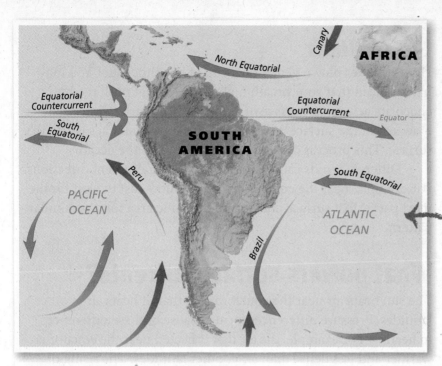

7 Identify Circle areas on the map where ocean currents have been deflected by a land mass.

Currents change direction when they meet continents.

Continental Deflections

If Earth's surface were covered only with water, surface currents would simply travel continually in one direction. However, water does not cover the entire surface of Earth. Continents rise above sea level over about one-third of Earth's surface. When surface currents meet continents, the currents are deflected and change direction. For example, the South Equatorial Current turns southward as it meets the coast of South America.

The Coriolis Effect

Earth's rotation causes all wind and ocean currents, except on the equator, to be deflected from the paths they would take if Earth did not rotate. The deflection of moving objects from a straight path due to Earth's rotation is called the **Coriolis effect** (kawr•ee•OH•lis ih•FEKT). Earth is spherical, so Earth's circumference at latitudes above and below the equator is shorter than the circumference at the equator. But the period of rotation is always 24 hours. Therefore, points on Earth near the equator travel faster than points closer to the poles.

The difference in speed of rotation causes the Coriolis effect. For example, wind and water traveling south from the North Pole actually go toward the southwest instead of straight south. Wind and water deflect to the right because the wind and water move east more slowly than Earth rotates beneath them. In the Northern Hemisphere, currents are deflected to the right. In the Southern Hemisphere, currents are deflected to the left.

The Coriolis effect is most noticeable for objects that travel over long distances, without any interruptions. Over short distances, the difference in Earth's rotational speed from one point to another point is not great enough to cause noticeable deflection.

In the Northern Hemisphere, currents are deflected to the right.

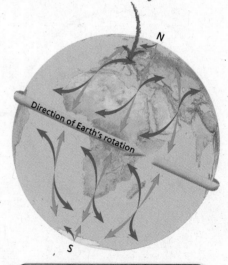

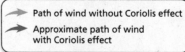

→ Path of wind without Coriolis effect

→ Approximate path of wind with Coriolis effect

Global Winds

Have you ever blown gently on a cup of hot chocolate? You may have noticed that your breath makes ripples that push the hot chocolate across the surface of the liquid. Similarly, winds that blow across the surface of Earth's oceans push water across Earth's surface. This process causes surface currents in the ocean.

Different winds cause currents to flow in different directions. For example, near the equator, the winds blow east to west for the most part. Most surface currents in the same area follow a similar pattern.

What powers surface currents?

The sun heats air near the equator more than it heats air at other latitudes. Pressure differences form because of these differences in heating. For example, the air that is heated near the equator is warmer and less dense than air at other latitudes. The rising of warm air creates an area of low pressure near the equator. Pressure differences in the atmosphere cause the wind to form. So, the sun causes winds to form, and winds cause surface currents to form. Therefore, the major source of the energy that powers surface currents is the sun.

8 Analyze Fill in the cause-and-effect chart to show how the sun's energy powers surface ocean currents.

The sun heats the atmosphere.

© Houghton Mifflin Harcourt Publishing Company • Image Credits: ©NASA/Photo Researchers, Inc.

Global Surface Winds

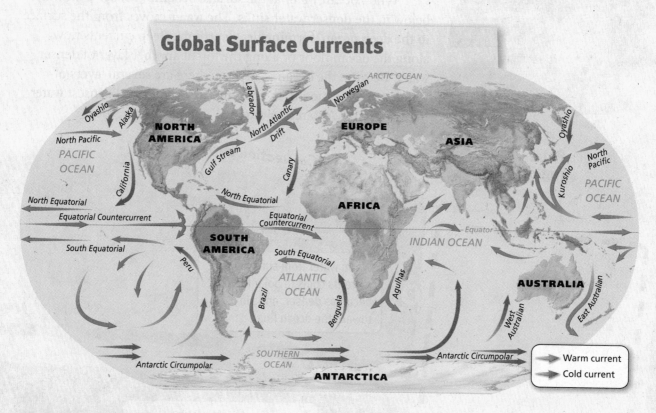

NORTH AMERICA

EUROPE

ASIA

PACIFIC OCEAN

PACIFIC OCEAN

AFRICA

Equator

SOUTH AMERICA

INDIAN OCEAN

AUSTRALIA

ATLANTIC OCEAN

SOUTHERN OCEAN

ANTARCTICA

→ Ocean surface wind

Global Surface Currents

ARCTIC OCEAN

Oyashio

Alaska

Labrador

Norwegian

Oyashio

North Pacific

NORTH AMERICA

North Atlantic Drift

EUROPE

ASIA

Kuroshio

North Pacific

PACIFIC OCEAN

Gulf Stream

Canary

PACIFIC OCEAN

California

AFRICA

North Equatorial

North Equatorial

Equatorial Countercurrent

Equatorial Countercurrent

Equator

INDIAN OCEAN

South Equatorial

SOUTH AMERICA

South Equatorial

Peru

ATLANTIC OCEAN

Brazil

Benguela

Agulhas

AUSTRALIA

West Australian

East Australian

Antarctic Circumpolar

SOUTHERN OCEAN

Antarctic Circumpolar

ANTARCTICA

→ Warm current
→ Cold current

Visualize It!

9 Analyze Circle the same area on each map. Describe what you observe about these two areas.

_____

_____

_____

Current Events

How do deep currents form?

Movements of ocean water far below the surface are called **deep currents**. Deep currents are caused by differences in water density. *Density* is the amount of matter in a given space or volume. The density of ocean water is affected by salinity (suh•LIN•ih•tee) and temperature. *Salinity* is a measure of the amount of dissolved salts or solids in a liquid. Water with high salinity is denser than water with low salinity. And cold water is denser than warm water. When water cools, it contracts and the water molecules move closer together. This contraction makes the water denser. When water warms, it expands and the water molecules move farther apart. The warm water is less dense, so it rises above the cold water.

When ocean water at the surface becomes denser than water below it, the denser water sinks. The water moves from the surface to the deep ocean, forming deep currents. Deep currents flow along the ocean floor or along the top of another layer of denser water. Because the ocean is so deep, there are several layers of water at any location in the ocean. The deepest and densest water in the ocean is Antarctic Bottom Water, near Antarctica.

© Houghton Mifflin Harcourt Publishing Company • Image Credits: (inset) ©Stephen J. Krasemann/Photographer's Choice/Getty Images

Polar region

10 Identify As you read, underline the cause of deep currents.

Convection current

B Warm water from surface currents cools in polar regions, becomes denser, and sinks toward the ocean floor.

C Deep currents carry colder, denser water in the deep ocean from polar regions to other parts of Earth.

Visualize It!

11 Illustrate Complete the drawing at part B on the diagram.

What are convection currents?

As you read about convection currents, refer to the illustration below. Surface currents and deep currents are linked in the ocean. Together they form convection currents. In the ocean, a **convection current** is a movement of water that results from density differences. Convection currents can be vertical, circular, or cyclical. Think of convection currents in the ocean as a conveyor belt. Surface currents make up the top part of the belt. Deep currents make up the bottom part of the belt. Water from a surface current may become a deep current in areas where water density increases. Deep current water then rises up to the surface in areas where the surface current is carrying low-density water away.

How do convection currents transfer energy?

Convection currents transfer energy. Water at the ocean's surface absorbs energy from the sun. Surface currents carry this energy to colder regions. The warm water loses energy to its surroundings and cools. As the water cools, it becomes denser and it sinks. The cold water travels along the ocean bottom. Then, the cold water rises to the surface as warm surface water moves away. The cold water absorbs energy from the sun, and the cycle continues.

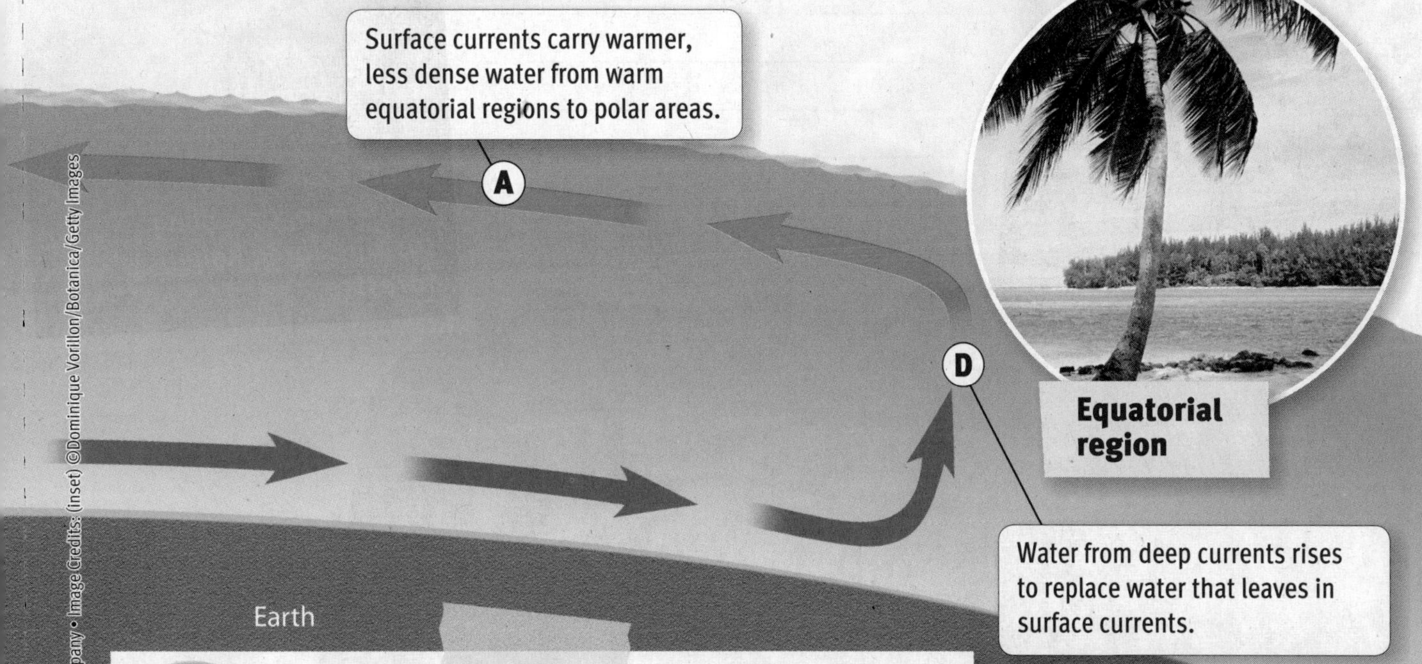

Think Outside the Book Inquiry

12 Apply Write an interview with a water molecule following a convection current. Be sure to include questions and answers. Can you imagine the temperature changes the molecule would experience?

Surface currents carry warmer, less dense water from warm equatorial regions to polar areas.

A

D

Equatorial region

Water from deep currents rises to replace water that leaves in surface currents.

Earth

Inquiry

13 Inquire How are convection currents important in the Earth system?

_____

_____

Note: Drawing is not to scale.

That's Swell!

Active Reading

14 Identify As you read, underline the steps that occur in upwelling.

What is upwelling?

At times, winds blow toward the equator along the northwest coast of South America and the west coast of North America. These winds cause surface currents to move away from the shore. The warm surface water is then replaced by cold, nutrient-rich water from the deep ocean in a process called **upwelling**. The deep water contains nutrients, such as iron and nitrate.

Upwelling is extremely important to ocean life. The nutrients that are brought to the surface of the ocean support the growth of phytoplankton (fy•toh•PLANGK•tuhn) and zooplankton. These tiny plants and animals are food for other organisms, such as fish and seabirds. Many fisheries are located in areas of upwelling because ocean animals thrive there. Some weather conditions can interrupt the process of upwelling. When upwelling is reduced, the richness of the ocean life at the surface is also reduced.

15 Predict What might happen to the fisheries if upwelling stopped?

_____

_____

_____

_____

_____

_____

The livelihood of these Peruvian fishermen depends on upwelling.

On the coast of California, upwelling sustains large kelp forests.

During upwelling, cold, nutrient-rich water from the deep ocean rises to the surface.

Why It Matters

Hitching a Ride!

What do coconuts, plankton, and sea turtles have in common? They get free rides on ocean currents.

World Travel
When baby sea turtles are hatched on a beach, they head for the ocean. They can then pick up ocean currents to travel. Some travel from Australia to South America on currents.

Sprouting Coconuts!
This sprouting coconut may be transported by ocean currents to a beach. This transport explains why coconut trees can grow in several areas.

Fast Food
Diatoms are a kind of phytoplankton. They are tiny, one-celled plants that form the basis of the food chain. Diatoms ride surface currents throughout the world.

Extend

Inquiry

16 Identify List three organisms transported by ocean currents.

17 Research Investigate the Sargasso Sea. State why a lot of plastic collects in this sea. Find out whether any plastic collects on the shoreline nearest you.

18 Explain Describe how plastic and other debris can collect in the ocean by doing one of the following:
- make a poster
- write a song
- write a poem
- write a short story

Traveling the World

What do ocean currents transport?

Ocean water circulates through all of Earth's ocean basins. The paths are like the main highway on which ocean water flows. If you could follow a water molecule on this path, you would find that the molecule takes more than 1,000 years to return to its starting point! Along with water, ocean currents also transport dissolved solids, dissolved gases, and energy around Earth.

Active Reading

19 Identify As you read, underline the description of how energy reaches the poles.

20 Describe Choose a location on the map. Using your finger, follow the route you would take if you could ride a current. Describe your route. Include the direction you go and the landmasses you pass.

Antarctica is not shown on this map, but the currents at the bottom of the map circulate around Antarctica.

Ocean Currents Transport Energy

Global ocean circulation is very important in the transport of energy in the form of heat. Remember that ocean currents flow in huge convection currents that can be thousands of kilometers long. These convection currents carry about 40% of the energy that is transported around Earth's surface.

Near the equator, the ocean absorbs a large amount of solar energy. The ocean also absorbs energy from the atmosphere. Ocean currents carry this energy from the equator toward the poles. When the warm water travels to cooler areas, the energy is released back into the atmosphere. Therefore, ocean circulation has an important influence on Earth's climate.

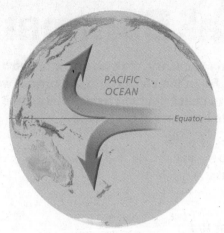

In the Pacific Ocean, surface currents transport energy from the tropics to latitudes above and below the equator.

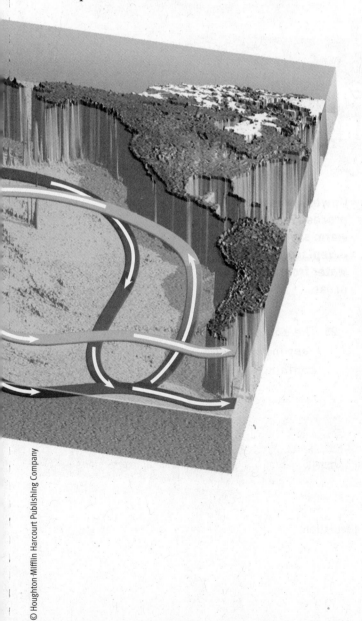

Ocean Currents Transport Matter

Besides water, ocean currents transport whatever is in the water. The most familiar dissolved solid in ocean water is sodium chloride, or table salt. Other dissolved solids are important to marine life. Ocean water contains many nutrients—such as nitrogen and phosphorus—that are important for plant and animal growth.

Ocean water also transports gases. Gases in the atmosphere are absorbed by ocean water at the ocean surface. As a result, the most abundant gases in the atmosphere—nitrogen, oxygen, argon, and carbon dioxide—are also abundant in the ocean. Dissolved oxygen and carbon dioxide are necessary for the survival of many marine organisms.

21 List Write three examples of matter besides water that are transported by ocean currents.

_____

_____

_____

_____

© Houghton Mifflin Harcourt Publishing Company

Visual Summary

To complete this summary, draw an arrow to show each type of
ocean current. Fill in the blanks with the correct word. Then use
the key below to check your answers. You can use this page to
review the main concepts of the lesson.

**Surface currents
are streamlike
movements of
water at or near the
surface of the ocean.**

22 The direction of a surface current
is affected by

_____ ,

_____ ,

and _____

**Deep currents are streamlike movements of
ocean water located far below the surface.**

23 Deep currents form
where the

_____

of ocean water
increases.

Ocean Currents

**A convection current in the ocean is any
movement of matter that results from
differences in density.**

24 A convection
current in the ocean
transports matter
and

_____

**Upwelling is the
process in which
warm surface water
is replaced by cold
water from the deep
ocean.**

25 The cold water from
deep in the ocean
contains

_____

Answers: 22 continental deflections, the Coriolis effect, global winds; 23 density; 24 energy; 25 nutrients

26 **Describe** State the two general patterns of global ocean circulation.

_____

_____

Lesson Review

Vocabulary

Fill in the blanks with the terms that best complete the following sentences.

1 _____ are streamlike movements of water in the ocean.

2 The _____ causes currents in open water to move in a curved path rather than a straight path.

3 _____ causes cold, nutrient-rich waters to move up to the ocean's surface.

Key Concepts

4 Explain List the steps that show how the sun provides the energy for surface ocean currents.

_____

_____

_____

_____

5 Explain State how a deep current forms.

_____

_____

_____

_____

6 Describe Explain how a convection current transports energy around the globe.

_____

_____

_____

7 List Write the three factors that affect surface ocean currents.

_____

_____

_____

Critical Thinking

Use this diagram to answer the following questions.

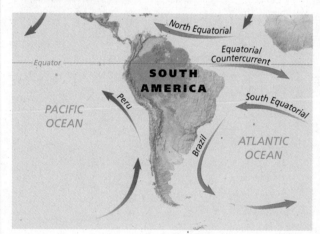

8 Apply Explain why the direction of the South Equatorial current changes.

_____

_____

_____

9 Apply If South America were not there, explain how the direction of the South Equatorial current would be different.

_____

_____

_____

_____

10 Apply Describe how surface currents would be affected if Earth did not rotate.

_____

_____

_____

_____

_____

My Notes

Unit 3 **Summary**

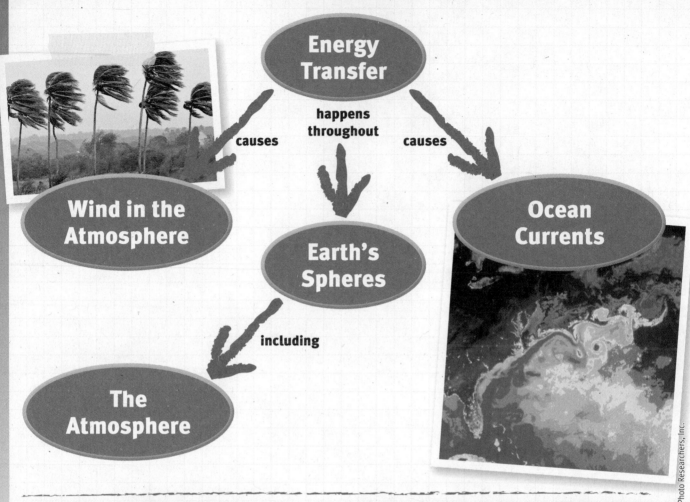

Energy Transfer

causes

happens throughout

causes

Wind in the Atmosphere

Earth's Spheres

Ocean Currents

including

The Atmosphere

1 Interpret The Graphic Organizer above shows that energy transfer causes wind in the atmosphere and ocean currents in the hydrosphere. Explain two ways in which wind in the atmosphere and ocean currents in the hydrosphere are similar.

_____

_____

_____

2 Contrast Describe the ways in which radiation, conduction, and convection transfer energy in the atmosphere.

_____

_____

_____

_____

3 Apply How could a lake be considered a part of one of Earth's spheres during one season and part of another sphere during another season?

_____

_____

_____

4 Justify Explain why the following statement is false: "The term *heat* applies to only those things that are considered hot."

_____

_____

_____

_____

ISTEP+ Review

Name _____

Multiple Choice

1 Maggie measures the wind speed every day for 7 weeks. She constructs the following line graph of the average daily wind speed.

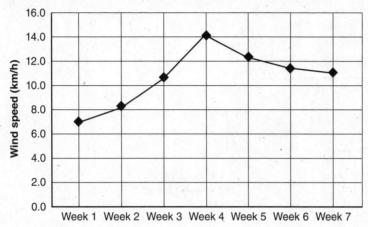

How many weeks have average wind speeds GREATER THAN 7.9 km/h?

A. 4 weeks

B. 5 weeks

C. 6 weeks

D. 7 weeks

2 Tanya is writing questions to use in a quiz show game that reinforces concepts about the movement of water in the ocean. To which of the following questions would the correct answer be DEEP CURRENT?

A. What type of current forms far below the ocean's surface because of differences in density?

B. What type of current forms when cold, nutrient-rich water rises to the ocean's surface?

C. What type of current transfers heat when warm water is moved into areas of cooler water?

D. What type of current is influenced by the Coriolis effect, continental deflection, and surface winds?

3 Which of the following processes transfers the sun's energy between particles as well as through empty space?

A. radiation only

B. conduction only

C. convection only

D. both conduction and convection

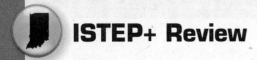

4 Carly draws a map of surface currents in the Atlantic Ocean. On her map, she includes the major wind belts for the same area. Her map is similar to the one shown.

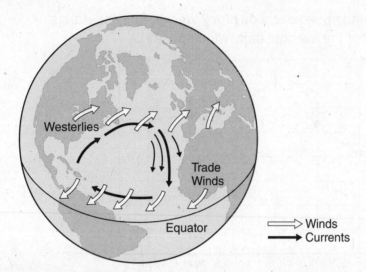

If Carly wants to add wind belts for the part of the Atlantic just south of the equator, how should she draw the arrows?

A. The arrows should curve upward to the left.

B. The arrows should curve upward to the right.

C. The arrows should curve downward to the left.

D. The arrows should curve downward to the right.

5 In the eighteenth century, the trade winds played an important role in England's merchant fleet crossing the Atlantic Ocean. This is how the trade winds got their name. In the tropics, in which DIRECTION do the trade winds drive equatorial ocean currents?

A. from the west to the east

B. from the south to the north

C. from the north to the south

D. from the east to the west

6 The gases that make up Earth's atmosphere are commonly referred to as air. Air consists of major gases, trace gases, water, and small particles. What type of substance is air?

A. Air is a mixture.

B. Air is a molecule.

C. Air is an element.

D. Air is a compound.

7 Throughout the day, Matthew and Mei measure the temperature of lake water as it is warmed by the sun. The following table shows their data at four different times.

Time	Temperature (°C)
9 a.m.	12
11 a.m.	14
3 p.m.	16
5 p.m.	13

At what time was the thermal energy of the lake water the GREATEST?

A. 9 a.m.

B. 11 a.m.

C. 3 p.m.

D. 5 p.m.

8 The continent of Antarctica is covered with an ice sheet. Which part of the Earth system includes the ice sheet?

A. biosphere

B. cryosphere

C. hydrosphere

D. atmosphere

9 Living things in the biosphere interact with other parts of the Earth system to exchange energy. Which picture represents the basic source of energy for the biosphere?

A.

C.

B.
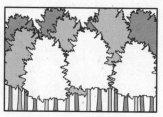

D.
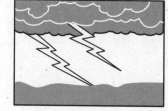

Constructed Response

10 The prefix *thermo-* means "heat." Explain why the name *thermosphere* is a fitting name for this layer of Earth's atmosphere.

_____

_____

_____

_____

Describe the location of the thermosphere within the Earth's atmosphere.

_____

_____

Extended Response

11 Many scientists agree that average temperatures on Earth are increasing. The increase in temperatures has caused melting at the poles. Describe the four steps that predict how this melting may affect ocean currents.

_____

_____

_____

_____

_____

_____

_____

UNIT 4
Weather and Climate

Houghton Mifflin Harcourt Publishing Company • Image Credits: (bkgd) ©Corbis; (br) ©AP Photo/Daniel R. Patmore

Core Standard

Explain how the sun's energy heats the air, land, and water driving the processes that result in wind, ocean currents, and the water cycle.

A tornado is a violently rotating column of air.

Damage caused by a tornado

What do you think?

The weather can change very quickly. In severe weather, people and pets can get hurt, and property can be damaged. Can you think of ways to keep people, pets, and property safe?

 **Indiana Standards**

CITIZEN SCIENCE
Exit Strategy

When there is an emergency, knowing what to do helps keep people as safe as possible. So, what's the plan?

1 Think About It

A Would you know what to do if there were a weather emergency while you were in school?

_____

B What kinds of information might you need to stay safe? List them below.

_____

_____

_____

_____

The electrical energy contained in lightning can make it a dangerous weather phenomenon.

② Ask a Question

Obtain a copy of the school's emergency evacuation plan. Read through the plan and answer the following questions as a class.

A Is the emergency evacuation plan/map easy for students to understand?

_____

B How would you know which way to go?

_____

_____

C How often do you have practice drills?

_____

EMERGENCY EVACUATION ROUTE

③ Propose and Apply Improvements

A Using what you have learned about your school's emergency evacuation plan, list your ideas for improvements below.

_____

_____

_____

_____

_____

B Develop and give a short oral presentation to your class about your proposal on ways to improve the school's emergency evacuation plan. Write the main points of your presentation below.

_____

_____

_____

_____

C As a class, practice the newly improved emergency evacuation plan. Describe how well the improved emergency evacuation plan worked.

_____

_____

_____

_____

_____

_____

_____

Take It Home

With an adult, create an emergency evacuation plan for your family or evaluate your family's emergency evacuation plan and propose improvements.

The Water Cycle

ESSENTIAL QUESTION

How does water change state and move around on Earth?

By the end of this lesson, you should be able to describe the water cycle and the different processes that are part of the water cycle on Earth.

When do clouds touch the sea? When it rains. This is one way in which water from the air returns to Earth's surface. Can you think of other ways in which water returns to Earth?

Indiana Standards

8.2.1 Recognize and demonstrate how the sun's energy drives convection in the atmosphere and in bodies of water, which results in ocean currents and weather patterns.

8.2.2 Describe and model how water moves through the earth's crust, atmosphere, and oceans in a cyclic way, as liquid, vapor, and solid.

Engage Your Brain

1 Predict Circle the word or phrase that best completes the following sentences.

The air inside a glass of ice would feel *warm/cold/room temperature*.

Ice would *melt/evaporate/remain frozen* if it were left outside on a hot day.

Water vapor will *condense on/evaporate from/melt into* the glass of ice from the air.

The ice *absorbs energy from/maintains its energy/releases energy into* the surroundings when it melts.

2 Analyze Using the photo above, solve the word scramble to answer the question: What happens to ice as it warms up?

TI GACNSEH EASTT

_____

Active Reading

3 Synthesize You can often define an unknown word if you know the meaning of the word's origin. Use the meaning of the words' origins and the sentence below to make an educated guess about the meaning of *precipitation* and *evaporation*.

Latin word	Meaning
praecipitare	fall
evaporare	spread out in vapor or steam

Example sentence
Precipitation, in the form of rain, helps replace the water lost by evaporation from the lake.

precipitation: _____

evaporation: _____

Vocabulary Terms

- water cycle
- evaporation
- transpiration
- sublimation
- condensation
- precipitation

4 Apply As you learn the definition of each vocabulary term in this lesson, write out a sentence using that term to help you remember the meaning of the term.

What goes up...

What is the water cycle?

Movement of water between the atmosphere, land, oceans, and even living things makes up the **water cycle**. Rain, snow, and hail fall on the oceans and land because of gravity. On land, ice and water flow downhill. Water flows in streams, rivers, and waterfalls such as the one in the photo, because of gravity. If the land is flat, water will collect in certain areas forming ponds, lakes, and marshland. Some water will soak through the ground and collect underground as groundwater. Even groundwater flows downhill.

Water and snow can move upward if they turn into water vapor and rise into the air. Plants and animals also release water vapor into the air. In the air, water vapor can travel great distances with the wind. Winds can also move the water in the surface layer of the ocean by creating ocean currents. When ocean currents reach the shore or colder climates, the water will sink if it is cold enough or salty enough. The sinking water creates currents at different depths in the ocean. These are some of the ways in which water travels all over Earth.

 Visualize It!

5 Analyze What is the relationship between gravity and water in this image?

_____

_____

_____

_____

How does water change state?

Water is found in three states on Earth: as liquid water, as solid water ice, and as gaseous water vapor. Water is visible as a liquid or a solid, but it is invisible as a gas in the air. Water can change from one state to another as energy is absorbed or released.

Water absorbs energy from its surroundings as it *melts* from solid to liquid. Water also absorbs energy when it *evaporates* from liquid to gas, or when it *sublimates* from solid to gas. Water releases energy into its surroundings when it *condenses* from gas to liquid. Water also releases energy when it *freezes* from liquid to solid, or *deposits* from gas to solid. No water is lost during these changes.

© Houghton Mifflin Harcourt Publishing Company • Image Credits: (t) ©Andrzej Tokarski/Alamy; (bl) ©Peter Lilja/The Image Bank/Getty Images; (br) ©Vincent MacNamara/Alamy

Active Reading

6 Identify As you read, underline each process in which energy is absorbed or released.

Visualize It!

7 Analyze Under each photo, write an example of where you might find water in that state of matter.

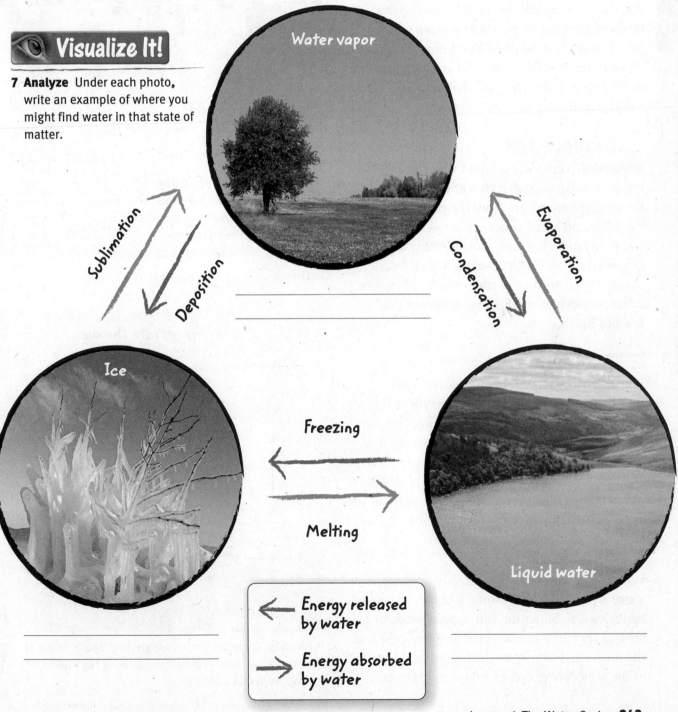

Water vapor

Sublimation

Deposition

Condensation

Evaporation

Ice

Freezing

Melting

Liquid water

← Energy released by water

→ Energy absorbed by water

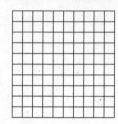

The evaporating water leaves behind a dry, cracked lake bed.

How does water reach the atmosphere?

Water reaches the atmosphere as water vapor in three ways: evaporation (i•VAP•uh•ray•shuhn), transpiration (tran•spuh•RAY•shuhn), and sublimation (suhb•luh•MAY•shuhn). It takes a lot of energy for liquid or solid water to turn into water vapor. The energy for these changes comes mostly from the sun, as solar energy.

◯ Evaporation

Evaporation occurs when liquid water changes into water vapor. About 90% of the water in the atmosphere comes from the evaporation of Earth's water. Some water evaporates from the water on land. However, most of the water vapor evaporates from Earth's oceans. This is because oceans cover most of Earth's surface. Therefore, oceans receive most of the solar energy that reaches Earth.

◯ Transpiration

Like many organisms, plants release water into the environment. Liquid water turns into water vapor inside the plant and moves into the atmosphere through stomata. Stomata are tiny holes that are found on some plant surfaces. This release of water vapor into the air by plants is called **transpiration**. About 10% of the water in the atmosphere comes from transpiration.

◯ Sublimation

When solid water changes directly to water vapor without first becoming a liquid, it is called **sublimation**. Sublimation can happen when dry air blows over ice or snow, where it is very cold and the pressure is low. A small amount of the water in the atmosphere comes from sublimation.

Do the Math **You Try It**

8 Graph Show the percentage of water vapor in the atmosphere that comes from the evaporation by coloring the equivalent number of squares in the grid.

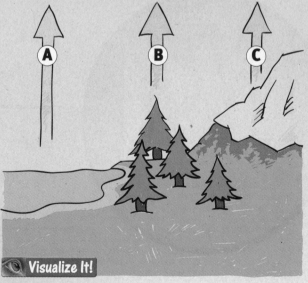

Water moves into the air.

Visualize It!

9 Identify Fill in the circles beside each red heading at left with the label of the arrow showing the matching process in this diagram.

What happens to water in the atmosphere?

Water reaches the atmosphere as water vapor. In the atmosphere, water vapor mixes with other gases. To leave the atmosphere, water vapor must change into liquid or solid water. Then the liquid or solid water can fall to Earth's surface.

○ Condensation

Remember, **condensation** (kahn•den•SAY•shuhn) is the change of state from a gas to a liquid. If air that contains water vapor is cooled enough, condensation occurs. Some of the water vapor condenses on small particles, such as dust, forming little balls or tiny droplets of water. These water droplets float in the air as clouds, fog, or mist. At the ground level, water vapor may condense on cool surfaces as dew.

○ Precipitation

In clouds, water droplets may collide and "stick" together to become larger. If a droplet becomes large enough, it falls to Earth's surface as precipitation (pri•sip•i•TAY•shuhn). **Precipitation** is any form of water that falls to Earth from clouds. Three common kinds of precipitation shown in the photos are rain, snow, and hail. Snow and hail form if the water droplets freeze. Most rain falls into the oceans because most water evaporates from ocean surfaces and oceans cover most of Earth's surface. But winds carry clouds from the ocean over land, increasing the amount of precipitation that falls on land.

Water returns to Earth's surface.

D

E

◉ Visualize It!

10 Identify Fill in the circle beside each red heading at left with the label of the arrow showing the matching process in this diagram.

11 Summarize Fill in the boxes to describe how precipitation forms.

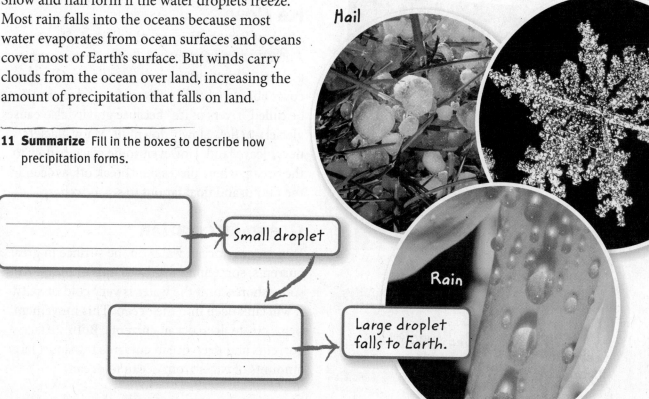

Hail

Snow

Rain

Small droplet

Large droplet falls to Earth.

How does water move on land and in the oceans?

After water falls to Earth, it flows and circulates all over Earth. On land, water flows downhill, both on the surface and underground. However, most of Earth's precipitation falls into the oceans. Ocean currents move water around the oceans.

Runoff and Infiltration

All of the water on land flows downhill because of gravity. Streams, rivers, and the water that flows over land are types of *runoff*. Runoff flows downhill toward oceans, lakes, and marshlands.

Some of the water on land seeps into the ground. This process is called *infiltration* (in•fil•TRAY•shuhn). Once undergound, the water is called *groundwater*. Groundwater also flows downhill through soil and rock.

Active Reading

12 Compare How do runoff and groundwater differ?

_____

_____

_____

Visualize It!

13 Summarize Write a caption describing how water is moving in the diagram above.

_____

_____

Ice Flow

Much of Earth's ice is stored in large ice caps in Antarctica and Greenland. Some ice is stored in glaciers at high altitudes all over Earth. Glaciers cover about 10% of Earth's surface. Glaciers can be called "rivers of ice" because gravity also causes glaciers to flow slowly downhill. Many glaciers never leave land. However, some glaciers flow to the ocean, where pieces may break off, as seen in the photo, and float far out to sea as icebergs.

Ocean Circulation

Winds move ocean water on the surface in great currents, sometimes for thousands of miles. At some shores, or if the water is very cold or salty, it will sink deep into the ocean. This movement helps create deep ocean currents. Both surface currents and deep ocean currents transport large amounts of water from ocean to ocean.

Icebergs can be carried over long distances by ocean currents.

Water Works

What does the water cycle transport?

In the water cycle, each state of water has some energy in it. This energy is released into or absorbed from its surroundings as water changes state. The energy in each state of water is then transported as the water moves from place to place. Matter is also transported as water and the materials in the water move all over Earth. Therefore, the water cycle moves energy and matter through Earth's atmosphere, land, oceans, and living things.

Think Outside the Book

14 Apply With a classmate, discuss how the water cycle transfers energy.

Energy

Energy is transported in the water cycle through changes of state and by the movement of water from place to place. For example, water that evaporates from the ocean carries energy into the atmosphere. This movement of energy can generate hurricanes. Also, cold ocean currents can cool the air along a coastline by absorbing the energy from the air and leaving the air cooler. This energy is carried away quickly as the current continues on its path. Such processes affect the weather and climate of an area.

Matter

Earth's ocean currents move vast amounts of water all over the world. These currents also transport the solids in the water and the dissolved salts and gases. Rivers transfer water from land into the ocean. Rivers also carry large amounts of sand, mud, and gravel as shown below. Rivers form deltas and floodplains, where some of the materials from upstream collect in areas downstream. Rivers also carve valleys and canyons, and carry the excess materials downstream. Glaciers also grind away rock and carry the ground rock with them as they flow.

Visualize It!

15 Identify What do rivers, such as the ones in the photo, transport?

_____

_____

© Houghton Mifflin Harcourt Publishing Company • Image Credits: ©Yann Arthus-Bertrand/Corbis

The Water Cycle

Water is continuously changing state and moving from place to place in the water cycle. This diagram shows these processes and movements.

16 Identify Label each arrow to show which process the arrow represents.

17 Identify Shade in the arrows that indicate where water is changing state.

Condensation

Evaporation

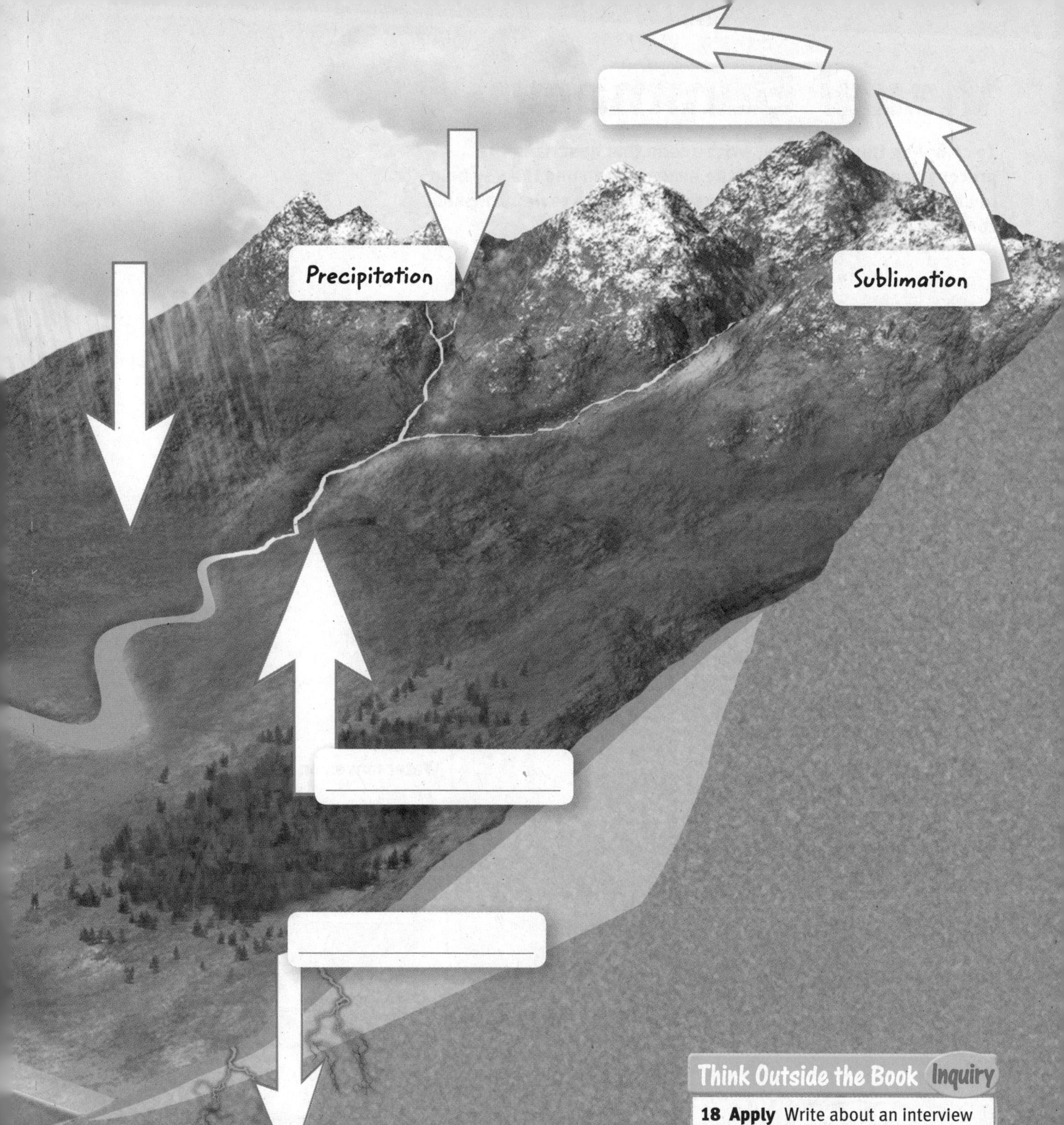

Precipitation

Sublimation

Think Outside the Book Inquiry

18 Apply Write about an interview with a water molecule. Write a story, or design a pamphlet describing one possible trip that a water molecule could take through the water cycle. Share your project with classmates.

Visual Summary

To complete this summary, write a term that describes the process happening in each of the images. Then use the key below to check your answers. You can use this page to review the main concepts of the lesson.

Water moves in the atmosphere.

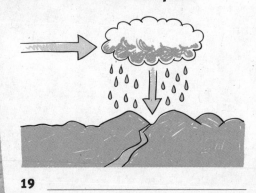

19 _____

The Water Cycle

Water moves into the atmosphere.

21 _____

Water moves on land and in oceans.

20 _____

Answers: 19 condensation or precipitation; 20 iceflow, runoff, infiltration, or ocean current; 21 evaporation, transpiration, or sublimation

22 Predict Describe what might happen to the water cycle if less solar energy reached Earth and how Earth's climate would be affected.

Lesson Review

Vocabulary

Write the correct label A, B, C, or D under each term to indicate the definition of that term.

1 water cycle

_____

2 evaporation

_____

3 precipitation

_____

4 condensation

_____

A The change of state from a liquid to a gas

B The change of state from a gas to a liquid

C The movement of water between the atmosphere, land, oceans, and living things

D Any form of water that falls to Earth's surface from the clouds

Key Concepts

5 Identify List the three ways in which water reaches the atmosphere and tell which way accounts for most of the water in the atmosphere.

_____

_____

_____

6 Classify Which of the processes of the water cycle occur by releasing energy?

_____

_____

7 Identify What happens to water once it reaches Earth's surface?

_____

_____

_____

8 Summarize Describe how three common types of precipitation form.

_____

_____

_____

_____

_____

Critical Thinking

Use the image below to answer the following question.

9 Apply Describe the energy changes occurring in the process shown above.

_____

_____

10 Infer Why does the amount of water that flows in a river change during the year?

_____

_____

11 Predict During a storm, a tree fell over into a river. What might happen to this tree?

_____

_____

_____

12 Evaluate Warm ocean currents cool as they flow along a coastline, away from the equator. Explain what is transported and how.

_____

_____

_____

_____

_____

Elements of Weather

ESSENTIAL QUESTION

What is weather and how can we describe different types of weather conditions?

By the end of this lesson, you should be able to describe elements of weather and explain how they are measured.

Weather stations placed all around the world allow scientists to measure the elements, or separate parts, of weather.

A researcher checks an automatic weather station on Alexander Island, Antarctica.

Indiana Standards

8.2.2 Describe and model how water moves through the earth's crust, atmosphere, and oceans in a cyclic way, as liquid, vapor, and solid.

8.2.5 Describe the conditions that cause Indiana weather and weather-related events such as tornadoes, lake effect snow, blizzards, thunderstorms, and flooding.

Engage Your Brain

1 Predict Check T or F to show whether you think each statement is true or false.

T   F

☐   ☐   Weather can change every day.

☐   ☐   Temperature is measured by using a barometer.

☐   ☐   Air pressure increases as you move higher in the atmosphere.

☐   ☐   Visibility is a measurement of how far we can see.

2 Describe Use at least three words that might describe the weather on a day when the sky looks like the picture above.

_____

_____

_____

_____

Active Reading

3 Distinguish The words *weather, whether,* and *wether* all sound alike but are spelled differently and mean entirely different things. You may have never heard of a wether—it is a neutered male sheep or ram.

Circle the correct use of the three words in the sentence below.

The farmer wondered *weather / whether / wether* the cold *weather / whether / wether* had affected his *weather / whether / wether*.

Vocabulary Terms

- **weather**
- **humidity**
- **relative humidity**
- **dew point**
- **precipitation**
- **air pressure**
- **wind**
- **visibility**

4 Apply As you learn the definition of each vocabulary term in this lesson, create your own definition or sketch to help you remember the meaning of the term.

Wonder about Weather?

What is weather?

Weather is the condition of Earth's atmosphere at a certain time and place. Different observations give you clues to the weather. If you see plants moving from side to side, you might infer that it is windy. If you see a gray sky and wet, shiny streets, you might decide to wear a raincoat. People talk about weather by describing factors such as temperature, humidity, precipitation, air pressure, wind, and *visibility* (viz•uh•BIL•i•tee).

What is temperature and how is it measured?

Temperature is a measure of how hot or cold something is. An instrument that measures and displays temperature is called a *thermometer*. A common type of thermometer uses a liquid such as alcohol or mercury to display the temperature. The liquid is sealed in a glass tube. When the air gets warmer, the liquid expands and rises in the tube. Cooler air causes the liquid to contract and fill less of the tube. A scale, often in Celsius (°C) or Fahrenheit (°F), is marked on the glass tube.

Another type of thermometer is an electrical thermometer. As the temperature becomes higher, electric current flow increases through the thermometer. The strength of the current is then translated into temperature readings.

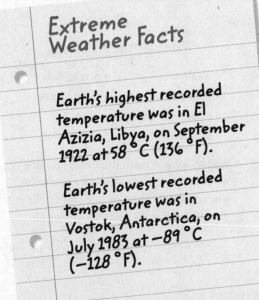

Extreme Weather Facts

Earth's highest recorded temperature was in El Azizia, Libya, on September 1922 at 58 °C (136 °F).

Earth's lowest recorded temperature was in Vostok, Antarctica, on July 1983 at −89 °C (−128 °F).

 **Visualize It!**

5 Identify Color in the liquid in the thermometer above to show Earth's average temperature in 2009 (58 °F). Write the Celsius temperature that equals 58 °F on the line below.

_____

What is humidity and how is it measured?

As water evaporates from oceans, lakes, and ponds, it becomes water vapor, or a gas that is in the air. The amount of water vapor in the air is called **humidity**. As more water evaporates and becomes water vapor, the humidity of the air increases.

Humidity is often described through relative humidity. **Relative humidity** is the amount of water vapor in the air compared to the amount of water vapor needed to reach saturation. As shown below, when air is saturated, the rates of evaporation and condensation are equal. Saturated air has a relative humidity of 100%. A psychrometer (sy•KRAHM•i•ter) is an instrument that is used to measure relative humidity.

Air can become saturated when evaporation adds water vapor to the air. Air can also become saturated when it cools to its dew point. The **dew point** is the temperature at which more condensation than evaporation occurs. When air temperature drops below the dew point, condensation forms. This can cause dew on surfaces cooler than the dew point. It also can form fog and clouds.

© Houghton Mifflin Harcourt Publishing Company • Image Credits: w(bkgd) ©Rick Lew/Stone/Getty Images

Active Reading

6 Identify Underline the name of the instrument used to measure relative humidity.

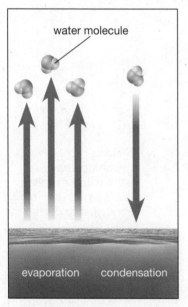

water molecule

evaporation   condensation

In unsaturated air, more water evaporates into the air than condenses back into the water.

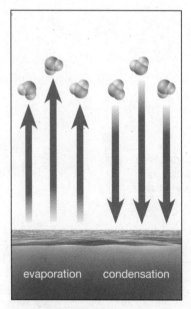

evaporation   condensation

In saturated air, the amount of water that evaporates equals the amount that condenses.

Visualize It!

7 Sketch In the space provided, draw what happens in air that is below the dew point.

When air cools below its dew point, more water vapor condenses into water than evaporates.

8 Explain Why does dew form on grass overnight?

_____

_____

What is precipitation and how is it measured?

Water vapor in the air condenses not only on Earth's surfaces, but also on tiny particles in the air to form clouds. When this water from the air returns to Earth's surface, it falls as precipitation. **Precipitation** is any form of water that falls to Earth's surface from the clouds. The four main forms of precipitation are rain, snow, hail, and sleet.

Rain is the most common form of precipitation. Inside a cloud, the droplets formed by condensation collide and form larger droplets. They finally become heavy enough to fall as raindrops. Rain is measured with a rain gauge, as shown in the picture below. A funnel or wide opening at the top of the gauge allows rain to flow into a cylinder that is marked in centimeters.

Snow forms when air temperatures are so low that water vapor turns into a solid. When a lot of snow has fallen, it is measured with a ruler or meterstick. When balls or lumps of ice fall from clouds during thunderstorms it is called *hail*. Sleet forms when rain falls through a layer of freezing air, producing falling ice.

Visualize It! (Inquiry)

9 Synthesize What are two ways in which all types of precipitation are alike?

_____

_____

Snow
Snow can fall as single ice crystals or ice crystals can join to form snowflakes.

Rain
Rain occurs when the water droplets in a cloud get so big they fall to Earth.

Sleet
Small ice pellets fall as sleet when rain falls through cold air.

Hail
Hailstones are layered lumps of ice that fall from clouds.

10 Measure How much rain has this rain gauge collected?

_____

Watching Clouds

Cirrus Clouds

Cumulus Clouds

Stratus Clouds

As you can see above, cirrus (SIR•uhs) clouds appear feathery or wispy. Their name means "curl of hair." They are made of ice crystals. They form when the wind is strong.

Cumulus (KYOOM•yuh•luhs) means "heap" or "pile." Usually these clouds form in fair weather but if they keep growing taller, they can produce thunderstorms.

Stratus (STRAY•tuhs) means "spread out." Stratus clouds form in flat layers. Low, dark stratus clouds can block out the sun and produce steady drizzle or rain.

If you watch the sky over a period of time, you will probably observe different kinds of clouds. Clouds have different characteristics because they form under different conditions. The shapes and sizes of clouds are mainly determined by air movement. For example, puffy clouds form in air that rises sharply or moves straight up and down. Flat, smooth clouds covering large areas form in air that rises gradually.

Extend

Inquiry

11 Reflect Think about the last time you noticed the clouds. When are you most likely to notice what type of cloud is in the sky?

12 Research Word parts are used to tell more about clouds. Look up the word parts -*nimbus* and *alto*-. What are cumulonimbus and altostratus clouds?

The Air Out There

What is air pressure and how is it measured?

Scientists use an instrument called a barometer (buh•RAHM•i•ter) to measure air pressure. **Air pressure** is the force of air molecules pushing on an area. The air pressure at any area on Earth depends on the weight of the air above that area. Although air is pressing down on us, we don't feel the weight because air pushes in all directions. So, the pressure of air pushing down is balanced by the pressure of air pushing up.

Air pressure and density are related; they both decrease with altitude. Notice in the picture that the molecules at sea level are closer together than the molecules at the mountain peak. Because the molecules are closer together, the pressure is greater. The air at sea level is denser than air at high altitude.

Air pressure and density are lower at a high altitude.

Air pressure and density are higher at sea level.

Visualize It!

13 Identify Look at the photos below and write whether wind direction or wind speed is being measured.

Anemometer

An anemometer measures:

_____

Wind vane

A wind vane measures:

_____

What is wind and how is it measured?

Wind is air that moves horizontally, or parallel to the ground. Uneven heating of Earth's surface causes pressure differences from place to place. These pressure differences set air in motion. Over a short distance, wind moves directly from higher pressure toward lower pressure.

An anemometer (an•uh•MAHM•i•ter) is used to measure wind speed. It has three or four cups attached to a pole. The wind causes the cups to rotate, sending an electric current to a meter that displays the wind speed.

Wind direction is measured by using a wind vane or a windsock. A wind vane has an arrow with a large tail that is attached to a pole. The wind pushes harder on the arrow tail due to its larger surface area. This causes the wind vane to spin so that the arrow points into the wind. A windsock is a cone-shaped cloth bag open at both ends. The wind enters the wide end and the narrow end points in the opposite direction, showing the direction the wind is blowing.

What is visibility and how is it measured?

Visibility is a measure of the transparency of the atmosphere. Visibility is the way we describe how far we can see, and it is measured by using three or four known landmarks at different distances. Sometimes not all of the landmarks will be visible. Poor visibility can be the result of air pollution or fog.

Poor visibility can be dangerous for all types of travel, whether by air, water, or land. When visibility is very low, roads may be closed to traffic. In areas where low visibility is common, signs are often posted to warn travelers.

 **Active Reading**

14 Explain What are two factors that can affect visibility?

_____

_____

Fog forms as land cools overnight, causing water vapor in the air above the land to condense.

What are some ways to collect weather data?

Many forms of technology are used to gather weather data. The illustration below shows some ways weather information can be collected. Instruments within the atmosphere can make measurements of local weather conditions. Satellites can collect data from above the atmosphere.

 **Visualize It!** **Inquiry**

15 Infer What are the benefits of stationary weather collection? Moving weather collection?

_____

_____

_____

_____

Satellite

Airplane

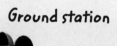
Ground station

Stationary
Some forms of technology provide measurements from set locations.

Moving
Some forms of technology report changing measurements along their paths.

Weather buoy

Ship

Visual Summary

To complete this summary, fill in the blanks with the correct word or phrase. Then use the key below to check your answers. You can use this page to review the main concepts of the lesson.

Elements of Weather

Weather is a condition of the atmosphere at a certain time and place.

16 Weather is often expressed by describing _____, humidity, precipitation, air pressure, wind, and visibility.

Humidity describes the amount of water vapor in the air.

17 The amount of moisture in the air is commonly expressed as _____ humidity.

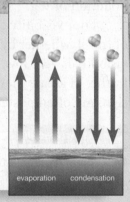

evaporation   condensation

Uneven heating of Earth's surface causes air pressure differences and wind.

18 Wind moves from areas of _____ pressure to areas of _____ pressure.

Visibility describes how far into the distance objects can be seen.

19 Visibility can be affected by air pollution and _____

Precipitation occurs when the water that condenses as clouds falls back to Earth in solid or liquid form.

20 The main types of precipitation are hail, snow, _____, and rain.

Answers: 16 temperature; 17 relative; 18 higher, lower; 19 fog; 20 sleet

21 Synthesize What instruments would you take along if you were going on a 3-month field study to measure how the weather on a mountaintop changes over the course of a season?

Lesson Review

Vocabulary

In your own words, define the following terms.

1 weather _____

_____

_____

2 humidity _____

_____

_____

3 air pressure _____

_____

_____

4 visibility _____

_____

_____

Key Concepts

Weather element	Instrument
5 Identify Measures temperature	
	6 Identify Is measured by using a barometer
7 Identify Measures relative humidity	
	8 Identify Is measured by using a rain gauge or meterstick
9 Identify Measures wind speed	

10 List What are four types of precipitation?

_____

_____

Critical Thinking

11 Apply Explain how wind is related to the uneven heating of Earth's surfaces by the sun.

_____

_____

_____

12 Explain Why does air pressure decrease as altitude increases?

_____

_____

_____

13 Synthesize What is the relative humidity when the air temperature is at its dew point?

_____

The weather data below was recorded from 1989–2009 by an Antarctic weather station similar to the station in the photo at the beginning of this lesson. Use these data to answer the questions that follow.

	Jan.	Apr.	July	Oct.
Mean max. temp. (°C)	2.1	−7.4	−9.9	−8.1
Mean min. temp. (°C)	−2.6	−14.6	−18.1	−15.1
Mean precip. (mm)	9.0	18.04	28.5	16.5

14 Identify Which month had the lowest mean minimum and maximum temperatures?

_____

_____

15 Infer The precipitation that fell at this location was most likely in what form?

_____

_____

What Influences Weather?

How do the water cycle and other global patterns affect local weather?

By the end of this lesson, you should be able to explain how global patterns in Earth's system influence weather.

Indiana Standards

8.2.1 Recognize and demonstrate how the sun's energy drives convection in the atmosphere and in bodies of water, which results in ocean currents and weather patterns.

8.2.2 Describe and model how water moves through the earth's crust, atmosphere, and oceans in a cyclic way, as liquid, vapor, and solid.

8.2.3 Describe the characteristics of ocean currents and identify their effects on weather patterns.

8.2.5 Describe the conditions that cause Indiana weather and weather-related events such as tornadoes, lake effect snow, blizzards, thunderstorms, and flooding.

The weather doesn't always turn out the way you want. But learning about the factors that affect weather can help you plan your next outing.

Engage Your Brain

1 Predict Check T or F to show whether you think each statement is true or false.

T   F

☐ ☐ The water cycle affects weather.

☐ ☐ Air can be warmed or cooled by the surface below it.

☐ ☐ Warm air sinks, cool air rises.

☐ ☐ Winds can bring different weather to a region.

2 Explain How can air temperatures along this coastline be affected by the large body of water that is nearby?

_____

_____

_____

Active Reading

3 Infer A military front is a contested armed frontier between opposing forces. A *weather front* occurs between two air masses, or bodies of air. What kind of weather do you think usually happens at a weather front?

_____

_____

_____

_____

_____

_____

Vocabulary Terms

- air mass
- front
- jet stream

4 Apply As you learn the definition of each vocabulary term in this lesson, create your own definition or sketch to help you remember the meaning of the term.

Water, Water

How does the water cycle affect weather?

Weather is the short-term state of the atmosphere, including temperature, humidity, precipitation, air pressure, wind, and visibility. These elements are affected by the energy received from the sun and the amount of water in the air. To understand what influences weather, then, you need to understand the water cycle.

In the water cycle, shown to the right, water is constantly being recycled between liquid, solid, and gaseous states. The water cycle is the continuous movement of water between the atmosphere, the land, the oceans, and living things. The water cycle involves the processes of evaporation, condensation, and precipitation.

Evaporation occurs when liquid water changes into water vapor, which is a gas. Condensation occurs when water vapor cools and changes from a gas to a liquid. A change in the amount of water vapor in the air affects humidity. Clouds and fog form through condensation of water vapor, so condensation also affects visibility. Precipitation occurs when rain, snow, sleet, or hail falls from the clouds onto Earth's surface.

Active Reading

5 List Name at least 5 elements of weather.

_____

_____

_____

Visualize It!

6 Summarize Describe how the water cycle influences weather by completing the sentences on the picture.

Ⓐ Evaporation **affects weather by** _____

_____

_____

Everywhere . . .

B Condensation **affects weather by** _____ _____ _____

C Precipitation **affects weather by** _____ _____ _____

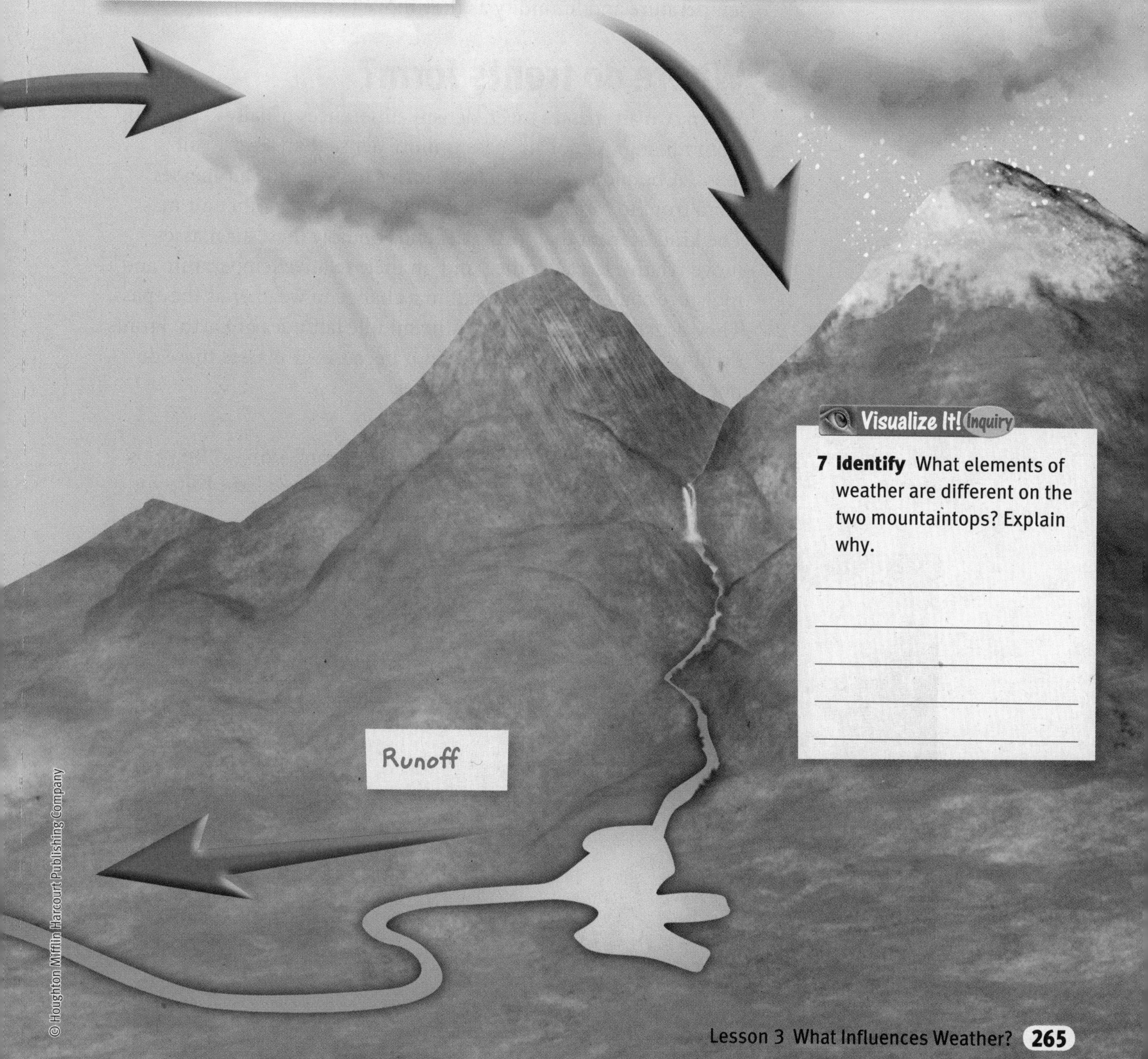

Visualize It! Inquiry

7 Identify What elements of weather are different on the two mountaintops? Explain why.

_____ _____ _____ _____ _____

Runoff

Putting Up a **Front**

How do air masses affect weather?

Active Reading

8 Identify As you read, underline how air masses form.

You have probably experienced the effects of air masses—one day is hot and humid, and the next day is cool and pleasant. The weather changes when a new air mass moves into your area. An **air mass** is a large volume of air in which temperature and moisture content are nearly the same throughout. An air mass forms when the air over a large region of Earth stays in one area for many days. The air gradually takes on the temperature and humidity of the land or water below it. When an air mass moves, it can bring these characteristics to new locations. Air masses can change temperature and humidity as they move to a new area.

Where do fronts form?

When two air masses meet, density differences usually keep them from mixing. A cool air mass is more dense than a warm air mass. A boundary, called a **front**, forms between the air masses. For a front to form, one air mass must run into another air mass. The kind of front that forms depends on how these air masses move relative to each other, and on their relative temperature and moisture content. Fronts result in a change in weather as they pass. They usually affect weather in the middle latitudes of Earth. Fronts do not often occur near the equator because air masses there do not have big temperature differences.

The boundary between air masses, or front, cannot be seen, but is shown here to illustrate how air masses can take on the characteristics of the surface below them.

Air masses that form above water are moist.

Air masses that form above land are dry.

Cold Fronts Form Where Cold Air Moves under Warm Air

Warm air is less dense than cold air is. So, a cold air mass that is moving can quickly push up a warm air mass. If the warm air is moist, clouds will form. Storms that form along a cold front are usually short-lived but can move quickly and bring heavy rain or snow. Cooler weather follows a cold front.

9 Apply If you hear that a cold front is headed for your area, what type of weather might you expect?

_____

_____

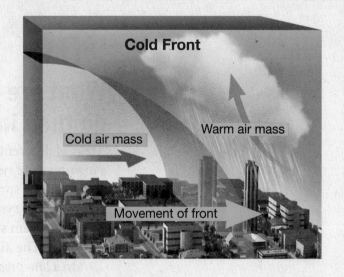

Cold Front

Warm air mass

Cold air mass

Movement of front

Warm Fronts Form Where Warm Air Moves over Cold Air

A warm front forms when a warm air mass follows a retreating cold air mass. The warm air rises over the cold air, and its moisture condenses into clouds. Warm fronts often bring drizzly rain and are followed by warm, clear weather.

10 Identify The rainy weather at the edge of a warm front is a result of

☐ the cold air mass that is leaving.

☐ the warm air rising over the cold air.

☐ the warm air mass following the front.

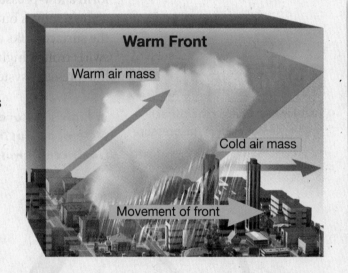

Warm Front

Warm air mass

Cold air mass

Movement of front

Stationary Fronts Form Where Cold and Warm Air Stop Moving

In a stationary front, there is not enough wind for either the cold air mass or the warm air mass to keep moving. So, the two air masses remain in one place. A stationary front can cause many days of unchanging weather, usually clear.

11 Infer When could a stationary front become a warm or cold front? Inquiry

_____

_____

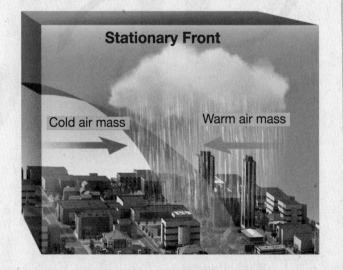

Stationary Front

Cold air mass

Warm air mass

Feeling the Pressure!

What are pressure systems, and how do they interact?

Areas of different air pressure cause changes in the weather. In a *high-pressure system*, air sinks slowly down. As the air nears the ground, it spreads out toward areas of lower pressure. Most high-pressure systems are large and change slowly. When a high-pressure system stays in one location for a long time, an air mass may form. The air mass can be warm or cold, humid or dry.

In a *low-pressure system*, air rises and so has a lower air pressure than the areas around it. As the air in the center of a low-pressure system rises, the air cools.

The diagram below shows how a high-pressure system can form a low-pressure system. Surface air, shown by the black arrows, moves out and away from high-pressure centers. Air above the surface sinks and warms. The green arrows show how air swirls from a high-pressure system into a low-pressure system. In a low-pressure system, the air rises and cools.

A high-pressure system can spiral into a low-pressure system, as illustrated by the green arrows below. In the Northern Hemisphere, air circles in the directions shown.

Visualize It!

12 Identify Choose the correct answer for each of the pressure systems shown below.

A In a high-pressure system, air

☐ rises and cools.

☐ sinks and warms.

B in a low-pressure system, air

☐ rises and cools.

☐ sinks and warms.

How do different pressure systems affect us?

When air pressure differences are small, air doesn't move very much. If the air remains in one place or moves slowly, the air takes on the temperature and humidity of the land or water beneath it. Each type of pressure system has it own unique weather pattern. By keeping track of high- and low-pressure systems, scientists can predict the weather.

High-Pressure Systems Produce Clear Weather

High-pressure systems are areas where air sinks and moves outward. The sinking air is denser than the surrounding air, and the pressure is higher. Cooler, denser air moves out of the center of these high-pressure areas toward areas of lower pressure. As the air sinks, it gets warmer and absorbs moisture. Water droplets evaporate, relative humidity decreases, and clouds often disappear. A high-pressure system generally brings clear skies and calm air or gentle breezes.

Low-Pressure Systems Produce Rainy Weather

Low-pressure systems have lower pressure than the surrounding areas. Air in a low-pressure system comes together, or converges, and rises. As the air in the center of a low-pressure system rises, it cools and forms clouds and rain. The rising air in a low-pressure system causes stormy weather.

A low-pressure system can develop wherever there is a center of low pressure. One place this often happens is along a boundary between a warm air mass and a cold air mass. Rain often occurs at these boundaries, or fronts.

 **Visualize It!**

13 Match Label each picture as a result of a high- or low-pressure system. Then, draw a line from each photo to its matching air-pressure diagram.

(A)

(B)

Warm air rises

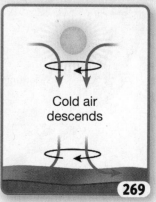

Cold air descends

Windy Weather

How do global wind patterns affect local weather?

Winds are caused by unequal heating of Earth's surface—which causes air pressure differences—and can occur on a global or on a local scale. On a local scale, air-pressure differences affect both wind speed and wind direction at a location. On a global level, there is an overall movement of surface air from the poles toward the equator. The heated air at the equator rises and forms a low-pressure belt. Cold air near the poles sinks and creates high-pressure centers. Because air moves from areas of high pressure to areas of low pressure, it moves from the poles to the equator. At high altitudes, the warmed air circles back toward the poles.

Temperature and pressure differences on Earth's surface also create regional wind belts. Winds in these belts curve to the east or the west as they blow, due to Earth's rotation. This curving of winds is called the *Coriolis effect* (kawr•ee•OH•lis eff•EKT). Winds would flow in straight lines if Earth did not rotate. Winds bring air masses of different temperatures and moisture content to a region.

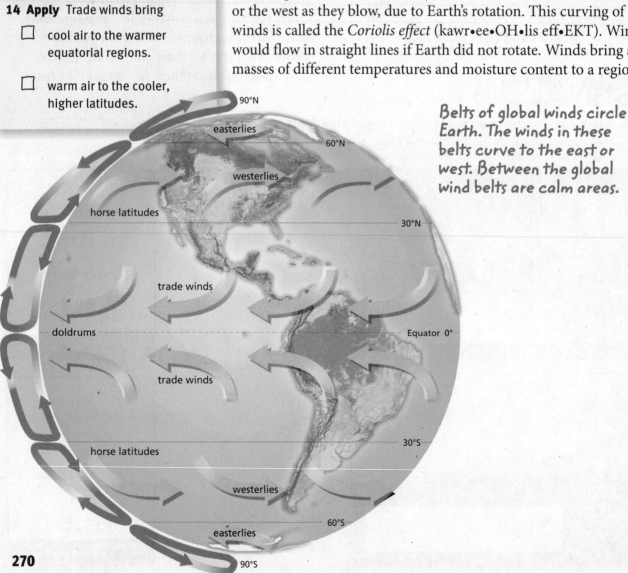

Belts of global winds circle Earth. The winds in these belts curve to the east or west. Between the global wind belts are calm areas.

Visualize It!

14 Apply Trade winds bring

☐ cool air to the warmer equatorial regions.

☐ warm air to the cooler, higher latitudes.

90°N
easterlies
60°N
westerlies
horse latitudes
30°N
trade winds
doldrums
Equator 0°
trade winds
horse latitudes
30°S
westerlies
60°S
easterlies
90°S

How do jet streams affect weather?

Long-distance winds that travel above global winds for thousands of kilometers are called **jet streams**. Air moves in jet streams with speeds that are at least 92 kilometers per hour and are often greater than 180 kilometers per hour. Like global and local winds, jet streams form because Earth's surface is heated unevenly. They flow in a wavy pattern from west to east.

Each hemisphere usually has two main jet streams, a polar jet stream and a subtropical jet stream. The polar jet streams flow closer to the poles in summer than in winter. Jet streams can affect temperatures. For example, a polar jet stream can pull cold air down from Canada into the United States and pull warm air up toward Canada. Jet streams also affect precipitation patterns. Strong storms tend to form along jet streams. Scientists must know where a jet stream is flowing to make accurate weather predictions.

Active Reading 15 **Identify** What are two ways jet streams affect weather?

_____

_____

_____

_____

In winter months, the polar jet stream flows across much of the United States.

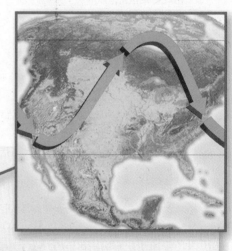

Polar jet stream

Subtropical jet streams

Polar jet stream

Visualize It!

16 **Infer** How does the polar jet stream influence the weather on the southern tip of South America?

_____

_____

_____

_____

Ocean Effects

How do ocean currents influence weather?

The same global winds that blow across the surface of Earth also push water across Earth's oceans, causing surface currents. Different winds cause currents to flow in different directions. The flow of surface currents moves energy as heat from one part of Earth to another. As the map below shows, both warm-water and cold-water currents flow from one ocean to another. Water near the equator carries energy from the sun to other parts of the ocean. The energy from the warm currents is transferred to colder water or to the atmosphere, changing local temperatures and humidity.

Oceans also have an effect on weather in the form of hurricanes and monsoons. Warm ocean water fuels hurricanes. Monsoons are winds that change direction with the seasons. During summer, the land becomes much warmer than the sea in some areas of the world. Moist wind flows inland, often bringing heavy rains.

Warm current
Cold current

Surface currents are caused by winds. They distribute energy across Earth's surface, changing local temperature and humidity.

Cool Ocean Currents Lower Coastal Air Temperatures

As currents flow, they warm or cool the atmosphere above, affecting local temperatures. The California current is a cold-water current that keeps the average summer high temperatures of coastal cities such as San Diego around 26 °C (78 °F). Cities that lie inland at the same latitude have warmer averages. The graph below shows average monthly temperatures for San Diego and El Centro, California.

Visualize It!

18 Explain Why are temperatures in San Diego, California, usually cooler than they are in El Centro, California?

_____

_____

_____

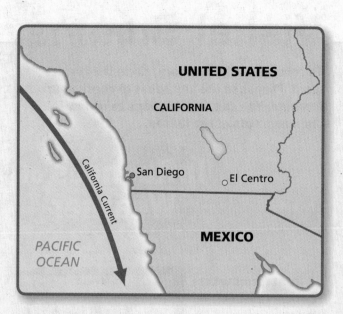

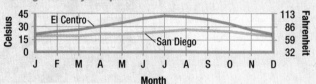

Average Monthly Temperatures

Source: weather.com

Warm Ocean Currents Raise Coastal Air Temperatures

In areas where warm ocean currents flow, coastal cities have warmer winter temperatures than inland cities at similar latitudes. For example, temperatures vary considerably from the coastal regions to the inland areas of Norway due to the warmth of the North Atlantic Current. Coastal cities such as Bergen have relatively mild winters. Inland cities such as Lillehammer have colder winters but temperatures similar to the coastal cities in summer.

Visualize It!

19 Identify Circle the city that is represented by each color in the graph.

■ Lillehammer/Bergen

■ Lillehammer/Bergen

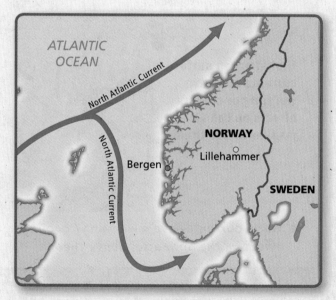

Average Monthly High Temperatures

Source: worldweather.org

Visual Summary

To complete this summary, circle the correct word. Then, use the key below to check your answers. You can use this page to review the main concepts of the lesson.

Influences of Weather

Understanding the water cycle is key to understanding weather.

20 Weather is affected by the amount of oxygen / water in the air.

A front forms where two air masses meet.

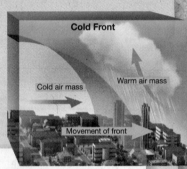

Cold Front

Cold air mass

Warm air mass

Movement of front

21 When a warm air mass and a cool air mass meet, the warm / cool air mass usually moves upward.

Low-pressure systems bring stormy weather, and high-pressure systems bring dry, clear weather.

Warm air rises

22 In a low-pressure system, air moves upward / downward.

Pressure differences from the uneven heating of Earth's surface cause predictable patterns of wind.

23 Global wind patterns occur as, due to temperature differences, air rises / sinks at the poles and rises / sinks at the equator.

Global ocean surface currents can have warming or cooling effects on the air masses above them.

24 Warm currents have a warming / cooling effect on the air masses above them.

Answers: 20 water; 21 warm; 22 upward; 23 sinks, rises; 24 warming

25 Synthesize How do air masses cause weather changes?

Lesson Review

Vocabulary

For each pair of terms, explain how the meanings of the terms differ.

1 *front* and *air mass*

_____

_____

_____

2 *high-pressure system* and *low-pressure system*

_____

_____

_____

3 *jet streams* and *global wind belts*

_____

_____

_____

Key Concepts

4 Apply If the weather becomes stormy for a short time and then becomes colder, which type of front has most likely passed?

_____

5 Describe Explain how an ocean current can affect the temperature and the amount of moisture of the air mass above the current and above nearby coastlines.

_____

_____

_____

_____

6 Synthesize How does the water cycle affect weather?

_____

_____

_____

_____

Critical Thinking

Use the diagram below to answer the following question.

Cool air descends   Warm air rises

7 Interpret How does the movement of air affect the type of weather that forms from high-pressure and low-pressure systems?

_____

_____

_____

_____

8 Explain How does the polar jet stream affect temperature and precipitation in North America?

_____

_____

_____

_____

9 Describe Explain how changes in weather are caused by the interaction of air masses.

_____

_____

_____

_____

_____

_____

Severe Weather and Weather Safety

ESSENTIAL QUESTION

How can humans protect themselves from hazardous weather?

By the end of this lesson, you should be able to describe the major types of hazardous weather and the ways human beings can protect themselves from hazardous weather and from sun exposure.

Lightning is often the most dangerous part of a thunderstorm. Thunderstorms are one type of severe weather that can cause a lot of damage.

Indiana Standards

8.2.5 Describe the conditions that cause Indiana weather and weather-related events such as tornadoes, lake effect snow, blizzards, thunderstorms, and flooding.

Engage Your Brain

1 Describe Fill in the blanks with the word or phrase that you think correctly completes the following sentences.

A _____ forms a funnel cloud and has high winds.

A flash or bolt of light across the sky during a storm is called _____

_____ is the sound that follows lightning during a storm.

One way to protect yourself from the sun's rays is to wear _____

2 Identify Name the weather event that is occurring in the photo. What conditions can occur when this event happens in an area?

_____

_____

_____

_____

Active Reading

3 Synthesize Use the sentence below to help you make an educated guess about what the term *storm surge* means. Write the meaning below.

Example sentence
Flooding causes tremendous damage to property and lives when a storm surge moves onto shore.

storm surge:

_____

_____

_____

Vocabulary Terms

- thunderstorm
- lightning
- thunder
- hurricane
- storm surge
- tornado

4 Apply As you learn the definition of each vocabulary term in this lesson, create your own definition or sketch to help you remember the meaning of the term.

☑ Take Cover!

What do we know about thunderstorms?

SPLAAAAAT! BOOOOM! The loud, sharp noise of thunder might surprise you, and maybe even make you jump. The thunder may have been joined by lightning, wind, and rain. A **thunderstorm** is an intense local storm that forms strong winds, heavy rain, lightning, thunder, and sometimes hail. A thunderstorm is an example of severe weather. Severe weather is weather that can cause property damage and sometimes death.

Thunderstorms Form from Rising Air

Thunderstorms get their energy from humid air. When warm, humid air near the ground mixes with cooler air above, the warm air creates an updraft that can build a thunderstorm quickly. Cold downdrafts bring precipitation and eventually end the storm by preventing more warm air from rising.

Step 1
In the first stage, warm air rises and forms a cumulus cloud. The water vapor releases energy when it condenses into cloud droplets. This energy increases the air motion. The cloud continues building up.

Step 2
Ice particles may form in the low temperatures near the top of the cloud. As the ice particles grow large, they begin to fall and pull cold air down with them. This strong downdraft brings heavy rain or hail.

Step 3
During the final stage, the downdraft can spread out and block more warm air from moving upward into the cloud. The storm slows down and ends.

5 Describe What role does warm air play in the formation of a thunderstorm?

_____

_____

_____

Lightning is a Discharge of Electrical Energy

If you have ever shuffled your feet on a carpet, you may have felt a small shock when you touched a doorknob. If so, you have experienced how lightning forms. **Lightning** is an electric discharge that happens between a positively charged area and a negatively charged area. While you walk around, electrical charges can collect on your body. When you touch someone or something else, the charges jump to that person or object in a spark of electricity. In a similar way, electrical charges build up near the tops and bottoms of clouds as pellets of ice move up and down through the clouds. Suddenly, a flash of lightning will spark from one place to another.

 **Visualize It!**

6 Label Fill in the positive and negative charges in the appropriate spaces provided.

Lightning forms between positive and negative charges. The upper part of a cloud usually carries a positive electric charge. The lower part of the cloud carries mainly negative charges. Lightning is a big spark that jumps between parts of clouds, or between a cloud and Earth's surface.

Thunder Is a Result of Rapidly Expanding Air

When lightning strikes, the air along its path is heated to a high temperature. The superheated air quickly expands. The rapidly moving air causes the air to vibrate and release sound waves. The result is **thunder**, the sound created by the rapid expansion of air along a lightning strike.

You usually hear thunder a few seconds after you see a lightning strike, because light travels faster than sound. You can count the seconds between a lightning flash and the sound of thunder to figure out about how far away the lightning is. For every 3 seconds between lightning and its thunder, add about 1 km to the lightning strike's distance from you.

Active Reading

7 Identify As you read, underline the explanation of what causes thunder during a storm.

☑ Plan Ahead!

What do we know about hurricanes?

A **hurricane** is a tropical low-pressure system with winds blowing at speeds of 119 km/h (74 mi/h) or more—strong enough to uproot trees. Hurricanes are called typhoons when they form over the western Pacific Ocean and cyclones when they form over the Indian Ocean.

Hurricanes Need Water to Form and Grow

A hurricane begins as a group of thunderstorms moving over tropical ocean waters. Thunderstorms form in areas of low pressure. Near the equator, warm ocean water provides the energy that can turn a low-pressure center into a violent storm. As water evaporates from the ocean, energy is transferred from the ocean water into the air. This energy makes warm air rise faster. Tall clouds and strong winds develop. As winds blow across the water from different directions into the low-pressure center, the paths bend into a spiral. The winds blow faster and faster around the low-pressure center, which becomes the center of the hurricane.

As long as a hurricane stays above warm water, it can grow bigger and more powerful. As soon as a hurricane moves over land or over cooler water, it loses its source of energy. The winds lose strength and the storm dies out. If a hurricane moves over land, the rough surface of the land reduces the winds even more.

Hurricanes in the Northern Hemisphere usually move westward with the trade winds. Near land, however, they will often move north or even back out to sea.

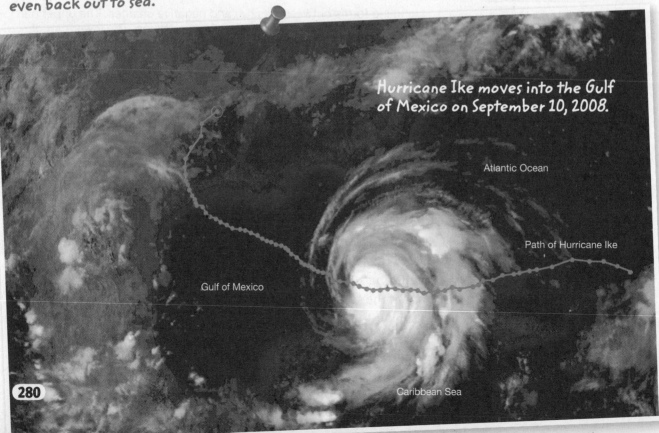

Hurricane Ike moves into the Gulf of Mexico on September 10, 2008.

Atlantic Ocean

Path of Hurricane Ike

Gulf of Mexico

Caribbean Sea

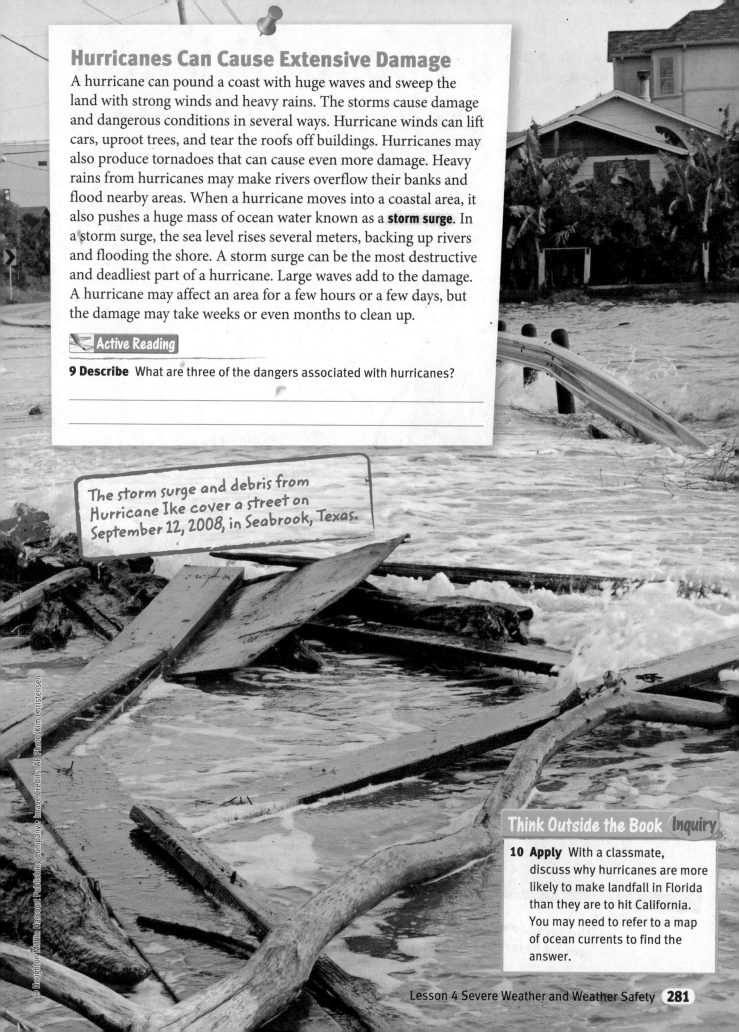

Hurricanes Can Cause Extensive Damage

A hurricane can pound a coast with huge waves and sweep the land with strong winds and heavy rains. The storms cause damage and dangerous conditions in several ways. Hurricane winds can lift cars, uproot trees, and tear the roofs off buildings. Hurricanes may also produce tornadoes that can cause even more damage. Heavy rains from hurricanes may make rivers overflow their banks and flood nearby areas. When a hurricane moves into a coastal area, it also pushes a huge mass of ocean water known as a **storm surge**. In a storm surge, the sea level rises several meters, backing up rivers and flooding the shore. A storm surge can be the most destructive and deadliest part of a hurricane. Large waves add to the damage. A hurricane may affect an area for a few hours or a few days, but the damage may take weeks or even months to clean up.

Active Reading

9 Describe What are three of the dangers associated with hurricanes?

_____

_____

The storm surge and debris from Hurricane Ike cover a street on September 12, 2008, in Seabrook, Texas.

Think Outside the Book Inquiry

10 Apply With a classmate, discuss why hurricanes are more likely to make landfall in Florida than they are to hit California. You may need to refer to a map of ocean currents to find the answer.

☑ Secure Loose Objects!

What do we know about tornadoes?

A **tornado** is a destructive, rotating column of air that has very high wind speeds and that is sometimes visible as a funnel-shaped cloud. A tornado forms when a thunderstorm meets horizontal winds at a high altitude. These winds cause the warm air rising in the thunderstorm to spin. A storm cloud may form a thin funnel shape that has a very low pressure center. As the funnel reaches the ground, the higher-pressure air rushes into the low-pressure area. The result is high-speed winds, which cause the damage associated with tornadoes.

Clouds begin to rotate, signaling that a tornado may form.

The funnel cloud becomes visible as the tornado picks up dust from the ground or particles from the air.

The tornado moves along the ground before it dies out.

Think Outside the Book

11 Illustrate Read the description of the weather conditions that cause tornadoes and draw a sketch of what those conditions might look like.

© Houghton Mifflin Harcourt Publishing Company • Image Credits: (t) ©Jim Edds/Photo Researchers, Inc.; (c) ©Digital Vision/Getty Images; (b) ©Reed Timmer/SPL/Photo Researchers, Inc.

Most Tornadoes Happen in the Midwest

Tornadoes happen in many places, but they are most common in the United States in *Tornado Alley*. Tornado Alley reaches from Texas up through the midwestern United States, including Iowa, Kansas, Nebraska, and Ohio. Many tornadoes form in the spring and early summer, typically along a front between cool, dry air and warm, humid air.

Tornadoes Can Cause Extensive Damage

The danger of a tornado is mainly due to the high speed of its winds. Winds in a tornado's funnel may have speeds of more than 400 km/h. Most injuries and deaths caused by tornadoes happen when people are struck by objects blown by the winds or when they are trapped in buildings that collapse.

12 Identify As you read, underline what makes a tornado so destructive.

13 Summarize In the overlapping sections of the Venn diagram, list the characteristics that are shared by the different types of storms. In the outer sections, list the characteristics that are specific to each type of storm.

Thunderstorms   Hurricanes

Tornadoes

14 Conclude Write a summary that describes the information in the Venn diagram.

_____

_____

_____

_____

☑ Be Prepared!

What can people do to prepare for severe weather?

Severe weather is weather that can cause property damage, injury, and sometimes death. Hail, lightning, high winds, tornadoes, hurricanes, and floods are all part of severe weather. Hailstorms can damage crops and cars and can break windows. Lightning starts many forest fires and kills or injures hundreds of people and animals each year. Winds and tornadoes can uproot trees and destroy homes. Flooding is also a leading cause of weather-related deaths. Most destruction from hurricanes results from flooding due to storm surges.

Think Outside the Book Inquiry

15 **Apply** Research severe weather in your area and come up with a plan for safety.

Plan Ahead

Have a storm supply kit that contains a battery-operated radio, batteries, flashlights, candles, rain jackets, tarps, blankets, bottled water, canned food, and medicines. Listen to weather announcements. Plan and practice a safety route. A safety route is a planned path to a safe place.

Listen for Storm Updates

During severe weather, it is important to listen to local radio or TV stations. Severe weather updates will let you know the location of a storm. They will also let you know if the storm is getting worse. A *watch* is given when the conditions are ideal for severe weather. A *warning* is given when severe weather has been spotted or is expected within 24 h. During most kinds of severe weather, it is best to stay indoors and away from windows. However, in some situations, you may need to evacuate.

Follow Flood Safety Rules

Sometimes, a place can get so much rain that it floods, especially if it is a low-lying area. So, like storms, floods have watches and warnings. However, little advance notice can usually be given that a flood is coming. A flash flood is a flood that rises and falls very quickly. The best thing to do during a flood is to find a high place to stay until it is over. You should always stay out of floodwaters. Even shallow water can be dangerous because it can move fast.

What can people do to stay safe during thunderstorms?

Stay alert when thunderstorms are predicted or when dark, tall clouds are visible. If you are outside and hear thunder, seek shelter immediately and stay there for 30 min after the thunder ends. Heavy rains can cause sudden, or flash, flooding, and hailstones can damage property and harm living things.

Lightning is one of the most dangerous parts of a thunderstorm. Because lightning is attracted to tall objects, it is important to stay away from trees if you are outside. If you are in an open area, stay close to the ground so that you are not the tallest object in the area. If you can, get into a car. Stay away from ponds, lakes, or other bodies of water. If lightning hits water while you are swimming or wading in it, you could be hurt or killed. If you are indoors during a thunderstorm, avoid using electrical appliances, running water, and phone lines.

How can people stay safe during a tornado?

Tornadoes are too fast and unpredictable for you to attempt to outrun, even if you are in a car. If you see or hear a tornado, go to a place without windows, such as basement, a storm cellar, or a closet or hallway. Stay away from areas that are likely to have flying objects or other dangers. If you are outside, lie in a ditch or low-lying area. Protect your head and neck by covering them with your arms and hands.

How can people stay safe during a hurricane?

If your family lives where hurricanes may strike, have a plan to leave the area, and gather emergency supplies. If a hurricane is in your area, listen to weather reports for storm updates. Secure loose objects outside, and cover windows with storm shutters or boards. During a storm, stay indoors and away from windows. If ordered to evacuate the area, do so immediately. After a storm, be aware of downed power lines, hanging branches, and flooded areas.

16 Apply What would you do in each of these scenarios?

Scenario	What would you do?
You are swimming at an outdoor pool when you hear thunder in the distance.	
You and your family are watching TV when you hear a tornado warning that says a tornado has been spotted in the area.	
You are listening to the radio when the announcer says that a hurricane is headed your way and may make landfall in 3 days.	

✓ Use Sun Sense!

How can people protect their skin from the sun?

Human skin contains melanin, which is the body's natural protection against ultraviolet (UV) radiation from the sun. The skin produces more melanin when it is exposed to the sun, but UV rays will still cause sunburn when you spend too much time outside. It is particularly important to protect your skin when the sun's rays are strongest, usually between 10 A.M and 4 P.M.

Active Reading

17 Identify As you read, underline when the sun's ray's are strongest during the day.

Have fun in the sun! Just be sure to protect your skin from harmful rays.

Know the Sun's Hazards

It's easy to notice the effects of a sunburn. Sunburn usually appears within a few hours after sun exposure. It causes red, painful skin that feels hot to the touch. Prolonged exposure to the sun will lead to sunburn in even the darkest-skinned people. Sunburn can lead to skin cancer and premature aging of the skin. The best way to prevent sunburn is to protect your skin from the sun, even on cloudy days. UV rays pass right through clouds and can give you a false feeling of protection from the sun.

Wear Sunscreen and Protective Clothing

Even if you tan easily, you should still use sunscreen. For most people, a sun protection factor (SPF) of 30 or more will prevent burning for about 1.5 h. Babies and people who have pale skin should use an SPF of 45 or more. In addition, you can protect your skin and eyes in different ways. Seek the shade, and wear hats, sunglasses, and perhaps even UV light-protective clothing.

How can people protect themselves from summer heat?

Heat exhaustion is a condition in which the body has been exposed to high temperatures for an extended period of time. Symptoms include cold, moist skin, normal or near-normal body temperature, headache, nausea, and extreme fatigue. *Heat stroke* is a condition in which the body loses its ability to cool itself by sweating because the victim has become dehydrated.

Limit Outdoor Activities

When outdoor temperatures are high, be cautious about exercising outdoors for long periods of time. Pay attention to how your body is feeling, and go inside or to a shady spot if you are starting to feel light-headed or too warm.

Drink Water

Heat exhaustion and heat stroke can best be prevented by drinking 6 to 8 oz of water at least 10 times a day when you are active in warm weather. If you are feeling overheated, dizzy, nauseous, or are sweating heavily, drink something cool (not cold). Drink about half a glass of cool water every 15 min until you feel like your normal self.

> Drinking water is one of the best things you can do to keep yourself healthy in hot weather.

Visualize It!

18 Describe List all the ways the people in the photo of the beach may have protected themselves from overexposure to the sun.

_____

_____

_____

_____

_____

_____

_____

Know the Signs of Heat Stroke

Active Reading **19 Identify** Underline signs of heat stroke in the paragraph below.

Heat stroke is life threatening, so it is important to know the signs and treatment for it. Symptoms of heat stroke include hot, dry skin; higher than normal body temperature; rapid pulse; rapid, shallow breathing; disorientation; and possible loss of consciousness.

What to Do In Case of Heat Stroke

☐ Seek emergency help immediately.

☐ If there are no emergency facilities nearby, move the person to a cool place.

☐ Cool the person's body by immersing it in a cool (not cold) bath or using wet towels.

☐ Do not give the person food or water if he or she is vomiting.

☐ Place ice packs under the person's armpits.

Visual Summary

To complete this summary, circle the correct word or phrase. Then use the key below to check your answers. You can use this page to review the main concepts of the lesson.

Severe Weather

Thunderstorms are intense weather systems that produce strong winds, heavy rain, lightning, and thunder.

20. One of the most dangerous parts of a thunderstorm is lightning / thunder.

A hurricane is a large, rotating tropical weather system with strong winds that can cause severe property damage.

21. An important step to plan for a hurricane is to buy raingear / stock a supply kit.

Tornadoes are rotating columns of air that touch the ground and can cause severe damage.

22. The damage from a tornado is mostly caused by associated thunderstorms / high-speed winds.

It is important to plan ahead and listen for weather updates in the event of severe weather.

23. One of the biggest dangers of storms that produce heavy rains or storm surges is flooding / low temperatures.

Prolonged exposure to the sun can cause sunburn, skin cancer, and heat-related health effects.

24. One of the best ways to avoid heat-related illnesses while in the sun is to stay active / drink water.

Answers: 20 lightning; 21 stock a supply kit; 22 high-speed winds; 23 flooding; 24 drink water.

25. **Synthesize** What are three ways in which severe weather can be dangerous?

Lesson Review

Vocabulary

Draw a line that matches the term with the correct definition.

1 hurricane

2 tornado

3 severe weather

4 thunderstorm

5 storm surge

A a huge mass of ocean water that floods the shore

B a storm with lightning and thunder

C a violently rotating column of air stretching to the ground

D weather that can potentially destroy property or cause loss of life

E a tropical low-pressure system with winds of 119 km/h or more

Key Concepts

6 Thunder is caused by _____

7 An electrical discharge between parts of clouds or a cloud and the ground is called _____

8 The sun's ultraviolet rays can cause skin damage including sunburn and even skin _____

9 Explain How can a person prepare for hazardous weather well in advance?

_____

_____

10 Describe What can people do to stay safe before and during a storm with high winds and heavy rains?

_____

_____

_____

Critical Thinking

Use the map below to answer the following question.

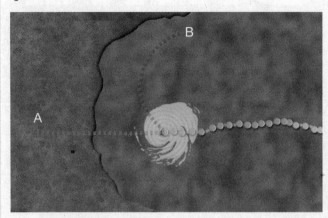

11 Interpret Would a hurricane be more likely to remain a hurricane if it reached point A or point B? Explain your answer.

_____

_____

_____

12 Explain Why do hurricanes form in tropical latitudes?

_____

_____

13 Describe What two weather conditions are needed for tornadoes to form?

_____

_____

14 Explain Why is hail sometimes dangerous?

_____

_____

_____

15 Summarize What can you do to avoid overexposure to the sun's rays?

_____

_____

_____

Climate

ESSENTIAL QUESTION

How is climate affected by energy from the sun and variations on Earth's surface?

By the end of this lesson, you should be able to describe the main factors that affect climate and explain how scientists classify climates.

Earth has a wide variety of climates, including polar climates like the one shown here. What kind of climate do you live in?

🔵 Indiana Standards

8.2.1 Recognize and demonstrate how the sun's energy drives convection in the atmosphere and in bodies of water, which results in ocean currents and weather patterns.

8.2.2 Describe and model how water moves through the earth's crust, atmosphere, and oceans in a cyclic way, as liquid, vapor, and solid.

8.2.3 Describe the characteristics of ocean currents and identify their effects on weather patterns.

Engage Your Brain

1 Predict Check T or F to show whether you think each statement is true or false.

T   F

☐   ☐   Locations in Florida and Oregon receive the same amount of sunlight on any given day.

☐   ☐   Temperature is an important part of determining the climate of an area.

☐   ☐   The climate on even the tallest mountains near the equator is too warm for glaciers to form.

☐   ☐   Winds can move rain clouds from one location to another.

2 Infer Volcanic eruptions can send huge clouds of gas and dust into the air. These dust particles can block sunlight. How might the eruption of a large volcano affect weather for years to come?

_____

_____

_____

_____

_____

Active Reading

3 Synthesize You can often define an unknown word if you know the meaning of its word parts. Use the word parts and sentence below to make an educated guess about the meaning of the word *topography*.

Word part	Meaning
topos-	place
-graphy	writing

Example sentence
The topography of the area is varied, because there are hills, valleys, and flat plains all within a few square miles.

topography:

_____

_____

Vocabulary Terms

- weather
- climate
- latitude
- topography
- elevation
- surface currents

4 Apply As you learn the definition of each vocabulary term in this lesson, create your own definition or sketch to help you remember the meaning of the term.

How's the **Climate?**

What determines climate?

Weather conditions change from day to day. **Weather** is the condition of Earth's atmosphere at a particular time and place. **Climate**, on the other hand, describes the weather conditions in an area over a long period of time. For the most part, climate is determined by temperature and precipitation (pree•SIP•uh•tay•shuhn). But what factors affect the temperature and precipitation rates of an area? Those factors include latitude, wind patterns, elevation, locations of mountains and large bodies of water, and nearness to ocean currents.

Temperature

Temperature patterns are an important feature of climate. Although the average temperature of an area over a period of time is useful information, using only average temperatures to describe climate can be misleading. Areas that have similar average temperatures may have very different temperature ranges.

A temperature range includes all of the temperatures in an area, from the coldest temperature extreme to the warmest temperature extreme. Organisms that thrive in a region are those that can survive the temperature extremes in that region. Temperature ranges provide more information about an area and are unique to the area. Therefore, temperature ranges are a better indicator of climate than are temperature averages.

Visualize It!

6 Infer How might the two different climates shown below affect the daily lives of the people who live there?

_____

_____

_____

_____

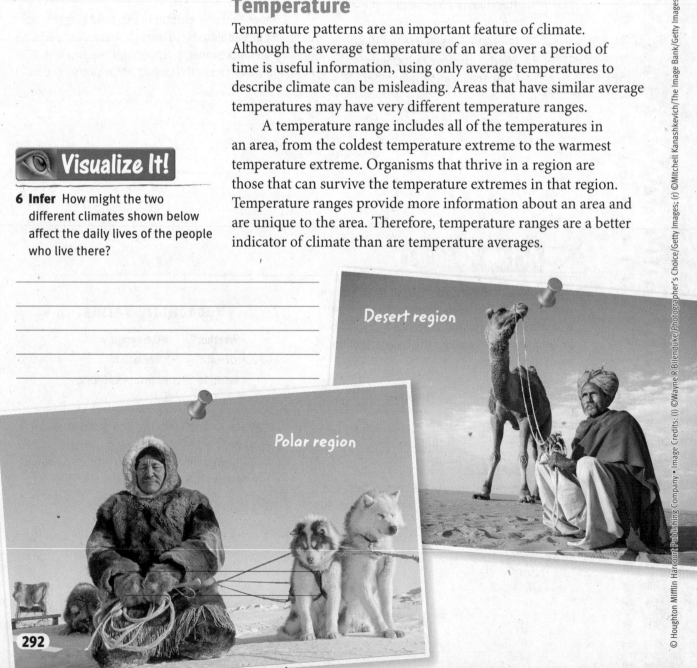

Desert region

Polar region

Precipitation

Precipitation, such as rain, snow, or hail, is also an important part of climate. As with temperature, the average yearly precipitation alone is not the best way to describe a climate. Two places that have the same average yearly precipitation may receive that precipitation in different patterns during the year. For example, one location may receive small amounts of precipitation throughout the year. This pattern would support plant life all year long. Another location may receive all of its precipitation in a few months of the year. These months may be the only time in which plants can grow. So, the pattern of precipitation in a region can determine the types of plants that grow there and the length of the growing season. Therefore, the pattern of precipitation is a better indicator of the local climate than the average precipitation alone.

Think Outside the Book Inquiry

8 Apply With a classmate, discuss what condition, other than precipitation, is likely related to better plant growth in the temperate area shown directly below than in the desert on the bottom right.

Visualize It!

7 Interpret Match the climates represented in the bar graph below to the photos by writing *A*, *B*, or *C* in the blank circles.

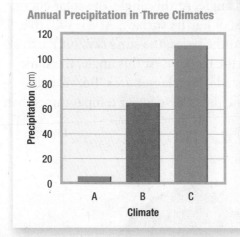

Annual Precipitation in Three Climates

○ There are enough resources in the area for plants to thickly cover the ground.

○ Some plants that grow in deserts have long roots to reach the water deep underground.

○ Conditions in a tropical forest allow lots of plants to grow quickly and closely together.

© Houghton Mifflin Harcourt Publishing Company • Image Credits: (t) ©Scott Kemper/Alamy; (c) ©Danita Delimont/Alamy; (b) ©Douglas Peebles Photography/Alamy

Here Comes the Sun!

How is the sun's energy related to Earth's climate?

The climate of an area is directly related to the amount of energy from the sun, or *solar energy*, that the area receives. This amount depends on the latitude (LAHT•ih•tood) of the area. **Latitude** is the angular distance in degrees north and south from the equator. Different latitudes receive different amounts of solar energy. The available solar energy powers the water cycle and winds, which affect the temperature, precipitation, and other factors that determine the local climate.

Latitude Affects the Amount of Solar Energy an Area Receives and that Area's Climate

Latitude helps determine the temperature of an area, because latitude affects the amount of solar energy an area receives. The figure below shows how the amount of solar energy reaching Earth's surface varies with latitude. Notice that the sun's rays travel in lines parallel to one another. Near the equator, the sun's rays hit Earth directly, at almost a 90° angle. At this angle, the solar energy is concentrated in a small area of Earth's surface. As a result, that area has high temperatures. At the poles, the sun's rays hit Earth at a lesser angle than they do at the equator. At this angle, the same amount of solar energy is spread over a larger area. Because the energy is less concentrated, the poles have lower temperatures than areas near the equator do.

Active Reading

9 Identify As you read, underline how solar energy affects the climate of an area.

Visualize It!

10 Analyze What is the difference between the sun's rays that strike at the equator and the sun's rays that strike at the poles?

_____

_____

_____

_____

The amount of solar energy an area receives depends on latitude.

Drawing is not to scale.

The Sun Powers the Water Cycle

It is easy to see how the water cycle affects weather and climate. For example, when it rains or snows, you see precipitation. In the water cycle, energy from the sun warms the surface of the ocean or other body of water. Some of the liquid water evaporates, becoming invisible water vapor, a gas. When cooled, some of the vapor condenses, turning into droplets of liquid water and forming clouds. Some water droplets collide, becoming larger. Once large enough, they fall to Earth's surface as precipitation.

Visualize It!

11 Apply Using the figure below, explain how the water cycle affects the climate of an area.

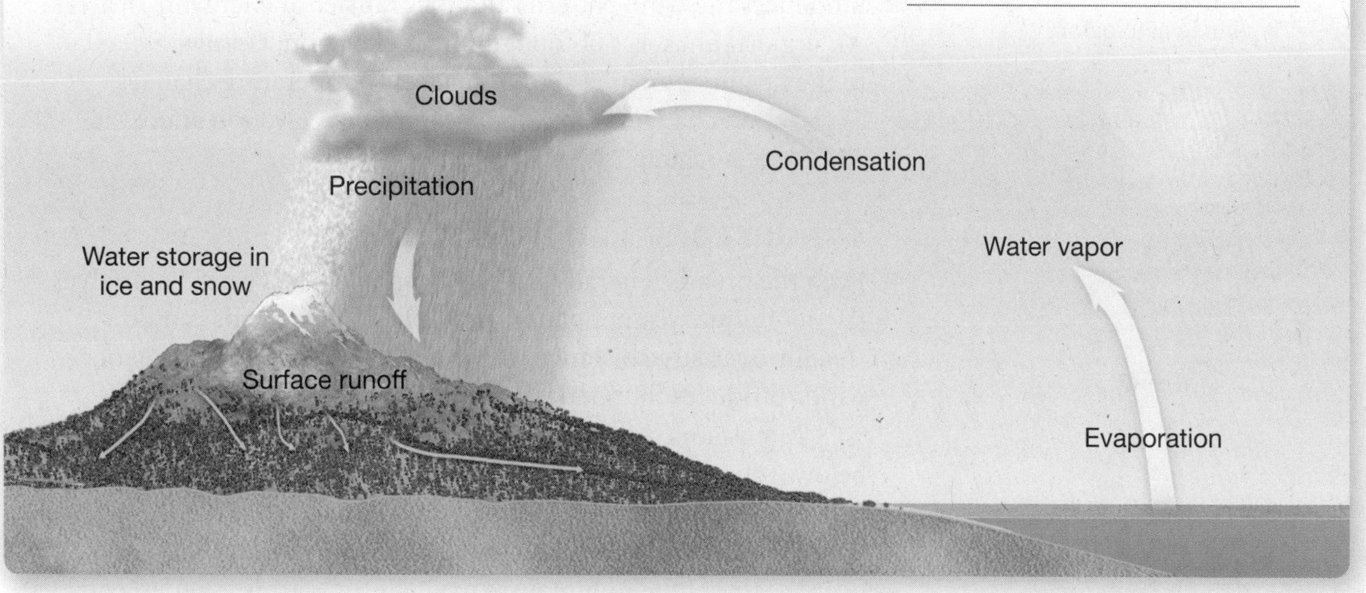

Clouds

Condensation

Precipitation

Water vapor

Water storage in ice and snow

Surface runoff

Evaporation

The Sun Powers Wind

The sun warms Earth's surface unevenly, creating areas of different air pressure. As air moves from areas of higher pressure to areas of lower pressure, it is felt as wind, as shown below. Global and local wind patterns transfer energy around Earth's surface, affecting global and local temperatures. Winds also carry water vapor from place to place. If the air cools enough, the water vapor will condense and fall as precipitation. The speed, direction, temperature, and moisture content of winds affect the climate and weather of the areas they move through.

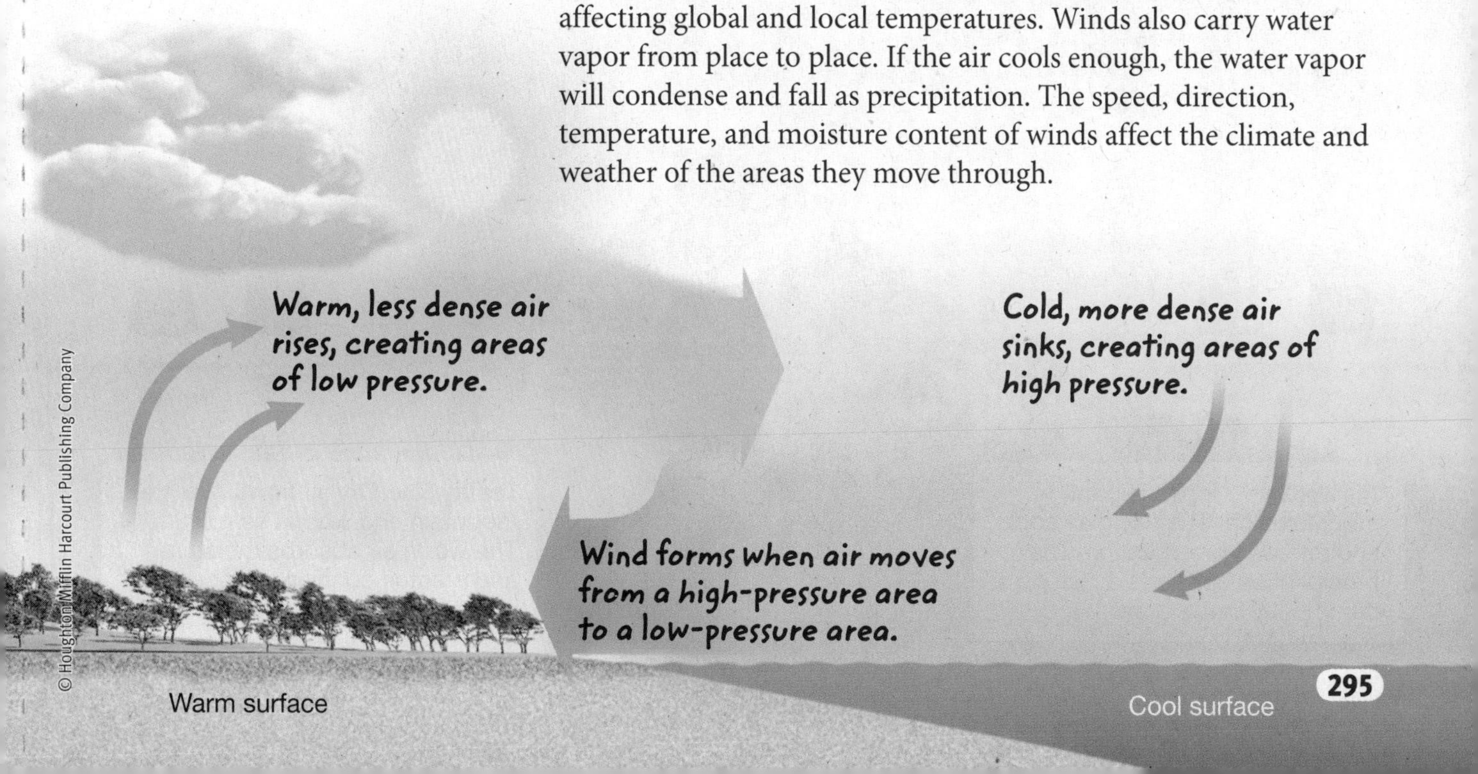

Warm, less dense air rises, creating areas of low pressure.

Cold, more dense air sinks, creating areas of high pressure.

Wind forms when air moves from a high-pressure area to a low-pressure area.

Warm surface

Cool surface

Latitude Isn't Everything

How do Earth's features affect climate?

On land, winds have to flow around or over features on Earth's surface, such as mountains. The surface features of an area combine to form its **topography** (tuh•POG•ruh•fee). Topography influences the wind patterns and the transfer of energy in an area. An important aspect of topography is elevation. **Elevation** refers to the height of an area above sea level. Temperature changes as elevation changes. Thus, topography and elevation affect the climate of a region.

Topography Can Affect Winds

Even the broad, generally flat topography of the Great Plains gives rise to unique weather patterns. On the plains, winds can flow steadily over large distances before they merge. This mixing of winds produces thunderstorms and even tornadoes.

Mountains can also affect the climate of an area, as shown below. When moist air hits a mountain, it is forced to rise up the side of the mountain. The rising air cools and often releases rain, which supports plants on the mountainside. The air that moves over the top of the mountain is dry. The air warms as it descends, creating a dry climate, which supports desert formation. Such areas are said to be in a *rain shadow,* because the air has already released all of its water by the time that it reaches this side of the mountain.

![Active Reading]

12 Identify As you read, underline how topography affects the climate of a region.

Visualize It!

13 Apply Circle the rain gauge in each set that corresponds to how much rain each side of the mountain is likely to receive.

The Rain Shadow Effect

The Wet Side Air rises up the mountainside. The rising air cools and releases precipitation. The precipitation supports a lush plant community in this area.

The Dry Side Dry air flows over the mountain and warms as it sinks. The warm air absorbs moisture and creates conditions under which deserts may develop.

Elevation Influences Temperature

Elevation has a very strong effect on the temperature of an area. If you rode a cable car up a mountain, the temperature would decrease by about 6.5 °C (11.7 °F) for every kilometer you rose in elevation. Why does it get colder as you move higher up? Because the lower atmosphere is mainly warmed by Earth's surface that is directly below it. The warmed air lifts to higher elevations, where it expands and cools. Even close to the equator, temperatures at high elevations can be very cold. For example, Mount Kilimanjaro in Tanzania is close to the equator, but it is still cold enough at the peak to support a permanent glacier. The example below shows how one mountain can have several types of climates.

Visualize It!

14 Apply Circle the thermometer that shows the most likely temperature for each photo at different elevations.

Effects of Elevation

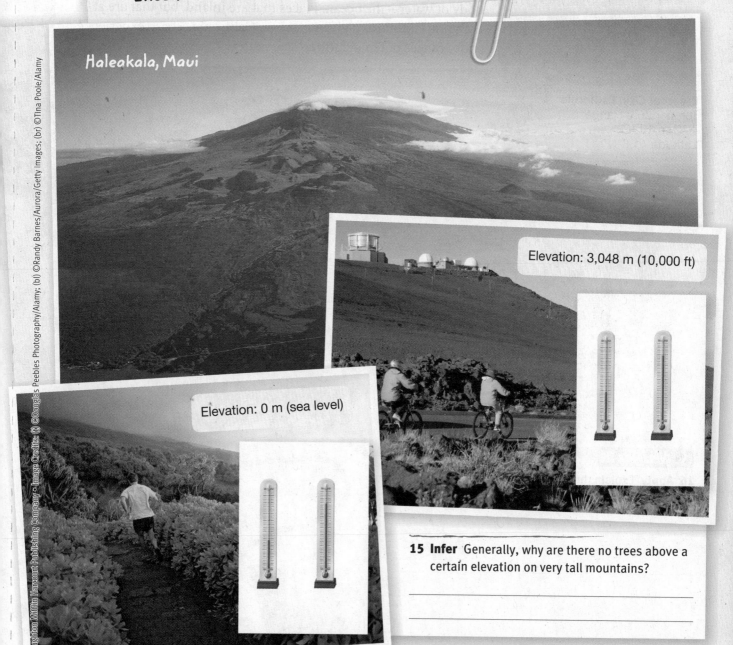

Haleakala, Maui

Elevation: 3,048 m (10,000 ft)

Elevation: 0 m (sea level)

15 Infer Generally, why are there no trees above a certain elevation on very tall mountains?

_____

_____

Waterfront Property

How do large bodies of water affect climate?

Large bodies of water, such as the ocean, can influence an area's climate. Water absorbs and releases energy as heat more slowly than land does. So, water helps moderate the temperature of nearby land. Sudden or extreme temperature changes rarely take place on land near large bodies of water. The state of Michigan, which is nearly surrounded by the Great Lakes, has more moderate temperatures than places far from large bodies of water at the same latitude. California's coastal climate is also influenced by a large body of water—the ocean. Places that are inland, but that are at the same latitude as a given place on California's coast, experience wider ranges of temperature.

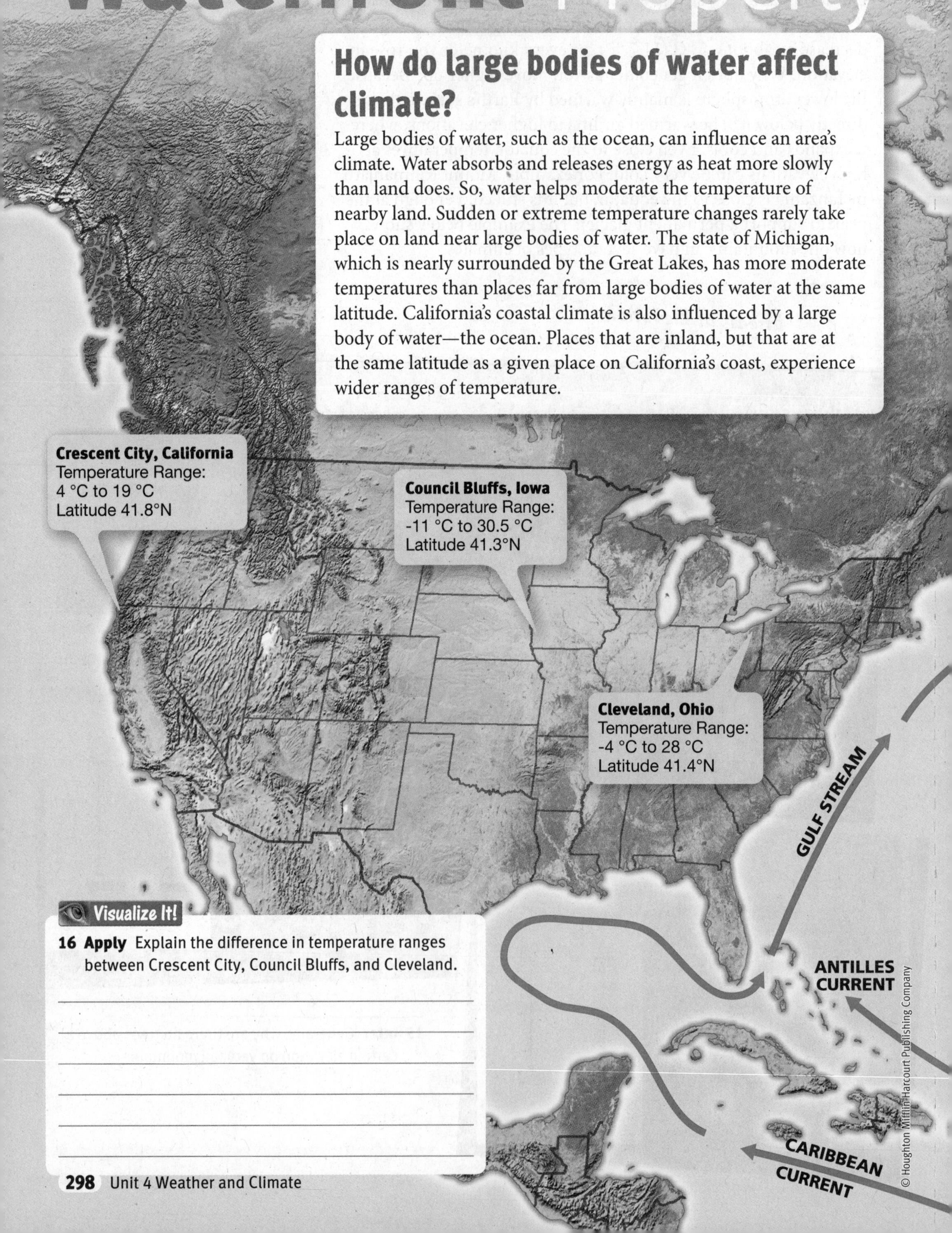

Crescent City, California
Temperature Range:
4 °C to 19 °C
Latitude 41.8°N

Council Bluffs, Iowa
Temperature Range:
-11 °C to 30.5 °C
Latitude 41.3°N

Cleveland, Ohio
Temperature Range:
-4 °C to 28 °C
Latitude 41.4°N

GULF STREAM

ANTILLES CURRENT

CARIBBEAN CURRENT

Visualize It!

16 Apply Explain the difference in temperature ranges between Crescent City, Council Bluffs, and Cleveland.

_____

_____

_____

_____

_____

_____

How do ocean currents affect climate?

An *ocean current* is the movement of water in a certain direction. There are many different currents in the oceans. Ocean currents move water and distribute energy and nutrients around the globe. The currents on the surface of the ocean are called **surface currents.** Surface currents are driven by winds and carry warm water away from the equator and carry cool water away from the poles.

Cold currents cool the air in coastal areas, while warm currents warm the air in coastal areas. Thus, currents moderate global temperatures. For example, the Gulf Stream is a surface current that moves warm water from the Gulf of Mexico northeastward, toward Great Britain and Europe. The British climate is mild because of the warm Gulf Stream waters. Polar bears do not wander the streets of Great Britain, as they might in Natashquan, Canada, which is at a similar latitude.

NORWAY CURRENT

Natashquan, Canada
Temperature Range:
-18 °C to 14 °C
Latitude: 50.2°N

LABRADOR CURRENT

London, England
Temperature Range:
2 °C to 22 °C
Latitude 51.5°N

GULF STREAM

NORTH ATLANTIC CURRENT

ATLANTIC OCEAN

17 Summarize How do currents distribute heat around the globe?

_____

_____

_____

👁 **Visualize It!**

18 Infer How do you think that the Canary current affects the temperature in the Canary Islands?

_____

_____

_____

CANARY CURRENT

Canary Islands, Spain
Temperature Range:
12 °C to 26 °C
Latitude 28°N

NORTH EQUATORIAL CURRENT

Zoning Out

What are the three major climate zones?

Earth has three major types of climate zones: tropical, temperate, and polar. These zones are shown below. Each zone has a distinct temperature range that relates to its latitude. Each of these zones has several types of climates. These different climates result from differences in topography, winds, ocean currents, and geography.

Active Reading

19 Identify Underline the factor that determines the temperature ranges in each zone.

Temperate

Temperate climates have an average temperature below 18 °C (64 °F) in the coldest month and an average temperature above 10 °C (50 °F) in the warmest month. There are five temperate zone subclimates: marine west coast climates, steppe climates, humid continental climate, humid subtropical climate, and Mediterranean climate. The temperate zone is characterized by lower temperatures than the tropical zone. It is located between the tropical zone and the polar zone.

Visualize It!

20 Label What climate zone is this?

_____

Polar

The polar zone, at latitudes of 66.5° and higher, is the coldest climate zone. Temperatures rarely rise above 10 °C (50 °F) in the warmest month. The climates of the polar regions are referred to as the *polar climates*. There are three types of polar zone subclimates: subarctic climates, tundra climates, and polar ice cap climates.

ARCTIC OCEAN

NORTH AMERICA

ATLANTIC OCEAN

23.5°N

0°–Equator

PACIFIC OCEAN

SOUTH AMERICA

23.5°S

66.5°S

SOUTH

21 Summarize Fill in the table for either the factor that affects climate or the effect on climate the given factor has.

Factor	Effect on climate
Latitude	
	Cooler temperatures as you travel up a tall mountain
Winds	
	Moderates weather so that highs and lows are less extreme
Surface ocean currents	
	Impacts wind patterns and the transfer of energy in an area

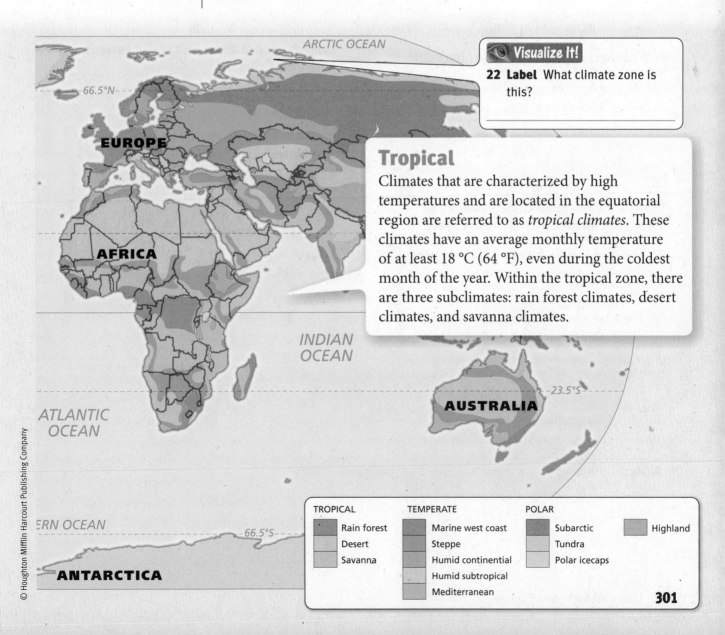

Visualize It!

22 Label What climate zone is this?

Tropical

Climates that are characterized by high temperatures and are located in the equatorial region are referred to as *tropical climates*. These climates have an average monthly temperature of at least 18 °C (64 °F), even during the coldest month of the year. Within the tropical zone, there are three subclimates: rain forest climates, desert climates, and savanna climates.

ARCTIC OCEAN

66.5°N

EUROPE

AFRICA

INDIAN OCEAN

ATLANTIC OCEAN

AUSTRALIA

-23.5°S

ERN OCEAN

66.5°S

ANTARCTICA

TROPICAL	TEMPERATE	POLAR	
Rain forest	Marine west coast	Subarctic	Highland
Desert	Steppe	Tundra	
Savanna	Humid continential	Polar icecaps	
	Humid subtropical		
	Mediterranean		

Visual Summary

To complete this summary, circle the correct word or phrase. Then, use the key below to check your answers. You can use this page to review the main concepts of the lesson.

Climate

Rain   Water vapor   Wind

Temperature and precipitation are used to describe climate.

23 Climate is the characteristic weather conditions in a place over a short/long period.

Winds transfer energy and moisture to new places.

24 Winds can affect the amount of precipitation in/elevation of an area.

Both topography and elevation affect climate.

25 Temperatures decrease as elevation increases/decreases.

Large bodies of water and ocean currents both affect climate.

26 Large bodies of water affect the climate of nearby land when cool waters absorb energy as heat from the warm air/cold land.

There are three main climate zones and many subclimates within those zones.

27 The three main types of climate zones are polar, temperate, and equatorial/tropical.

28 The three main climate zones are determined by elevation/latitude.

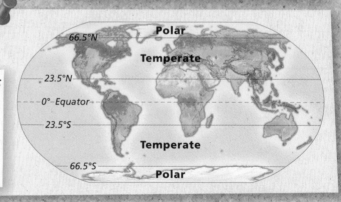

66.5°N   Polar
Temperate
23.5°N
0° Equator
23.5°S
Temperate
66.5°S   Polar

29 **Analyze** How does temperature change with elevation and latitude?

Lesson Review

Vocabulary

In your own words, define the following terms.

1 topography

_____

_____

2 climate

_____

_____

Key Concepts

Fill in the table below.

Factor	Effect on Climate
3 Identify Latitude	
4 Identify Elevation	
5 Identify Large bodies of water	
6 Identify Wind	

7 Explain What provides Great Britain with a moderate climate? How?

_____

_____

8 Identify What are two characteristics used to describe the climate of an area?

_____

_____

Critical Thinking

Use the image below to answer the following question.

9 Explain Location A receives nearly 200 cm of rain each year, while Location B receives only 30 cm. Explain why Location A gets so much more rain. Use the words *rain shadow* and *precipitation* in your answer.

_____

_____

_____

_____

_____

_____

10 Analyze What climate zone are you in if the temperatures are always very warm? Where is this zone located on Earth?

_____

11 Analyze How does the sun's energy affect the climate of an area?

_____

_____

_____

J. Marshall Shepherd

METEOROLOGIST AND CLIMATOLOGIST

J. Marshall Shepherd

Dr. Marshall Shepherd, who works at the University of Georgia, has been interested in weather since he made his own weather-collecting instruments for a school science project. Although the instruments he uses today, like computers and satellites, are much larger and much more powerful than the ones he made in school, they give him some of the same information.

In his work, Dr. Shepherd tries to understand weather events, such as hurricanes and thunderstorms, and relate them to current weather and climate change. He once led a team that used space-based radar to measure rainfall over urban areas. The measurements confirmed that the areas downwind of major cities experience more rainfall in summer than other areas in the same region. He explained that the excess heat retained by buildings and roads changes the way the air circulates, and this causes rain clouds to form.

While the most familiar field of meteorology is weather forecasting, research meteorology is also used in air pollution control, weather control, agricultural planning, climate change studies, and even criminal and civil investigations.

Social Studies Connection

An almanac is a type of calendar that contains various types of information, including weather forecasts and astronomical data, for every day of the year. Many people used almanacs before meteorologists started to forecast the weather. Use an almanac from the library or the Internet to find out what the weather was on the day that you were born.

JOB BOARD

Atmospheric Scientist

What You'll Do: Collect and analyze data on Earth's air pressure, humidity, and winds to make short-range and long-range weather forecasts. Work around the clock during weather emergencies like hurricanes and tornadoes.

Where You Might Work: Weather data collecting stations, radio and television stations, or private consulting firms.

Education: A bachelor's degree in meteorology, or in a closely related field with courses in meteorology, is required. A master's degree is necessary for some jobs.

Airplane Pilot

What You'll Do: Fly airplanes containing passengers or cargo, or for crop dusting, search and rescue, or fire-fighting. Before flights, check the plane's control equipment and weather conditions. Plan a safe route. Pilots communicate with air traffic control during flight to ensure a safe flight and fill out paperwork after the flight.

Where You Might Work: Flying planes for airlines, the military, radio and tv stations, freight companies, flight schools, farms, national parks, or other businesses that use airplanes.

Education: Most pilots will complete a four-year college degree before entering a pilot program. Before pilots become certified and take to the skies, they need a pilot license and many hours of flight time and training.

Snow Plow Operator

What You'll Do: In areas that receive snowfall, prepare the roads by spreading a mixture of sand and salt on the roads when snow is forecast. After a snowfall, drive snow plows to clear snow from roads and walkways.

Where You Might Work: For public organizations or private companies in cities and towns that receive snowfall.

Education: In most states, there is no special license needed, other than a driver's license.

Indiana Weather and Climate

ESSENTIAL QUESTION

What are the weather and climate like in Indiana?

By the end of this lesson, you should be able to describe Indiana's weather and climate.

This winter storm is bringing snow to much of Indiana. It might even produce a blizzard. Indiana has a wide range of weather, including blizzards, thunderstorms, and warm, sunny days.

⊙ Houghton Mifflin Harcourt Publishing Company • Image Credits: (bkgd) ©Frank Cezus/Photographer's Choice/Getty Images; (c) ©NOAA

Indiana Standards

8.2.5 Describe the conditions that cause Indiana weather and weather-related events such as tornadoes, lake effect snow, blizzards, thunderstorms, and flooding.

Engage Your Brain

1 Describe Fill in the blank with the word or phrase that you think correctly completes the following sentences.

Most thunderstorms in Indiana happen during

the _____

Blizzards are _____ storms

that happen during the _____

Indiana has _____ distinct seasons.

Temperatures in the northern part of the state

generally are _____ than temperatures in the southern part of the state.

2 Create Draw a sketch of your neighborhood during the season of your choice. Then write a caption that describes how that season affects your neighborhood.

Active Reading

3 Apply Use context clues to write your own definitions for the words *contribute* and *dominate*.

Example sentence
Factors that <u>contribute</u> to the climate of a region include latitude and distance from large bodies of water.

contribute

_____

_____

Example sentence
Polar air masses <u>dominate</u> the weather of the northern states.

dominate

_____

_____

Vocabulary Terms

- lake-effect snow
- blizzzard

4 Identify As you read, place a question mark next to any words that you don't understand. When you finish reading the lesson, go back and review the text that you marked. If the information is still confusing, consult a classmate or a teacher.

Today's Forecast: Mixed

What is the weather like in Indiana?

Recall that weather is the state of the atmosphere at a given time and place. Midwestern states generally experience a mix of weather, and Indiana is no exception. One day might be sunny and dry. The next day might be cloudy and wet. The weather most days is relatively mild. But Indiana can have severe weather any time of year.

Active Reading **5 Identify** As you read, underline the characteristics of the different kinds of weather that occur in Indiana.

Thunderstorms and Tornadoes

Indiana has about 30 to 50 thunderstorm days each year. Most happen between May and August. Some states have fewer than 10 thunderstorm days and other states have more than 90. So, Indiana has an average number of thunderstorms each year.

The state has an above average number of tornadoes, however. Indiana is the sixth most tornado-prone state, and many scientists consider it part of Tornado Alley. These powerful storms can occur in any part of the state.

Flooding

Floods are linked to heavy rains that occur during severe storms. A *flash flood* is a flood that occurs with little or no warning in which water levels rise quite rapidly.

According to the National Weather Service, flash flooding in Indiana is most common in late spring and summer. Some of the worst flooding in Indiana history happened in June 2008. Up to 280 mm (11 in) of rain fell in parts of Indiana in a 24-hour period. About one-third of Indiana counties were declared disaster areas.

Floods occur at lower elevations, especially near bodies of water.

Lake-effect Snow

If you look at a map of Indiana, you'll notice that part of the state borders Lake Michigan. During the winter, this area can experience lake-effect snow. **Lake-effect snow** is a weather phenomenon that occurs when cold, dry air passes over a large body of water. The air picks up moisture, and then drops it as heavy snowfall.

Lake-effect snow occurs mainly near the Great Lakes. Lake-effect snow events happen because of temperature differences between cold, dry air moving down from Canada and the warmer air above the water surface. As the cold air moves over the water, it becomes warmer and wetter. The warm air rises and water vapor condenses, forming clouds. The clouds dump the moisture as snow over the lake and land downwind of the lake. Parts of northern Indiana can receive about 196 cm (77 in) of lake-effect snow each year. The term *snowbelt* is used for areas that are affected by lake-effect snow events.

Blizzards

In addition to lake-effect snow, Indiana has blizzards. A **blizzard** is a storm that produces large amounts of snow or blowing snow, has winds of at least 56 kph (35 mph), and low visibility for at least three hours. Frostbite and hypothermia are two dangers due to the strong winds and cold temperatures of blizzards. One of the worst blizzards in Indiana occurred in 1978. A wind chill factor of –46 °C (–50 °F) was recorded in Indianapolis. Winds reached 88 kph (55 mph), and more than 37.5 cm (15 in) of snow fell.

Think Outside the Book

6 Research Find out about a severe weather event that happened in your area. When did the event happen? How did it impact your area in terms of property damage or environmental changes?

Visualize It!

7 Analyze Would lake-effect snow form if the air above the surface of the water were the same temperature as the cold air moving across the water? Explain your answer.

Lake-effect snow forms when cold, dry, arctic air moves across a large body of water. The air picks up moisture and drops it as snow over nearby areas.

Spring into Summer

What is the climate like in Indiana during spring and summer?

The term *climate* describes the average weather conditions in an area over a long period of time. Indiana's location on the North American continent determines its climate. Indiana has a humid continental climate. A humid continental climate is usually found in middle latitudes where cold, dry, arctic air meets warm, moist, tropical air.

In general, Indiana has four distinct seasons with marked temperature differences between the warmest and coldest months. Nearby Lake Michigan has a moderating effect on the climate of northern Indiana. During spring and summer, Indiana's weather is dominated by the clash of cold, arctic air that makes its way down from Canada and warm, moist air that makes its way up from the Gulf of Mexico.

Active Reading **8 Identify** Underline the average temperatures in different parts of Indiana during spring and summer.

Spring Is Often Stormy

Most precipitation in Indiana happens during spring. On average, the southern part of the state receives more precipitation than the northern part of the state does. Spring storms generally occur when warm, moist air from the Gulf of Mexico meets cold, dry air driven down from Canada by the jet stream. Most thunderstorms occur during the months of March and April. April also is peak tornado time in Indiana.

Temperatures generally are cooler in the north than in the south. South Bend in northern Indiana has an average temperature of almost 3 °C (37 °F) during March, the first month of spring. Evansville in the south has an average March temperature of nearly 8 °C (46 °F).

Summer Is Often Hot

Summers can be hot and humid in Indiana. This is particularly true in the southernmost part of the state, which borders on a humid, subtropical climate. Average high temperatures in Evansville, for example, reach 26 °C (79 °F) in July, the height of summer. In contrast, average high temperatures in South Bend for July are a more comfortable 23 °C (73 °F). The interplay of dry, arctic air and warm, moist, tropical air continues throughout the summer. If polar air masses dominate, summers tend to be cooler than normal. If tropical air masses dominate, summers tend to be quite hot. Levels of precipitation decrease slightly from spring to summer, and mid-summer droughts are not uncommon.

This graph shows average temperatures and precipitation during the spring and summer months for Indianapolis, which is located in central Indiana.

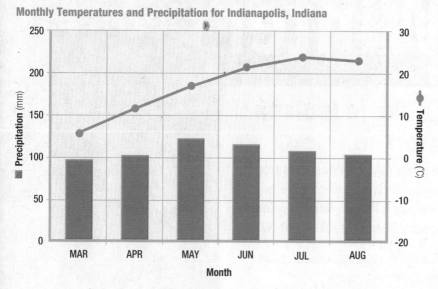

Monthly Temperatures and Precipitation for Indianapolis, Indiana

Source: Average Temperatures and Precipitation 1971–2000, National Climatic Data Center

9 Identify What is the wettest month in Indianapolis during spring and summer?

_____

10 Analyze Describe the temperature pattern in Indianapolis from March through August.

_____

_____

_____

11 Predict Based on these data, during which month would Indianapolis most likely experience a drought? Explain your answer.

_____

_____

_____

_____

_____

Average July Temperatures in Indiana

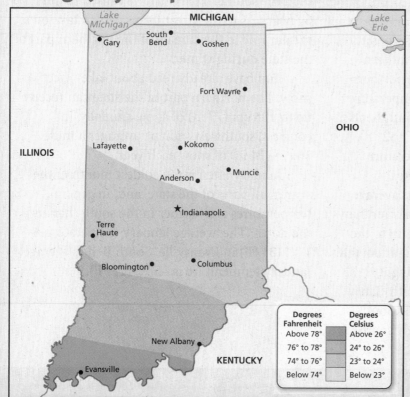

Visualize It!

12 Analyze Study the map and its key. How do average summer temperatures differ in different parts of Indiana?

_____

_____

_____

_____

_____

_____

_____

_____

_____

_____

Fall into Winter

What is the climate like in Indiana during fall and winter?

The clash of contrasting air masses, latitude, and nearness to the Great Lakes—the same factors that affect Indiana's climate in spring and summer—are in play during fall and winter. For many state residents, fall is a favorite season. Read on to find out why.

> **Active Reading** **13 Identify** Underline the average temperatures in different parts of Indiana during fall and winter.

Fall Is Often Sunny and Mild

Summers can be hot and humid in Indiana. But when summer turns to fall, temperature and humidity levels drop. The sun shines, too. Fall is the least cloudy season in the state.

On average, Indiana gets about 7.6 cm (3 in) of rainfall during the fall. That compares to nearly 12.7 cm (5 in) in the spring. Temperatures are mild throughout the state, with southern Indiana generally being warmer than northern Indiana. Evansville has an average temperature of nearly 14 °C (57 °F) in October. South Bend's average October temperature is 11 °C (52 °F).

This north-south trend in temperature varies somewhat due to the Great Lakes. South Bend is near Lake Michigan. Its average temperatures in fall and winter are warmer than those of Kokomo, about 133 km (83 mi) to the south. The influence of Lake Michigan moderates the temperature of South Bend, making it warmer than places slightly to the south. The opposite is true in spring and summer. South Bend is a bit cooler than places slightly south because of the lake's moderating effect.

Winter Is Often Cloudy and Cold

Winter is a cold, cloudy time of year in Indiana. About 70 percent of winter days are cloudy, compared to only 35 percent of summer days. The northern part of the state usually is cloudier than the southern part. This is caused mainly by nearness to the Great Lakes, which take on a greater role in the climate of the northern part of the state during winter.

You have already read about lake-effect snow. The northern part of the state can receive up to 196 cm (77 in) of snow annually. In contrast, southwest Indiana averages a mere 36 cm (14 in) of snow each year.

January often is the coldest month of the year in all parts of the state, and, in general, temperatures are warmer in the south than in the north. The average January temperature is 1 °C (31 °F) in Evansville. South Bend's average January temperature is –5 °C (23 °F).

Do the Math You Try It

This graph shows average temperatures and precipitation during the fall and winter months for Indianapolis, which is located in central Indiana.

Monthly Temperatures and Precipitation for Indianapolis, Indiana

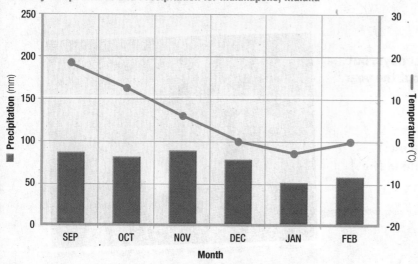

Source: Average Temperatures and Precipitation 1971–2000, National Climatic Data Center

14 Identify What is the driest month in Indianapolis during fall and winter?

_____

15 Calculate What is the mean temperature in Indianapolis from September to February?

. . . .

Solve

A. Identify the average temperature for each month in the data set.

September =

October =

November =

December =

January =

February =

B. Add these numbers together.

C. Divide by the number of months in the data set (6).

Average January Temperatures in Indiana

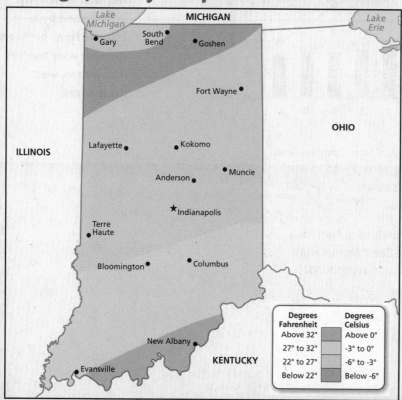

Visualize It! Inquiry

16 Infer Notice that the region around Gary and South Bend has slightly higher January temperatures than does the region to the south. What do you think might be influencing the temperatures in this region? Explain your reasoning.

_____

_____

_____

_____

_____

_____

_____

Visual Summary

To complete this summary, check the box that indicates true or false. Then, use the key below to check your answers. You can use this page to review the main concepts of the lesson.

Weather and Climate in Indiana

The weather in Indiana is mild most days, but severe weather can occur throughout the year.

T F

17 ☐ ☐ Indiana is the sixth most tornado-prone state in the United States.

Indiana has a humid continental climate and experiences four distinct seasons.

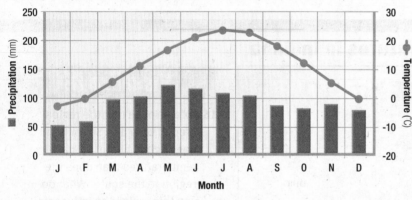

Monthly Temperatures and Precipitation for Indianapolis, Indiana

Source: Average Temperatures and Precipitation 1971–2000, National Climatic Data Center

T F

18 ☐ ☐ The climate of Indiana is heavily influenced by interactions between cold, dry air masses and warm, wet air masses.

Answers: 17 F; 18 T

19 **Predict** How would your life change if Indiana did not have four distinct seasons? What would it be like if temperature and precipitation remained nearly the same year-round?

Lesson Review

Vocabulary

Circle the term that best completes the following sentences.

1 *Weather/Climate* describes the state of the atmosphere in Indiana at a given time.

2 *Weather/Climate* describes temperature, precipitation, and other atmospheric conditions over a long period of time.

3 *Blizzards/Lake-effect snow events* have strong winds and low visibility.

4 *Blizzards/Lake-effect snow events* occur in the northern part of Indiana because it is located near Lake Michigan.

Key Concepts

5 Compare How do spring and fall differ in Indiana?

_____
_____
_____

6 Categorize What types of severe weather are most likely to occur in Indiana during summer? What types of severe weather are most likely to occur during winter?

_____
_____
_____
_____
_____

7 Apply City A and City B are both in Indiana. City A is 100 km north of City B. However, City A is warmer in the winter and cooler in the summer than City B. What factor could contribute to this difference in climate?

_____
_____
_____

Critical Thinking

Use the information in the table to answer the following question.

Average Climate Data for Indiana				
	A	**B**	**C**	**D**
Temperature	24 °C	0 °C	12 °C	14 °C
Precipitation	10 cm	7.4 cm	10.7 cm	8.2 cm

8 Conclude This chart shows average seasonal data for Indiana. Decide which season each set of data represents. Fill in your answers in the spaces provided below.

A. _____

B. _____

C. _____

D. _____

9 Infer Fall generally is the sunniest time of the year in Indiana. What can you infer about interactions between conflicting air masses in fall? Explain your answer.

_____
_____
_____
_____

10 Produce Imagine you are a meteorologist employed by a television news program in northern Indiana. Write a script explaining the formation of lake-effect snow for your viewing audience.

_____
_____
_____
_____
_____
_____
_____

My Notes

Unit 4 Summary

What Influences Weather? → **Elements of Weather**

averaged
over time
determine

The Water Cycle

Climate

Severe Weather and Weather Safety — are connected to → **Indiana Weather**

1 Interpret The Graphic Organizer above shows that the water cycle influences weather and climate. Explain why this is true.

_____

_____

_____

_____

_____

2 Explain Suppose you were writing a weather safety brochure for Indiana residents alone. Explain what type of information would you include in the brochure and why.

_____

_____

_____

_____

3 Distinguish Describe the difference between weather and climate.

_____

_____

_____

_____

_____

4 Justify *Weather safety* includes preparing for certain types of good weather. Explain why this is true.

_____

_____

_____

_____

_____

ISTEP+ Review

Name _____

Multiple Choice

1 Latitude plays a major role in determining the climate, or long-term weather patterns, of an area. Because of differences in the intensity of solar energy, climates in higher latitudes are generally colder than climates in lower latitudes. What causes some areas of Earth to receive less intense solar energy than others?

A. the mass of Earth

B. the elevation of Earth

C. the curve of Earth

D. the density of Earth

2 Kevin was carrying out the following steps as part of an experiment.

Step	Procedure
1	Fill a tray with cold water.
2	Add several drops of food coloring to a glass of warm water.
3	Slowly pour the warm water into the tray.
4	Observe what happens to the water in the tray.

What was the TOPIC of this experiment?

A. the water cycle

B. the circulation of global winds

C. the formation of ocean currents

D. the formation of a hurricane over water

3 One type of weather event develops when some of the warm air in a thunderstorm rises into high-altitude, horizontal winds. This causes the rising air to rotate. What type of weather event is being described?

A. hurricane

B. lightning

C. thunder

D. tornado

4 Which conditions are associated with a BLIZZARD?

A. lightning and thunder

B. low visibility and large amounts of hail

C. low visibility and large amounts of snow

D. strong winds and storm surges

ISTEP+ Review

5 The sun's energy influences climate in different ways. For example, the latitudes at the equator receive more intense energy from the sun and therefore have warmer temperatures. How does the sun's energy MOST DIRECTLY influence precipitation in an area?

A. The sun's energy drives the water cycle, which determines precipitation.

B. The sun's energy creates surface currents in oceans that bring precipitation to different areas.

C. The sun's energy controls the amount of condensation and therefore precipitation.

D. The sun's energy powers the water cycle by causing runoff, which leads to precipitation.

6 The following graph shows the temperature in Tallahassee at different times of a day. Each temperature was determined at the same location.

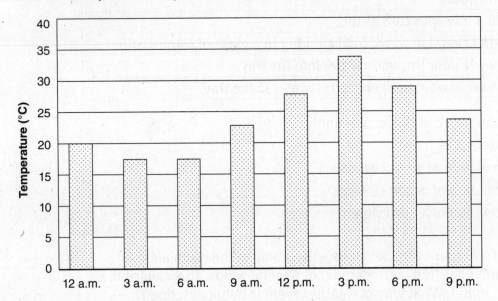

What is MOST responsible for the warmer temperatures at midday?

A. the sun

B. the wind

C. the altitude

D. the dew point

7 Tania drew the following diagram to represent the water cycle.

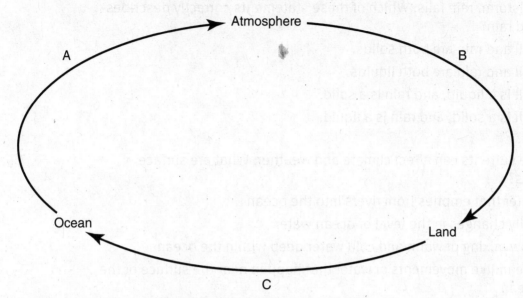

Tania wants to improve her diagram by adding labels to the arrows. What would be the BEST label for arrow A?

A. evaporation

B. precipitation

C. runoff

D. transpiration

8 Which conditions would MOST LIKELY lead to the formation of lake-effect snow?

A. A cold, dry air mass moves over a relatively warm body of water.

B. A warm, maritime air mass clashes with a cool, continental air mass.

C. A low-pressure system forms over a tropical ocean.

D. High-altitude winds cause the rising air in a thunderstorm to rotate.

9 On an island near the equator, the sun's energy causes ocean water to evaporate during the day. In the afternoon, heavy rains fall. This process is repeated during the summer months. What does this example BEST show?

A. how most water on Earth is in the form of water vapor

B. how the sun is the main source of energy for the water cycle

C. how land is the main source of water during the water cycle

D. how the ocean is large enough that it never runs out of water

10 During a winter storm, Annabelle observes hail falling in her yard. After the hailstorm, rain falls. Which of these statements correctly describes hail and rain?

   A. Hail and rain are both solids.

   B. Hail and rain are both liquids.

   C. Hail is a liquid, and rain is a solid.

   D. Hail is a solid, and rain is a liquid.

11 Surface currents can affect climate and weather. What are surface currents?

   A. water that empties from rivers into the ocean

   B. daily changes in the level of ocean water

   C. slow mixing of warm and cold water deep within the ocean

   D. streamlike movements of water that happen near the surface of the ocean

12 Surface currents carry warm water or cool water to different locations. Which of the following would be MOST STRONGLY influenced by a surface current?

   A. the wind speed over land located 50 km from the ocean

   B. the pressure of air above a coastal mountain range

   C. the humidity of air above a tropical zone

   D. the temperature of air above the surface current

13 Condensation is part of the water cycle. During condensation, water vapor cools and changes from a gas to a liquid. What happens when this process occurs near Earth's surface?

   A. Fog forms.

   B. Precipitation falls.

   C. Water runs off into lakes and streams.

   D. Water evaporates from oceans and lakes.

14 The following table shows the temperature and precipitation levels of four different cities on the same day. In only one city on this day, it snowed.

	City A	City B	City C	City D
Low Temperature (°C)	15	19	−9	−11
High Temperature (°C)	22	26	−3	−5
Precipitation (mm)	14	11	25	0

Which city experienced snow on this day?

A. City A

B. City B

C. City C

D. City D

Constructed Response

15 Describe the temperature and density of air at the EQUATOR.

_____

_____

Describe the temperature and density of air at the POLES.

_____

_____

Explain what causes this difference in air temperature and density.

_____

_____

_____

Extended Response

16 What is weather?

_____

_____

_____

Describe the following elements of weather.

Temperature: _____

_____

_____

Humidity: _____

_____

_____

Precipitation: _____

_____

_____

Human Impact on Earth

Core Standard

Describe how human activities have changed the land, water, and atmosphere.

Human actions, such as cutting down trees to build large housing developments, affect the surrounding ecosystem.

Factories cause pollution.

What do you think?

Human activities can affect Earth's air, water, and land resources in a variety of ways. What are some specific ways in which human activities affect the environment?

CITIZEN SCIENCE
Investigating Water Resources

Water is an important natural resource. Over one half of Indiana's population relies on underground aquifers for drinking and household uses.

1 Think About It

A What makes fresh surface water and groundwater such valuable resources?

_____

_____

_____

B How does human activity affect the availability of fresh water?

_____

_____

_____

Rain barrels collect rainwater for home use.

A Describe the environment that surrounds your local water source.

_____

_____

B Describe threats to your local water supply and how your water supply can be protected.

Threats to Water Supply	Ways to Protect Water Supply

Where does your water come from?

With a partner, research the source of the water used by your community. Consider contacting your local utility company for information.

Things to Consider

☐ How do our water supplies get replenished?

☐ What are the most common uses for water?

C Choose one of the ideas for protecting the water supply that you listed above. Describe how this method of protection might be implemented by your community.

_____

_____

_____

_____

Take It Home

Trace the water used in your home to its source. Use a map to determine the route by which the water you use must be transported from its source.

Natural Resources

ESSENTIAL QUESTION

What are Earth's natural resources?

By the end of this lesson, you should be able to understand the types and uses of Earth's natural resources.

Light produced from electrical energy helps people see at night. Some regions of Earth are still mostly dark once the sun sets. The people living in some of these regions rely more on sunlight.

Indiana Standards

8.2.7 Recognize that some of Earth's resources are finite and describe how recycling, reducing consumption and the development of alternatives can reduce the rate of their depletion.

Engage Your Brain

1 Predict Check T or F to show whether you think each statement is true or false.

T   F

☐   ☐   Energy from the sun can be used to make electricity.

☐   ☐   All of Earth's resources will last forever.

☐   ☐   Food, cloth, rope, lumber, paper, and rubber come from plants.

☐   ☐   Human activity can negatively affect Earth's resources.

2 Describe Name one item that you use everyday. Describe how you think that item is made.

_____

_____

_____

_____

_____

_____

_____

Active Reading

3 Apply Many scientific words, such as *natural* and *resource*, also have everyday meanings. Use context clues to write your own definition for each underlined word.

Oranges are a <u>natural</u> source of vitamin C.

natural:

_____

_____

His curly hair is <u>natural</u>.

natural:

_____

_____

A dictionary is a useful <u>resource</u> for learning words.

resource:

_____

_____

In the desert, water is a limited <u>resource</u>.

resource:

_____

_____

Vocabulary Terms

- natural resource
- renewable resource
- nonrenewable resource
- fossil fuel
- material resource
- energy resource

4 Identify This list contains the key terms you'll learn in this lesson. As you read, circle the definition of each term.

It's Only Natural

What are natural resources?

What do the water you drink, the paper you write on, the gasoline used in cars, and the air you breathe have in common? All of these come from Earth's natural resources. A **natural resource** is any natural material that is used by humans, such as air, soil, minerals, water, petroleum, plants, and animals.

The Earth's natural resources provide everything needed for life. The energy we get from many of these resources, such as petroleum and wind, originally comes from the sun's energy. The atmosphere contains the air we breathe, controls air temperatures, and produces rain. Rainfall from the atmosphere renews the water in oceans, rivers, lakes, and streams in the water cycle. In turn, these water sources provide food and water for drinking, cleaning, and other uses. The Earth's soil provides nutrients and a place for plants to grow. Plants provide food for some animals and humans. Petroleum is used to make fuels for cars and other machines, and also to make plastics. All of these natural resources are used to make products that make people's lives more convenient.

Active Reading

5 Identify As you read, underline examples of natural resources.

Bauxite is a rock that is used to make aluminum.

Visualize It!

6 Illustrate Draw or label the missing natural resources.

A

How can we categorize natural resources?

There are many different types of natural resources. Some can be replaced more quickly than others. Thus, a natural resource may be categorized as a renewable resource or a nonrenewable resource.

Think Outside the Book Inquiry

7 Debate Research and summarize why water can be a renewable or nonrenewable resource. Discuss your points with a classmate.

Renewable

Some natural resources can be replaced in a relatively short time. A **renewable resource** is a natural resource that can be replaced at the same rate at which the resource is consumed. Solar energy, water, and air are considered renewable resources. However, renewable resources can be used up too quickly. For example, trees are renewable. But some forests are being cut down faster than new forests can grow to replace them. Some renewable resources are considered to be *inexhaustible resources* (in'•ig•ZAW•stuh•buhl REE•sawrs•iz) because the resources can never be used up. Solar energy and wind energy from the sun are examples of these resources.

Nonrenewable

A **nonrenewable resource** is a resource that forms at a rate that is much slower than the rate at which it is consumed. Some natural resources, like minerals, form very slowly. Iron ore, aluminum, and copper are important minerals. A **fossil fuel** is a nonrenewable resource formed from buried remains of plants and animals that lived long ago. For example, coal is a fossil fuel that takes millions of years to form. Oil and natural gas are other types of fossil fuels. Once these resources are used up, humans will have to find other resources to use instead. Some renewable resources, such as water, may also be considered nonrenewable if they are not used wisely.

8 Compare List some examples of renewable and nonrenewable resources.

Renewable Resources	Nonrenewable Resources

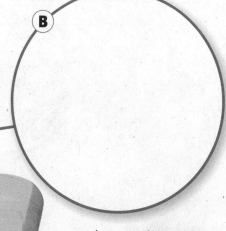

Natural fibers from cotton plants are processed to make fabric.

B

Material World

How do we use natural resources?

When you turn on a computer, take a shower, or eat food, you are using natural resources. A variety of natural resources are used to make common objects. The energy required for many of the activities that we do also comes from natural resources. Earth's natural resources can be divided into material resources and energy resources depending on how the resource is used.

As Material Resources

A **material resource** is a natural resource that humans use to make objects or to consume as food or drink. These resources can come from Earth's atmosphere, crust, fresh waters and oceans, and from organisms, such as plants and animals.

Earth's atmosphere provides the oxygen needed by plants and animals, including humans. Minerals and rock in Earth's crust are used for construction and other industries. Salt, a mineral, comes from ocean water. Fresh water sources and the oceans provide drinking water and food. Some plants, such as cotton, produce fibers that are woven into cloth or braided into ropes. Trees supply fruit crops, lumber, and paper. The sap of some trees is used to make rubber and maple syrup. Animals provide meat, leather, and dairy and egg products.

10 Apply What other items can you think of that are made of wood?

_____

_____

_____

_____

Cedar tree

Trees are a material resource when they are used to make products, such as this guitar.

As Energy Resources

Energy resources drive the world. An **energy resource** is a natural resource that humans use to generate energy. Most of the energy used by humans comes from fossil fuels. When fossil fuels are burned, they release energy, usually in the form of heat. Power plants and machines use that heat to produce mechanical and electrical energy. In turn, electrical energy is used to power lights and most of the appliances we use every day.

Other energy resources include moving water, solar power, and wind power. Trees supply fuel in the form of heat. Horses, camels, and other animals are used as transportation in some places. All of these resources are renewable energy resources.

Trees are energy resources when they are burned in a campfire.

11 Infer What two types of energy are generated from fire?

_____

_____

12 List Think about all the products you use every day. Fill in the chart with three of these products and the resources needed to make them or use them.

Product	Material and Energy Resources Needed
computer	plastic, metal, glass, electricity

Visual Summary

To complete this summary, circle the correct word. Then use the key below to check your answers. You can use this page to review the main concepts of the lesson.

Natural resources can be categorized as nonrenewable resources or renewable resources depending on how quickly they can be replaced.

13 Bauxite is a nonrenewable / renewable resource.

14 Cotton plants are a nonrenewable / renewable resource.

Natural Resources

A material resource can be used to make objects or to consume as food or drink. An energy resource is used to generate energy.

15 Trees that are used to make paper products are material resources / energy resources.

Answers: 13 nonrenewable; 14 renewable; 15 material resources

16 Summarize Explain how a natural resource could be used as both a material resource and an energy resource.

Lesson Review

Vocabulary

Fill in the blank with the term that best completes the following sentences.

1 Nonrenewable and renewable are the two

categories of _____

2 A(n) _____ can be used to
make objects.

Key Concepts

3 Evaluate Why are natural resources important
to humans?

_____

_____

_____

4 Identify Give one example of a material
resource and one example of an energy
resource.

_____

_____

5 Compare How do nonrenewable resources and
renewable resources differ?

_____

_____

_____

_____

6 List Name two material resources, one
renewable and one nonrenewable. Explain your
answer.

_____

_____

_____

_____

_____

Critical Thinking

Use the graph to answer the following three
questions.

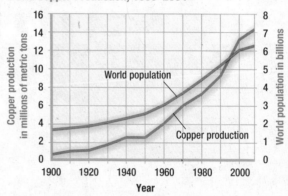

World Copper Production, 1900–2004

Sources: U.S. Bureau of Mines, U.S. Geological Survey,
and U.S. Census Bureau

7 Interpret In what year was the most copper
produced?

_____

8 Analyze What is the trend in copper
production over the past 100 years?

_____

_____

_____

9 Apply Copper is used in making electronic
devices. Describe how the use of copper might
change as copper becomes more scarce.

_____

_____

_____

_____

10 Infer How does human activity affect Earth's
natural resources? Explain.

_____

_____

_____

_____

Human Impact on Land

Human activities can carve up land features. A tunnel was cut into this mountain in Zion National Park, Utah, so that people may move around easily.

ESSENTIAL QUESTION

What impact can human activities have on land resources?

By the end of this lesson, you should be able to identify the impact that human activity has on Earth's land.

Indiana Standards

8.2.6 Identify, explain, and discuss some effects human activities have on the biosphere, such as air, soil, light, noise and water pollution.

8.2.8 Explain that human activities, beginning with the earliest herding and agricultural activities, have drastically changed the environment and have affected the capacity of the environment to support native species. Explain current efforts to reduce and eliminate these impacts and encourage sustainability.

Engage Your Brain

1 Predict Check T or F to show whether you think each statement is true or false.

T   F

☐ ☐ Urban areas have more open land than rural areas do.

☐ ☐ Many building materials are made from land resources.

☐ ☐ Soil provides habitat for plants but not animals.

☐ ☐ Soil can erode when trees are removed from an area.

2 Illustrate Draw a picture of an object or material that is taken from the land and that is commercially important.

Active Reading

3 Synthesize You can often define an unknown word if you know the meaning of its word parts. Use the word parts to make an educated guess about the meaning of the words *land degradation* and *deforestation*.

Word part	Meaning
degrade	to damage something
deforest	to remove trees from an area
-ation	action or process

Vocabulary Terms

- urbanization
- land degradation
- deforestation
- desertification

4 Apply As you learn the definition of each vocabulary term in this lesson, create your own definition or sketch to help you remember the meaning of the term.

land degradation:

_____

_____

deforestation:

_____

_____

Land of Plenty

Why is land important?

It is hard to imagine human life without land. Land supplies a solid surface for buildings and roads. The soil in land provides nutrients for plants and hiding places for animals. Minerals below the land's surface can be used for construction materials. Fossil fuels underground can be burned to provide energy. Land and its resources affect every aspect of human life.

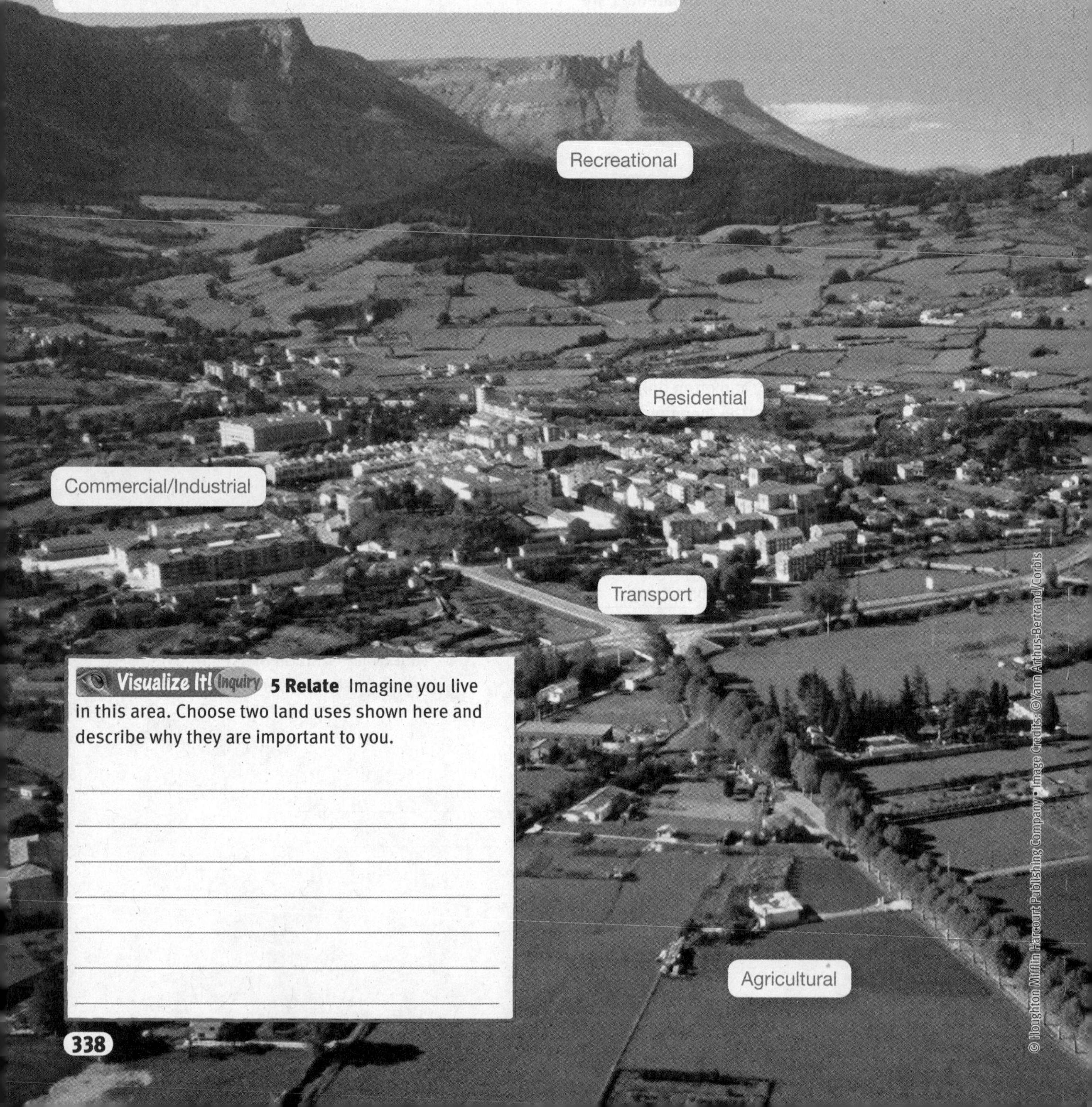

Recreational

Residential

Commercial/Industrial

Transport

Agricultural

Visualize It! (Inquiry) **5 Relate** Imagine you live in this area. Choose two land uses shown here and describe why they are important to you.

_____

_____

_____

_____

_____

_____

What are the different types of land use?

We live on land in urban or rural areas. Cities and towns are urban areas. Rural areas are open lands that may be used for farming. Humans use land in many ways. We use natural areas for *recreation*. We use roads that are built on land for *transport*. We grow crops and raise livestock on *agricultural* land. We live in *residential* areas. We build *commercial* businesses on land and extract resources such as metals and water from the land.

Recreational

Natural areas are places that humans have left alone or restored to a natural state. These wild places include forests, grasslands, and desert areas. People use natural areas for hiking, bird-watching, mountain-biking, hunting, and other fun or recreational activities.

Transport

A large network of roads and train tracks connect urban and rural areas all across the country. Roads in the U.S. highway system cover 4 million miles of land. Trucks carry goods on these highways and smaller vehicles carry passengers. Railroads carrying freight or passengers use over 120,000 miles of land for tracks. Roads and train tracks are often highly concentrated in urban areas.

Agricultural

Much of the open land in rural areas is used for agriculture. Crops such as corn, soybeans, and wheat are grown on large, open areas of land. Land is also needed to raise and feed cattle and other livestock. Agricultural land is open, but very different from the natural areas that it has replaced. Farmland generally contains only one or two types of plants such as corn or cotton. Natural grasslands, forests, and other natural areas contain many species of plants and animals.

Active Reading **6 Identify** As you read, underline the ways rural areas differ from urban areas.

Residential

Where do you call home? People live in both rural and urban areas. Rural areas have large areas of open land and low densities of people. Urban areas have dense human populations and small areas of open land. This means that more people live in a square mile of an urban area than live in a square mile of a rural area. **Urbanization** is the growth of urban areas caused by people moving into cities. When cities increase in size, the population of rural areas near the city may decrease. When an area becomes urbanized, its natural land surface is replaced by buildings, parking lots, and roads. City parks, which contain natural surfaces, may also be built in urban areas.

Commercial and Industrial

As cities or towns expand, commercial businesses are built too, and replace rural or natural areas. Industrial businesses also use land resources. For example, paper companies and furniture manufacturers use wood from trees harvested on forest land. Cement companies, fertilizer manufacturers, and steel manufacturers use minerals that are mined from below the land's surface. Commercial and industrial development usually includes development of roads or railways. Transporting goods to market forms the basis of commerce.

Active Reading

7 Identify What effects does urbanization have on land?

_____

_____

_____

_____

Why is soil important?

Soil is a mixture of mineral fragments, organic material, water, and air. Soil forms when rocks break down and dead organisms decay. There are many reasons why soil is important. Soil provides habitat for organisms such as plants, earthworms, fungi, and bacteria. Many plants get the water and nutrients they need from the soil. Because plants form the base of food webs, healthy soil is important for most land ecosystems. Healthy soil is also important for agricultural land, which supplies humans with food.

8 Identify As you read, underline the ways that soil is important to plants.

It Is a Habitat for Organisms

Earthworms, moles, badgers, and other burrowing animals live in soil. These animals also find food underground. *Decomposers* are organisms that break down dead animal and plant material, releasing the nutrients into the soil. Decomposers such as fungi and bacteria live in soil. Soil holds plant roots in place, providing support for the plant. In turn, plants are food for herbivores and are habitats for organisms such as birds and insects. Many animals on Earth depend on soil for shelter or food.

It Stores Water and Nutrients

Falling rain soaks into soil and is stored between soil particles. Different types of soil can store different amounts of water. Wetland soils, for example, store large amounts of water and reduce flooding. Soils are also part of the nutrient cycle. Plants take up nutrients and water stored in soil. Plants and animals that eat them die and are broken down by decomposers such as bacteria and earthworms. Nutrients are released back into the soil and the cycle starts again.

Visualize It!

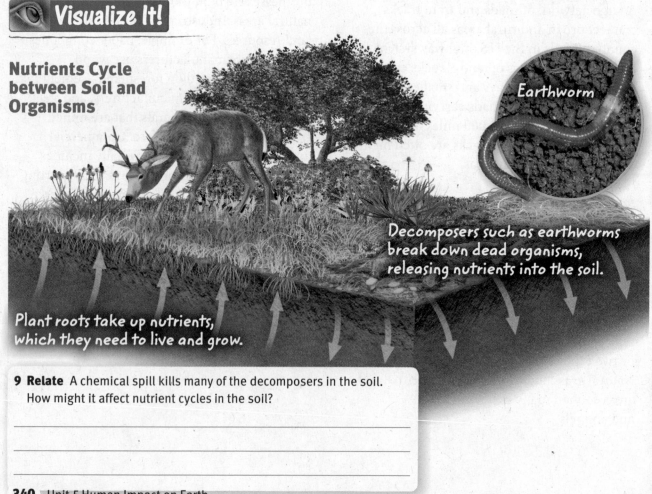

Nutrients Cycle between Soil and Organisms

Earthworm

Decomposers such as earthworms break down dead organisms, releasing nutrients into the soil.

Plant roots take up nutrients, which they need to live and grow.

9 Relate A chemical spill kills many of the decomposers in the soil. How might it affect nutrient cycles in the soil?

_____

_____

_____

Dust Bowl

In the 1930s, huge clouds of dusty soil rolled across the southern Great Plains of the United States. Areas that were once farmlands and homesteads were wiped out. What caused the soil to blow away?

Drought and Overuse

Farmers who settled in the southern Great Plains overplowed and overgrazed their land. When severe drought hit in 1931, topsoil dried out. Winds lifted the soil and carried it across the plains in huge storms that farmers called "black blizzards." The drought and dust storms continued for years.

Modern Day Dust Bowl

Today in northwest China another dust bowl is forming. Large areas of farmland were made there by clearing the natural vegetation and plowing the soil. Herds of sheep and cattle are overgrazing the land, and large dust storms are common.

Extend

Inquiry

10 Identify What type of land use by people contributed to the Dust Bowl? Does it remain a common use of land today?

11 Compare Research another area under threat from overuse that differs from the feature. What type of land use is causing the problem?

12 Illustrate Do one of the following to show how the Dust Bowl or the area you researched affected society: make a poster, write a play, write a song, or draw a cartoon strip. Present your findings to the class.

Footprints

How can human activities affect land and soil?

Human activities can have positive and negative effects on land and soil. Some activities restore land to its natural state, or increase the amount of fertile soil on land. Other activities can degrade land. **Land degradation** is the process by which human activity and natural processes damage land to the point that it can no longer support the local ecosystem. Urbanization, deforestation, and poor farming practices can all lead to land degradation.

Active Reading

14 Identify As you read, underline the effects that urbanization can have on land.

Urban Sprawl

When urbanization occurs at the edge of a city or town, it is called *urban sprawl*. Urban sprawl replaces forests, fields, and grasslands with houses, roads, schools, and shopping areas. Urban sprawl decreases the amount of farmland that is available for growing crops. It decreases the amount of natural areas that surround cities. It increases the amount of asphalt and concrete that covers the land. Rainwater runs off hard surfaces and into storm drains instead of soaking into the ground and filling aquifers. Rainwater runoff from urban areas can increase the erosion of nearby soils.

Erosion

Erosion (ih•ROH•zhuhn) is the process by which wind, water, or gravity transports soil and sediment from one place to another. Some type of erosion occurs on most land. However, erosion can speed up when land is degraded. Roots of trees and plants act as anchors to the soil. When land is cleared for farming, the trees and plants are removed and the soil is no longer protected. This exposes soil to blowing wind and running water that can wash away the soil, as shown in this photo.

Nutrient Depletion and Land Pollution

Crops use soil nutrients to grow. If the same crops are planted year after year, the same soil nutrients get used up. Plants need the right balance of nutrients to grow. Farmers can plant a different crop each year to reduce nutrient loss. Pollution from industrial activities can damage land. Mining wastes, gas and petroleum leaks, and chemical wastes can kill organisms in the soil. U.S. government programs such as Superfund help to clean up polluted land.

EPA QUANTA RESOURCES SUPERFUND SITE

WARNING : Hazardous substances present in soil and sediment. No Trespassing.

For further information call the U.S. Environmental Protection Agency (800) 346-5009

Desertification

When too many livestock are kept in one area, they can overgraze the area. Overgrazing removes the plants and roots that hold topsoil together. Overgrazing and other poor farming methods can cause desertification. **Desertification** (dih•zer•tuh•fih•KAY•shuhn) is the process by which land becomes more desertlike and unable to support life. Without plants, soil becomes dusty and prone to wind erosion. Deforestation and urbanization can also lead to desertification.

Deforestation

The removal of trees and other vegetation from an area is called **deforestation**. Logging for wood can cause deforestation. Surface mining causes deforestation by removing vegetation and soil to get to the minerals below. Deforestation also occurs in rain forests, as shown in the photo, when farmers cut or burn down trees so they can grow crops. Urbanization can cause deforestation when forests are replaced with buildings. Deforestation leads to increased soil erosion.

👁 Visualize It!

15 Relate How has human activity affected the forest in this photo?

_____

_____

_____

_____

_____

Visual Summary

To complete this summary, circle the correct word or phrase. Then use the key below to check your answers. You can use this page to review the main concepts of the lesson.

Humans use land in different ways.

16 Crops are grown on recreational/agricultural land.

Soil is important to all organisms, including humans.

17 Decomposers/plants that live in soil break down dead matter in the soil.

Human Impact on Land

Human activities can affect land and soil.

18 Poor farming practices and drought can lead to desertification/urbanization.

Answers: 16 agricultural; 17 decomposers; 18 desertification

19 Apply How could concentrating human populations in cities help to conserve agricultural and recreational lands?

Lesson Review

Vocabulary

Draw a line to connect the following terms to their definitions.

1 urbanization

2 deforestation

3 land degradation

4 desertification

A the removal of trees and other vegetation from an area

B the process by which land becomes more desertlike

C the process by which human activity can damage land

D the formation and growth of cities

Key Concepts

5 Contrast How are natural areas different from rural areas?

_____

_____

_____

_____

6 Relate How might deforestation lead to desertification?

_____

_____

_____

7 Relate Think of an animal that eats other animals. Why would soil be important to this animal?

_____

_____

_____

_____

Critical Thinking

Use this photo to answer the following questions.

8 Analyze What type of land degradation is occurring in this photo?

_____

9 Predict This type of soil damage can happen in urban areas too. Outline how urbanization could lead to this type of degradation.

_____

_____

_____

_____

_____

10 Apply What kinds of land uses are around your school? Write down each type of land use. Then describe how one of these land uses might affect natural systems.

_____

_____

_____

_____

_____

_____

_____

Human Impact on Water

ESSENTIAL QUESTION

What impact can human activities have on water resources?

By the end of this lesson, you should be able to explain the impacts that humans can have on the quality and supply of fresh water.

Humans and other organisms depend on clean water to survive. More than half of the material inside humans is water.

Indiana Standards

8.2.6 Identify, explain, and discuss some effects human activities have on the biosphere, such as air, soil, light, noise and water pollution.

8.2.8 Explain that human activities, beginning with the earliest herding and agricultural activities, have drastically changed the environment and have affected the capacity of the environment to support native species. Explain current efforts to reduce and eliminate these impacts and encourage sustainability.

Engage Your Brain

1 Analyze Write a list of the reasons humans need water. Next to this list, write a list of reasons fish need water. Are there similarities between your two lists?

2 Identify Circle the word that correctly completes the following sentences.
The man in this photo is testing *water/air* quality.
The flowing body of water next to the man is a *river/lake*.

Active Reading

3 Synthesize You can often define an unknown word if you know the meaning of its word parts. Use the word parts and the sentence below to make an educated guess about the meaning of the word *nonrenewable*.

Word part	Meaning
renew	restore, make like new
-able	able to be
non-	not

Example sentence
Some of Earth's <u>nonrenewable</u> resources include coal and oil.

nonrenewable:

_____

_____

_____

_____

Vocabulary Terms

- water pollution
- point-source pollution
- nonpoint-source pollution
- thermal pollution
- eutrophication
- potable
- reservoir

4 Identify This list contains the key terms you'll learn in this lesson. As you read, circle the definition of each term.

Water, Water

Close up of a mayfly larva

Organisms need clean water for life and good health. For example, young mayflies live in water, humans drink water, and brown pelicans eat fish they catch in water.

Why is water important?

Earth is the only planet with large amounts of water. Water shapes Earth's surface and affects Earth's weather and climates. Most importantly, water is vital for life. Every living thing is made mostly of water. Most life processes use water. Water is an important natural resource. For humans and other organisms, access to clean water is important for good health.

There is lots of water, so what's the problem?

About 97% of Earth's water is salty, which leaves only 3% as fresh water. However, as you can see from the graph, over two-thirds of Earth's fresh water is frozen as ice and snow. But a lot of the liquid water seeps into the ground as groundwater. That leaves much less than 1% of Earth's fresh liquid water on the surface. Water is vital for people, so this small volume of fresh surface and groundwater is a limited resource.

Areas with high densities of people, such as cities, need lots of fresh water. Cities are getting bigger, and so the need for fresh water is increasing. *Urbanization* (ER•buh•ny•zhay•shuhn) is the growth of towns and cities that results from the movement of people from rural areas into the urban areas. The greater demand for fresh water in cities is threatening the availability of water for many people. Fresh water is becoming a natural resource that cannot be replaced at the same rate at which it is used.

Distribution of Earth's Fresh Water

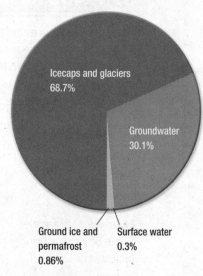

Icecaps and glaciers
68.7%

Groundwater
30.1%

Ground ice and permafrost
0.86%

Surface water
0.3%

👁 Visualize It!

5 Interpret What percentage of fresh water on Earth is frozen? What percentage of fresh water is liquid?

_____

_____

Everywhere...

Where do we get fresh water?

Fresh water may fall directly as precipitation, or may melt from ice and snow. Earth's fresh liquid water is found as surface water and groundwater. *Surface water* is any body of water above the ground. It includes liquid salt or fresh water, or solid water, like snow and ice. Water may seep below the surface to become *groundwater*. Groundwater is found under Earth's surface, in spaces in rocks or in soil, where it can be liquid or frozen.

Aquifers and Groundwater

Aquifers and ground ice are forms of groundwater. An *aquifer* is a body of rock or sediment that can store a lot of water, and that allows water to flow easily through it. Aquifers store water in spaces, called *pores,* between particles of rock or sediment. Wells are dug into aquifers to reach the water. In polar regions, water is often frozen in a layer of soil called *permafrost*.

Rivers, Streams, and Lakes

Rivers, streams, and most lakes are fresh surface waters. A stream or river may flow into a bowl-shaped area, which may fill up to form a lake. Many millions of people around the world depend on fresh water that is taken from rivers and fresh water lakes.

What are water quality and supply?

Water quality is a measure of how clean or polluted water is. Water quality is important because humans and other organisms depend on clean water to survive. It is vital for living things to not only have water, but also to have clean water. Dirty, contaminated water can make us sick or even kill us.

Water supply is the availability of water. Water supply influences where and when farmers grow crops, and where people can build cities. *Water supply systems* carry water from groundwater or surface waters so people can use the water. The systems can be a network of underground pipes, or a bucket for scooping water from a well. A shortage of clean, fresh water reduces quality of life for people. Many people in developing countries do not have access to clean, fresh water.

Active Reading

6 List What are the different sources of fresh water?

_____

_____

Think Outside the Book Inquiry

7 Observe Keep a water diary for a day. Record every time you use water at school, at home, or elsewhere. At the end of the day, review your records. How could you reduce your water usage?

Many people do not have a water supply to their homes. Instead, they have to go to a local stream, well, or pump to gather water for cooking, cleaning, and drinking.

Under Threat

What threatens fresh water quality?

When waste or other material is added to water so that it is harmful to organisms that use it or live in it, **water pollution** (WAW•ter puh•LOO•shuhn) occurs. It is useful to divide pollution sources into two types. **Point-source pollution** comes from one specific site. For example, a major chemical spill is point-source pollution. Usually this type of pollution can be controlled once its source is found. **Nonpoint-source pollution** comes from many small sources and is more difficult to control. Most nonpoint-source pollution reaches water supplies by runoff or by seeping into groundwater. The main sources of nonpoint-source pollution are city streets, roads and drains, farms, and mines.

Active Reading

8 Identify As you read, underline the sources of water pollution.

Thermal Pollution

Any heating of natural water that results from human activity is called **thermal pollution**. For example, water that is used for cooling some power plants gets warmed up. When that water is returned to the river or lake it is at a higher temperature than the lake or river water. The warm water has less oxygen available for organisms that live in the water.

Chemical Pollution

Chemical pollution occurs when harmful chemicals are added to water supplies. Two major sources of chemical pollution are industry and agriculture. For example, refineries that process oil or metals and factories that make metal or plastic products or electronic items all produce toxic chemical waste. Chemicals used in agriculture include pesticides, herbicides, and fertilizers. These pollutants can reach water supplies by seeping into groundwater. Once in groundwater, the pollution can enter the water cycle and can be carried far from the pollution source. *Acid rain* is another form of chemical pollution. It forms when gases formed by burning fossil fuels mix with water in the air. Acid rain can harm both plants and animals. It can lower the pH of soil and water, and make them too acidic for life.

Biological Pollution

Many organisms naturally live in and around water, but they are not normally polluters. *Biological pollution* occurs when live or dead organisms are added to water supplies. Wastewater may contain disease-causing microbes from human or animal wastes. *Wastewater* is any water that has been used by people for such things as flushing toilets, showering, or washing dishes. Wastewater from feed lots and farms may also contain harmful microbes. These microbes can cause diseases such as dysentery, typhoid, or cholera.

Eutrophication

Fresh water often contains nutrients from decomposing organisms. An increase in the amount of nutrients in water is called **eutrophication** (yoo•TRAWF•ih•kay•shuhn). Eutrophication occurs naturally in water. However, *artificial eutrophication* occurs when human activity increases nutrient levels in water. Wastewater and fertilizer runoff that gets into waterways can add extra nutrients which upset the natural biology of the water. These extra nutrients cause the fast growth of algae over the water surface. An overgrowth of algae and aquatic plants can reduce oxygen levels and kill fish and other organisms in the water.

Visualize It!

Water can become polluted by human activities in many different ways.

Chemical Pollution
Sulfur in smoke and vehicle exhausts contributes to the acidification of rain, leading to acid rain. Acid rain can affect areas far from the point of pollution.

Biological pollution

Biological Pollution
Animal and human wastes can get washed into a water supply in runoff, or through leaking pipes.

Thermal pollution

Eutrophication

Chemical pollution

9 Describe How is human activity impacting water quality in this image?

_____

_____

_____

_____

10 Apply Identify one point-source and one nonpoint-source of pollution in this image.

_____

_____

_____

_____

How is water quality measured?

Before there were scientific methods of testing water, people could only look at water, taste it, and smell it to check its quality. Scientists can now test water with modern equipment, so the results are more reliable. Modern ways of testing water are especially important for finding small quantities of toxic chemicals or harmful organisms in water.

Water is a good solvent. So, water in nature usually contains dissolved solids, such as salt and other substances. Because most dissolved solids cannot be seen, it is important to measure them. Measurements of water quality include testing the levels of dissolved oxygen, pH, temperature, dissolved solids, and the number and types of microbes in the water. Quality standards depend on the intended use for the water. For example, drinking water needs to meet much stricter quality standards than environmental waters such as river or lake waters do.

Water Quality Measurement

Quality measurement	What is it?	How it relates to water quality
Dissolved solids	a measure of the amount of ions or microscopic suspended solids in water	Some dissolved solids could be harmful chemicals. Others such as calcium could cause scaling or build-up in water pipes.
pH	a measure of how acidic or alkaline water is	Aquatic organisms need a near neutral pH (approx. pH 7). Acid rain can drop the pH too low (acidic) for aquatic life to live.
Dissolved oxygen (DO)	the amount of oxygen gas that is dissolved in water	Aquatic organisms need oxygen. Animal waste and thermal pollution can decrease the amount of oxygen dissolved in water.
Turbidity	a measure of the cloudiness of water that is caused by suspended solids	High turbidity increases the chance that harmful microbes or chemicals are in the water.
Microbial load	the identification of harmful bacteria, viruses or protists in water	Microbes such as bacteria, viruses, and protists from human and animal wastes can cause diseases.

11 Predict Why might increased turbidity increase the chance of something harmful being in the water?

_____

_____

How is water treated for human use?

Active Reading **12 Identify** As you read, number the basic steps in the water treatment process.

Natural water may be unsafe for humans to drink. So, water that is to be used as drinking water is treated to remove harmful chemicals and organisms. Screens take out large debris. Then chemicals are added that make suspended particles stick together. These particles drop out of the water in a process called *flocculation*. Flocculation also removes harmful bacteria and other microbes. Chlorine is often added to kill microbes left in the water. In some cities, fluoride is added to water supplies to help prevent tooth decay. Finally, air is bubbled through the water. Water that is suitable to drink is called **potable** water. Once water is used, it becomes wastewater. It enters the sewage system where pipes carry it to a wastewater treatment plant. There the wastewater is cleaned and filtered before being released back into the environment.

Drinking water is often mixed in large basins to help remove chemicals and harmful organisms. Paddles stir the water in the basins.

Who monitors and protects our water quality?

Active Reading **13 Identify** As you read, underline the government agency that is responsible for enforcing water quality rules.

If a public water supply became contaminated, many people could get very sick. As a result, public water supplies are closely monitored so that any problems can be fixed quickly. The Safe Drinking Water Act is the main federal law that ensures safe drinking water for people in the United States. The act sets strict limits on the amount of heavy metals or certain types of bacteria that can be in drinking water, among other things. The Environmental Protection Agency (EPA) has the job of enforcing this law. It is responsible for setting the standards drinking water must meet before the water can be pumped into public water systems. Water quality tests can be done by trained workers or trained volunteers.

Samples of water are routinely taken to make sure the water quality meets the standards required by law.

Supply and Demand

How does water get to the faucet?

In earlier times, humans had to live near natural sources of fresh water. Over time, engineers developed ways to transport and store large amounts of water. So, humans can now live in places where fresh water is supplied by water pipes and other infrastructure. The ability to bring fresh water safely from its source to a large population has led to the urbanization of cities.

Creating Water Supply Systems

Freshwater supply is often limited, so we have found ways to store and transport water far from its source to where it is used. Surface water is collected and pumped to places where people need it. Groundwater can be found by digging wells into aquifers. Water can be lifted from a well by hand in buckets. It can be pumped into pipes that supply homes, farms, factories and cities. Piped water supply systems can deliver water over great distances to where humans need it. Water supply and storage systems are expensive to build and maintain.

👁 Visualize It!

A public water supply includes the water source, the treatment facilities, and the pipes and pumps that send it to homes, industries, businesses, and public facilities.

Water treatment and distribution

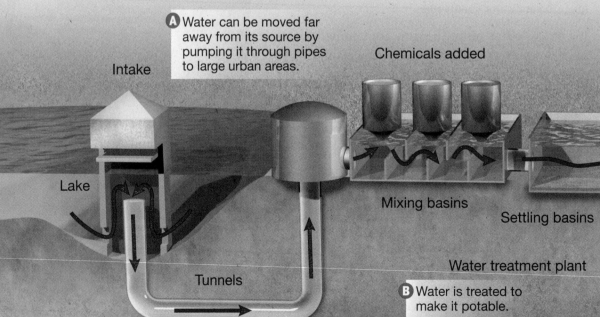

A Water can be moved far away from its source by pumping it through pipes to large urban areas.

Intake

Chemicals added

Lake

Mixing basins

Settling basins

Tunnels

Water treatment plant

B Water is treated to make it potable.

Changing the Flow of Water

Pumping and collecting groundwater and surface water changes how water flows in natural systems. For example, a **reservoir** (REZ•er•vwar) is a body of water that usually forms behind a dam. Dams stop river waters from flowing along their natural course. The water in a reservoir would naturally have flowed to the sea. Instead, the water can be diverted into a pipeline or into artificial channels called *canals* or *aqueducts*.

What threatens our water supply?

Active Reading **14 Identify** As you read, underline the things that are a threat to water supply.

As the human use of water has increased, the demand for fresh water has also increased. Demand is greater than supply in many areas of the world, including parts of the United States. The larger a population or a city gets, the greater the demand for fresh water. Increased demand for and use of water can cause water shortages. Droughts or leaking water pipes can also cause water shortages. Water is used to keep our bodies clean and healthy. It is also used to grow crops for food. Water shortages threaten these benefits.

15 Infer Why would a larger city have a larger demand for water?

_____
_____
_____
_____
_____

C The infrastructure shown here is used to supply clean water. Once water is used, it becomes wastewater. A different system, called a sewage system, carries wastewater away from urban areas to wastewater treatment plants.

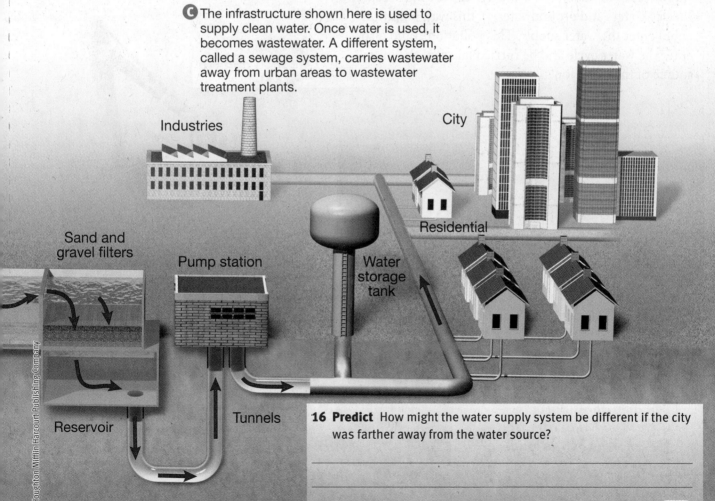

Industries

City

Sand and gravel filters

Pump station

Water storage tank

Residential

Reservoir

Tunnels

16 Predict How might the water supply system be different if the city was farther away from the water source?

_____
_____

How do efforts to supply water to humans affect the environment?

Growing urban populations place a greater demand on water supplies. Efforts to increase water supply can affect the environment. For example, building dams and irrigation canals changes the natural flow of water. The environment is physically changed by construction work. The local ecology changes too. Organisms that live in or depend on the water may lose their habitat and move away.

Aquifers are often used as freshwater sources for urban areas. When more water is taken from an aquifer than can be replaced by rain or snow, the water table can drop below the reach of existing wells. Rivers and streams may dry up and the soil that once held aquifer waters may collapse, or *subside*. In coastal areas, the overuse of groundwater can cause seawater to seep into the aquifer in a process called *saltwater intrusion*. In this way, water supplies can become contaminated with salt water.

Increasing population in an area can also affect water quality. The more people that use a water supply in one area, the greater the volume of wastewater that is produced in that area. Pollutants such as oil, pesticides, fertilizers, and heavy metals from city runoff, from industry, and from agriculture may seep into surface waters and groundwater. In this way, pollution could enter the water supply. This pollution could also enter the water cycle and be carried far from the initial source of the pollution.

Active Reading

17 Relate How can the increased demand on water affect water quality?

_____

_____

_____

_____

_____

Building dams disrupts water flow and affects the ecology of the land and water.

Digging irrigation canals changes the flow of rivers.

Irrigating arid areas changes the ecology of those areas.

© Houghton Mifflin Harcourt Publishing Company • Image Credits: (l) ©Travel Ink/Gallo Images/Getty Images; (r) ©Derrick Francis Furlong/Alamy; (bc) ©Tony Roberts/Corbis

Death of a Sea

The Aral Sea in Central Asia was once the world's fourth-largest inland salty lake. But it has been shrinking since the 1960s. In the 1940s, the courses of the rivers that fed the lake were changed to irrigate the desert, so that crops such as cotton and rice could be grown. By 2004, the lake had shrunk to 25% of its original size. The freshwater flow into the lake was reduced and evaporation caused the lake to become so salty that most of the plants and animals in it died or left the lake.

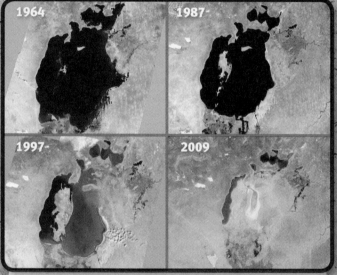

1964

1987

1997

2009

By 2007, the lake had shrunk to 10% of its original size and had split into three separate, smaller lakes.

Polluted Land

The Aral Sea is also heavily polluted by industrial wastes, pesticides, and fertilizer runoff. Salty dust that is blown from the dried seabed damages crops and pollutes drinking water. The salt- and dust-laden air cause serious public health problems in the Aral Sea region. One of the more bizarre reminders of how large the lake once was are the boats that lie abandoned on the exposed sea floor.

Extend

Inquiry

18 Identify What human activity has created the situation in the Aral Sea?

19 Apply Research the impact that of one of these two large water projects has had on people and on the environment: The Three Gorges Dam or the Columbia Basin Project.

20 Relate Research a current or past water project in the area where you live. What benefits will these projects have for people in the area? What risks might there be to the environment?

Visual Summary

To complete this summary, fill in the blanks with the correct word or phrase. Then use the key below to check your answers. You can use this page to review the main concepts of the lesson.

Human Impact on Water

Organisms need clean water for life and good health.

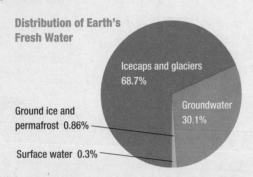

Distribution of Earth's Fresh Water

Icecaps and glaciers 68.7%

Groundwater 30.1%

Ground ice and permafrost 0.86%

Surface water 0.3%

21 Earth's fresh liquid water is found as surface water and _____

Water pollution can come from many different sources.

22 Runoff from farmland into a river is an example of _____ source pollution.

Federal laws set the standards for potable water quality. Water quality is constantly monitored.

23 Dissolved solids, pH, temperature, and dissolved oxygen are measures of _____ .

Ensuring a constant supply of water for people can change the environment.

24 A _____ is a body of water that forms when a dam blocks a river.

Answers: 21 groundwater; 22 nonpoint; 23 water quality; 24 reservoir

25 Compare What is the difference between water quality and water supply?

Lesson Review

Vocabulary

Fill in the blank with the term that best completes the following sentences.

1 _____ water is a term used to describe water that is safe to drink.

2 The addition of nutrients to water by human activity is called artificial _____.

3 _____ pollution comes from many small sources.

Key Concepts

Complete the table below with the type of pollution described in each example.

Example	Type of pollution (chemical, thermal, or biological)
4 Identify A person empties an oil can into a storm drain.	
5 Identify A factory releases warm water into a local river.	
6 Identify Untreated sewage is washed into a lake during a rain storm.	

7 Describe Name two ways in which humans can affect the flow of fresh water.

_____

_____

_____

8 Explain Why does water quality need to be monitored?

_____

_____

Critical Thinking

Use this graph to answer the following questions.

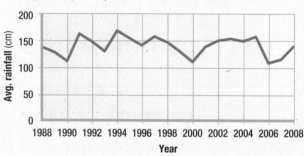

Average Yearly Precipitation in Florida from 1988 to 2008

Source: Florida State University Climate Center

9 Analyze Which year had the least precipitation?

_____

10 Infer What effect might many years of low precipitation have on water supply?

_____

11 Explain Could a single person or animal be a cause of point-source pollution? Explain.

_____

_____

_____

_____

12 Apply In times of hot, dry, weather, some cities ban the use of garden sprinklers. Why do you think there is such a rule?

_____

_____

_____

_____

Angel Montoya

CONSERVATION BIOLOGIST

In 1990, Angel Montoya was a student intern working at Laguna Atascosa National Wildlife Refuge in Texas. He became interested in the Aplomado falcon, a bird of prey that disappeared from the southwestern United States during the first half of the 20th century. Montoya decided to go looking for the raptors. He found a previously unknown population of Aplomados in Chihuahua, Mexico. His work helped to make it possible for the falcons to be reintroduced to an area near El Paso, Texas.

Restoration of the Aplomado falcon became Angel's lifework. He has monitored and researched the falcon since 1992. He helps release falcons that have been raised in captivity back into the wild and monitors falcons that have already been released. It isn't easy to keep tabs on a falcon, however. "Their first year they are pretty vulnerable, because they haven't had parents," Montoya says. "Just like juveniles, they're always getting into trouble. But I think they will do just fine."

Angel Montoya releases an Aplomado falcon back into the wild.

JOB BOARD

Environmental Engineering Technician

What You'll Do: Work closely with environmental engineers and scientists to prevent or fix environmental damage. Take care of water and wastewater treatment systems, as well as equipment used for recycling. Test water and air quality and keep good records.

Where You Might Work: In a water treatment facility, or an environmental laboratory.

Education: an associate's degree in engineering technology.

Other Job Requirements: Good communication skills and the ability to work well with others.

Agronomist

What You'll Do: Study the best ways to grow crops and work with farmers to help them use their land better, and get better yields. Agronomists are scientists who study crops and soil.

Where You Might Work: On a farm, in an agricultural business, for the U.S. Department of Agriculture or state or local government agencies, or for seed companies. Agronomists may work both in fields and in laboratories.

Education: a four-year college degree in agronomy, agriculture, or soil conservation.

PEOPLE IN SCIENCE NEWS

YUMI Someya

Fueling the Family Business

Yumi Someya's family had worked in recycling for three generations, cleaning and recycling used cooking oil. In Japan, many people enjoy fried foods. They often throw out the used cooking oil. Yumi's family business collected used oil, cleaned it, and sold it for reuse.

When Yumi traveled to Nepal, she was caught in a landslide. She learned that deforestation was one cause of the landslide and began to think about environmental issues. When she returned home, she worked with her father to find new uses for the used cooking oil. They experimented with fertilizer and soap. Then, in 1992, they learned about biodiesel—fuel made from recycled soybean oil. They thought that used cooking oil might work to fuel cars, too. With a team of researchers, they created Vegetable Diesel Fuel (VDF).

Now, VDF fuels the company's oil-collecting trucks and some Tokyo buses. Yumi hopes to eventually recycle all of the cooking oil used in Japan.

Human Impact on the Atmosphere

ESSENTIAL QUESTION

How do humans impact Earth's atmosphere?

By the end of this lesson, you should be able to identify the impact that humans have had on Earth's atmosphere.

Indiana Standards

8.2.6 Identify, explain, and discuss some effects human activities have on the biosphere, such as air, soil, light, noise and water pollution.

8.2.8 Explain that human activities, beginning with the earliest herding and agricultural activities, have drastically changed the environment and have affected the capacity of the environment to support native species. Explain current efforts to reduce and eliminate these impacts and encourage sustainability.

Human activities that involve burning fuels, such as driving vehicles and keeping buildings cool, can cause air pollution.

Engage Your Brain

1 Identify Check T or F to show whether you think each statement is true or false.

T	F	
☐	☐	Human activities can cause air pollution.
☐	☐	Air pollution cannot affect you if you stay indoors.
☐	☐	Air pollution does not affect places outside of cities.
☐	☐	Air pollution can cause lung diseases.

2 Analyze The photo above shows the same city as the photo on the left, but on a different day. How are these photos different?

_____

_____

_____

_____

Active Reading

3 Apply Use context clues to write your own definitions for the words *contamination* and *quality*.

Example Sentence
You can help prevent food <u>contamination</u> by washing your hands after touching raw meat.

contamination:

_____

_____

_____

Example Sentence
The good sound <u>quality</u> coming from the stereo speakers indicated they were expensive.

quality:

_____

_____

_____

Vocabulary Terms

- greenhouse effect
- air pollution
- particulate
- smog
- acid precipitation
- air quality

4 Apply As you learn the definition of each vocabulary term in this lesson, create your own definition or sketch to help you remember the meaning of the term.

AIR
What Is It Good For?

Why is the atmosphere important?

If you were lost in a desert, you could survive a few days without food and water. But you wouldn't last more than a few minutes without air. Air is an important natural resource. The air you breathe forms part of Earth's atmosphere. The *atmosphere* (AT•muh•sfeer) is a mixture of gases that surrounds Earth. Most organisms on Earth have adapted to the natural balance of gases found in the atmosphere.

It Provides Gases That Organisms Need to Survive

Oxygen is one of the gases that make up Earth's atmosphere. It is used by most living cells to get energy from food. Every breath you take brings oxygen into your body. The atmosphere also contains carbon dioxide. Plants need carbon dioxide to make their own food through photosynthesis (foh•toh•SYN•thuh•sys).

It Absorbs Harmful Radiation

High-energy radiation from space would harm life on Earth if it were not blocked by the atmosphere. Fast-moving particles, called *cosmic rays,* enter the atmosphere every second. These particles collide with oxygen, nitrogen, and other gas molecules and are slowed down. A part of the atmosphere called the *stratosphere* contains ozone gas. The ozone layer absorbs most of the high-energy radiation from the sun, called *ultraviolet radiation* (UV), that reaches Earth.

It Keeps Earth Warm

Without the atmosphere, temperatures on Earth would not be stable. It would be too cold for life to exist. The **greenhouse effect** is the way by which certain gases in the atmosphere, such as water vapor and carbon dioxide, absorb and reradiate thermal energy. This slows the loss of energy from Earth into space. The atmosphere acts like a warm blanket that insulates the surface of Earth, preventing the sun's energy from being lost. For this reason, carbon dioxide and water vapor are called *greenhouse gases.*

Active Reading **5 Explain** How is Earth's atmosphere similar to a warm blanket?

_____

_____

What is air pollution?

The contamination of the atmosphere by pollutants from human and natural sources is called **air pollution**. Natural sources of air pollution include volcanic eruptions, wildfires, and dust storms. In cities and suburbs, most air pollution comes from the burning of fossil fuels such as oil, gasoline, and coal. Oil refineries, chemical manufacturing plants, dry-cleaning businesses, and auto repair shops are just some potential sources of air pollution. Scientists classify air pollutants as either gases or particulates.

Active Reading

6 Identify As you read, underline sources of air pollution.

Visualize It!

7 Analyze Which one of these images could be both a natural or a human source of air pollution? Give reasons for your answer.

_____

_____

_____

_____

_____

Factory emissions

Vehicle exhaust

Forest fires and wildfires

Gases

Gas pollutants include carbon monoxide, sulfur dioxide, nitrogen oxide, and ground-level ozone. Some of these gases occur naturally in the atmosphere. These gases are considered pollutants only when they are likely to cause harm. For example, ozone is important in the stratosphere, but at ground level it is harmful to breathe. Carbon monoxide, sulfur dioxide, and nitrogen dioxide are released from burning fossil fuels in vehicles, factories, and homes. They are a major source of air pollution.

Particulates

Particle pollutants can be easier to see than gas pollutants. A **particulate** (per•TIK•yuh•lit) is a tiny particle of solid that is suspended in air or water. Smoke contains ash, which is a particulate. The wind can pick up particulates such as dust, ash, pollen, and tiny bits of salt from the ocean and blow them far from their source. Ash, dust, and pollen are common forms of air pollution. Vehicle exhaust also contains particulates. The particulates in vehicle exhaust are a major cause of air pollution in cities.

It Stinks!

What pollutants can form from vehicle exhaust?

In urban areas, vehicle exhaust is a common source of air pollution. Gases such as carbon monoxide and particulates such as soot and ash are in exhaust fumes. Vehicle exhaust may also react with other substances in the air. When this happens, new pollutants can form. Ground-level ozone and smog are two types of pollutants that form from vehicle exhaust.

Active Reading

8 Identify As you read, underline how ground-level ozone and smog can form.

Ground-Level Ozone

Ozone in the ozone layer is necessary for life, but ground-level ozone is harmful. It is produced when sunlight reacts with vehicle exhaust and oxygen in the air. You may have heard of "Ozone Action Days" in your community. When such a warning is given, people should limit outdoor activities because ozone can damage their lungs.

Smog

Smog is another type of pollutant formed from vehicle exhaust. **Smog** forms when ground-level ozone and vehicle exhaust react in the presence of sunlight. Smog is a problem in large cities because there are more vehicles on the roads. It can cause lung damage and irritate the eyes and nose. In some cities, there can be enough smog to make a brownish haze over the city.

Visualize It!

Some compounds in smoke and exhaust are harmful by themselves. And some compounds in smoke and exhaust can react in the atmosphere to form other pollutants such as smog and acid precipitation.

Smog
Smog forms when ground-level ozone and vehicle exhaust react in the presence of sunlight.

smog

sunlight

ground-level ozone

vehicle exhaust

How does pollution from human activities produce acid precipitation?

Active Reading **9 Identify** As you read, underline how acid precipitation forms.

Precipitation (prih•sip•ih•TAY•shuhn) such as rain, sleet, or snow that contains acids from air pollution is called **acid precipitation**. Burning fossil fuels releases sulfur dioxide and nitrogen oxides into the air. When these gases mix with water in the atmosphere, they form sulfuric acid and nitric acid. Precipitation is naturally slightly acidic. When carbon dioxide in the air and water mix, they form carbonic acid. Carbonic acid is a weak acid. Sulfuric acid and nitric acid are strong acids. They can make precipitation so acidic that it is harmful to the environment.

What are some effects of acid precipitation?

Acid precipitation can cause soil and water to become more acidic than normal. Plants have adapted over long periods of time to the natural acidity of the soils in which they live. When soil acidity rises, some nutrients that plants need are dissolved. These nutrients get washed away by rainwater. Bacteria and fungi that live in the soil are also harmed by acidic conditions.

Acid precipitation may increase the acidity of lakes or streams. It also releases toxic metals from soils. The increased acidity and high levels of metals in water can sicken or kill aquatic organisms. This can disrupt habitats and result in decreased biodiversity in an ecosystem. Acid precipitation can also erode the stonework on buildings and statues.

10 Analyze Explain how pollution from one location can affect the environment far away from the source of the pollution.

_____

_____

_____

blowing winds

Smoke and fumes from factories and vehicles contain sulfur dioxide and nitrogen oxide gases, which can be blown long distances by winds.

Acid Precipitation
These gases dissolve in water vapor, and form sulfuric acids and nitric acids, which fall to Earth as acid precipitation.

How's the AIR?

What are measures of air quality?

Measuring how clean or polluted the air is tells us about **air quality**. Pollutants reduce air quality. Two major threats to air quality are vehicle exhausts and industrial pollutants. The air quality in cities can be poor. As more people move into cities, the cities get bigger. This leads to increased amounts of human-made pollution. Poor air circulation, such as a lack of wind, allows air pollution to stay in one area where it can build up. As pollution increases, air quality decreases.

Air Quality Index

The Air Quality Index (AQI) is a number used to describe the air quality of a location such as a city. The higher the AQI number, the more people are likely to have health problems that are linked to air pollution. Air quality is measured and given a value based on the level of pollution detected. The AQI values are divided into ranges. Each range is given a color code and a description. The Environmental Protection Agency (EPA) has AQIs for the pollutants that pose the greatest risk to public health, including ozone and particulates. The EPA can then issue advisories to avoid exposure to pollution that may harm health.

Indoor Air Pollution

The air inside a building can become more polluted than the air outside. This is because buildings are insulated to prevent outside air from entering the building. Some sources of indoor air pollution include chlorine and ammonia from household cleaners and formaldehyde from furniture. Harmful chemicals can be released from some paints and glues. Radon is a radioactive gas released when uranium decays. Radon can seep into buildings through gaps in their foundations. It can build up inside well-insulated buildings. *Ventilation,* or the mixing of indoor and outside air, can reduce indoor air pollution. Another way to reduce indoor air pollution is to limit the use of items that create the pollution.

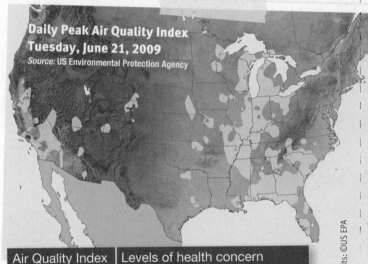

Daily Peak Air Quality Index Tuesday, June 21, 2009
Source: US Environmental Protection Agency

Air Quality Index (AQI) values	Levels of health concern
0–50	Good
51–100	Moderate
101–150	Unhealthy for sensitive groups
151–200	Unhealthy
201–300	Very unhealthy

Source: **US Environmental Protection Agency**

Color codes based on the Air Quality Index show the air quality in different areas.

👁 Visualize It!

11 Recommend If you were a weather reporter using this map, what would you recommend for people living in areas that are colored orange?

_____

_____

_____

_____

_____

12 Apply If this was your house, how might you decrease the sources of indoor air pollution?

_____

_____

_____

_____

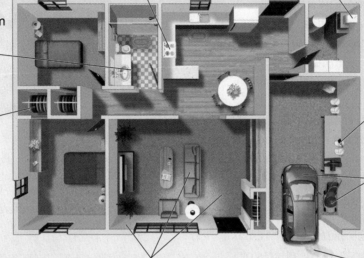

Nitrogen oxides from unvented gas stove, wood stove, or kerosene heater

Chlorine and ammonia from household cleaners

Chemicals from dry cleaning

Formaldehyde from furniture, carpeting, particleboard, and foam insulation

Fungi and bacteria from dirty heating and air conditioning ducts

Chemicals from paint strippers and thinners

Gasoline from car and lawn mower

Carbon monoxide from car left running

How can air quality affect health?

Daily exposure to small amounts of air pollution can cause serious health problems. Children, elderly people, and people with asthma, allergies, lung problems, and heart problems are especially vulnerable to the effects of air pollution. The short-term effects of air pollution include coughing, headaches, and wheezing. Long-term effects, such as lung cancer and emphysema, are dangerous because they can cause death.

Think Outside the Book Inquiry

13 Evaluate Think about the community in which you live. What different things in your community and the surrounding areas might affect the air quality where you live?

Air Pollution and Your Health

Short-term effects	Long-term effects
coughing	asthma
headaches	emphysema
difficulty breathing	allergies
burning/itchy eyes	lung cancer
	chronic bronchitis

14 Identify Imagine you are walking next to a busy road where there are a lot of exhaust fumes. Circle the effects listed in the table that you are most likely to have while walking.

Things Are CHANGING

How might humans be changing Earth's climates?

The burning of fossil fuels releases greenhouse gases, such as carbon dioxide, into the atmosphere. The atmosphere today contains about 37% more carbon dioxide than it did in the mid-1700s, and that level continues to increase. Average global temperatures have also risen in recent decades.

Many people are concerned about how the greenhouse gases from human activities add to the observed trend of increasing global temperatures. Earth's atmosphere and other systems work together in complex ways, so it is hard to know exactly how much the extra greenhouse gases change the temperature. Climate scientists make computer models to understand the effects of climate change. Models predict that average global temperatures are likely to rise another 1.1 to 6.4 °C (2 to 11.5 °F) by the year 2100.

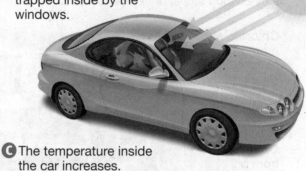

Ⓐ Sunlight (radiant energy) passes through the windows of the car.

Ⓑ Energy as heat is trapped inside by the windows.

Ⓒ The temperature inside the car increases.

👁 **Visualize It!**

15 Synthesize How is a car with closed windows a good analogy of the atmosphere's greenhouse effect?

_____

_____

_____

What are some predicted effects of climate change?

📖 **Active Reading** **16 Identify** As you read, underline some effects of an increasing average global temperature.

Scientists have already noticed many changes linked to warmer temperatures. For example, some glaciers and the Arctic sea ice are melting at the fastest rates ever recorded. A warmer Earth may lead to changes in rainfall patterns, rising sea levels, and more severe storms. These changes will have many negative impacts for life on Earth. Other predicted effects include drought in some regions and increased precipitation in others. Farming practices and the availability of food is also expected to be impacted by increased global temperatures. Such changes will likely have political and economic effects on the world, especially in developing countries.

Melt water pours from an iceberg that broke away from the Jakobshavn Glacier in West Greenland.

How is the ozone layer affected by air pollution?

In the 1980s, scientists reported an alarming discovery about Earth's protective ozone layer. Over the polar regions, the ozone layer was thinning. Chemicals called *chlorofluorocarbons* (klor•oh•flur•oh•kar•buhns) (CFCs) were causing ozone to break down into oxygen, which does not block harmful ultraviolet (UV) rays. The thinning of the ozone layer allows more UV radiation to reach Earth's surface. UV radiation is dangerous to organisms, including humans, as it causes sunburn, damages DNA (which can lead to cancer), and causes eye damage.

CFCs once had many industrial uses, such as coolants in refrigerators and air-conditioning units. CFC use has now been banned, but CFC molecules can stay in the atmosphere for about 100 years. So, CFCs released from a spray can 30 years ago are still harming the ozone layer today. However, recent studies show that breakdown of the ozone layer has slowed.

The dark blue area on this map shows the size of the ozone hole over the South Pole.

17 Infer How might these penguins near the South Pole be affected by the ozone hole?

_____

_____

_____

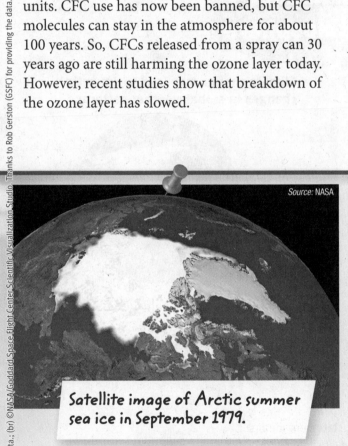

Source: NASA

Satellite image of Arctic summer sea ice in September 1979.

Source: NASA

Satellite image of Arctic summer sea ice in September 2007.

Inquiry

18 Relate What effect might melting sea ice have for people who live in coastal areas?

_____

_____

_____

© Houghton Mifflin Harcourt Publishing Company • Image Credits: (bkgd) ©Paul Souders/Corbis; (tl) ©NASA images courtesy Goddard Space Flight Center Ozone Processing Team; (tr) Kyodo via AP Images; (bl) ©NASA/Goddard Space Flight Center Scientific Visualization Studio.; (br) ©NASA/Goddard Space Flight Center Scientific Visualization Studio. Thanks to Rob Gerston (GSFC) for providing the data.

Visual Summary

To complete this summary, fill in the blanks with the correct word or phrase. Then use the key below to check your answers. You can use this page to review the main concepts of the lesson.

smog

Human activities are a major cause of air pollution.

19 Two types of air pollutants are gases and _____.

Car exhaust is a major source of air pollution in cities.

20 _____ is formed when exhausts and ozone react in the presence of sunlight.

Human Impact on the Atmosphere

Air quality and levels of pollution can be measured.

Air Quality Index (AQI) values	Levels of health concern
0–50	Good
51–100	Moderate
101–150	Unhealthy for sensitive groups
151–200	Unhealthy
201–300	Very unhealthy

21 As pollution increases, _____ decreases.

Climate change may lead to dramatic changes in global weather patterns.

22 The melting of polar ice is one effect of _____ .

Answers: 19 particulates; 20 smog; 21 air quality; 22 global warming/climate change

23 Apply Explain in your own words what the following statement means: Each of your breaths, every tree that is planted, and every vehicle on the road affects the composition of the atmosphere.

Lesson Review

Vocabulary

Draw a line to connect the following terms to their definitions.

1 Air pollution

2 Greenhouse effect

3 Air quality

4 Particulate

5 Smog

A tiny particle of solid that is suspended in air or water

B the contamination of the atmosphere by the introduction of pollutants from human and natural sources

C pollutant that forms when ozone and vehicle exhaust react with sunlight

D a measure of how clean or polluted the air is

E the process by which gases in the atmosphere, such as water vapor and carbon dioxide, absorb and release energy as heat

Key Concepts

6 Identify List three effects that an increase in urbanization can have on air quality.

_____

_____

7 Relate How are ground-level ozone and smog related?

_____

_____

_____

8 Explain How can human health be affected by changes in air quality?

_____

_____

_____

Critical Thinking

Use this graph to answer the following questions.

Concentration of a CFC in the Atmosphere Over Time

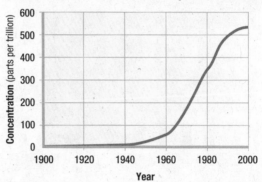

9 Analyze At what time in the graph did CFCs begin building up in the atmosphere?

_____

_____

10 Synthesize Since the late 1970s, the use of CFCs has been reduced, with a total ban in 2010. But CFCs can stay in the atmosphere for up to 100 years. In the space below, draw a graph showing the concentration of CFCs in the atmosphere over the next 100 years.

11 Apply Do you think it is important that humans control the amount of human-made pollution? Explain your reasoning.

_____

_____

_____

_____

_____

Protecting Earth's Water, Land, and Air

ESSENTIAL QUESTION

How can Earth's resources be used wisely?

By the end of this lesson, you should be able to summarize the value of conserving Earth's resources and the effect that wise stewardship has on land, water, and air resources.

Indiana Standards

8.2.6 Identify, explain, and discuss some effects human activities have on the biosphere, such as air, soil, light, noise and water pollution.

8.2.7 Recognize that some of Earth's resources are finite and describe how recycling, reducing consumption and the development of alternatives can reduce the rate of their depletion.

8.2.8 Explain that human activities, beginning with the earliest herding and agricultural activities, have drastically changed the environment and have affected the capacity of the environment to support native species. Explain current efforts to reduce and eliminate these impacts and encourage sustainability.

Picking up litter to clean streams or rivers is one way we can help preserve Earth's natural resources.

Engage Your Brain

1 Predict Check T or F to show whether you think each statement is true or false.

T	F	
☐	☐	Conservation is the overuse of natural resources.
☐	☐	It is everybody's job to be a good steward of the Earth's resources.
☐	☐	Reforestation is the planting of trees to repair degraded lands.
☐	☐	Alternative energy sources, like solar power, increase the amount of pollution released into the air.

2 Describe Have you ever done something to protect a natural resource? Draw a picture showing what you did. Include a caption.

Active Reading

3 Synthesize You can often guess the meaning of a word from its context, or how it is used in a sentence. Use the sentence below to guess the meaning of the word *stewardship*.

Example sentence
Stewardship of water resources will ensure that there is plenty of clean water for future generations.

stewardship:

_____

_____

Vocabulary Terms
- conservation
- stewardship

4 Apply As you learn the definition of each vocabulary term in this lesson, create your own definition or sketch to help remember the meaning of the term.

Keeping It Clean

What are conservation and stewardship?

In the past, some people have used Earth's resources however they wanted, without thinking about the consequences. They thought it didn't matter if they cut down hundreds of thousands of trees or caught millions of fish. They also thought it didn't matter if they dumped trash into bodies of water. Now we know that it does matter how we use resources. Humans greatly affect the land, water, and air. If we wish to keep using our resources in the future, we need to conserve and care for them.

Conservation: Wise Use of Resources

Conservation (kahn•sur•VAY•shuhn) is the wise use of natural resources. By practicing conservation, we can help make sure that resources will still be around for future generations. It is up to everybody to conserve and protect resources. When we use energy or create waste, we can harm the environment. If we conserve whenever we can, we reduce the harm we do to the environment. We can use less energy by turning off lights, computers, and appliances. We can reuse shopping bags, as in the picture below. We can recycle whenever possible, instead of just throwing things away. By doing these things, we take fewer resources from Earth and put less pollution into the water, land, and air.

This old tire is being used as a planter instead of being thrown away.

Stewardship: Managing Resources

Stewardship (stoo•urd•SHIP) is the careful and responsible management of a resource. If we are not good stewards, we will use up a resource or pollute it. Stewardship of Earth's resources will ensure that the environment stays clean enough to help keep people and other living things healthy. Stewardship is everybody's job. Governments pass laws that protect water, land, and air. These laws determine how resources can be used and what materials can be released into the environment. Individuals can also act as stewards. For example, you can plant trees or help clean up a habitat in your community. Any action that helps to maintain or improve the environment is an act of stewardship.

7 Compare Fill in the Venn diagram to compare and contrast conservation and stewardship.

Stewardship

Both

Conservation

Turning empty lots into gardens improves the environment and provides people with healthy food.

© Houghton Mifflin Harcourt Publishing Company • Image Credits: (l) ©Jeff Greenberg/Alamy; (r) ©Tyrone Turner/National Geographic/Getty Images

 Visualize It!

8 Identify How is the person in the picture to the right practicing stewardship?

_____
_____
_____

Sea turtles are endangered. Scientists help sea turtles that have just hatched find their way to the sea.

Water Wise!

How can we preserve water resources?

Most of the Earth's surface is covered by water, so you might think there is lots of water for humans to use. However, there is actually very little fresh water on Earth, so people should use freshwater resources very carefully. People should also be careful to avoid polluting water, because the quality of water is important to the health of both humans and ecosystems. Because water is so important to our health, we need to keep it clean!

By Conserving Water

If we want to make sure there is enough water for future generations, we need to reduce the amount of water we use. In some places, if people aren't careful about using water wisely, there soon won't be enough water for everyone. There are many ways to reduce water usage. We can use low-flow toilets and showerheads. We can take shorter showers. In agriculture and landscaping, we can reduce water use by installing efficient irrigation systems. We can also use plants that don't need much water. Only watering lawns the amount they need and following watering schedules saves water. The photo below shows a simple way to use less water—just turn off the tap while brushing your teeth!

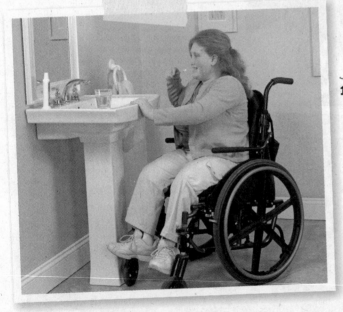

Do the Math

You Try It

9 Calculate How much fresh water is on Earth?

Solve

Each square on the grid equals 1%. Use the grid to fill in the percentage of each type of water found on Earth.

Earth's Water

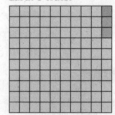

☐ Salt water _____

☐ Ice (fresh water) _____

☐ Fresh liquid water _____

10 Identify What are some ways you can reduce the amount of water you use?

- Turn off the tap when brushing my teeth.

- _____

- _____

- _____

With Water Stewardship

Humans and ecosystems need clean water. The diagram below shows how a community keeps its drinking water clean. The main way to protect drinking water is to keep pollution from entering streams, lakes, and other water sources. Laws like the Clean Water Act and Safe Drinking Water Act were passed to protect water sources. These laws indicate how clean drinking water must be and limit the types of chemicals that businesses and private citizens can release into water. These laws also help finance water treatment facilities. We can help protect water by not throwing chemicals in the trash or dumping them down the drain. We can also use nontoxic chemicals whenever possible. Reducing the amount of fertilizer we use on our gardens also reduces water pollution.

For healthy ecosystems and safe drinking water, communities need to protect water sources. The first step to protecting water sources is keeping them from becoming polluted.

Protecting Water Resources

Water testing makes sure water is safe for people to drink. It also helps us find out if there is a pollution problem that needs to be fixed.

Without clean water to drink, people can get sick. Clean water is also important for agriculture and natural ecosystems.

Water treatment plants remove pollution from wastewater before it is reused or put back into the environment.

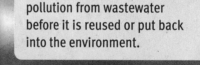

Visualize It!

11 Apply What steps should a community take to manage its water resources?

_____

_____

_____

_____

This Land Is Your Land

How can we preserve land resources?

People rely on land resources for recreation, agriculture, transportation, commerce, industry, and housing. If we manage land resources carefully, we can make sure that these resources will be around for generations and continue to provide resources for humans to use. We also need to make sure that there are habitats for wild animals. To do all these things, we must protect land resources from overuse and pollution. Sometimes we need to repair damage that is already done.

Through Preservation

Preservation of land resources is very important. *Preservation* means protecting land from being damaged or changed. Local, state, and national parks protect many natural areas. These parks help ensure that many species survive. Small parks can protect some species. Other species, such as predators, need larger areas. For example, wolves roam over hundreds of miles and would not be protected by small parks. By protecting areas big enough for large predators, we also protect habitats for many other species.

Yosemite National Park is one of the oldest national parks in the country. Like other national, state, and local parks, Yosemite was formed to preserve natural habitats.

© Houghton Mifflin Harcourt Publishing Company • Image Credits: ©Panoramic Images/Getty Images

Through Reforestation

People use the wood from trees for many things. We use it to make paper and to build houses. We also use wood to heat homes and cook food. In many places, huge areas of forest were cut down to use the wood and nothing was done to replant the forests. Now when we cut trees down, they are often replanted, as in the picture at right. We also plant trees in areas where forests disappeared many years ago in order to help bring the forests back. The process of planting trees to reestablish forestland is called *reforestation*. Reforestation is important, but we can't cut down all forests and replant them. It is important to keep some old forests intact for the animals that need them to survive.

Through Reclamation

In order to use some resources, such as coal, metal, and minerals, the resources first have to be dug out of the ground. In the process, the land is damaged. Sometimes, large areas of land are cleared and pits are dug to reach the resource. Land can also be damaged in other ways, including by development and agriculture. *Reclamation* is the process by which a damaged land area is returned to nearly the condition it was in before people used it. Land reclamation, shown in the lower right photo, is required for mines in many states once the mines are no longer in use. Many national and state laws, such as the Surface Mining and Reclamation Act and the Resource Conservation and Recovery Act, guide land reclamation.

Reforestation

A mine being reclaimed

Visualize It!

14 Compare What are the similarities between reforestation and reclamation?

_____

_____

_____

_____

One way to reduce urban sprawl is to locate homes and businesses close together.

Through Reducing Urban Sprawl

Urban sprawl is the outward spread of suburban areas around cities. As we build more houses and businesses across a wider area, there is less land for native plants and animals. Reducing urban sprawl helps to protect land resources. One way to reduce sprawl is to locate more people and businesses in a smaller area. A good way to do this is with vertical development—that means constructing taller buildings. Homes, businesses, and even recreational facilities can be placed within high-rise buildings. We also can reduce sprawl using mixed-use development. This development creates communities with businesses and houses very close to one another. Mixed-use communities are also better for the environment, because people can walk to work instead of driving.

Through Recycling

Recycling is one of the most important things we can do to preserve land resources. *Recycling* is the process of recovering valuable materials from waste or scrap. We can recycle many of the materials that we use. By recycling materials like metal, plastic, paper, and glass, we use fewer raw materials. Recycling aluminum cans reduces the amount of bauxite that is mined. We use bauxite in aluminum smelting. Everyone can help protect land resources by recycling. Lots of people throw away materials that can be recycled. Find out what items you can recycle!

Bauxite mine

15 Apply Aluminum is mined from the ground. Recycling aluminum cans decreases the need for mining bauxite. Paper can also be recycled. How does recycling paper preserve trees?

_____

_____

Through Using Soil Conservation Methods

Soil conservation protects soil from erosion or degradation by overuse or pollution. For example, farmers change the way they plow in order to conserve soil. Contour plowing creates ridges of soil across slopes. The small ridges keep water from eroding soils. In strip cropping, two types of crops are planted in rows next to each other to reduce erosion. Terracing is used on steep hills to prevent erosion. Areas of the hill are flattened to grow crops. This creates steps down the side of the hill. *Crop rotation* means that crops with different needs are planted in alternating seasons. This reduces the prevalence of plant diseases and makes sure there are nutrients for each crop. It also ensures that plants are growing in the soil almost year-round. In no-till farming, soils are not plowed between crop plantings. Stalks and cover crops keep water in the soils and reduce erosion by stopping soil from being blown away.

 **Active Reading**

16 Identify As you read this page, underline five methods of soil conservation.

Visualize It!

Terracing involves building leveled areas, or steps, to grow crops on.

In contour plowing, crop rows are planted in curved lines along land's natural contours.

Strip cropping prevents erosion by creating natural dams that stop water from rushing over a field.

17 Analyze Which two soil conservation techniques would be best to use on gentle slopes?

☐ contour plowing

☐ crop terracing

☐ strip cropping

18 Analyze Which soil conservation technique would be best to use on very steep slopes?

☐ contour plowing

☐ crop terracing

☐ strip cropping

Into Thin Air

How can we reduce air pollution?

Polluted air can make people sick and harm organisms. Air pollution can cause the atmosphere to change in ways that are harmful to the environment and to people. There are many ways that we can reduce air pollution. We can use less energy. Also, we can develop new ways to get energy that produces less pollution. Everybody can help reduce air pollution in many different ways.

Through Energy Conservation

Energy conservation is one of the most important ways to reduce air pollution. Fossil fuels are currently the most commonly used energy resource. When they are burned, they release pollution into the air. If we use less energy, we burn fewer fossil fuels.

There are lots of ways to conserve energy. We can turn off lights when we don't need them. We can use energy-efficient lightbulbs and appliances. We can use air conditioners less in the summer and heaters less in the winter. We can unplug electronics when they are not in use. Instead of driving ourselves to places, we can use public transportation. We can also develop alternative energy sources that create less air pollution. Using wind, solar, and geothermal energy will help us burn less fossil fuel.

Active Reading

19 Identify Underline the sentences that explain the relationship between burning fossil fuels and air pollution.

Using public transportation, riding a bike, sharing rides, and walking reduce the amount of air pollution produced by cars.

Energy can be produced with very little pollution. These solar panels help us use energy from the sun and replace the use of fossil fuels.

Many cities, such as Los Angeles, California, have air pollution problems.

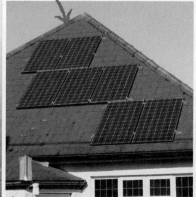

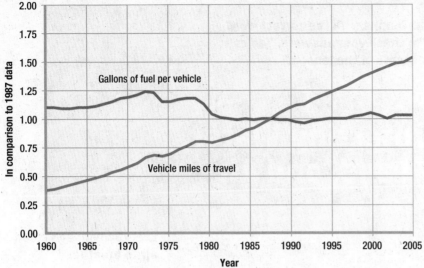

Vehicle Fuel Consumption and Miles Traveled, 1960–2005

In comparison to 1987 data

- Gallons of fuel per vehicle
- Vehicle miles of travel

Year

Source: U.S. Department of Transportation

20 Analyze How has vehicle fuel consumption in comparison to miles traveled changed since 1960? What is the likely cause for this change?

Through Technology

There are lots of ways to generate energy without creating much air pollution. By developing these alternative energy sources, we can reduce the amount of pollution created by burning fossil fuels. Wind turbines generate clean power. So do solar panels that use energy from the sun. We also can use power created by water flowing through rivers or moving with the tides. Geothermal energy from heat in Earth's crust can be used to generate electricity. Hybrid cars get energy from their brakes and store it in batteries. They burn less gas and release less pollution. Driving smaller cars that can go farther on a gallon of gas also reduces air pollution.

Through Laws

Governments in many countries work independently and together to reduce air pollution. They monitor air quality and set limits on what can be released into the air. In the United States, the Clean Air Act limits the amount of toxic chemicals and other pollutants that can be released into the atmosphere by factories and vehicles. It is up to the Environmental Protection Agency to make sure that these limits are enforced. Because air isn't contained by borders, some solutions must be international. The Kyoto Protocol is a worldwide effort to limit the release of greenhouse gases— pollution that can warm the atmosphere.

21 Summarize List three ways air pollution can be reduced.

- _____
- _____
- _____

New technologies, such as this compact fluorescent lightbulb (CFL), help limit air pollution. CFL bulbs use less energy to make the same amount of light.

Visual Summary

To complete this summary, fill in the blanks with the correct word or phrase. Then use the key below to check your answers. You can use this page to review the main concepts of the lesson.

Protecting Water, Land, and Air

Water resources are important to our health.

22 A community's water supply can be protected by:
- conserving water
- preventing pollution
- _____
- treating wastewater

Land resources are used to grow food and make products.

23 Land resources can be protected by:
- preservation
- reclamation and reforestation
- reducing urban sprawl
- _____
- soil conservation

Everybody needs clean air to breathe.

24 The main way to reduce air pollution is to:

_____
_____
_____
_____
_____
_____

25 **Relate** How can you personally act as a steward of water, land, and air resources?

Lesson Review

Vocabulary

Fill in the blank with the term that best completes the following sentences.

1 _____ is the wise use of natural resources.

2 _____ is the careful and responsible management of a resource.

Key Concepts

3 Describe How can water pollution be prevented?

_____

_____

_____

_____

Fill in the table below.

Example	Type of land resource conservation
4 Identify A county creates a park to protect a forest.	
5 Identify A mining company puts soil back in the hole and plants grass seeds on top of it.	
6 Identify A logging company plants new trees after it has cut some down.	
7 Identify A plastic milk bottle is turned into planks for a boardwalk to the beach.	
8 Identify Instead of building lots of single houses, a city builds an apartment building with a grocery store.	

9 Determine How has technology helped decrease air pollution in recent years?

_____

_____

_____

10 Explain Why is it important to protect Earth's water, land, and air resources?

_____

_____

_____

_____

Critical Thinking

11 Explain Land reclamation can be expensive. Why might recycling materials lead to spending less money on reclamation?

_____

_____

_____

Use the graph to answer the following question.

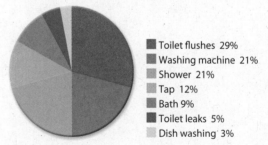

Average Water Usage of U.S. Household

- Toilet flushes 29%
- Washing machine 21%
- Shower 21%
- Tap 12%
- Bath 9%
- Toilet leaks 5%
- Dish washing 3%

Source: U.S. Environmental Protection Agency

12 Analyze The graph above shows water use in the average U.S. household. Using the graph, identify three effective ways a household could conserve water.

_____

_____

_____

My Notes

Unit 5 **Summary**

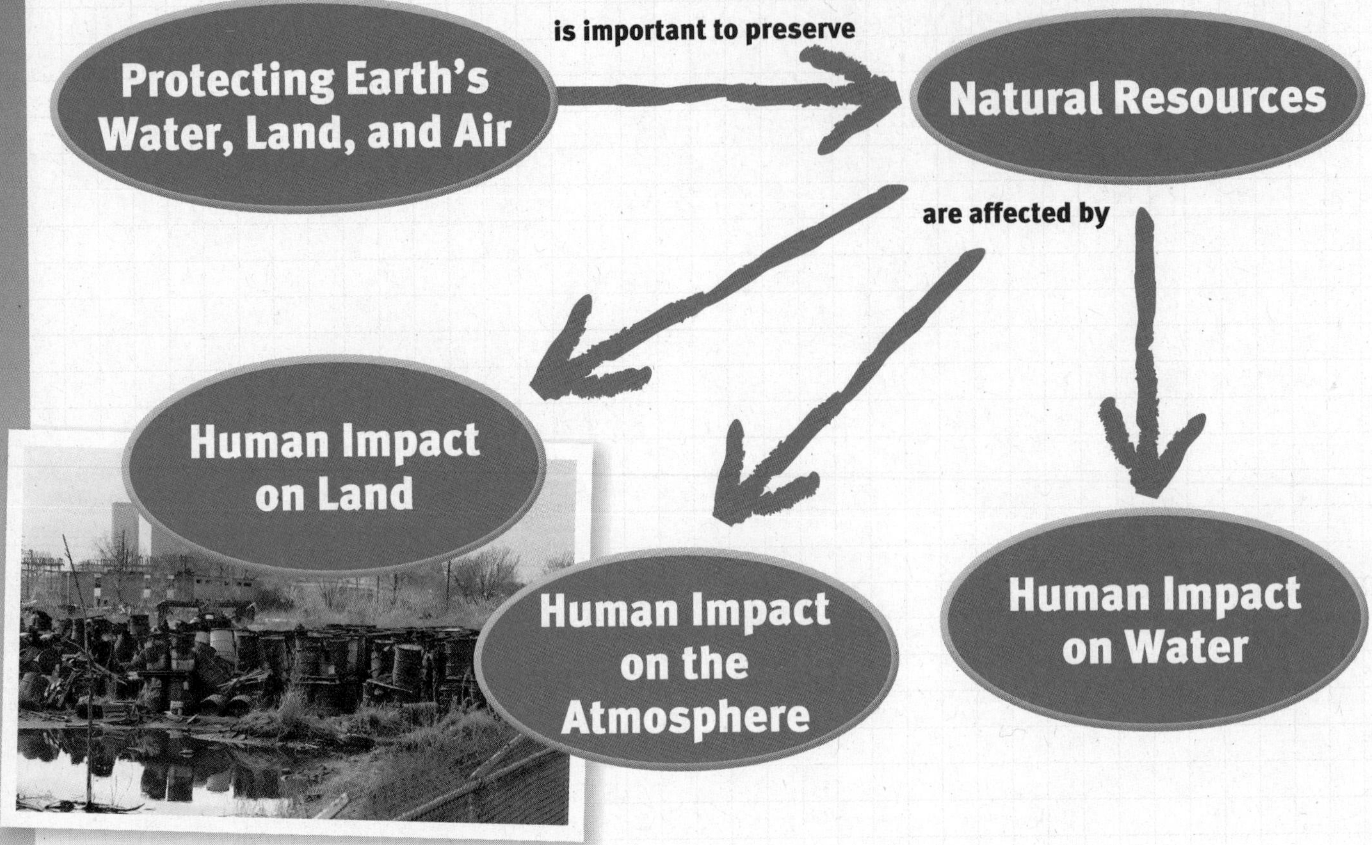

Protecting Earth's Water, Land, and Air

is important to preserve

Natural Resources

are affected by

Human Impact on Land

Human Impact on the Atmosphere

Human Impact on Water

1 Interpret The Graphic Organizer above shows that humans can have an impact on Earth's natural resources. List two examples of ways in which humans can have an impact on natural resources.

_____

_____

_____

_____

_____

2 Integrate How can erosion on land impact water quality?

_____

_____

_____

_____

3 Relate How does increasing human population affect land resources, water resources, and the atmosphere?

_____

_____

_____

_____

_____

_____

_____

_____

_____

ISTEP+ Review

Name _____

Multiple Choice

1 Which of the following items is sometimes considered a renewable resource and at other times considered a nonrenewable resource?

A. steel

B. wildlife

C. sunlight

D. limestone

2 Humans can cause different types of pollution. When fertilizers and pesticides make their way into water systems, which type of pollution has taken place?

A. air

B. biological

C. chemical

D. thermal

3 The line graph below shows the average amount of dissolved nutrients in a body of water each year from 1996 to 2005.

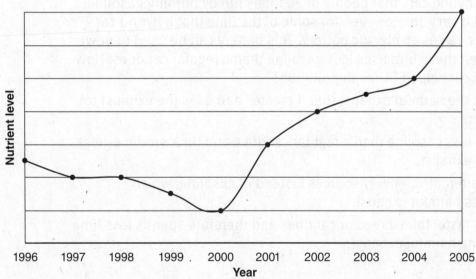

Dissolved Nutrients

Which human activity MOST LIKELY affected this body of water between 2000 and 2005?

A. burning fossil fuels

B. adding chemical fertilizers to water

C. dumping litter in the water

D. discharging warm water into the body of water

4 Which of the following choices is an example of environmental stewardship?

A. building a shopping center that is far from where most people live and work

B. choosing a building location that reduces the amount of trees that are cut down

C. saving money by burning fossil fuels instead of using alternative energy sources

D. passing laws that place the rights of wildlife over the health and safety of people

5 Humans need fresh, clean water to survive. Which of these statements is TRUE about fresh water?

A. An unlimited amount of fresh water is available on Earth.

B. In some places on Earth, fresh water is being used up faster than it can be replaced.

C. The global population is currently decreasing, and people are using less fresh water.

D. Fresh water was once considered a renewable resource, but now is considered an inexhaustible resource.

6 Many of the hybrid cars that people drive today run by burning gasoline, just as regular cars do. However, for some of the time that a hybrid car runs, it also charges an electric battery. This battery can be used to power the car so that the hybrid uses less gasoline than a regular car does. How can a hybrid car help REDUCE air pollution?

A. It stores the harmful exhaust that it creates and uses the exhaust to power the car.

B. It burns less gasoline than a regular car does and thus produces less harmful exhaust.

C. It uses alternative energy sources instead of gasoline, which produces harmful exhaust.

D. It drives faster than a regular car does and therefore spends less time producing harmful exhaust.

7   Earth's surface is mostly water. However, only a small amount of water on Earth is clean fresh water. Why is it important to maintain water quality?

A.   to keep clean fresh water from evaporating

B.   to keep levels of water in the ocean from lowering

C.   to keep the clean fresh water in the polar ice caps from melting

D.   to keep clean fresh water from becoming a nonrenewable resource

8   Acid precipitation harms vegetation and reduces soil quality. Which of the following is MOST responsible for acid precipitation?

A.   decrease in ozone levels

B.   burning of fossil fuels

C.   changes in the atmosphere

D.   changes in climate

9   Different areas are classified according to land use. Which of these areas would LIKELY have the largest human population and the highest levels of air pollution?

A.   a rural area

B.   an urban area

C.   a natural area

D.   a suburban area

Constructed Response

10   How does urbanization affect air pollution?

_____

_____

_____

Suggest ONE strategy for how an individual can reduce air pollution related to urbanization.

_____

_____

_____

_____

Extended Response

11 The diagram below shows a type of crop rotation.

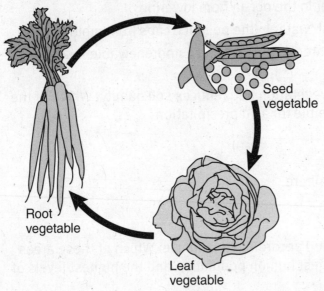

Root vegetable

Seed vegetable

Leaf vegetable

Define crop rotation in your own words.

_____

_____

Explain the purpose of crop rotation.

_____

_____

How might soil quality be affected if crops were not rotated each year?

_____

_____

Use the diagram to give an example of how a farmer could carry out crop rotation.

_____

_____

_____

_____

Life over Time

Core Standard

Explain how a particular environment selects for traits that increase the likelihood of survival and reproduction by individuals bearing those traits.

Fossils provide valuable information about life over time. Some species, such as the ginkgo tree, have lived on Earth for millions of years.

Modern ginkgo leaf

What do you think?

Over Earth's history, life forms change as the environment changes. What kinds of organisms lived in your area during prehistoric times?

Unit 6
Life over Time

CITIZEN SCIENCE

Prehistoric Life

Scientists have learned a lot about prehistoric times from fossils. We know that life on Earth was very different in the geologic past, and that it changes over time. A changing environment causes changes in the types of organisms that are able to survive.

Jurassic Period
206 m.y.a.–140 m.y.a.

The central United States was covered by a huge ocean during the age of the dinosaurs! Many fossils from that time period are from aquatic organisms.

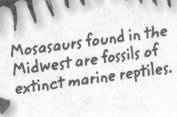

Mosasaurs found in the Midwest are fossils of extinct marine reptiles.

What clues does this fossil give you about the type of food the animal ate?

Wood fossilizes when minerals replace all the organic material.

Mammals such as this saber-toothed cat once roamed Indiana grasslands.

Great white egrets live in Indiana's wetlands.

Tertiary Period
65 m.y.a.–2 m.y.a.

Land began to emerge from the water. Early mammals and some plants left many kinds of fossils behind, telling us a lot about this period.

Early Holocene
12,000–10,000 years ago

As humans occupied the land, many large animals, including mammoths, mastodons, saber-toothed cats, and giant sloths, disappeared.

Present Day

Humans have a large impact on the organisms living in the Midwest. Some species, such as the piping plover, are threatened with extinction due to human activities. Protecting these species helps to ensure that Midwestern habitats will remain diverse.

Take It Home) Your Neighborhood over Time

Your neighborhood has also changed over time. Do some research to find out when your town was founded. Create a timeline similar to the one above that shows the details of what changes your neighborhood and town might have experienced in the time since it was founded.

Theory of Evolution by Natural Selection

ESSENTIAL QUESTION

What is the theory of evolution by natural selection?

By the end of this lesson, you should be able to describe the role of genetic and environmental factors in the theory of evolution by natural selection.

Because this grass snake's skin color looks like the plant stalk, it is able to hide from predators! This form of camouflage is the result of natural selection.

🦭 Indiana Standards

8.3.7 Recognize and explain that small genetic differences between parents and offspring can accumulate in successive generations so that descendants may be different from their ancestors.

8.3.8 Examine traits of individuals within a population of organisms that may give them an advantage in survival and reproduction in a given environment or when the environment changes.

8.3.9 Describe the effect of environmental changes on populations of organisms when their adaptive characteristics put them at a disadvantage for survival. Describe how extinction of a species can ultimately result.

Engage Your Brain

1 Predict Check T or F to show whether you think each statement is true or false.

T **F**

☐ ☐ Skin color can protect an animal from danger.

☐ ☐ The amount of available food can impact an organism's survival.

☐ ☐ Your parents' characteristics are not passed on to you.

☐ ☐ A species can go extinct if its habitat is destroyed.

2 Imagine How do you think phones have changed from the type in the photo below to what is used today?

_____

_____

_____

_____

_____

Active Reading

3 Synthesize You can often define an unknown word by clues provided in the sentence. Use the sentence below to make an educated guess about the meaning of the word *artificial*.

Example sentence
Many people prefer real sugar to <u>artificial</u> sweeteners made by humans.

_____

_____

_____

Vocabulary Terms

- evolution
- artificial selection
- natural selection
- variation
- adaptation
- extinction

4 Apply As you learn the definition of each vocabulary term in this lesson, create your own definition or sketch to help you remember the meaning of the term.

© Houghton Mifflin Harcourt • Image Credits: (bkg) ©DLILLC/Corbis; (tr) ©Corbis

Darwin's Voyage

What did Darwin observe?

You have already seen an example of how the telephone has changed over time. In biology, **evolution** refers to the process in which populations gradually change over time. A population is all the individuals of a species that live together in an area. A species is a group of closely-related organisms that can produce fertile offspring. A scientist named Charles Darwin developed a theory of how evolution takes place.

Charles Darwin was born in England in 1809. When he was 22 years old, Darwin graduated from college with a degree in theology. But he was most interested in plants and animals. So he signed on as the naturalist—a scientist who studies nature—on the British ship HMS *Beagle*. With the observations he made on this almost five-year journey, Darwin formed a theory about how biological evolution could happen.

Darwin kept a log during his voyage and this was published as *The Voyage of the Beagle*. Darwin observed and collected many living and fossil specimens. Darwin made his most influential observations on the Galápagos Islands of South America.

Darwin left England on December 27, 1831. He returned 5 years later.

The plants and animals on the Galápagos Islands differed from island to island. This is where Darwin studied birds called finches.

NORTH AMERICA

EUROPE

ENGLAND

ATLANTIC OCEAN

AFRICA

Galápagos Islands

Equator

SOUTH AMERICA

Cape of Good Hope

Think Outside the Book · Inquiry

5 Explore Trace Darwin's route on the map, and choose one of the following stops on his journey: Galápagos Islands, Andes Mountains, Australia. Do some research to find out what plants and animals live there. Then write an entry in Darwin's log to describe what you saw.

Differences Among Species

Darwin collected birds from the Galápagos Islands and nearby islands. He observed that these birds differed slightly from those on the nearby mainland of South America. And the birds on each island were different from the birds on the other islands. After careful analysis back in England, he realized that they were all finches!

The most obvious difference between the finches was the shape of their beaks. Perhaps these differences related to the birds' diets. Birds with shorter, heavier beaks could eat harder foods than those that had skinnier, thinner beaks. Based on these observations, Darwin wondered if the birds had evolved from one species of finch.

This cactus finch has a narrow beak that it uses to cut into cactus and eat the tissue.

The vegetarian finch has a curved beak, ideal for taking large berries from a branch.

ASIA

👁 **Visualize It!**

6 Infer How do you think the pointed beak of this woodpecker finch helps it to get food?

_____

_____

_____

Woodpecker finch

Equator

INDIAN OCEAN

Darwin saw many plants and animals that were only found on certain continents, such as Australia.

AUSTRALIA

NEW ZEALAND

km 0   1,000   2,000

mi 0   1,000   2,000

Darwin's Homework

What other ideas influenced Darwin?

The ideas of many scientists and observations of the natural world influenced Darwin's thinking. Darwin was influenced by ideas about how traits are passed on in selective breeding, Earth's history, and the growth of populations. All of these ideas helped him develop his theory of how populations could change over time.

This chicken has been bred to have large tail feathers and a big red comb.

Organisms Pass Traits On to Offspring

Farmers and breeders have been producing many kinds of domestic animals and plants for thousands of years. These plants and animals had traits that were desired by the farmers and breeders. A *trait* is a form of an inherited characteristic. For example, large tail feathers is a trait, and tail feather length is the corresponding characteristic. The practice by which humans select plants or animals for breeding based on desired traits is **artificial selection**. Artificial selection shows that traits can change and can spread through populations.

This chicken has been bred to have large head feathers.

7 List Darwin studied artificial selection in the pigeons that he bred. List three other animals that have many different breeds.

_____

_____

_____

_____

This chicken has been bred to have feathers on its feet.

8 Identify As you read, underline the names of other important thinkers that influenced Darwin's theory.

Organisms Acquire Traits

Scientist Jean Baptiste Lamarck thought that organisms could bring about the changes they needed to survive in the environment. For example, a man could acquire stronger muscles over time. If the muscles were an advantage in the environment, he would pass these stronger muscles on to his offspring. We know now that acquired traits do not become part of an organism's DNA, and can't be passed on to offspring. But the idea that an organism's traits help them survive influenced Darwin's theory.

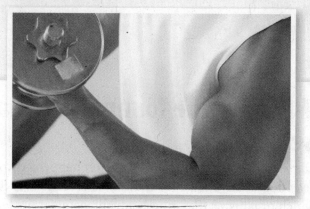

9 Apply Is the size of your muscles an acquired trait or part of your DNA? Explain.

_____

_____

_____

These rock layers formed over millions of years.

The Earth Changes Over Time

The presence of different rock layers, such as in the Grand Canyon to the left, show that Earth has changed over time. Geologist Charles Lyell theorized that small changes in rock have collected over hundreds of millions of years. Darwin reasoned that if Earth were very old, then there would be enough time for very small changes in life forms to collect over a very long period of time as well.

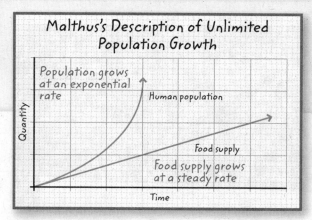

Malthus's Description of Unlimited Population Growth

Population grows at an exponential rate

Human population

Quantity

Food supply

Food supply grows at a steady rate

Time

Visualize It!

10 Infer What can you infer from the two red growth lines on this graph?

_____

_____

A Struggle for Survival Exists

After his journey Darwin read an essay about population growth by economist Thomas Malthus. The essay helped Darwin understand how the environment could influence which organisms survive and which organisms die. All populations are affected by factors that limit population growth, such as disease, predation, and competition for food. Darwin reasoned that the survivors probably have traits that help them survive, and that some of these traits could be passed on from parent to offspring.

Natural Selection

What are the four parts of natural selection?

Darwin proposed that most evolution happens through the natural selection of advantageous traits. **Natural selection** is the process by which organisms that inherit advantageous traits tend to reproduce more successfully than the other organisms do.

Overproduction

When a plant or animal reproduces, it usually makes more offspring than the environment can support. For example, a female jaguar may have up to four pups. Only some of them will survive to adulthood, and a smaller number of them will successfully reproduce.

---

11 Infer A fish may have hundreds of offspring at a time, and only a small number will survive. What characteristics of fish might allow them to survive?

_____

_____

_____

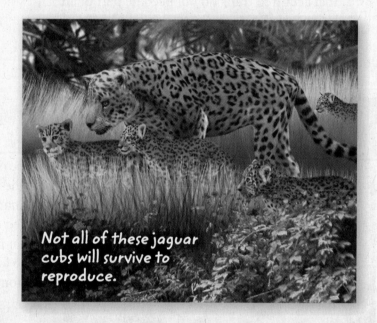

Not all of these jaguar cubs will survive to reproduce.

Variation exists in the jaw size between these two jaguars. This variation will get passed on to the next generation.

Genetic Variation

Within a species there are natural differences, or **variations**, in traits. For example, the jaw size of the two jaguar skulls to the left is different. This difference results from a difference in the genetic material of the jaguars. Genetic variations can be passed on from parent to offsrping. Sometimes a mutation occurs that changes genetic material.

As each new generation is produced, new genetic differences may be introduced into a population. In this way, genetic variations can add up in a population. The more genetic variation a population has, the more likely it is that some individuals might have traits that will be advantageous if the environment changes.

Selection

Individuals try to get the resources they need to survive. These resources include food, water, space and, in most cases, mates for reproduction. About 11,000 years ago jaguars faced a shortage of food because the climate changed and many species died. A genetic variation in jaw size became important for survival. Jaguars with larger jaws could eat hard-shelled reptiles when other prey were hard to find.

Darwin reasoned that individuals with a particular trait, like a large jaw, are more likely to survive long enough to reproduce. As a result, the trait is "selected," or becomes more common in the next generation of offspring.

12 Summarize How did large jaws and teeth become typical characteristics of jaguars?

_____

_____

_____

A larger jaw makes it easier for this jaguar to eat hard-shelled turtles.

Adaptation

An inherited characteristic that helps an organism survive and reproduce in its environment is an **adaptation**. A larger jaw size helped jaguars survive when food was hard to find. As the process of natural selection repeats from generation to generation, these adaptations become more common in the population, and new adaptations may arise. Over time, the population becomes better adapted to the environment.

Large jaw size is one adaptation of jaguars.

13 Explain In the table below, explain how each part of natural selection works.

Principles of natural selection	How it works
Overproduction	
Inherited Variation	
Selection	
Adaptation	

Well-adapted

How do species change over time?

Life first appeared on Earth nearly 4 billion years ago. Since then, many species—such as dinosaurs—appeared, survived for a time, and then died. An incredible diversity of life exists because species have changed over time, or evolved.

Sometimes a population changes so much that it can no longer reproduce with the rest of the species. That population becomes a new species. An early form of a species, called an *ancestor*, may give rise to many new *descendent* species over time.

The skin of this frog looks like a dead leaf.

14 Apply How does this frog's color help it survive?

_____

_____

_____

_____

This butterfly has a long tongue to reach nectar deep inside a flower.

Species Change in Response to Their Environment

Adaptations are genetic variations that help a species survive and reproduce in a particular environment. Some adaptations, such as a butterfly's long tongue, are physical. Other adaptations, such as a bird's mating ritual, are behaviors that help it find food, protect itself, or reproduce. The frog above is adapted to its environment because it can hide from predators.

The male frigate bird uses his red throat pouch to attract a female and hopefully reproduce.

A venus flytrap is well-adapted to catch prey!

This dinosaur went extinct about 65 million years ago.

Why is adaptation important for survival?

The traits that help an organism survive depend on both the needs of the species and environmental factors. For example, a snake that lives in tall, green grass may benefit from being green. In this environment, a green snake will be able to hide from predators more easily than a brown snake will. Therefore, green snakes will survive and reproduce more than brown snakes will. But being brown may be more beneficial if the snake lives on a forest floor that has a large amount of dead leaves. On a forest floor, a brown snake will probably survive and reproduce more than a green snake will.

Species Not Adapted to the Environment May Go Extinct

What happens when the environment that a species has adapted to changes? The environmental change could be gradual, or it could happen suddenly. Changes in environmental conditions can affect the survival of individuals with a particular trait. The species may be able to survive at first. But, if no individuals were born with traits that help them to survive and reproduce in the changed environment, the species will become extinct.

Extinction is when all of the members of a species have died. Competition, new predators, and the loss of habitat are environmental pressures that can limit the growth of populations and could lead to extinction. The fossil record is a record of the things that have lived in a particular location. It shows that many species, like the dinosaur above, have gone extinct in the course of the history of life on Earth.

👁 **Visualize It!**

15 Summarize Examine the four photos of adaptations. Describe how each of the adaptations below help the species survive and or reproduce.

Organism	Adaptation	Role in survival or reproduction
venus flytrap	trap helps catch prey	
frog	skin looks like a dead leaf	
bird	male has large red throat pouch	
butterfly	long tongue to reach inside flower	

Visual Summary

To complete this summary, circle the correct word. Then use the key below to check your answers. You can use this page to review the main concepts of the lesson.

Darwin's theory of natural selection was influenced by his own observations and the work of other scientists.

Evolution is Change Over Time

16 During natural / artificial selection, breeders choose the traits that are passed on to the next generation.

The theory of evolution by natural selection states that organisms with advantageous traits produce more offspring.

17 Natural selection can only act on acquired traits / inherited variation.

Species that are not adapted to their environment may go extinct.

18 Dinosaurs are an example of organisms that have undergone variation / extinction.

19 **Infer** How does the environment influence natural selection?

Lesson Review

Vocabulary

Use a term from the lesson to complete the sentences below.

1 _____ is the natural difference between members of a species.

2 Owners of cattle herds who only choose to breed cows that produce the most milk are engaging in _____ selection.

3 A characteristic that improves an individual's ability to survive and reproduce in a specific environment is called an _____

Key Concepts

4 Summarize Describe what Darwin observed during his voyage on the HMS *Beagle*.

_____

_____

_____

_____

5 Explain How does the environment impact a species's survival?

_____

_____

_____

_____

6 Compare Why are only inherited traits, not acquired ones, necessary for the process of natural selection?

_____

_____

_____

_____

7 Describe How are fish adapted to their environment?

_____

_____

_____

Critical Thinking

Use the diagram to answer the following question.

8 Apply How are each of these lizards adapted to their environment?

_____

_____

_____

_____

_____

_____

_____

_____

9 Infer How can natural selection account for the long snout of an anteater?

_____

_____

_____

_____

_____

_____

Scientific Debate

Indiana Standards

NOS 8.8 Analyze data, using appropriate mathematical manipulation as required, and use it to identify patterns and make inferences based on these patterns.

NOS 8.11 Communicate findings using graphs, charts, maps and models through oral and written reports.

Not all scientific knowledge is gained through experimentation. It is also the result of a great deal of debate and confirmation.

Tutorial

As you prepare for a debate, look for information from the following sources.

Controlled Experiments Consider the following points when planning or examining the results of a controlled experiment.

- Only one factor should be tested at a time. A factor is anything in the experiment that can influence the outcome.

- Samples are divided into experimental group(s) and a control group. All of the factors of the experimental group(s) and the control group are the same except for one variable.

- A variable is a factor that can be changed. If there are multiple variables, only one variable should be changed at a time.

Independent Studies The results of a different group may provide stronger support for your argument than your own results. And using someone else's results helps to avoid the claim that your results are biased. Bias is the tendency to think about something from only one point of view. The claim of bias can be used to argue against your point.

Comparison with Similar Objects or Events If you cannot gather data from an experiment to help support your position, finding a similar object or event might help. The better your example is understood, the stronger your argument will be.

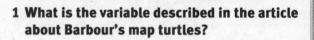

Read the passage below and answer the questions.

Many people want to protect endangered species but do not agree on the best methods to use. Incubating, or heating eggs to ensure hatching, is commonly used with bird eggs. It was logical to apply the same technique to turtle eggs. The Barbour's map turtle is found in Florida, Georgia, and Alabama. To help more turtles hatch, people would gather eggs and incubate them. However, debate really began when mostly female turtles hatched. Were efforts to help the turtles really harming them? Scientists learned that incubating eggs at 25°C (77°F) produces males and at 30°C (86°F) produces females. As a result, conservation programs have stopped artificially heating the eggs.

1 What is the variable described in the article about Barbour's map turtles?

_____

2 Write a list of factors that were likely kept the same between the sample groups described in the article.

_____

_____

_____

3 What argument could people have used who first suggested incubating the turtle eggs?

_____

_____

_____

You Try It!

Fossils from the Burgess Shale Formation in Canada include many strange creatures that lived over 500 million years ago. The fossils are special because the soft parts of the creatures were preserved. Examine the fossil of the creature *Marrella* and the reconstruction of what it might have looked like.

Fossil

Reconstruction

1 Recognizing Relationships Find four features on the reconstruction that you can also identify in the fossil. Write a brief description of each feature.

_____

_____

_____

_____

_____

_____

_____

2 Applying Concepts *Marrella* is extinct. How do you think *Marrella* behaved when it was alive? What did it eat? How did it move? On what do you base your argument?

_____

_____

_____

_____

_____

_____

_____

_____

_____

3 Communicating Ideas Share your description with a classmate. Discuss and debate your positions. Complete the table to show the points on which you agree and disagree.

Agree	Disagree

Take It Home

Research more about the creatures of the Burgess Shale Formation. Find at least one other fossil creature and its reconstruction. What do you think the creature was like?

Evidence of Evolution

ESSENTIAL QUESTION

What evidence supports the theory of evolution?

By the end of this lesson, you should be able to describe the evidence that supports the theory of evolution by natural selection.

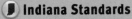**Indiana Standards**

8.3.6 Observe anatomical structures of a variety of organisms and describe their similarities and differences. Use the data collected to organize the organisms into groups and predict their relatedness.

Fossils show us what a dinosaur looks like. This dinosaur lived millions of years ago!

Engage Your Brain

1 Predict Check T or F to show whether you think each statement is true or false.

T	F	
☐	☐	Fossils provide evidence of organisms that lived in the past.
☐	☐	The wing of a bat has similar bones to those in a human arm.
☐	☐	DNA can tell us how closely related two organisms are.
☐	☐	Whales are descended from land-dwelling mammals.

2 Infer This is a Petoskey stone, which is made up of tiny coral fossils. What can you infer if you find a coral fossil on land?

Petoskey stone

_____

_____

_____

_____

Active Reading

3 Synthesize You can often define an unknown word if you understand the parts of the word. Use the words below to make an educated guess about the meaning of the word *fossil record*.

Word	Meaning
fossil	the remains or trace of once-living organisms
record	an account that preserves information about facts or events

fossil record:

_____

_____

_____

Vocabulary Terms

- fossil
- fossil record

4 Apply As you learn the definition of each vocabulary term in this lesson, create your own definition or sketch to help you remember the meaning of the term.

Fossil Hunt

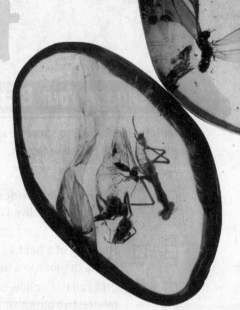

How do fossils form?

Evidence that organisms have changed over time can be found in amber, ice, or sedimentary rock. Sedimentary rock is formed when particles of sand or soil are deposited in horizontal layers. Often this occurs as mud or silt hardens. After one rock layer forms, newer rock layers form on top of it. So, older layers are found below or underneath younger rock layers. The most basic principle of dating such rocks and the remains of organisms inside is "the deeper it is, the older it is."

Amber fossils form when small creatures are trapped in tree sap and the sap hardens.

5 Examine What features of the organism are preserved in amber?

_____

_____

_____

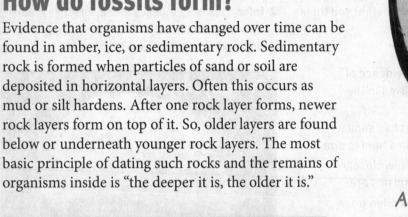

This flying dinosaur is an example of a cast fossil.

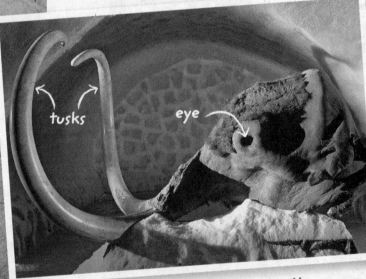

tusks

eye

Because this woolly mammoth was frozen in ice, its skin and hair were preserved.

Many Fossils Form in Sedimentary Rock

Rock layers preserve evidence of organisms that were once alive. The remains or imprints of once-living organisms are called **fossils**. Fossils commonly form when a dead organism is covered by a layer of sediment or mud. Over time, more sediment settles on top of the organism. Minerals in the sediment may seep into the organism and replace the body's material with minerals that harden over time. This process produces a cast fossil. Many familiar fossils are casts of hard parts, such as shells and bones. If the organism rots away completely after being covered, it may leave an imprint of itself in the rock. Despite all of the fossils that have been found, it is rare for an organism to become a fossil. Most often, the dead organism is recycled back into the biological world by scavengers, decomposers, or the process of weathering.

Active Reading

6 Identify As you read, underline the steps that describe how a cast fossil forms.

How do fossils show change over time?

All of the fossils that have been discovered make up the **fossil record**. The fossil record provides evidence about the order in which species have existed through time, and how they have changed over time. By examining the fossil record, scientists can learn about the history of life on Earth.

Despite all the fossils that have been found, there are gaps in the fossil record. These gaps represent chunks of geologic time for which a fossil has not been discovered. Also, the transition between two groups of organisms may not be well understood. Fossils that help fill in these gaps are *transitional fossils*. The illustration on the right is based on a transitional fossil.

Fossils found in newer layers of Earth's crust tend to have physical or molecular similarities to present-day organisms. These similarities indicate that the fossilized organisms were close relatives of the present-day organisms. Fossils from older layers are less similar to present-day organisms than fossils from newer layers are. Most older fossils are of earlier life-forms such as dinosaurs, which don't exist anymore.

Visualize It!

A transitional form between fish and four-legged land vertebrates may be this creature called *Tiktaalik roseae*.

7 Identify Describe the environment in which this organism lives.

_____

_____

_____

8 Infer How is this organism like both a fish and a four-legged vertebrate, such as an amphibian?

_____

_____

_____

_____

More clues . . .

What other evidence supports evolution?

Many fields of study provide evidence that modern species and extinct species share an ancestor. A *common ancestor* is the most recent species from which two different species have evolved. Structural data, DNA, developmental patterns, and fossils all support the theory that populations change over time. Sometimes these populations become new species. Biologists observe that all living organisms have some traits in common and inherit traits in similar ways. Evidence of when and where those ancestors lived and what they looked like is found in the fossil record.

Active Reading

9 List What is a common ancestor?

_____

_____

_____

Common Structures

Scientists have found that related organisms share structural traits. Structures reduced in size or function may have been complete and functional in the organism's ancestor. For example, snakes have traces of leglike structures that are not used for movement. These unused structures are evidence that snakes share a common ancestor with animals like lizards and dogs.

Scientists also consider similar structures with different functions. The arm of a human, the front leg of a cat, and the wing of a bat do not look alike and are not used in the same way. But as you can see, they are similar in structure. The bones of a human arm are similar in structure to the bones in the front limbs of a cat and a bat. These similarities suggest that cats, bats, and humans had a common ancestor. Over millions of years, changes occurred. Now, these bones perform different functions in each type of animal.

front limb of a bat

front limb of a cat

Visualize It!

10 Relate Do you see any similarities between the bones of the bat and cat limbs and the bones of the human arm? If so, use the colors of the bat and cat bones to color similar bones in the human arm. If you don't have colored pencils, label the bones with the correct color names.

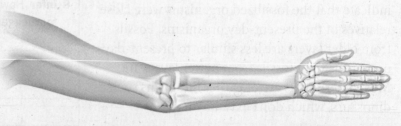

Similar DNA

The genetic information stored in an organism's DNA determines the organism's traits. Because an organism's DNA stays almost exactly the same throughout its entire lifetime, scientists can compare the DNA from many organisms. The greater the number of similarities between the molecules of any two species, the more recently the two species most likely shared a common ancestor.

Recall that DNA determines which amino acids make up a protein. Scientists have compared the amino acids that make up cytochrome c proteins in many species. Cytochrome c is involved in cellular respiration. Organisms that have fewer amino acid differences are more likely to be closely related.

Frogs also have cytochrome c proteins, but they're a little different from yours.

Cytochrome C Comparison

Organism	Number of amino acid differences from human cytochrome c
Chimpanzee	0
Rhesus monkey	1
Whale	10
Turtle	15
Bullfrog	18
Lamprey	20

Source: M.Dayhoff, *Atlas of Protein Sequence and Structure*

Visualize It!

11 Infer The number of amino acids in human cytochrome c differs between humans and the species at left. Which two species do you infer are the least closely related to humans?

_____

_____

_____

_____

Developmental Similarities

The study of development is called *embryology*. Embryos undergo many physical and functional changes as they grow and develop. If organisms develop in similar ways, they also likely share a common ancestor.

Scientists have compared the development of different species to look for similar patterns and structures. Scientists think that such similarities come from an ancestor that the species have in common. For example, at some time during development, all animals with backbones have a tail. This observation suggests that they shared a common ancestor.

These embryos are at a similar stage of development.

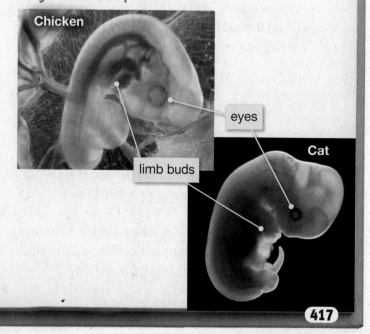

Chicken

limb buds

eyes

Cat

Visualize It!

How do we know organisms are related?

Scientists examine organisms carefully for clues about their ancestors. In a well-studied example, scientists looked at the characteristics of whales that made them different from other ocean animals. Unlike fish and sharks, whales breathe air, give birth to live young, and produce milk. Fossil and DNA evidence support the hypothesis that modern whales evolved from hoofed mammals that lived on land.

Fossil Evidence

Scientists have examined fossils of extinct species that have features in between whales and land mammals. These features are called *transitional characters*. None of these species are directly related to modern whales. But their skeletons suggest how a gradual transition from land mammal to aquatic whale could have happened.

Ⓐ Pakicetus   52 million years ago
- whale-shaped skull and teeth adapted for hunting fish
- ran on four legs
- ear bones in between those of land and aquatic mammals

Ⓑ Ambulocetus natans   50 million years ago
- name means "the walking whale that swims"
- hind limbs that were adapted for swimming
- a fish eater that lived on water and on land

Ⓒ Dorudon   About 40 million years ago
- lived in warm seas and propelled itself with a long tail
- tiny hind legs could not be used for swimming
- pelvis and hind limbs not connected to spine, could not support weight for walking

Unused Structures

Most modern whales have pelvic bones and some have leg bones. These bones do not help the animal move.

Molecular Evidence

The DNA of whales is very similar to the DNA of hoofed mammals. Below are some DNA fragments of a gene that makes a type of milk protein.

Hippopotamus   TCC TGGCA GTCCA GTGGT
Humpback whale CCC TGGCA GTGCA GTGCT

12 Identify Circle the pairs of nitrogen bases (G, T, C, or A) that differ between the hippopotamus and humpback whale DNA.

13 Infer How do you think these bones are involved in a whale's movement?

_____

_____

_____

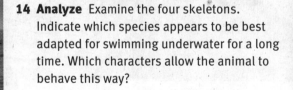

Modern Whale   *Present day*

- no hind limbs, front limbs are flippers
- some whales have tiny hip bones left over from their hoofed-mammal ancestors
- breathe air with lungs like other mammals do

14 Analyze Examine the four skeletons. Indicate which species appears to be best adapted for swimming underwater for a long time. Which characters allow the animal to behave this way?

_____

_____

_____

_____

_____

_____

Visual Summary

To complete this summary, circle the correct word. Then use the key below to check your answers. You can use this page to review the main concepts of the lesson.

Evidence of Evolution

Fossil evidence shows that life on Earth has changed over time.

15 The remains of once-living organisms are called fossils / ancestors.

Scientists use evidence from many fields of research to study the common ancestors of living organisms.

Evolutionary theory is also supported by structural, genetic, and developmental evidence.

16 Similarities / Differences in internal structures support evidence of common ancestry.

17 The tiny leg bones / large dorsal fins of modern whales are an example of unused structures.

Answers: 15 fossils; 16 similarities; 17 tiny leg bones

18 Summarize How does the fossil record provide evidence of the diversity of life?

Lesson Review

Vocabulary

1 Which word means "the remains or imprints of once-living organisms found in layers of rock?"

_____

2 Which word means "the history of life in the geologic past as indicated by the imprints or remains of living things?"

_____

Key Concepts

3 Identify What are two types of evidence that suggest that evolution has occurred?

_____

_____

4 Explain How do fossils provide evidence that evolution has taken place?

_____

_____

5 Apply What is the significance of the similar number and arrangement of bones in a human arm and a bat wing?

_____

_____

_____

Critical Thinking

6 Imagine If you were a scientist examining the DNA sequence of two unknown organisms that you hypothesize share a common ancestor, what evidence would you expect to find?

_____

_____

_____

Use this table to answer the following questions.

Cytochrome C Comparison	
Organism	Number of amino acid differences from human cytochrome c
Chimpanzee	0
Turtle	15
Tuna	21

Source: M. Dayhoff, *Atlas of Protein Sequence and Structure*

7 Identify What do the data suggest about how related turtles are to humans compared to tuna and chimpanzees?

_____

_____

_____

8 Infer If there are no differences between the amino acid sequences in the cytochrome c protein of humans and chimpanzees, why aren't we the same species?

_____

_____

_____

_____

9 Apply Explain why the pattern of differences that exists from earlier to later fossils in the fossil record supports the idea that evolution has taken place on Earth.

_____

_____

_____

_____

Classification of Living Things

ESSENTIAL QUESTION

How are organisms classified?

By the end of this lesson, you should be able to describe how people sort living things into groups based on shared characteristics.

Scientists use physical and chemical characteristics to classify organisms. Is that an ant? Look again. It's an ant-mimicking jumping spider!

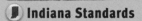 **Indiana Standards**

8.3.6 Observe anatomical structures of a variety of organisms and describe their similarities and differences. Use the data collected to organize the organisms into groups and predict their relatedness.

© Houghton Mifflin Harcourt Publishing Company • Image Credits: ©Simon D. Pollard/Photo Researchers, Inc.

Engage Your Brain

1 Predict Check T or F to show whether you think each statement is true or false.

T	F	
☐	☐	The classification system used today has changed very little since it was introduced.
☐	☐	To be classified as an animal, organisms must have a backbone.
☐	☐	Organisms can be classified by whether they have nuclei in their cells.
☐	☐	Scientists can study genetic material to classify organisms.
☐	☐	Organisms that have many physical similarities may be related.

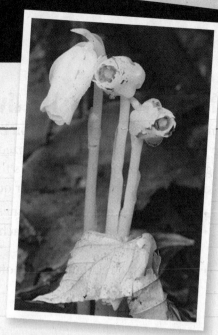

2 Analyze The flowering plant shown above is called an Indian pipe. It could be mistaken for a fungus. Write down how the plant is similar to and different from other plants you know.

_____

_____

_____

_____

Active Reading

3 Synthesize Often, you can define an unknown word if you know the meaning of its word parts. Use the word parts and sentence below to make an educated guess about the meaning of the term *dichotomous key*.

Word part	Meaning
dich-	in two
-tomous	to cut

Example sentence
Sophie used the paired statements in a <u>dichotomous key</u> to identify the animal she found during the field trip.

dichotomous key:

_____

_____

_____

Vocabulary Terms

- species
- genus
- domain
- Bacteria
- Archaea
- Eukarya
- Animalia
- Plantae
- Protista
- Fungi
- dichotomous key

4 Apply As you learn the definition of each vocabulary term in this lesson, write your own definition or make a sketch to help you remember the meaning of each term.

Sorting Things Out!

Why do we classify living things?

There are millions of living things on Earth. How do scientists keep all of these living things organized? Scientists *classify* living things based on characteristics that living things share. Classification helps scientists answer questions such as:

- How many kinds of living things are there?
- What characteristics define each kind of living thing?
- What are the relationships among living things?

Sharks have fins and gills.

Dolphins also have fins, but not gills.

Visualize It!

5 Analyze The photos below show two organisms. In the table, place a check mark in the box for each characteristic that the organisms have.

Miami blue butterfly

Scrub jay

	Wings	Antennae	Beak	Feathers
Miami blue butterfly				
Scrub jay				

6 Summarize What characteristics do Miami blue butterflies have in common with scrub jays? How do they differ?

_____

_____

_____

How do scientists know living things are related?

If two organisms look similar, are they related? To classify organisms, scientists compare physical characteristics. For example, they may look at size or bone structure. Scientists also compare the chemical characteristics of living things.

Active Reading

7 Identify As you read this page, underline the characteristics used to classify living things.

Physical Characteristics

How are chickens similar to dinosaurs? If you compare dinosaur fossils and chicken skeletons, you'll see that chickens and dinosaurs share many physical characteristics. Scientists look at physical characteristics, such as skeletal structure. They also study how organisms develop from an egg to an adult. Organisms that have similar skeletons and development may be related.

Chemical Characteristics

Scientists can identify the relationships among organisms by studying genetic material such as DNA and RNA. They use mutations and genetic similarities to find relationships among organisms. Organisms that have very similar gene sequences or have the same mutations are likely related. Other chemicals, such as proteins and hormones, can also be studied to learn how organisms are related.

Kaibab squirrels live on the North Rim of the Grand Canyon.

Abert's squirrels live on the South Rim of the Grand Canyon.

Kaibab squirrels and Abert's squirrels look different, and they are separated by the Grand Canyon. However, DNA testing showed that these squirrels are very closely related.

8 Synthesize In addition to canyons, what other kinds of geologic formations might separate similar organisms?

_____

_____

_____

What's in a Name?

How are living things named?

Early scientists used names as long as 12 words to identify living things, and they also used common names. So, classification was confusing. In the 1700s, a scientist named Carolus Linnaeus (KAR•uh•luhs lih•NEE•uhs) simplified the naming of living things. He gave each kind of living thing a two-part *scientific name*.

Scientific Names

Each species has its own scientific name. A **species** (SPEE•sheez) is a group of organisms that are very closely related. They can mate and produce fertile offspring. Consider the scientific name for a mountain lion: *Puma concolor.* The first part, *Puma,* is the genus name. A **genus** (JEE•nuhs; plural, *genera*) includes similar species. The second part, *concolor,* is the specific, or species, name. No other species is named *Puma concolor.*

A scientific name always includes the genus name followed by the specific name. The first letter of the genus name is capitalized, and the first letter of the specific name is lowercase. The entire scientific name is written either in italics or underlined.

HELLO
my name is
Carolus Linnaeus

The A.K.A. Files

Some living things have many common names. Scientific names prevent confusion when people discuss organisms.

Scientific name:
Puma concolor

Common names:
Mountain lion
Puma
Cougar
Panther

Scientific name:
Acer rubrum

Common names:
Red maple
Swamp maple
Soft maple

9 Apply In the scientific names above, circle the genus name and underline the specific name.

What are the levels of classification?

Linnaeus's ideas became the basis for modern taxonomy (tak•SAHN•uh•mee). *Taxonomy* is the science of describing, classifying, and naming living things. At first, many scientists sorted organisms into two groups: plants and animals. But many organisms did not fit into either group.

Today, scientists use an eight-level system to classify living things. Each level gets more definite. Therefore, it contains fewer kinds of living things than the level before it. Living things in the lower levels are more closely related to each other than they are to organisms in the higher levels. From most general to most definite, the levels of classification are domain, kingdom, phylum (plural, *phyla*), class, order, family, genus, and species.

Classifying Organisms

Domain **Domain Eukarya** includes all protists, fungi, plants, and animals.

Kingdom **Kingdom Animalia** includes all animals.

Phylum Animals in **Phylum Chordata** have a hollow nerve cord in their backs. Some have a backbone.

Class Animals in **Class Mammalia**, or mammals, have a backbone and nurse their young.

Order Animals in **Order Carnivora** are mammals that have special teeth for tearing meat.

Family Animals in **Family Felidae** are cats. They are carnivores that have retractable claws.

Genus Animals in **Genus *Felis*** are cats that cannot roar. They can only purr.

Species The **species *Felis domesticus***, or the house cat, has unique traits that other members of genus *Felis* do not have.

From domain to species, each level of classification contains a smaller group of organisms.

Visualize It!

11 Apply How does the shape of a pyramid relate to the number of organisms in each level of the classification system?

Triple Play

What are the three domains?

Once, kingdoms were the highest level of classification. Scientists used a six-kingdom system. But scientists noticed that organisms in two of the kingdoms differed greatly from organisms in the other four kingdoms. So, scientists added a new classification level: domains. A **domain** represents the largest differences among organisms. The three domains are Bacteria (bak•TIR•ee•uh), Archaea (ar•KEE•uh), and Eukarya (yoo•KEHR•ee•uh).

Active Reading

12 Identify As you read, underline the three domains of life.

Bacteria

All bacteria belong to domain Bacteria. Domain **Bacteria** is made up of prokaryotes that usually have a cell wall and reproduce by cell division. *Prokaryotes* are single-celled organisms that lack a nucleus in their cells. Bacteria live in almost any environment—soil, water, and even inside the human body!

Archaea

Domain **Archaea** is also made up of prokaryotes. They differ from bacteria in their genetics and in the makeup of their cell walls. Archaea were discovered living in harsh environments, such as hot springs and thermal vents, where other organisms could not survive. Some archaea are found in the open ocean and soil.

Bacteria from the genus *Streptomyces* are commonly found in soil.

Archaea from genus *Sulfolobus* are found in hot springs.

Eukarya

What do algae, mushrooms, trees, and humans have in common? All of these organisms are *eukaryotes*. Eukaryotes are made up of cells that have a nucleus and membrane-bound organelles. The cells of eukaryotes are more complex than the cells of prokaryotes. For this reason, the cells of eukaryotes are usually larger than the cells of prokaryotes. Some eukaryotes, such as many protists and some fungi, are single-celled. Many eukaryotes are multicellular organisms. Some protists and many fungi, plants, and animals are multicellular eukaryotes. Domain **Eukarya** is made up of all eukaryotes.

It may look like a pinecone, but the pangolin is actually an animal from Africa. It is in domain Eukarya.

13 Analyze To demonstrate your understanding of domains, fill in the concept map below.

The Three Domains

include

A _____

Archaea

B _____

which are

which includes

protists

C _____

D _____

E _____

F _____

My Kingdom for a Eukaryote!

What kingdoms are in Eukarya?

Eukaryotes are found throughout the world. They vary in size from single-celled organisms, such as plankton, to multicellular organisms, such as blue whales. Currently, four kingdoms make up the domain Eukarya: Protista, Fungi, Plantae, and Animalia.

Kingdom Animalia

Kingdom **Animalia** contains multicellular organisms that lack cell walls, are usually able to move around, and have specialized sense organs. They eat other organisms for food. Birds, fish, reptiles, insects, and mammals are just a few examples of animals.

Kingdom Plantae

Kingdom **Plantae** consists of multicellular organisms that have cell walls, cannot move around, and make their own food. Plants are found on land and in water that light can pass through.

Kingdom Protista

Members of the kingdom **Protista**, called *protists*, are single-celled or simple multicellular organisms such as algae, protozoans, and slime molds. Protists are a very diverse group of organisms, with plantlike, animal-like, or funguslike characteristics.

Kingdom Fungi

The members of kingdom **Fungi** get energy by absorbing materials and have cells with cell walls but no chloroplasts. Fungi are single-celled or multicellular. Yeasts, molds, and mushrooms are fungi. Fungi use digestive juices to break down materials around them for food.

Visualize It!

14 Synthesize For which kingdom would you most likely need a magnifying lens or microscope to study the organisms?

_____

How do classification systems change?

Thousands of organisms have been identified, but millions remain to be named. Many new organisms fit into the existing system. However, scientists often find organisms that don't fit. Not only do scientists identify new species, but they find new genera and even phyla. In fact, many scientists argue that protists are so different from each other that they should be classified into several kingdoms instead of one. Classification continues to change as scientists learn more about living things.

15 Predict How might the classification of protists change in the future?

_____

_____

_____

_____

How are classification relationships illustrated?

How do you organize your closet? What about your books? People organize things in many different ways. Scientists use different tools to organize information about classification. Among those tools are *branching diagrams*.

Branching Diagrams

Scientists often use a type of branching diagram called a *cladogram* (KLAD•uh•gram). A cladogram shows relationships among species. Organisms are grouped based on common characteristics. Usually, these characteristics are listed along a line that points to the right. Branches extend from this line. Organisms on branches to the right of each characteristic have the characteristic. Organisms on branches to the left lack the characteristic.

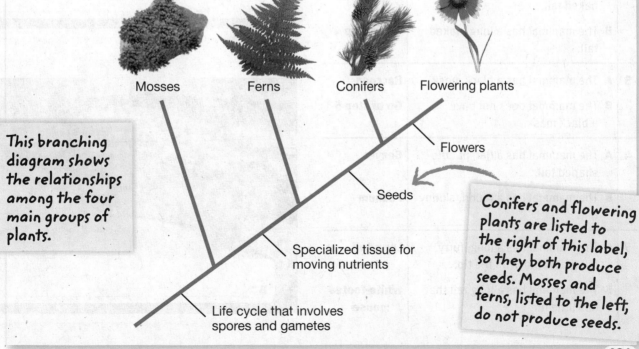

Mosses   Ferns   Conifers   Flowering plants

Flowers

Seeds

Specialized tissue for moving nutrients

Life cycle that involves spores and gametes

This branching diagram shows the relationships among the four main groups of plants.

Conifers and flowering plants are listed to the right of this label, so they both produce seeds. Mosses and ferns, listed to the left, do not produce seeds.

Keys to Success

How can organisms be identified?

Imagine walking through the woods. You see an animal sitting on a rock. It has fur, whiskers, and a large, flat tail. How can you find out what kind of animal it is? You can use a dichotomous key.

Dichotomous Keys

A **dichotomous key** (di•KOT•uh•muhs KEE) uses a series of paired statements to identify organisms. Each pair of statements is numbered. When identifying an organism, read each pair of statements. Then choose the statement that best describes the organism. Either the chosen statement identifies the organism or you will be directed to another pair of statements. By working through the key, you can eventually identify the organism.

16 Apply Use the dichotomous key below to identify the animals shown in the photographs.

Dichotomous Key to Six Mammals in the Eastern United States

1	A	The mammal has no hair on its tail.	Go to step 2
	B	The mammal has hair on its tail.	Go to step 3
2	A	The mammal has a very short, naked tail.	Eastern mole
	B	The mammal has a long, naked tail.	Go to step 4
3	A	The mammal has a black mask.	Raccoon
	B	The mammal does not have a black mask.	Go to step 5
4	A	The mammal has a flat, paddle-shaped tail.	Beaver
	B	The mammal has a round, skinny tail.	Possum
5	A	The mammal has a long, furry tail that is black on the tip.	Long-tail weasel
	B	The mammal has a long tail that has little fur.	White-footed mouse

A _____

B _____

17 Apply Some dichotomous keys are set up as diagrams instead of tables. Work through the key below to identify the unknown plant.

18 Summarize With a partner, choose six plants or animals in a local ecosystem. Then design a dichotomous key that can be used to identify the organisms. When you have finished, trade keys with your classmates and work through their keys with your partner.

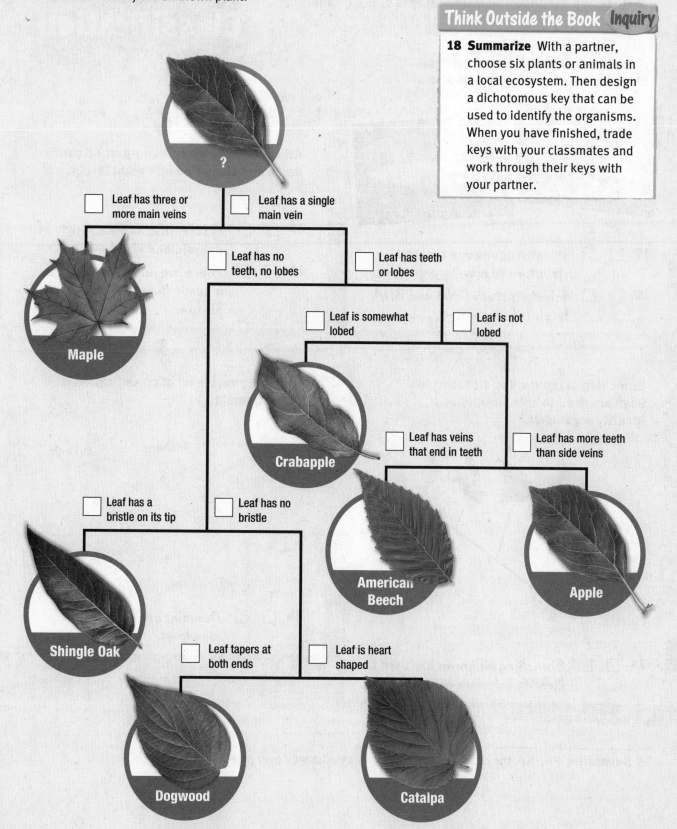

Leaf has three or more main veins

Leaf has a single main vein

Leaf has no teeth, no lobes

Leaf has teeth or lobes

Leaf is somewhat lobed

Leaf is not lobed

Maple

Leaf has veins that end in teeth

Leaf has more teeth than side veins

Crabapple

Leaf has a bristle on its tip

Leaf has no bristle

American Beech

Apple

Shingle Oak

Leaf tapers at both ends

Leaf is heart shaped

Dogwood

Catalpa

Visual Summary

To complete this summary, check the box that indicates true or false. Then use the key below to check your answers. You can use this page to review the main concepts of the lesson.

Classification

Scientists use physical and chemical characteristics to classify organisms.

	T	F	
19	☐	☐	Scientists compare skeletal structure to classify organisms.
20	☐	☐	Scientists study DNA and RNA to classify organisms.

All species are given a two-part scientific name and classified into eight levels.

	T	F	
21	☐	☐	A scientific name consists of domain and kingdom.
22	☐	☐	There are more organisms in a genus than there are in a phylum.

Branching diagrams and dichotomous keys are used to help classify and identify organisms.

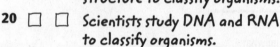

	T	F	
23	☐	☐	Branching diagrams are used to identify unknown organisms.

The highest level of classification is the domain.

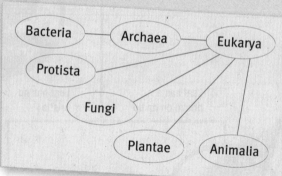

	T	F	
24	☐	☐	Domains are divided into kingdoms.

Answers: 19 T; 20 T; 21 F; 22 F; 23 F; 24 T

25 Summarize How has the classification of living things changed over time?

Lesson Review

Vocabulary

Fill in the blanks with the term that best completes the following sentences.

1 A _____ contains paired statements that can be used to identify organisms.

2 The kingdoms of eukaryotes are _____, Fungi, Plantae, and Animalia.

3 Domains _____ and _____ are made up of prokaryotes.

Key Concepts

4 List Name the eight levels of classification from most general to most definite.

_____

_____

5 Explain How did scientific names impact classification?

_____

_____

_____

6 Identify What two types of evidence are used to classify organisms?

_____

_____

7 Compare Dichotomous keys and branching diagrams organize different types of information about classification. How are these tools used differently?

_____

_____

_____

_____

_____

Critical Thinking

Use the figure to answer the following questions.

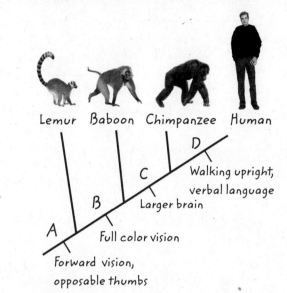

8 Identify Which traits do baboons have?

_____

_____

9 Analyze Which animal shares the most traits with humans?

_____

10 Synthesize Do both lemurs and humans have the trait listed at point D? Explain.

_____

_____

_____

_____

11 Classify A scientist finds an organism that cannot move. It has many cells, produces spores, and gets food from its environment. In which kingdom does it belong? Explain.

_____

_____

_____

_____

My Notes

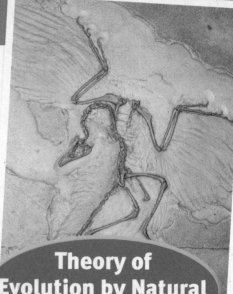

Evidence of Evolution — supports the → **Theory of Evolution by Natural Selection**

provides a basis for ↓

Classification of Living Things

1 Interpret The Graphic Organizer above shows that evidence of evolution can help scientists to classify living things. Name two types of evidence that support evolution.

_____

_____

_____

_____

2 Identify Describe the four eukaryotic kingdoms and give an example from each one.

_____

_____

_____

_____

_____

_____

3 Contrast How is natural selection different from evolution?

_____

_____

_____

_____

_____

4 Explain The fossil record reveals changes over time in the environment. Why might a scientist studying evolution be interested in how the environment has changed over time?

_____

_____

_____

_____

_____

ISTEP+ Review

Name _____

Multiple Choice

1 The diagram below shows the proposed evolutionary relationships among some groups of mammals.

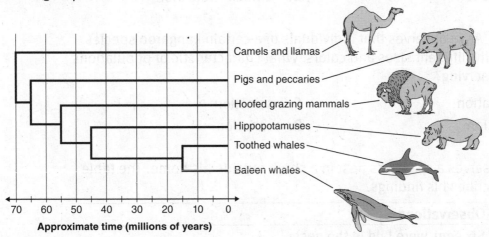

Camels and llamas

Pigs and peccaries

Hoofed grazing mammals

Hippopotamuses

Toothed whales

Baleen whales

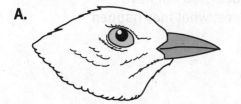
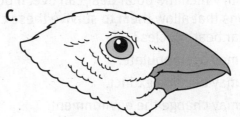

70 60 50 40 30 20 10 0

Approximate time (millions of years)

Which of these organisms is MOST CLOSELY related to whales?

A. bison

B. camel

C. hippopotamus

D. pig

2 When Charles Darwin observed finches on the Galápagos Islands, he noted differences in the shapes of the birds' beaks. He observed that finches that ate insects had longer, narrower beaks than finches that crushed and ate seeds. Crushing seeds requires a larger, powerful beak. Based on this information, which finch shown below would MOST LIKELY have an advantage for survival in an environment where seeds are the main source of food?

A.

B.

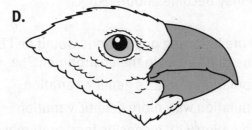

C.

D.

3 When farmers want two desirable traits in cows, they often breed individuals that have those traits in the hopes that the offspring will have both desirable traits. What is this practice called?

A. variation

B. adaptation

C. natural selection

D. artificial selection

4 At the zoo, Anya observes that individuals of a certain kangaroo species have slightly different sizes and colors. What characteristic of populations is Anya observing?

A. adaptation

B. evolution

C. selection

D. variation

5 Ronald observes a sparrow's nest in a shrub outside his home. The table below describes his findings.

Week	Observations
1	Six eggs were laid in the nest.
2	Five eggs hatched, and one egg did not hatch.
4	One of the chicks disappeared.
7	Three of the chicks learned to fly, and another one disappeared.

What part of natural selection did Ronald observe?

A. adaptation

B. overproduction

C. selection

D. variation

6 Polar bears live in the Arctic. Ice in the Arctic is melting rapidly, reducing the range in which the polar bear can live. If polar bears do not have adaptations that allow them to survive these changes, what may happen to the polar bear species?

A. They may overpopulate.

B. They may become extinct.

C. They may change the environment.

D. They may become another species.

7 Which of the following populations would be LEAST LIKELY to become extinct due to changes in the environment?

A. a population with less genetic variation

B. a population with more genetic variation

C. a population with a specific food preference

D. a population who experienced high competition for food

8 Serena knows that scientists use physical similarities to classify organisms. She studies the figures of four different organisms.

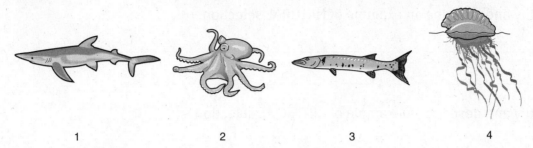

1   2   3   4

Which two organisms should Serena conclude are MOST closely related?

A. 1 and 2   **C.** 2 and 3

B. 1 and 3   **D.** 2 and 4

9 Joaquin's teacher gives him a list and a branching diagram. She asks Joaquin to match the numbers on the diagram to the characteristics on the list.

Joaquin's list	
spinal cord	jaws and vertebral column
teeth for eating meat	eggs with internal membrane
hair and mammary glands	

Lamprey (jawless fish)   Perch (freshwater fish)   Lizard   Mouse   Cat

5

4

3

2

1

Look at the similarities and differences between the organisms. What characteristic should appear at point 4?

A. spinal cord   **C.** hair and mammary glands

B. teeth for eating meat   **D.** jaws and vertebral column

Constructed Response

10 Identify and describe an example of NATURAL selection.

_____

_____

Identify and describe an example of ARTIFICIAL selection.

_____

_____

Extended Response

11 The diagram below shows the forelimbs of four different organisms.

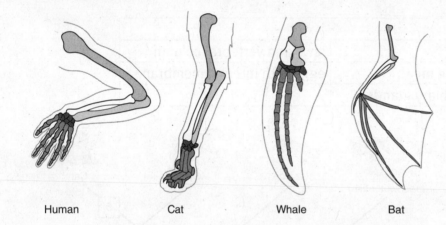

Human   Cat   Whale   Bat

How are the forelimbs of the human, cat, whale, and bat SIMILAR?

_____

How are they DIFFERENT?

_____

What can you infer about how closely the organisms are related?

_____

_____

How does the diagram provide structural evidence for evolution?

_____

_____

Reproduction and Heredity

Core Standard

Understand the predictability of characteristics being passed from parents to offspring.

Characteristics of each variety of apple are passed along through heredity.

What do you think?

We can see some of the traits that parents share with their offspring. How are an organism's traits passed on to the next generation?

This dog was bred to have a curly coat.

Unit 7
Reproduction and Heredity

Indiana Standards

As citizens of the constructed world, students will participate in the design process. Students will learn to use materials and tools safely and employ the basic principles of the engineering design process in order to find solutions to problems.

DP 8.1 Identify a need or problem to be solved.

DP 8.4 Select a solution to the need or problem.

DP 8.10 Communicate the solution including evidence using mathematical representations (graphs, data tables), drawings or prototypes.

CITIZEN SCIENCE

Pass It On

Heredity was a mystery that scientists worked to crack over hundreds of years. The modern field of genetics is vital to the understanding of hereditary diseases. The study of genetics can also predict which traits will be passed from parent to offspring.

1856–1863
Many people consider Gregor Mendel the father of modern genetics. His famous pea plant experiments helped to illustrate and establish the laws of inheritance.

Gregor Mendel

Can you predict the characteristics Mendel might have examined in pea plants? What traits might a fruit or vegetable plant inherit from a parent plant?

_____

_____

_____

_____

_____

Pairs of chromosomes, viewed under a microscope

Fruit fly

DNA samples

1882
Walther Flemming discovered chromosomes while observing the process of cell division. He didn't know it, but chromosomes pass traits from parents to offspring.

1908
Thomas Hunt Morgan was the first to actually realize that chromosomes carry traits. Morgan's fruit fly studies established that genes are located on chromosomes. Fruit flies are still commonly used in genetic studies.

2003
Our DNA carries information about all of our traits. In fact, the human genome is made up of 20,000–25,000 genes! In 2003, the Human Genome Project successfully mapped the first human genome.

Take It Home · Making Trait Predictions

① Think About It

Different factors influence appearance. Family members may look similar in some ways but different in others. What factors influence a person's appearance?

_____
_____
_____
_____

② Ask Some Questions

Can you spot any physical traits, like bent or straight pinky fingers, that people in your family share?

_____
_____
_____
_____

③ Make a Plan

Consider the traits that are most distinctive in your family. How can you trace the way these traits have been passed through the family? Design an investigation of hereditary traits in your family.

_____
_____
_____
_____

Describe how these traits might be the same or different as they are passed on to offspring. What factors might influence this? Make notes here, and illustrate your descriptions on a separate sheet of paper.

_____
_____
_____
_____

Mitosis

ESSENTIAL QUESTION

How do cells divide?

By the end of this lesson, you should be able to relate the process of mitosis to its functions in single-celled and multicellular organisms.

A human skin cell divides, producing two new cells that are identical to the original cell.

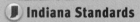

Indiana Standards

8.3.1 Explain that reproduction is essential for the continuation of every species and is the mechanism by which all organisms transmit genetic information.

8.3.3 Explain that genetic information is transmitted from parents to offspring mostly by chromosomes.

8.3.4 Understand the relationship between deoxyribonucleic acid (DNA), genes, and chromosomes.

Engage Your Brain

1 Predict Check T or F to show whether you think each statement is true or false.

T	F	
☐	☐	Single-celled organisms can reproduce by cell division.
☐	☐	The only function of cell division is reproduction.
☐	☐	In multicellular organisms, cell division can help repair injured areas.
☐	☐	Cell division produces two cells that are different from each other.

2 Infer An old sequoia tree weighs many tons and has billions of cells. These trees start out as tiny seeds. Predict how these trees get so large.

_____

_____

_____

_____

Active Reading

3 Synthesize You can often define an unknown word if you know the meaning of its word parts. Use the word parts and sentence below to make an educated guess about the meaning of the word *cytokinesis*.

Word part	Meaning
cyto-	hollow vessel
-kinesis	division

Example sentence
When a dividing cell undergoes <u>cytokinesis</u>, two cells are produced.

cytokinesis:

_____

_____

_____

Vocabulary Terms

- DNA
- chromosomes
- cell cycle
- interphase
- mitosis
- cytokinesis

4 Apply As you learn the definition of each vocabulary term in this lesson, write your own definition or make a sketch to help you remember the meaning of the term.

Splitsville!

Why do cells divide?

Cell division happens in all organisms. Cell division takes place for different reasons. For example, single-celled organisms reproduce through cell division. In multicellular organisms, cell division is involved in growth, development, and repair, as well as reproduction.

Reproduction

Cell division is important for asexual reproduction, which involves only one parent organism. In single-celled organisms, the parent divides in two, producing two identical offspring. In single-celled and some multicellular organisms, offspring result when a parent organism buds, producing offspring. In multicellular organisms, reproduction by cell division can include plant structures such as runners and plantlets.

Growth and Repair

One characteristic of all living things is that they grow. You are probably bigger this year than you were last year. Your body is made up of cells. Although cells themselves grow, most growth in multicellular organisms happens because cell division produces new cells.

Cell division also produces cells for repair. If you cut your hand or break a bone, the damaged cells are replaced by new cells that form during cell division.

 Visualize It!

5 Apply Take a look at the photos below. Underneath each photo, describe the role of cell division in what is taking place.

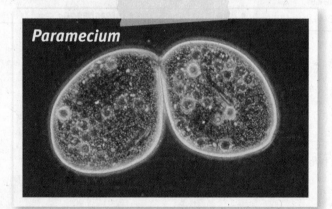

Paramecium

Starfish

Role of cell division:

_____

_____

_____

Role of cell division:

_____

_____

_____

What happens to genetic material during cell division?

The genetic material in cells is called DNA (deoxyribonucleic acid). A **DNA** molecule contains the information that determines the traits that a living thing inherits and needs to live. It contains instructions for an organism's growth, development, and activities. In eukaryotes, DNA is found in the nucleus.

During most of a cell's life cycle, DNA, along with proteins, exists in a complex material called *chromatin* (KROH•muh•tin). Before cell division, DNA is duplicated, or copied. Then, in an early stage of cell division, the chromatin is compacted into visible structures called **chromosomes** (KROH•muh•sohmz). A duplicated chromosome consists of two identical structures called *chromatids* (KROH•muh•tidz). The chromatids are held together by a *centromere* (SEN•truh•mir).

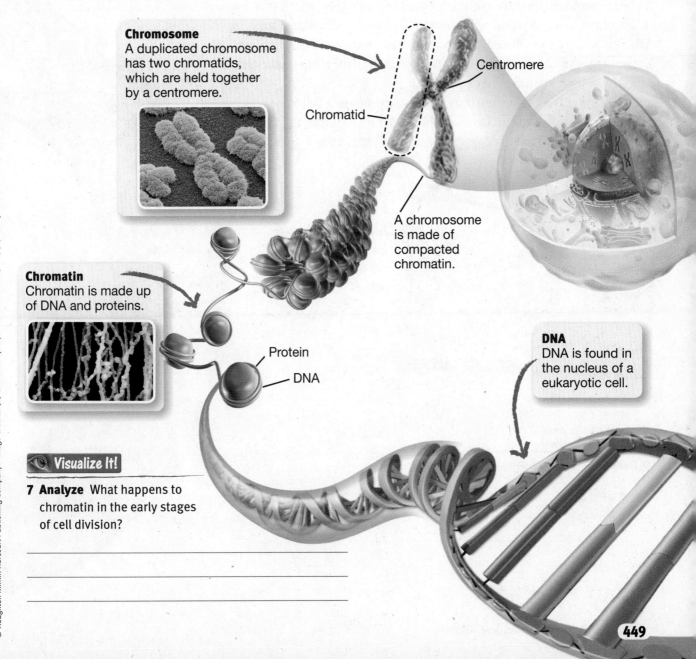

Chromosome
A duplicated chromosome has two chromatids, which are held together by a centromere.

Centromere

Chromatid

A chromosome is made of compacted chromatin.

Chromatin
Chromatin is made up of DNA and proteins.

Protein

DNA

DNA
DNA is found in the nucleus of a eukaryotic cell.

👁 **Visualize It!**

7 Analyze What happens to chromatin in the early stages of cell division?

_____

_____

_____

Around and Around

What are the stages of the cell cycle?

The life cycle of an organism includes birth, growth, reproduction, and death. The life cycle of a eukaryotic cell, called the **cell cycle,** can be divided into three stages: interphase, mitosis, and cytokinesis. During the cell cycle, a parent cell divides into two new cells. The new cells are identical to the parent.

Active Reading

8 Identify As you read, underline the main characteristics of each stage of the cell cycle.

Interphase

The part of the cell cycle during which the cell is not dividing is called **interphase** (IN•ter•fayz). A lot of activity takes place in this stage of the cell's life. The cell grows to about twice the size it was when it was first produced. It also produces various organelles. The cell engages in normal life activities, such as transporting materials into the cell and getting rid of wastes.

Changes that occur during interphase prepare a cell for division. Before a cell can divide, DNA must be duplicated. This ensures that, after cell division, each new cell gets an exact copy of the genetic material in the original cell.

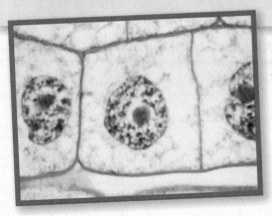

During interphase, the cell carries out normal life activities.

INTERPHASE

Active Reading

9 Describe What happens during interphase?

_____

_____

_____

_____

Mitosis

In eukaryotic cells, **mitosis** (my•TOH•sis) is the part of the cell cycle during which the nucleus divides. Prokaryotes do not undergo mitosis because they do not have a nucleus. Mitosis results in two nuclei that are identical to the original nucleus. So, the two new cells formed after cell division have the same genetic material. During mitosis, chromosomes condense from chromatin. When viewed with a microscope, chromosomes are visible inside the nucleus. At the end of mitosis, the cell has two identical sets of chromosomes in two separate nuclei.

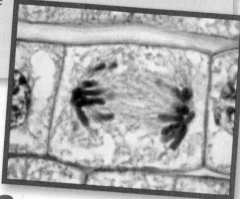

During mitosis, the cell's nucleus divides into two identical nuclei.

MITOSIS

Prophase

Metaphase

Anaphase

Telophase

CYTOKINESIS

Cytokinesis

Cytokinesis (sy•toh•kuh•NEE•sis) is the division of the parent cell's cytoplasm. Cytokinesis begins during the last step of mitosis. During cytokinesis, the cell membrane pinches inward between the new nuclei. Eventually, it pinches all the way, forming two complete cells.

In a cell that has a cell wall, such as a plant cell, a cell plate forms. The cell plate becomes cell membranes that separate the new cells. New cell walls form where the plate was.

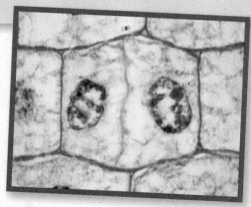

During cytokinesis, the cytoplasm divides and two new cells are produced.

Visualize It!

10 Interpret Based on this diagram, in what stage does a cell spend most of its time?

_____

Phasing Out

What are the phases of mitosis?

Mitosis has four phases: prophase (PROH•fayz), metaphase (MET•uh•fayz), anaphase (AN•uh•fayz), and telophase (TEE•luh•fayz). By the end of these phases, the cell will have two identical nuclei and cytokinesis will begin.

 **Active Reading**

11 Identify As you read, underline the major events that take place in each phase of mitosis.

During interphase, DNA is duplicated.

Prophase

During prophase, the chromatin in the nucleus of a cell condenses and becomes visible under a microscope. Each chromosome consists of two chromatids held together by a centromere. The membrane around the nucleus breaks down.

Prophase

Metaphase

During metaphase, chromosomes line up in the middle of the cell. Centromeres of the chromosomes are the same distance from each side of the cell.

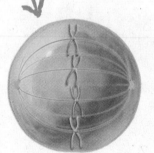

Metaphase

Anaphase

During anaphase, the chromatids separate. They are pulled to opposite sides of the cell. Each side of the cell ends up with a complete set of chromosomes.

Anaphase

12 Model With a small group, write a play that acts out the steps of mitosis. Trade your play with another group, and perform the play for your classmates.

13 Apply Use the table below to draw a picture for each step of the cell cycle.

Step	Drawing
Interphase	
Mitosis: Prophase	
Mitosis: Metaphase	
Mitosis: Anaphase	
Mitosis: Telophase	
Cytokinesis	

Both new cells start the cycle again.

After mitosis, cytokinesis results in two new cells.

Telophase

Telophase

The last phase of mitosis is telophase. A new nuclear membrane forms around each group of chromosomes. So, the cell now has two identical nuclei. The chromosomes become less condensed. Cytokinesis begins during this phase.

Visual Summary

To complete this summary, fill in the blanks with the correct word or phrase. Then, use the key below to check your answers. You can use this page to review the main concepts of the lesson.

During the cell cycle, cells divide to produce two identical cells.

14 Three reasons that cells divide are

_____

_____

_____

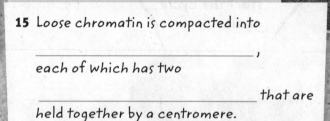

DNA is duplicated before cell division.

15 Loose chromatin is compacted into

_____,

each of which has two

_____ that are

held together by a centromere.

Mitosis

The cell cycle is the life cycle of a cell.

16 They lack nuclei, so prokaryotes do not undergo _____

17 The cell produces organelles during

_____

18 _____ results in the formation of two new cells.

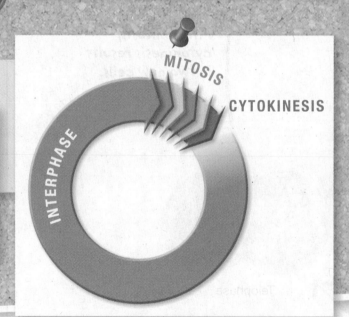

MITOSIS

CYTOKINESIS

INTERPHASE

Answers: 14 reproduction, growth, repair; 15 chromosomes, chromatids; 16 mitosis; 17 interphase; 18 Cytokinesis

19 **Summarize** Briefly describe the four phases of mitosis.

© Houghton Mifflin Harcourt Publishing Company • Image Credits: (tl) ©Jeff Rotman/Photo Researchers, Inc.; (tr) ©Andrew Syred/Photo Researchers, Inc.

Lesson Review

Vocabulary

Fill in the blanks with the term that best completes the following sentences.

1 _____ provides the information for cell growth and function.

2 The cell spends most of its time in the _____ stage of the cell cycle.

3 After _____ , the nucleus of the parent cell has divided into two new nuclei.

4 A _____ is the condensed, visible form of chromatin.

Key Concepts

5 Relate What happens in a cell during interphase?

_____

_____

_____

_____

6 Compare Describe the functions of cell division in single-celled and multicellular organisms.

_____

_____

_____

_____

7 Explain Why is it important for DNA to be duplicated before mitosis?

_____

_____

_____

_____

Critical Thinking

Use the figures below to answer the questions that follow.

8 Sequence Starting with prophase, what is the correct order of the four diagrams above?

_____

9 Identify What phase is shown in each of the diagrams above?

_____

_____

_____

_____

10 Describe What is happening to the cell in diagram B?

_____

_____

_____

_____

11 Predict What would happen if the cell went through mitosis but not cytokinesis?

_____

_____

_____

_____

_____

Meiosis

© Houghton Mifflin Harcourt Publishing Company • Image Credits: ©3D4Medical.com/Getty Images

ESSENTIAL QUESTION

How do cells divide for sexual reproduction?

By the end of this lesson, you should be able to describe the process of meiosis and its role in sexual reproduction.

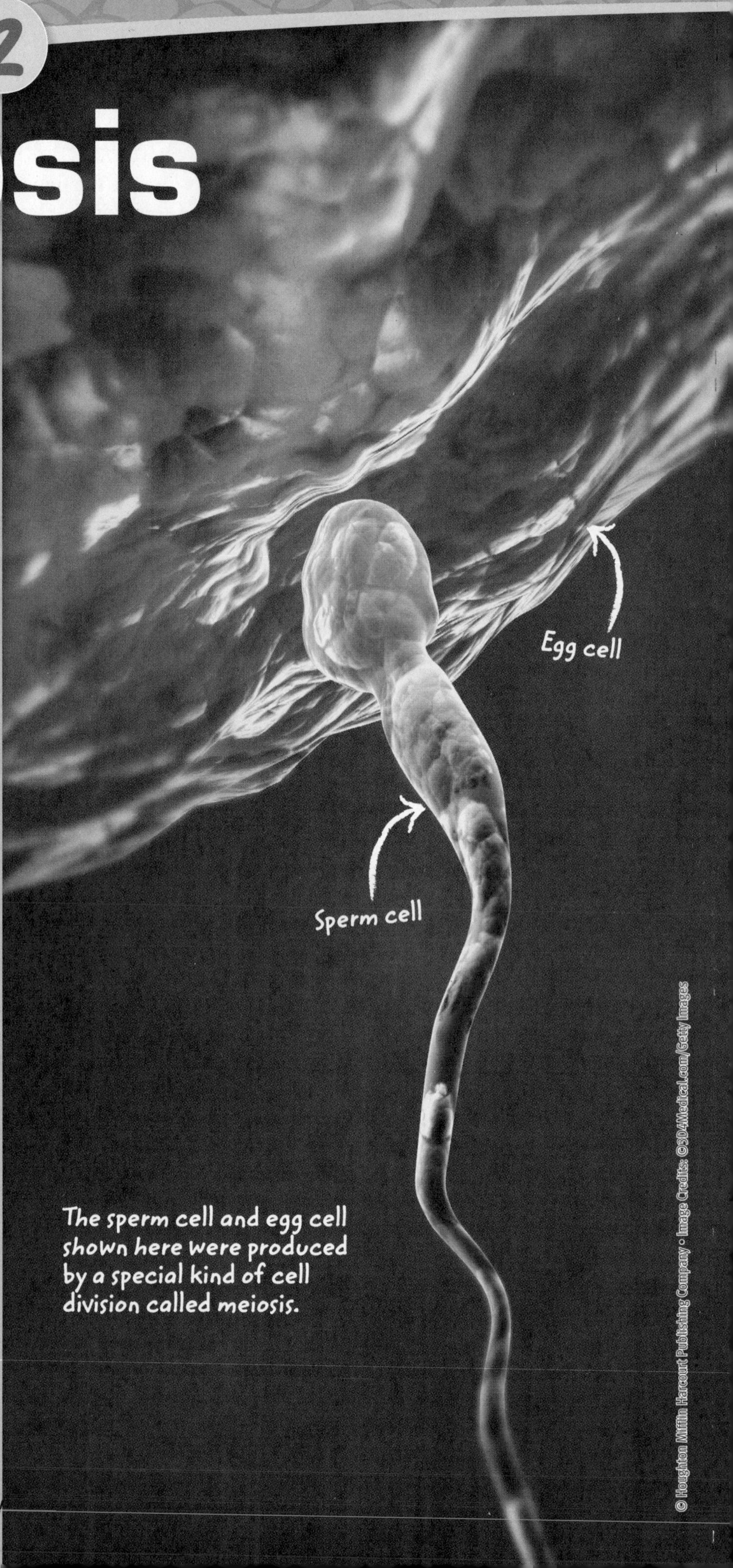

Egg cell

Sperm cell

The sperm cell and egg cell shown here were produced by a special kind of cell division called meiosis.

🔊 Indiana Standards

8.3.3 Explain that genetic information is transmitted from parents to offspring mostly by chromosomes.

Engage Your Brain

1 Predict Check T or F to show whether you think each statement is true or false.

T **F**

☐ ☐ The offspring of sexual reproduction have fewer chromosomes than their parents have.

☐ ☐ During sexual reproduction, two cells combine to form a new organism.

☐ ☐ Sex cells are produced by cell division.

☐ ☐ Sex cells have half the normal number of chromosomes.

2 Calculate Organisms have a set number of chromosomes. For example, humans have 46 chromosomes in body cells and half that number (23) in sex cells. In the table below, fill in the number of chromosomes for different organisms.

Organism	Full set of chromosomes	Half set of chromosomes
Human	46	23
Fruit fly		4
Chicken		39
Salamander	24	
Potato	48	

Active Reading

3 Synthesize You can often define an unknown word if you know the meaning of its word parts. Use the word parts and the sentence below to make an educated guess about the meaning of the term *homologous*.

Word part	Meaning
homo-	same
-logos	word, structure

Example sentence
Homologous chromosomes are a pair of chromosomes that look similar and have the same genes.

homologous:

_____

_____

_____

Vocabulary Terms

- **homologous chromosomes**
- **meiosis**

4 Apply As you learn the definition of each vocabulary term in this lesson, write your own definition or make a sketch to help you remember the meaning of the term.

Number Off!

How do sex cells differ from body cells?

Before sexual reproduction can take place, each parent produces sex cells. *Sex cells* have half of the genetic information that body cells have. Thus, when the genetic information from two parents combines, the offspring have a full set of genetic information. The offspring will have the same total number of chromosomes as each of its parents.

Active Reading **5 Relate** Describe sex cells.

This photo shows the 23 chromosome pairs in a human male. Body cells contain all of these chromosomes. Sex cells contain one chromosome from each pair.

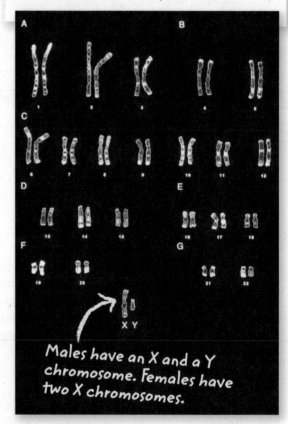

Males have an X and a Y chromosome. Females have two X chromosomes.

Chromosome Number

In body cells, most chromosomes are found in pairs that have the same structure and size. These **homologous chromosomes** (huh•MAHL•uh•guhs KROH•muh•sohmz) carry the same genes. A homologous chromosome pair may have different versions of the genes they carry. One chromosome pair is made up of *sex chromosomes*. Sex chromosomes control the development of sexual characteristics. In humans, these chromosomes are called X and Y chromosomes. Cells with a pair of every chromosome are called *diploid* (DIP•loyd). Many organisms, including humans, have diploid body cells.

Visualize It! **Inquiry**

6 Predict The cell shown is a body cell that has two pairs of homologous chromosomes. Use the space to the right to draw a sex cell for the same organism.

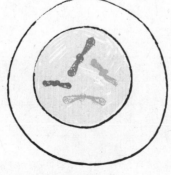

Body cell   Sex cell

© Houghton Mifflin Harcourt Publishing Company • Image Credits: (tr) ©Leonard Lessin/Photo Researchers, Inc.

Why do organisms need sex cells?

Most human body cells contain 46 chromosomes. Think about what would happen if two body cells were to combine. The resulting cell would have twice the normal number of chromosomes. A sex cell is needed to keep this from happening.

Sex cells are also known as *gametes* (GAM•eetz). Gametes contain half the usual number of chromosomes—one chromosome from each homologous pair and one sex chromosome. Cells that contain half the usual number of chromosomes are known as *haploid* (HAP•loyd).

Gametes are found in the reproductive organs of plants and animals. An egg is a gamete that forms in female reproductive organs. The gamete that forms in male reproductive organs is called a sperm cell.

How are sex cells made?

You know that body cells divide by the process of mitosis. Mitosis produces two new cells, each containing exact copies of the chromosomes in the parent cell. Each new cell has a full set of chromosomes. But to produce sex cells, a different kind of cell division is needed.

Meiosis

A human egg and a human sperm cell each have 23 chromosomes. When an egg is joined with, or *fertilized* by, a sperm cell, a new diploid cell is formed. This new cell has 46 chromosomes, or 23 pairs of chromosomes. One set is from the mother, and the other set is from the father. The newly formed diploid cell may develop into an offspring. **Meiosis** (my•OH•sis) is the type of cell division that produces haploid sex cells such as eggs and sperm cells.

Visualize It!

For the example of fertilization shown, the egg and sperm cells each have one chromosome.

Egg cell (female gamete)

Haploid

Sperm cell (male gamete)

Haploid

— Fertilization —→

Fertilized egg cell (zygote)

Diploid

7 Summarize Based on the figure, describe the process of fertilization.

_____

_____

_____

What are the stages of meiosis?

Meiosis results in the formation of four haploid cells. Each haploid cell has half the number of chromosomes found in the original cell. Meiosis has two parts: meiosis I and meiosis II.

Meiosis I

Remember that homologous chromosomes have the same genes, but they are not exact copies of each other. Before meiosis I begins, each chromosome is duplicated, or copied. Each half of a duplicated chromosome is called a *chromatid* (KROH•muh•tid). Chromatids are connected to each other by *centromeres* (SEN•truh•mirz). Duplicated chromosomes are drawn in an **X** shape. Each side of the **X** represents a chromatid, and the point where they touch is the centromere.

During meiosis I, pairs of homologous chromosomes and sex chromosomes split apart into two new cells. These cells each have one-half of the chromosome pairs and their duplicate chromatids. The steps of meiosis I are shown below.

Active Reading

8 Sequence As you read, underline what happens to chromosomes during meiosis.

Duplicated homologous chromosomes

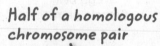
Half of a homologous chromosome pair

Prophase I
The chromosomes are copied before meiosis begins. The duplicated chromosomes, each made up of two chromatids, pair up.

Metaphase I
After the nuclear membrane breaks down, the chromosome pairs line up in the middle of the cell.

Anaphase I
The chromosomes separate from their partners, and then move to opposite ends of the cell.

Telophase I and cytokinesis
The nuclear membranes re-form, and the cell divides into two cells. The chromatids are still joined.

Visualize It!

9 Contrast How does meiosis II differ from meiosis I?

_____

_____

_____

_____

Telophase II and cytokinesis

The nuclear membranes re-form and the cells divide. Four new haploid cells are formed. Each has half the usual number of chromosomes.

Centromere

Chromatid

Anaphase II

The chromatids are pulled apart and move to opposite sides of the cell.

Metaphase II

The chromosomes line up in the middle of each cell.

Prophase II

The chromosomes are not copied again before meiosis II. The nuclear membrane breaks down.

Think Outside the Book

10 Summarize Work with a partner to make a poster that describes all the steps of meiosis.

Meiosis II

Meiosis II involves both of the new cells formed during meiosis I. The chromosomes of these cells are not copied before meiosis II begins. Both of the cells divide during meiosis II. The steps of meiosis II are shown above.

Meiosis II results in four haploid sex cells. In male organisms, these cells develop into sperm cells. In female organisms, these cells become eggs. In females of some species, three of the cells are broken down and only one haploid cell becomes an egg.

11 Identify At the end of meiosis II, how many cells have formed?

_____

How does meiosis compare to mitosis?

The processes of meiosis and mitosis are similar in many ways. However, they also have several very important differences.

- Only cells that will become sex cells go through meiosis. All other cells divide by mitosis.
- During meiosis, chromosomes are copied once, and then the nucleus divides twice. During mitosis, the chromosomes are copied once, and then the nucleus divides once.
- The cells produced by meiosis contain only half of the genetic material of the parent cell—one chromosome from each homologous pair and one sex chromosome. The cells produced by mitosis contain exactly the same genetic material as the parent—a full set of homologous chromosomes and a pair of sex chromosomes.

Single chromosome   Single chromosome

Cell produced by meiosis (haploid)

Chromosome pair   Chromosome pair

Cell produced by mitosis (diploid)

12 Summarize Using the table below, compare meiosis and mitosis.

Characteristic	Meiosis	Mitosis
Number of nuclear divisions		
Number of cells produced		
Number of chromosomes in new cells (diploid or haploid)		
Type of cell produced (body cell or sex cell)		
Steps of the process		

Down Syndrome

Down syndrome is a genetic disease. It is usually caused by an error during meiosis. During meiosis, the chromatids of chromosome 21 do not separate. So, a sex cell gets two copies of chromosome 21 instead of one copy. When this sex cell joins with a normal egg or sperm, the fertilized egg has three copies of chromosome 21 instead of two copies.

Beating the Odds
Down syndrome causes a number of health problems and learning difficulties, but many people with Down syndrome have fulfilling lives.

One Too Many
Someone who has Down syndrome has three copies of chromosome 21 instead of two copies.

Extend

Inquiry

13 Identify What type of error in meiosis causes Down syndrome?

14 Investigate Research the characteristics of Down syndrome. How can some of the difficulties caused by the disorder be overcome?

15 Recommend Research the Special Olympics. Then make an informative brochure, poster, or oral presentation that describes how the Special Olympics gives people with Down syndrome and other disabilities the chance to compete in sports.

Visual Summary

To complete this summary, fill in the blanks with the correct word or phrase. Then use the key below to check your answers. You can use this page to review the main concepts of the lesson.

Meiosis

Meiosis produces haploid cells that can become sex cells.

16 List the steps of meiosis I.

_____
_____
_____
_____

17 List the steps of meiosis II.

_____
_____
_____
_____

Sex cells have half as many chromosomes as body cells.

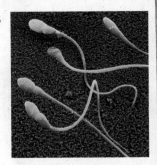

18 Sex cells produced by males are called _____, and sex cells produced by females are called _____

Mitosis and meiosis have similarities and differences.

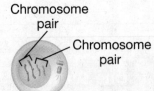

Single chromosome
Single chromosome
Cell produced by meiosis (haploid)

Chromosome pair
Chromosome pair
Cell produced by mitosis (diploid)

19 During _____, chromosomes are copied once and the nucleus divides twice.

20 During _____, chromosomes are copied once and the nucleus divides once.

Answers: 16 prophase I, metaphase I, anaphase I, telophase I and cytokinesis; 17 prophase II, metaphase II, anaphase II, telophase II and cytokinesis; 18 sperm cells, eggs; 19 meiosis; 20 mitosis

21 Summarize Briefly describe what happens during meiosis I and meiosis II.

Lesson Review

Vocabulary

Fill in the blanks with the term that best completes the following sentences.

1 _____ chromosomes are found in body cells but not sex cells.

2 The process of _____ produces haploid cells.

Key Concepts

3 Compare How does the number of chromosomes in sex cells compare with the number of chromosomes in body cells?

_____

_____

4 Identify What is the function of meiosis?

_____

_____

5 List Identify the steps of meiosis.

_____

_____

_____

_____

6 Compare How are mitosis and meiosis alike and different?

_____

_____

_____

_____

_____

_____

Critical Thinking

Use the figure to answer the following questions.

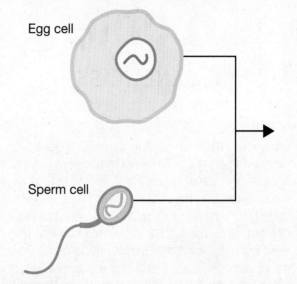

Egg cell

Sperm cell

7 Identify By what process did these cells form?

_____

8 Identify How many chromosomes does a body cell for the organism shown have?

_____

9 Predict Draw a picture of the cell that would form if the sperm cell fused with the egg cell. What is this cell called?

10 Synthesize What would happen if meiosis did not occur?

_____

_____

_____

_____

_____

Michael Coble

GENETICIST

Michael Coble's interest in genetics began when, as young child, he learned about Gregor Mendel's discoveries. While Coble was in college, his interest increased due to a science project in which he had to find dominant and recessive genes in fruit flies. Little did Coble know at the time that his work in genetics would lead him to solve one of history's greatest mysteries: What happened to Russia's royal family, the Romanovs, during the Russian revolution?

The whole family had supposedly been executed in 1918. However, many people believed there was a chance that at least one of the children had escaped.

Coble says that "since 1918, over 200 individuals have claimed to be one of the five 'surviving' Romanov children." Fueling the mystery was the fact that there were no remains in the Romanov's grave for two of the children.

However, in 2007, a grave with the remains of two people was found. Coble and his team used the DNA evidence to identify the remains as the missing Romanov children.

Coble continues his work in genetics today. He says, "It is very rewarding to know that something you were involved with will be used for finding criminals, exonerating the innocent, or helping to identify missing persons."

If the bands of DNA on the film line up correctly, you have a match.

Dr. Coble solved the mystery of Princess Anastasia and the other Romanov children.

Social Studies Connection

Research Find out more about what happened to the Romanovs, including the mystery around Princess Anastasia. Put together a slideshow or a video to report your findings.

JOB BOARD

Genetic Counselor

What You'll Do: Analyze a family's risk factors for inherited conditions and disorders

Where You Might Work: At a doctor's office, a health clinic, or a hospital

Education: A graduate degree in genetic counseling

Other Job Requirements: Certification from the American Board of Genetic Counseling

Plant Nursery Manager

What You'll Do: Grow plants from seeds, cuttings, or by other methods. Manage a plant-related business or organization.

Where You Might Work: At a botanical garden, a garden center, or a plant nursery

Education: A degree in plant science and/or business management

Other Job Requirements: A green thumb!

PEOPLE IN SCIENCE NEWS

MULTIPLE Births

Not so rare anymore

Dr. Brian Kirshon and his medical team made history in December 1998. They delivered the world's first known set of surviving octuplets. Octuplets are a very rare type of multiple birth in which the mother carries eight fetuses in her uterus at once. There have been only 19 recorded instances of octuplets. Only two of those sets survived past birth—the first in 1998, and another in 2009. Considering how rare octuplets are, how is it possible that two pairs were born so recently?

The birth rate for twins increased by 70% from 1980 to 2004. In 2006, the birth rate for twins was up to 32 for every 1,000 births. The birth rate in 2006 for having triplets or a larger birth was 153 for every 100,000 births.

What's going on? Doctors point to modern fertility drugs and treatments. In addition, many women are now waiting until later in life to have children. This increases the chance of having a multiple birth.

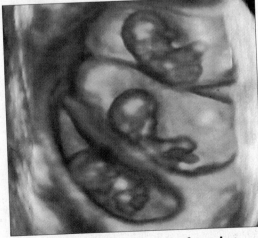

3D ultrasound image of triplets

Sexual and Asexual Reproduction

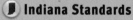

ESSENTIAL QUESTION

How do organisms reproduce?

By the end of this lesson, you should be able to describe asexual and sexual reproduction and list the advantages and disadvantages of each.

Female wolf spiders carry their young on their backs for a short period of time after the young hatch.

Indiana Standards

8.3.1 Explain that reproduction is essential for the continuation of every species and is the mechanism by which all organisms transmit genetic information.

8.3.2 Compare and contrast the transmission of genetic information in sexual and asexual reproduction.

8.3.3 Explain that genetic information is transmitted from parents to offspring mostly by chromosomes.

© Houghton Mifflin Harcourt Publishing Company • Image Credits: (bkgd) ©Gary Meszaros/Photo Researchers, Inc.

Engage Your Brain

1 Predict Check T or F to show whether you think each statement is true or false.

T	F	
☐	☐	Reproduction requires two parents.
☐	☐	Some organisms reproduce by cell division.
☐	☐	New plants can grow from parts of a parent plant, such as roots and stems.
☐	☐	Offspring of two parents always look like one of their parents.

2 Describe How is the young wolf in the photo below similar to its mother?

_____

_____

_____

_____

_____

Active Reading

3 Synthesize You can often define an unknown word if you know the meaning of its word parts. Use the word parts and sentence below to make an educated guess about the meaning of the word *reproduction*.

Word part	Meaning
re-	again
produce	to make
-ion	act or process

Example sentence
Flowers are plant organs that are used for <u>reproduction</u>.

reproduction:

_____

_____

Vocabulary Terms

- asexual reproduction
- sexual reproduction
- fertilization

4 Apply As you learn the definition of each vocabulary term in this lesson, write your own definition or make a sketch to help you remember the meaning of the term.

One Becomes Two

What is asexual reproduction?

An individual organism does not live forever. The survival of any species depends on the ability to reproduce. Reproduction lets genetic information be passed on to new organisms. Reproduction involves various kinds of cell division.

Most single-celled organisms and some multicellular organisms reproduce asexually. In **asexual reproduction** (ay•SEHK•shoo•uhl ree•pruh•DUHK•shuhn), one organism produces one or more new organisms that are identical to itself. These organisms live independently of the original organism. The organism that produces the new organism or organisms is called a *parent*. Each new organism is called an *offspring*. The parent passes on all of its genetic information to the offspring. So, the offspring produced by asexual reproduction are genetically identical to their parents. They may differ only if a genetic mutation happens.

Active Reading

5 Relate Describe the genetic makeup of the offspring of asexual reproduction.

_____

_____

_____

Dandelions usually reproduce asexually. The dandelions in this field may all be genetically identical!

© Houghton Mifflin Harcourt Publishing Company • Image Credits: (bkgd) ©Peter Cade/Iconica/Getty Images

Think Outside the Book Inquiry

6 Summarize Research five organisms that reproduce asexually. Make informative flash cards that describe how each organism reproduces asexually. When you have finished, trade flashcards with a classmate to learn about five more organisms.

How do organisms reproduce asexually?

Organisms reproduce asexually in many ways. In prokaryotes, which include bacteria and archaea, asexual reproduction happens by cell division. In eukaryotes, which include single-celled and multicellular organisms, asexual reproduction is a more involved process. It often involves a type of cell division called *mitosis* (my•TOH•sis). Mitosis produces genetically identical cells.

Binary Fission

Binary fission (BY•nuh•ree FISH•uhn) is the form of asexual reproduction in prokaryotes. It is a type of cell division. During binary fission, the parent organism splits in two, producing two new cells. Genetically, the new cells are exactly like the parent cell.

Budding

During *budding,* an organism develops tiny buds on its body. A bud grows until it forms a new full-sized organism that is genetically identical to the parent. Budding is the result of mitosis. Eukaryotes such as single-celled yeasts and multicellular hydras reproduce by budding.

Spores

A *spore* is a specialized cell that can survive harsh conditions. Both prokaryotes and eukaryotes can form spores. Spores are produced asexually by one parent. Spores are light and can be carried by the wind. In the right conditions, a spore develops into an organism, such as a fungus.

Vegetative Reproduction

Some plants are able to reproduce asexually by *vegetative reproduction.* Mitosis makes vegetative reproduction possible. New plants may grow from stems, roots, or leaves. Runners are aboveground stems from which a new plant can grow. Tubers are underground stems from which new plants can grow. Plantlets are tiny plants that grow along the edges of a plant's leaves. They drop off the plant and grow on their own.

Visualize It!

7 Infer Pick one of the pictures below. Describe how the type of asexual reproduction can help the organism reproduce quickly.

_____

_____

Bacteria reproduce by binary fission.

Hydras reproduce by budding.

Spores can survive long periods of time in harsh conditions.

New potato plants can grow from tubers.

Two Make One

What is sexual reproduction?

Most multicellular organisms can reproduce sexually. In **sexual reproduction** (SEHK•shoo•uhl ree•pruh•DUHK•shuhn), two parents each contribute a sex cell to the new organism. Half the genes in the offspring come from each parent. So, the offspring are not identical to either parent. Instead, they have a combination of traits from each parent.

Fertilization

Usually, one parent is male and the other is female. Males produce sex cells called *sperm cells*. Females produce sex cells called *eggs*. Sex cells are produced by a type of cell division called *meiosis* (my•OH•sis). Sex cells have only half of the full set of genetic material found in body cells.

A sperm cell and an egg join together in a process called **fertilization** (fer•tl•i•ZAY•shuhn). When an egg is fertilized by a sperm cell, a new cell is formed. This cell is called a *zygote* (ZY•goht). It has a full set of genetic material. The zygote develops into a new organism. The zygote divides by mitosis, which increases the number of cells. This increase in cells produces growth. You are the size that you are today because of mitosis.

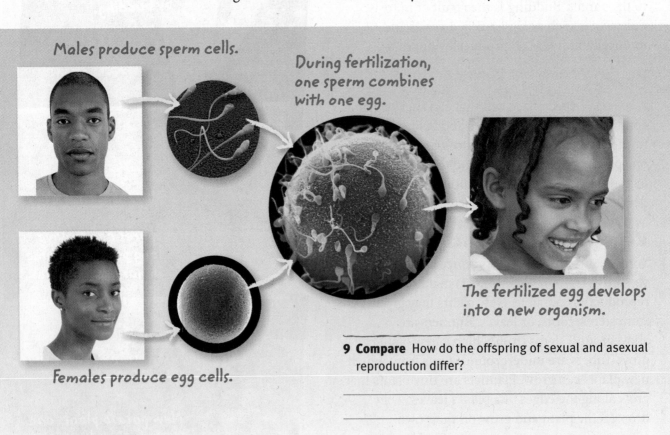

Males produce sperm cells.

During fertilization, one sperm combines with one egg.

The fertilized egg develops into a new organism.

Females produce egg cells.

9 Compare How do the offspring of sexual and asexual reproduction differ?

_____

_____

_____

Odd Reproduction

It may seem like only single-celled organisms undergo asexual reproduction. However, many multicellular organisms reproduce asexually.

Original arm

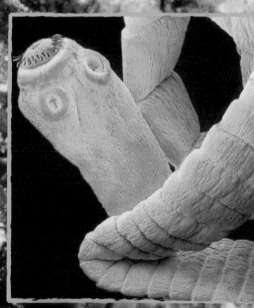

Appearing Act
Some organisms, such as aphids, reproduce asexually by *parthenogenesis*. A female produces young without fertilization.

Falling to Pieces
Tapeworms can reproduce asexually by *fragmentation*. Each segment of the worm can become a new organism if it breaks off of the worm.

Newly grown body and arms

Seeing Stars
Organisms such as starfish reproduce asexually by *regeneration*. Even a small part of the starfish can grow into a new organism.

Extend

Inquiry

10 Identify Which types of asexual reproduction involve part of an organism breaking off?

11 Investigate Research the advantages and disadvantages of a type of reproduction shown on this page.

12 Hypothesize A female shark was left alone in an aquarium tank. She was not pregnant when placed in the tank. But scientists were surprised one morning to find a baby shark in the tank. Form a hypothesis about what type of reproduction took place in this scenario.

Added Advantage

What are the advantages of each type of reproduction?

Organisms reproduce asexually, sexually, or both. Each type of reproduction has advantages. For example, sexual reproduction involves complex structures, such as flowers and other organs. These are not needed for asexual reproduction. But the offspring of sexual reproduction may be more likely to survive in certain situations. Read on to find out more about the advantages of each.

13 Compare Use the Venn diagram below to compare asexual and sexual reproduction.

Asexual Reproduction

_____
_____
_____
_____

Both

_____
_____
_____

Sexual Reproduction

_____
_____
_____
_____

Advantages of Asexual Reproduction

Asexual reproduction has many advantages. First, an organism can reproduce very quickly. Offspring are identical to the parent. So, it also ensures that any favorable traits the parent has are passed on to offspring. Also, a parent organism does not need to find a partner to reproduce. Finally, all offspring—not just females—are able to produce more offspring.

14 List Identify four advantages of asexual reproduction.

_____
_____
_____
_____

Cholla cactuses reproduce asexually by vegetative reproduction. They drop off small pieces that grow into new plants.

Cats reproduce sexually. Offspring are similar to, but not exactly like, their parents.

Advantages of Sexual Reproduction

Sexual reproduction is not as quick as asexual reproduction. Nor does it produce as many offspring. However, it has advantages. First, it increases genetic variation. Offspring have different traits that improve the chance that at least some offspring will survive. This is especially true if the environment changes. Offspring are not genetically identical to the parents. So, they may have a trait that the parents do not have, making them more likely to survive.

15 Explain How can increased genetic variation help some offspring survive?

_____

_____

_____

_____

Advantages of Using Both Types of Reproduction

Some organisms can use both types of reproduction. For example, when conditions are favorable, many plants and fungi will reproduce asexually. Doing so lets them spread quickly and take over an area. When the environment changes, these organisms will switch to sexual reproduction. This strategy increases the chance that the species will survive. Because of genetic variation, at least some of the offspring may have traits that help them make it through the environmental change.

16 Compare In the table below, place a check mark in the cells that describe a characteristic of asexual or sexual reproduction.

	Quick	Increases chance of survival in changing environments	Produces genetic variation	Doesn't need a partner	Requires complex structures
Asexual reproduction					
Sexual reproduction					

© Houghton Mifflin Harcourt Publishing Company • Image Credits: ©Petra Wegner/Alamy

Visual Summary

To complete this summary, circle the correct word that completes each statement. Then use the key below to check your answers. You can use this page to review the main concepts of the lesson.

Reproduction

Asexual reproduction involves one parent.

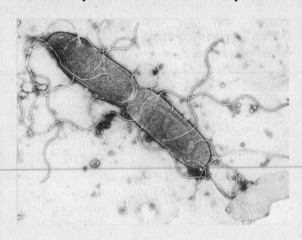

Sexual reproduction involves two parents.

17 The offspring of asexual reproduction are genetically identical / similar to the parent organisms.

18 Prokaryotes reproduce by budding / binary fission.

19 Specialized reproductive structures called runners / spores can survive harsh conditions.

20 A benefit of asexual reproduction is that it is fast / slow.

21 Male organisms produce sex cells called eggs / sperm cells.

22 Male and female sex cells join during fertilization / meiosis.

23 Sexual reproduction increases genetic variation / similarity.

Answers: 17 Identical; 18 binary fission; 19 spores; 20 fast; 21 sperm cells; 22 fertilization; 23 variation

24 Explain How can both asexual reproduction and sexual reproduction allow for the survival of a species?

Lesson Review

Vocabulary

Fill in the blanks with the term that best completes the following sentences.

1 After _____ , the zygote develops into a larger organism.

2 An advantage of _____ reproduction is the ability to reproduce quickly.

3 The offspring of _____ reproduction are more likely to survive changes in the environment.

Key Concepts

4 Identify What are some advantages of asexual and sexual reproduction?

_____

_____

_____

_____

5 Compare In sexual reproduction, how do the offspring compare to the parents?

_____

_____

_____

6 Identify List four types of asexual reproduction.

_____

_____

_____

7 Explain Why do some organisms use both types of reproduction?

_____

_____

_____

_____

Critical Thinking

Use the graph to answer the following questions.

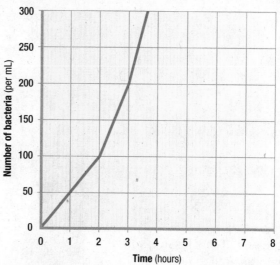

Growth of a Bacterial Population Over Time

8 Infer What type of reproduction is most likely taking place?

_____

_____

9 Analyze Which advantage of reproduction does the graph show? Explain.

_____

_____

_____

10 Predict How might the graph change if the environmental conditions of the bacteria suddenly change? Explain.

_____

_____

_____

_____

_____

_____

Heredity

ESSENTIAL QUESTION

How are traits inherited?

By the end of this lesson, you should be able to analyze the inheritance of traits in individuals.

Members of the same family share certain traits. Can you think of some traits that family members share?

Indiana Standards

8.3.3 Explain that genetic information is transmitted from parents to offspring mostly by chromosomes.

8.3.4 Understand the relationship between deoxyribonucleic acid (DNA), genes, and chromosomes.

8.3.5 Identify and describe the difference between inherited traits and physical and behavioral traits that are acquired or learned.

Engage Your Brain

1 Predict Check T or F to show whether you think each statement is true of false.

T	F	
☐	☐	Siblings look similar because they each have some traits of their parents.
☐	☐	Siblings always have the same hair color.
☐	☐	Siblings have the same DNA.

2 Describe Do you know any identical twins? How are they similar? How are they different?

_____

_____

_____

_____

Active Reading

3 Infer Use context clues to write your own definition for the words *exhibit* and *investigate*.

Example sentence
You may <u>exhibit</u> a certain trait, such as brown eye color.

exhibit:

_____

_____

Example sentence
Gregor Mendel began to <u>investigate</u> the characteristics of pea plants.

investigate:

_____

_____

Vocabulary Terms

- heredity
- gene
- allele
- genotype
- phenotype
- dominant
- recessive
- incomplete dominance
- codominance

4 Identify This list contains the key terms you'll learn in this lesson. As you read, circle the definition of each term.

Give Peas a Chance

What is heredity?

Imagine a puppy. The puppy has long floppy ears like his mother has, and the puppy has dark brown fur like his father has. How did the puppy get these traits? The traits are a result of information stored in the puppy's genetic material. The passing of genetic material from parents to offspring is called **heredity**.

What did Gregor Mendel discover about heredity?

The first major experiments investigating heredity were performed by a monk named Gregor Mendel. Mendel lived in Austria in the 1800s. Before Mendel became a monk, he attended a university and studied science and mathematics. This training served him well when he began to study the inheritance of traits among the pea plants in the monastery's garden. Mendel studied seven different characteristics of pea plants: plant height, flower and pod position, seed shape, seed color, pod shape, pod color, and flower color. A *characteristic* is a feature that has different forms in a population. Mendel studied each pea plant characteristic separately, always starting with plants that were true-breeding for that characteristic. A true-breeding plant is one that will always produce offspring with a certain trait when allowed to self-pollinate. Each of the characteristics that Mendel studied had two different forms. For example, the color of a pea could be green or yellow. These different forms are called *traits*.

5 Apply Is flower color a characteristic or a trait?

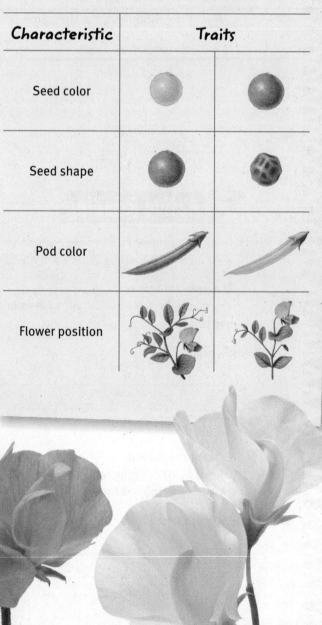

Characteristics of Pea Plants

Characteristic	Traits	
Seed color		
Seed shape		
Pod color		
Flower position		

© Houghton Mifflin Harcourt Publishing Company • Image Credits: (b) ©Nature Alan King/Alamy

Traits Depend on Inherited Factors

In his experiments with seed pod color, Mendel took two sets of plants, one true-breeding for plants that produce yellow seed pods and the other true-breeding for plants that produce green seed pods. Instead of letting the plants self-pollinate as they do naturally, he paired one plant from each set. He did this by fertilizing one plant with the pollen of another plant. Mendel called the plants that resulted from this cross the first generation. All of the plants from this first generation produced green seed pods. Mendel called this trait the *dominant* trait. Because the yellow trait seemed to recede, or fade away, he called it the *recessive* trait.

Then Mendel let the first-generation plants self-pollinate. He called the offspring that resulted from this self-pollination the second generation. About three-fourths of the second-generation plants had green seed pods, but about one-fourth had yellow pods. So the trait that seemed to disappear in the first generation reappeared in the second generation. Mendel hypothesized that each plant must have two heritable "factors" for each trait, one from each parent. Some traits, such as yellow seed pod color, could only be observed if a plant received two factors—one from each parent—for yellow pod color. A plant with one yellow factor and one green factor would produce green pods because producing green pods is a dominant trait. However, this plant could still pass on the yellow factor to the next generation of plants.

6 Identify As you read, underline Mendel's hypothesis about how traits are passed from parents to offspring.

Visualize It!

7 Apply Which pod color is recessive?

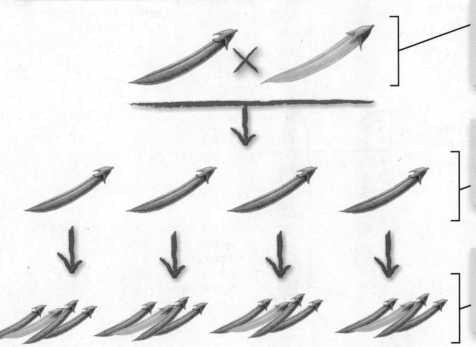

Parent plants Mendel crossed true-breeding green-pod plants with true-breeding yellow-pod plants.

First generation All of the first generation plants had green pods. Mendel let these plants self-pollinate.

Second generation About three-fourths of the second generation had green pods, and one-fourth had yellow pods.

It's in your genes!

Genes are made up of DNA.

How are traits inherited?

Mendel's experiments and conclusions have been the basis for much of the scientific thought about heredity. His ideas can be further explained by our modern understanding of the genetic material DNA. What Mendel called "factors" are actually segments of DNA known as genes!

Genes Are Passed from Parents to Offspring

Genes are segments of DNA found in chromosomes that give instructions for producing a certain characteristic. Humans, like many other organisms, inherit their genes from their parents. Each parent gives one set of genes to the offspring. The offspring then has two versions, or forms, of the same gene for every characteristic—one version from each parent. The different versions of a gene are known as **alleles** (uh•LEELZ). Genes are often represented by letter symbols. Dominant alleles are shown with a capital letter, and recessive alleles are shown with a lowercase version of the same letter. An organism with two dominant or two recessive alleles is said to be *homozygous* for that gene. An organism that has one dominant and one recessive allele is *heterozygous*.

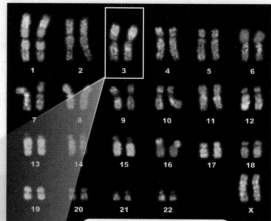

Humans have 23 pairs of chromosomes.

In humans, cells contain pairs of chromosomes. One chromosome of each pair comes from each of two parents. Each chromosome contains sites where specific genes are located.

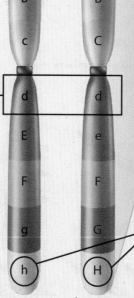

A gene occupies a specific location on both chromosomes in a pair.

Alleles are alternate forms of the same gene.

 **Visualize It!**

8 Apply Circle a gene pair for which this person is heterozygous.

This girl has dimples.

This girl does not have dimples.

9 **Apply** The girls in this photograph have different types of hair. Is hair type a genotype or a phenotype?

Genes Influence Traits

The alternate forms of genes, called alleles, determine the traits of all living organisms. The combination of alleles that you inherited from your parents is your **genotype** (JEEN•uh•typ). Your observable traits make up your **phenotype** (FEEN•uh•typ). The phenotypes of some traits follow patterns similar to the ones that Mendel discovered in pea plants. That is, some traits are dominant over others. For example, consider the gene responsible for producing dimples, or creases in the cheeks. This gene comes in two alleles: one for dimples and one for no dimples. If you have even one copy of the allele for dimples, you will have dimples. This happens because the allele for producing dimples is dominant. The **dominant** allele contributes to the phenotype if one or two copies are present in the genotype. The no-dimples allele is recessive. The **recessive** allele contributes to the phenotype only when two copies of it are present. If one chromosome in the pair contains a dominant allele and the other contains a recessive allele, the phenotype will be determined by the dominant allele. If you do not have dimples, it is because you inherited two no-dimples alleles—one from each parent. This characteristic shows *complete dominance*, because one trait is completely dominant over another. However, not all characteristics follow this pattern.

Active Reading

11 **Identify** What is the phenotype of an individual with one allele for dimples and one allele for no dimples?

_____

_____

Think Outside the Book (Inquiry)

10 **Imagine** Write a short story about a world in which you could change your DNA and your traits. What would be the advantages? What would be the disadvantages?

© Houghton Mifflin Harcourt Publishing Company • Image Credits: (t) ©Stockbyte/Getty Images

Many Genes Can Influence a Single Trait

Some characteristics, such as the color of your skin, hair, and eyes, are the result of several genes acting together. Different combinations of alleles can result in different shades of eye color. Because there is not always a one-to-one relationship between a trait and a gene, many traits do not have simple patterns of inheritance.

A Single Gene Can Influence Many Traits

Sometimes, one gene influences more than one trait. For example, a single gene causes the tiger shown below to have white fur. If you look closely, you will see that the tiger also has blue eyes. The gene that affects fur color also influences eye color.

Many genetic disorders in humans are linked to a single gene but affect many traits. For example, the genetic disorder sickle cell anemia occurs in individuals who have two recessive alleles for a certain gene. This gene carries instructions for producing a protein in red blood cells. When a person has sickle cell anemia alleles, the body makes a different protein. This protein causes red blood cells to be sickle or crescent shaped when oxygen levels are low. Sickle-shaped blood cells can stick in blood vessels, sometimes blocking the flow of blood. These blood cells are also more likely to damage the spleen. With fewer healthy red blood cells, the body may not be able to deliver oxygen to the body's organs. All of the traits associated with sickle cell anemia are due to a single gene.

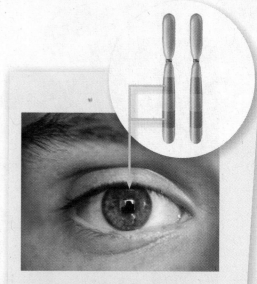

Visualize It!

12 Identify How many genes are responsible for eye color in this example?

_____

_____

This single gene affects the tiger's fur color and eye color.

The Environment Can Influence Traits

Sometimes, the environment influences an organism's phenotype. For example, the arctic fox has a gene that is responsible for coat color. This gene is affected by light. In the winter, there are fewer hours of daylight, and the hairs that make up the arctic fox's coat grow in white. In the summer, when there are more daylight hours, the hairs in the coat grow in brown. In this case, both genes and the environment contribute to the organism's phenotype. The environment can influence human characteristics as well. For example, your genes may make it possible for you to grow to be tall, but you need a healthy diet to reach your full height potential.

Traits that are learned in one's environment are not inherited. For example, your ability to read and write is an acquired trait—a skill you learned. You were not born knowing how to ride a bike, and if you have children, they will not be born knowing how to do it either. They will have to learn the skill just as you did.

**Active Reading**

13 Identify Give an example of an acquired trait.

_____

_____

In the summer, the arctic fox has a brown coat.

In the winter, the arctic fox has a white coat.

14 Predict What advantage does white fur give the arctic fox in winter?

_____

_____

_____

Bending the Rules

What are the exceptions to complete dominance?

The characteristics that Mendel chose to study demonstrated complete dominance, meaning that heterozygous individuals show the dominant trait. Some human traits, such as freckles and dimples, follow the pattern of complete dominance, too. However, other traits do not. For traits that show incomplete dominance or codominance, one trait is not completely dominant over another.

Incomplete Dominance

In **incomplete dominance**, each allele in a heterozygous individual influences the phenotype. The result is a phenotype that is a blend of the phenotypes of the parents. One example of incomplete dominance is found in the snapdragon flower, shown below. When a true-breeding red snapdragon is crossed with a true-breeding white snapdragon, all the offspring are pink snapdragons. Both alleles of the gene have some influence. Hair texture is an example of incomplete dominance in humans. A person with one straight-hair allele and one curly-hair allele will have wavy hair.

Active Reading

15 Identify As you read, underline examples of incomplete dominance and codominance.

Visualize It!

16 Analyze How can you tell that these snapdragons do not follow the pattern of complete dominance?

_____

_____

_____

_____

Pink snapdragons are produced by a cross between a red snapdragon and a white snapdragon.

Codominance

For a trait that shows **codominance**, both of the alleles in a heterozygous individual contribute to the phenotype. Instead of having a blend of the two phenotypes, heterozygous individuals have both of the traits associated with their two alleles. An example of codominance is shown in the genes that determine human blood types. There are three alleles that play a role in determining a person's blood type: *A, B,* and *O.* The alleles are responsible for producing small particles on the surface of red blood cells called antigens. The *A* allele produces red blood cells coated with A antigens. The *B* allele produces red blood cells coated with B antigens. The *O* allele does not produce antigens. The *A* and *B* alleles are codominant. So, someone with one *A* allele and one *B* allele will have blood cells that are coated with A antigens and B antigens. This person would have type AB blood.

 **18 Identify** What antigens coat the red blood cells of a person with type AB blood?

Think Outside the Book Inquiry

17 Research Blood type is an important factor when people give or receive blood. Research the meanings of the phrases "universal donor" and "universal recipient." What are the genotypes of each blood type?

_____

Visualize It!

19 Predict The color of these imaginary fish is controlled by a single gene. Sketch or describe their offspring if the phenotypes follow the pattern of complete dominance, incomplete dominance, or codominance.

Complete dominance (Blue is dominant to yellow.)	Incomplete dominance	Codominance

Visual Summary

To complete this summary, circle the correct word or phrase. Then use the key below to check your answers. You can use this page to review the main concepts of the lesson.

Heredity

Gregor Mendel studied patterns of heredity in pea plants.

20 Traits that seemed to disappear in Mendel's first-generation crosses were dominant / recessive traits.

Inherited genes influence the traits of an individual.

21 An individual with the genotype BB is heterozygous / homozygous.

Phenotypes can follow complete dominance, incomplete dominance, or codominance.

22 When these imaginary fish cross, their offspring are all green. This is an example of codominance / incomplete dominance.

Answers: 20 recessive; 21 homozygous; 22 incomplete dominance

23 **Apply** If a child has blonde hair and both of her parents have brown hair, what does that tell you about the allele for blonde hair?

Lesson Review

Vocabulary

Draw a line to connect the following terms to their definitions.

1 heredity

2 gene

3 phenotype

A an organism's appearance or other detectable characteristic

B a section of DNA that contains instructions for a particular characteristic

C the passing of genetic material from parent to offspring

Key Concepts

4 Describe What did Mendel discover about genetic factors in pea plants?

_____

_____

_____

_____

_____

_____

5 Describe What is the role of DNA in determining an organism's traits?

_____

_____

_____

_____

_____

6 Apply Imagine that a brown horse and a white horse cross to produce an offspring whose coat is made up of some brown hairs and some white hairs. Which pattern of dominance is this an example of?

_____

_____

7 Identify Give an example of a trait that is controlled by more than one gene.

_____

Use this diagram to answer the following questions.

8 Identify What is the genotype at the Q gene?

_____

9 Apply For which genes is this individual heterozygous?

_____

_____

Critical Thinking

10 Describe Marfan syndrome is a genetic disorder caused by a dominant allele. Describe how Marfan syndrome is inherited.

_____

_____

_____

11 Describe Jenny, Jenny's mom, and Jenny's grandfather are all good basketball players. Give an example of an inherited trait and an acquired trait that could contribute to their skill at basketball.

_____

_____

_____

_____

Interpreting Tables

Indiana Standards

NOS 8.8 Analyze data, using appropriate mathematical manipulation as required, and use it to identify patterns and make inferences based on these patterns.

Visual displays, such as diagrams, tables, or graphs, are useful ways to show data collected in an experiment. A table is the most direct way to communicate this information. Tables are also used to summarize important trends in scientific data. Making a table may seem easy. However, if tables are not clearly organized, people will have trouble reading them. Below are a few strategies to help you improve your skills in interpreting scientific tables.

Tutorial

Use the following instructions to study the parts of a table about heredity in Brittanies and to analyze the data shown in the table.

Offspring from Cross of Black Solid and Liver Tricolor Brittanies		
Color	**Pattern**	**Number of Offspring**
orange and white	solid	1
black and white	solid	1
	tricolor	3
liver and white	solid	1
	tricolor	3

Reading the Title
Every table should have an informative title. By reading the title of the table to the left, we know that the table contains data about the offspring of a cross between a black solid Brittany and a liver tricolor Brittany.

Summarizing the Title
Sometimes it is helpful to write a sentence to summarize a table's title. For example, you could write, "This table shows how puppies that are the offspring of a black solid Brittany and a liver tricolor Brittany might look."

Analyzing the Headings
Row and column headings describe the data in the cells. Headings often appear different from the data in the cells, such as being larger, bold, or being shaded. The row headings in the table to the left organize three kinds of data: the coat color of the puppies, the coat pattern of the puppies, and the number of puppies that have each combination of coat color and pattern.

Describing the Data
In complete sentences, record the information that you read in the table. For example, you could write, "There are five different kinds of offspring. Tricolor puppies are most common, and puppies with a solid coat pattern are least common. There are twice as many tricolor puppies as solid puppies."

Analyzing the Data
Now that you have seen how the table is organized, you can begin to look for trends in the data. Which combinations are most common? Which combinations are least common?

You Try It!

The table below shows the characteristics of Guinea pig offspring. Look at the table, and answer the questions that follow.

Characteristics of Guinea Pig Offspring from Controlled Breeding			
Hair Color	Coat Texture	Hair Length	Number of Guinea Pigs
black	rough	short	27
		long	9
	smooth	short	9
		long	3
white	rough	short	9
		long	3
	smooth	short	3
		long	1

1 Summarizing the Title Circle the title of the table. Write a one-sentence description of the information shown in the table.

_____

_____

2 Analyzing the Headings Shade the column headings in the table. What information do they show? How many combinations of hair color, coat texture, and hair length are shown?

_____

_____

_____

3 Analyzing the Data Circle the most common type of Guinea pig. Box the least common type of Guinea pig. Write sentences to describe the characteristics of each.

_____

_____

_____

_____

4 Applying Mathematics Calculate the total number of Guinea pig offspring. Write this total at the bottom of the table. What percentage of the total number of Guinea pigs has short hair? What percentage of the total number of Guinea pigs has long hair?

_____

_____

_____

_____

5 Observing Trends Based on your data from Step 4, which characteristic is dominant in Guinea pigs: long hair or short hair?

_____

_____

6 Applying Concepts What is one advantage of displaying data in tables? What is one advantage of describing data in writing?

_____

_____

_____

_____

Take It Home

With an adult, practice making tables. You can categorize anything that interests you. Make sure your table has a title and clearly and accurately organizes your data using headings. If possible, share your table with your class.

Punnett Squares and Pedigrees

ESSENTIAL QUESTION

How are patterns of inheritance studied?

By the end of this lesson, you should be able to explain how patterns of heredity can be predicted by Punnett squares and pedigrees.

These cattle are bred for their long, curly hair, which keeps them warm in cold climates. This trait is maintained by careful breeding of these animals.

Engage Your Brain

1 Infer Why do you think that children look like their parents?

2 Apply Color or label each circle with the color that results when the two paints mix. As you read the lesson, think about how this grid is similar to and different from a Punnett square.

Active Reading

3 Apply Use context clues to write your own definition for the words *occur* and *outcome*.

Example sentence
Tools can be used to predict the likelihood that a particular genetic combination will <u>occur</u>.

occur:

Example sentence
A Punnett square can be used to predict the <u>outcome</u> of a genetic cross.

outcome:

Vocabulary Terms

- **Punnett square**
- **probability**
- **ratio**
- **pedigree**

4 Apply As you learn the definition of each vocabulary term in this lesson, create your own definition or sketch to help you remember the meaning of the term.

Squared Away

How are Punnett squares used to predict patterns of heredity?

When Gregor Mendel studied pea plants, he noticed that traits are inherited in patterns. One tool for understanding the patterns of heredity is a diagram called a *Punnett square*. A **Punnett square** is a graphic used to predict the possible genotypes of offspring in a given cross. Each parent has two alleles for a particular gene. An offspring receives one allele from each parent. A Punnett square shows all of the possible allele combinations in the offspring.

The Punnett square below shows how alleles are expected to be distributed in a cross between a pea plant with purple flowers and a pea plant with white flowers. The top of the Punnett square shows one parent's alleles for this trait (*F* and *F*). The left side of the Punnett square shows the other parent's alleles (*f* and *f*). Each compartment within the Punnett square shows an allele combination in potential offspring. You can see that in this cross, all offspring would have the same genotype (*Ff*). Because purple flower color is completely dominant to white flower color, all of the offspring would have purple flowers.

Active Reading

5 Identify In a Punnett square, where are the parents' alleles written?

_____

_____

_____

_____

This Punnett square shows the possible offspring combinations in pea plants with different flower colors.

Key:

F Purple flower allele

f White flower allele

Genotype: FF
Phenotype: purple flower

Genotype: ff
Phenotype: white flower

One parent's alleles

The other parent's alleles

	F	F
f	Ff	Ff
f	Ff	Ff

6 Apply Fill in the genotypes and phenotypes of the parents and offspring in this Punnett square. Sketch the resulting offspring possibilities in the white boxes below. (Hint: Assume complete dominance.)

Key:

R Round pea allele

r Wrinkled pea allele

Genotype: _____

Phenotype: _____

Genotype: _____

Phenotype: _____

	R	r
R	Genotype: _____ Phenotype: _____	Genotype: _____ Phenotype: _____
r	Genotype: _____ Phenotype: _____	Genotype: _____ Phenotype: _____

7 Analyze What does each compartment of the Punnett square represent?

_____

_____

_____

_____

_____

_____

_____

How can a Punnett square be used to make predictions about offspring?

A Punnett square does not tell you what the exact results of a certain cross will be. A Punnett square only helps you find the probability that a certain genotype will occur. **Probability** is the mathematical chance of a specific outcome in relation to the total number of possible outcomes.

Probability can be expressed in the form of a **ratio** (RAY•shee•oh), an expression that compares two quantities. A ratio written as 1:4 is read as "one to four." The ratios obtained from a Punnett square tell you the probability that any one offspring will get certain alleles. Another way of expressing probability is as a *percentage*. A percentage is like a ratio that compares a number to 100. A percentage states the number of times a certain outcome might happen out of a hundred chances.

1:4 is the ratio of red squares to total squares.

Do the Math   Sample Problem

In guinea pigs, the dominant *B* allele is responsible for black fur, while the recessive *b* allele is responsible for brown fur. Use the Punnett square to find the probability of this cross resulting in offspring with brown fur.

	B	b
b	Bb	bb
b	Bb	bb

Identify

A. What do you know?

Parent genotypes are Bb and bb. Possible offspring genotypes are Bb and bb.

B. What do you want to find out?

Probability of the cross resulting in offspring with brown fur

Plan

C. Count the total number of offspring allele combinations: 4

D. Count the number of allele combinations that will result in offspring with brown fur: 2

Solve

E. Write the probability of offspring with brown fur as a ratio: 2:4

F. Rewrite the ratio to express the probability out of 100 offspring by multiplying each side of the ratio by the same number (such as 25): 50:100

G. Convert the ratio to a percentage: 50%

Answer: 50% chance of offspring with brown fur

Do the Math   You Try It

8 Calculate This Punnett square shows a cross between two *Bb* guinea pigs. What is the probability of the cross resulting in offspring with black fur?

	B	b
B	BB	Bb
b	Bb	bb

Identify

A. What do you know?

B. What do you want to find out?

Plan

C. Count the total number of offspring allele combinations:

D. Count the number of allele combinations that will result in offspring with black fur:

Solve

E. Write the probability of offspring with black fur as a ratio:

F. Rewrite the ratio to express the probability out of 100 offspring by multiplying each side of the ratio by the same number:

G. Convert the ratio to a percentage:

Answer:

9 Graph In the cross above, what is the ratio of each of the possible genotypes? Show your results by filling in the pie chart at the right. Fill in the key with color or shading to show which pieces of the chart represent the different genotypes.

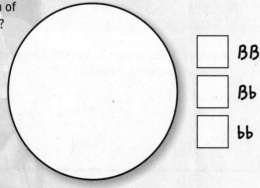

☐ BB
☐ Bb
☐ bb

How can a pedigree trace a trait through generations?

A pedigree is another tool used to study patterns of inheritance. A **pedigree** traces the occurrence of a trait through generations of a family. Pedigrees can be created to trace any inherited trait—even hair color!

Pedigrees can be useful in tracing a special class of inherited disorders known as *sex-linked disorders*. Sex-linked disorders are associated with an allele on a sex chromosome. Many sex-linked disorders, such as hemophilia and colorblindness, are caused by an allele on the X chromosome. Women have two X chromosomes, so a woman can have one allele for colorblindness without being colorblind. A woman who is heterozygous for this trait is called a *carrier,* because she can carry or pass on the trait to her offspring. Men have just one X chromosome. In men, this single chromosome determines if the trait is present.

The pedigree below traces a disease called *cystic fibrosis*. Cystic fibrosis causes serious lung problems. Carriers of the disease have one recessive allele. They do not have cystic fibrosis, but they are able to pass the recessive allele on to their children. If a child receives a recessive allele from each parent, then the child will have cystic fibrosis. Other genetic conditions follow a similar pattern.

Think Outside the Book Inquiry

10 **Design** Create a pedigree chart that traces the occurrence of dimples in your family or in the family of a friend. Collect information for as many family members as you can.

Visualize It!

Pedigree for Cystic Fibrosis

11 **Analyze** Does anyone in the third generation have cystic fibrosis? Explain.

_____

_____

_____

12 **Calculate** What is the probability that the child of two carriers will have cystic fibrosis?

_____

_____

_____

Saving the European Mouflon

The European mouflon is an endangered species of sheep. Scientists at the University of Teramo in Italy used genetic tools and techniques to show how the population of mouflon could be preserved.

Maintaining Genetic Diversity

When a very small population of animals interbreeds, there is a greater risk that harmful genetic conditions can appear in the animals. This is one issue that scientists face when trying to preserve endangered species. One way to lower this risk is to be sure that genetically-similar animals do not breed.

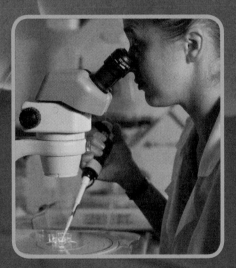

Genetics to the Rescue!

Researchers combined the sperm and egg of genetically-dissimilar European mouflons in a laboratory. The resulting embryo was implanted into a mother sheep. By controlling the combination of genetic material, scientists hope to lower the risk of inherited disorders.

Extend

Inquiry

13 Explain Why are small populations difficult to preserve?

14 Research Research another population of animals that has been part of a captive breeding program.

15 Describe Describe these animals and the results of the breeding program by doing one of the following:
• make a poster
• write a song
• write a short story
• draw a graphic novel

Visual Summary

To complete this summary, fill in the blanks with the correct word or phrase. Then use the key below to check your answers. You can use this page to review the main concepts of the lesson.

Predicting Patterns of Inheritance

Punnett squares can be used to make predictions about possible offspring.

	F	F
f	Ff	Ff
f	Ff	Ff

16 A Punnett square shows combinations of different _____ received from each parent.

Pedigrees trace a trait through generations.

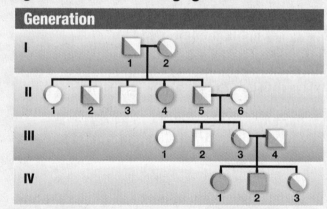

17 An allele responsible for a _____ is found on a sex chromosome.

18 Compare How is a heterozygous individual represented in the Punnett square and pedigree shown above?

Lesson Review

Vocabulary

Circle the term that best completes the following sentences.

1 A *Punnett square / ratio* is a tool that can be used to predict the genotypes of potential offspring in a given cross.

2 The results from a Punnett square can be used to find the *pedigree / probability* that a certain allele combination will occur in offspring.

3 A mathematical expression that compares one number to another is called a *pedigree / ratio*.

Key Concepts

Use this diagram to answer the following questions.

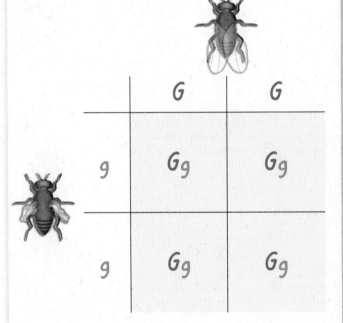

4 Analyze What is gene G responsible for in these fruit flies?

_____

_____

5 Analyze What is the ratio of heterozygous offspring to total offspring in the Punnett square?

_____

_____

6 Define What is a sex-linked disorder?

_____

_____

_____

_____

Critical Thinking

7 Infer Imagine a pedigree that traces an inherited disorder found in individuals with two recessive alleles for gene D. The pedigree shows three siblings with the genotypes *DD*, *Dd*, and *dd*. Did the parents of these three children have the disorder? Explain.

_____

_____

_____

_____

8 Explain A *Bb* guinea pig crosses with a *Bb* guinea pig, and four offspring are produced. All of the offspring are black. Explain how this could happen.

_____

_____

_____

_____

9 Synthesize You are creating a pedigree to trace freckles, a recessive trait, in a friend's family. You find out which of her family members have freckles and which do not. When you complete the pedigree, what can you learn about members of your friend's family that you could not tell just by looking at them?

_____

_____

_____

My Notes

Unit 7 Summary

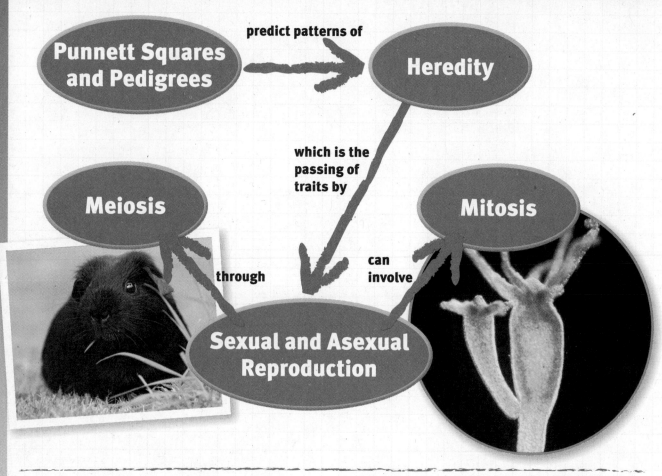

Punnett Squares and Pedigrees → predict patterns of → Heredity

which is the passing of traits by

Meiosis

Mitosis

through

can involve

Sexual and Asexual Reproduction

1 Interpret The Graphic Organizer above shows that Punnett squares are used to make predictions about heredity. Are Punnett squares more useful for predicting the results of sexual or asexual reproduction? Explain.

_____

_____

_____

_____

_____

_____

_____

_____

_____

_____

2 Compare How are meiosis and mitosis similar? How are they different?

_____

_____

_____

_____

_____

_____

_____

3 Relate Compare the phenotype and genotype of a parent to the phenotype and genotype of its offspring produced by asexual reproduction.

_____

_____

_____

ISTEP+ Review

Multiple Choice

1 Lucinda decides to investigate what would happen if there is an error at different stages of the cell cycle. She examines interphase, mitosis, and cytokinesis. Which of these statement MOST LIKELY describes what happens if DNA is not duplicated during interphase?

A. The new cells would be more numerous.

B. The new cells would have too many chromosomes.

C. The new cells would have too many or too few nuclei.

D. The new cells would have an incorrect number of chromosomes.

2 Noriko discovers a new plant in a forest. She observes it for some time, and when it reproduces, she tests the offspring and finds that they are genetically identical to the parent. Which of these statements is TRUE about Noriko's find?

A. The plant reproduces sexually, and two parents are required.

B. The plant reproduces asexually, and two parents are required.

C. The plant reproduces sexually, and only one parent is required.

D. The plant reproduces asexually, and only one parent is required.

3 John sees some bright flowers growing on an azalea plant in Leah's garden, and he tells her how much he likes them. Leah cuts a small stem from one of the azaleas and gives it to John. John takes the cutting home and plants it in his garden. In a few months, the small stem has grown into a full-sized, new plant. Which of these choices CORRECTLY describes this situation?

A. The parent plant reproduced sexually by budding, and the plant in John's garden has genes that are different than those of the plant in Leah's garden.

B. The parent plant reproduced asexually by budding, and the plant in John's garden has genes identical to those of the plant in Leah's garden.

C. The parent plant reproduced sexually by vegetative reproduction, and the plant in John's garden has genes that are different than those of the plant in Leah's garden.

D. The parent plant reproduced asexually by vegetative reproduction, and the plant in John's garden has genes identical to those of the plant in Leah's garden.

4 Delia is teaching her sister about important molecules in the body. She tells her sister that one molecule contains genes that determine traits, such as eye color or hair color. Which molecule is Delia describing?

A. DNA

B. glucose

C. cellulose

D. cholesterol

5 A species of rabbit can have brown fur or white fur. One rabbit with two alleles for brown fur (BB) has brown fur. A second rabbit with two alleles for white fur (bb) has white fur. Which statement is TRUE about the alleles B and b?

A. They are two different genes.

B. They result in the same phenotype.

C. They are two different versions of the same gene.

D. They provide identical instructions about different traits.

6 Hank was studying how genetic information is passed on during sexual reproduction. He drew these pictures, each on a different flash card, to show different stages of meiosis.

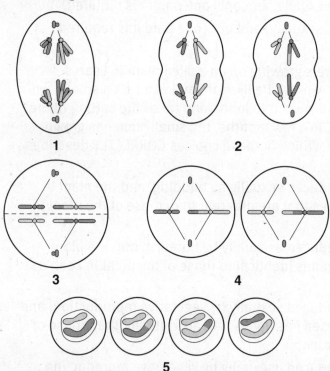

Which choice below lists the stages that Hank drew in the correct order? Hint: Remember that meiosis involves two cell divisions: meiosis I and meiosis II.

A. 1, 2, 4, 3, 5

B. 3, 4, 1, 2, 5

C. 3, 1, 4, 2, 5

D. 5, 2, 4, 1, 3

7 Which of these descriptions correctly defines the term DNA?

A. one-half of a copied chromosome

B. area where chromatids are attached

C. molecule inside chromosomes that determines the traits of living things

D. long strand made up of genetic material and protein

8 Scientists have discovered that a type of shark called a *hammerhead shark* can reproduce asexually. How does this type of reproduction give the hammerhead shark an advantage?

A. It increases the genetic diversity of the hammerhead shark species.

B. It allows hammerhead sharks to reproduce without investing energy in finding a mate.

C. It requires two parents and produces hammerhead offspring genetically different from each other.

D. It gives hammerhead sharks a better chance of surviving if conditions change and suddenly become unfavorable.

9 The diagram below shows the results of crossing a pea plant with round seeds and a pea plant with wrinkled seeds.

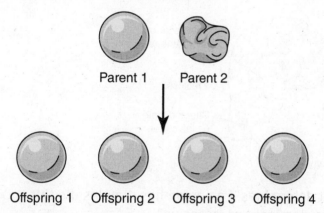

Parent 1   Parent 2

Offspring 1   Offspring 2   Offspring 3   Offspring 4

What can be determined from the results of the experiment?

A. Smooth shape and wrinkled shape are both recessive traits.

B. Smooth shape and wrinkled shape are both dominant traits.

C. Smooth shape is a dominant trait, and wrinkled shape is a recessive trait.

D. Smooth shape is a recessive trait, and wrinkled shape is a dominant trait.

Constructed Response

10 Identify one advantage for asexual reproduction AND one advantage for sexual reproduction.

_____

_____

Some organisms can use both types of reproduction. Under what type of conditions would it be beneficial to use sexual reproduction? Explain.

_____

_____

Extended Response

11 This girl has dimples, an inherited trait. Dimples are completely dominant over no dimples. This girl's mother has dimples and her father does not.

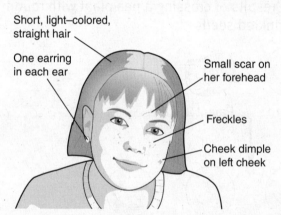

Short, light–colored, straight hair

One earring in each ear

Small scar on her forehead

Freckles

Cheek dimple on left cheek

What form of the gene that determines if a person has dimples did this girl inherit from her mother, dominant or recessive?

_____

What form of the gene did the girl inherit from her father?

_____

Explain why this girl's phenotype is dimples.

_____

Identify TWO other inherited characteristics that are shown in this figure.

_____

DNA and Modern Genetics

Core Standard

Understand the predictability of characteristics being passed from parents to offspring.

A centrifuge can be used to separate blood into its components.

What do you think?

Not all clues are large! Biological evidence gathered at crime scenes can tell forensic scientists many things. How do detectives in forensics labs use genetics to interpret evidence?

CRIME SCEN

509

Unit 8
DNA and Modern Genetics

CITIZEN SCIENCE

Solved with Forensics

Modern crime labs use genetics, the study of how traits are inherited, to interpret evidence found at the scene of a crime. In the following scenario, a bike has been stolen and you will use genetic evidence to figure out what happened.

Stolen!
Have you seen my bike?

① Ask A Question

What should a detective at a crime scene look for?

Determine what types of evidence a detective could find at a crime scene. Consider that some evidence might be microscopic! In this case, you have found an empty juice box and a lock of hair.

② Think About It

A List some of the traits (like fingerprints) that are unique to every individual.

_____

_____

_____

_____

B What biological evidence might be found on the juice box and lock of hair left behind at the crime scene? What could they tell you about the crime?

_____

_____

_____

_____

③ Apply Your Knowledge

A The hair sample you gathered is in a sealed bag. Why is it important to protect samples?

_____

_____

_____

B When lab technicians analyze DNA, it doesn't have a name on it. How can you match your sample to an individual and solve the crime?

_____

_____

_____

C Can forensics determine for sure that the person identified by the evidence committed the crime? Explain.

_____

_____

_____

_____

Take It Home

Find out how DNA forensics is applied in our justice system. How accurate is it? Has it been used to reverse any court decisions or overturn any convictions?

DNA Structure and Function

ESSENTIAL QUESTION

What is DNA?

By the end of this lesson, you should be able to describe the structure and main functions of DNA.

This bacterium was treated with a special chemical, causing a twisted maze of DNA to burst from the cell.

© Houghton Mifflin Harcourt Publishing Company • Image Credits: ©Dr. Gopal Murti/Photo Researchers, Inc.

Indiana Standards

8.3.4 Understand the relationship between deoxyribonucleic acid (DNA), genes, and chromosomes.

1 Predict Check T or F to show whether you think each statement is true or false.

T	F	
☐	☐	DNA is found in the cells of all living things.
☐	☐	All DNA mutations are harmful.
☐	☐	The cell can make copies of its DNA.

2 Describe DNA is sometimes called the *blueprint of life*. Why do you think that is?

_____

_____

_____

_____

_____

Active Reading

3 Synthesize Many English words have their roots in other languages. Use the Latin words below to make an educated guess about the meanings of the words *replication* and *mutation*.

Latin word	Meaning
mutare	to change
replicare	to repeat

Example sentence
DNA can undergo <u>mutation</u>.

mutation:

_____

_____

Example sentence
Before cell division, DNA <u>replication</u> occurs.

replication:

_____

_____

Vocabulary Terms

- DNA
- nucleotide
- replication
- mutation
- RNA
- ribosome

4 Identify This list contains the key terms you'll learn in this lesson. As you read, circle the definition of each term.

Cracking the CODE

ATTAGCGATCACTAAATTAGC

Active Reading

5 Identify As you read, underline the meaning of the word *code*.

What is DNA?

The genetic material of a cell contains information needed for the cell's growth and other activities. It also determines the inherited characteristics of an organism. The genetic material in cells is contained in a molecule called deoxyribonucleic (dee•OK•see•ry•boh•noo•KLAY•ik) acid, or **DNA** for short. You could compare the information in DNA to the books in your local library. You might find a book describing how to bake a cake or complete your favorite video game. The books, however, don't actually do any of those things—you do. Similarly, the "books" that make up the DNA "library" carry the information that a cell needs to function, grow, and divide. However, DNA doesn't do any of those things. Proteins do most of the work of a cell and also make up much of the structure of a cell.

Scientists describe DNA as containing a code. A *code* is a set of rules and symbols used to carry information. For example, your computer uses a code of ones and zeroes that is translated into numbers, letters, and graphics on a computer screen. To understand how DNA functions as a code, you first need to learn about the structure of the DNA molecule.

DNA Timeline

Review this timeline to learn about some of the important scientific contributions to our understanding of DNA.

1875	1900	1925

1869 Friedrich Miescher identifies a substance that will later be known as DNA.

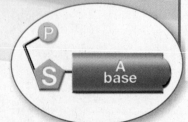

1919 Phoebus Levene publishes a paper on nucleic acids. His research helps scientists determine that DNA is made up of sugars, phosphate groups, and four nitrogen-containing bases: adenine, thymine, guanine, and cytosine. Bases are often referred to by their first letter: A, T, C, or G. Each base has a different shape.

6 Analyze In this model, what do *P, S,* and *A bases* represent?

_____

_____

How was DNA discovered?

The discovery of the structure and function of DNA did not happen overnight. Many scientists from all over the world contributed to our current understanding of this important molecule. Some scientists discovered the chemicals that make up DNA. Others learned how these chemicals fit together. Still others determined the three-dimensional structure of the DNA molecule. The timeline below shows some of the key steps in this process of discovery.

© Houghton Mifflin Harcourt Publishing Company • Image Credits: (l) ©NLM/Science Source/Photo Researchers, Inc; (c) ©Omikron/Photo Researchers, Inc.; (r) ©A. Barrington Brown/Photo Researchers, Inc.

Think Outside the Book Inquiry

7 Research Use the Internet or library resources to research a scientist who contributed to the discovery of DNA. Then, create a poster about the scientist. Share your findings with your class.

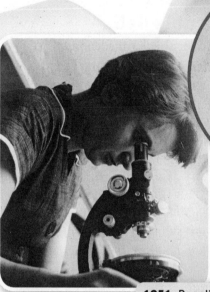

An image of DNA produced by using x-rays.

1951 Rosalind Franklin and Maurice Wilkins make images of DNA using x-rays. When an x-ray passes through the molecule, the ray bends and creates a pattern that is captured on film.

1953 James Watson and Francis Crick use Chargaff's rules and the x-ray images of DNA to conclude that DNA looks like a long, twisted ladder. They build a large-scale model of DNA using simple materials from their laboratory.

1950

1975

1950 Erwin Chargaff observes that the amount of guanine always equals the amount of cytosine, and the amount of adenine equals the amount of thymine. His findings are now known as *Chargaff's rules*.

1952 Alfred Hershey and Martha Chase perform experiments with viruses to confirm that DNA, not proteins, carries genetic information.

Unraveling DNA

What does DNA look like?

The chemical components that make up DNA are too small to be observed directly. But experiments and imaging techniques have helped scientists to infer the shape of DNA and the arrangement of its parts.

The Shape of DNA Is a Double Helix

The structure of DNA is a twisted ladder shape called a *double helix*. The two sides of the ladder, often referred to as the DNA backbone, are made of alternating sugars and phosphate groups. The rungs of the ladder are made of a pair of bases, each attached to one of the sugars in the backbone.

Active Reading **8 Describe** Where are phosphate groups found in a DNA molecule?

_____

_____

DNA is found in the nucleus of eukaryotic cells.

The DNA molecule has a double-helix shape.

Visualize It!

9 Compare Explain how the double-helix structure of DNA is like a spiral staircase.

_____

_____

_____

_____

_____

_____

DNA Is Made Up of Nucleotides

A base, a sugar, and a phosphate group make a building block of DNA known as a **nucleotide**. These repeating chemical units join together to form the DNA molecule. There are four different nucleotides in DNA, identified by their bases: adenine (A), thymine (T), cytosine (C), and guanine (G). Because of differences in size and shape, adenine always pairs with thymine (A-T) and cytosine always pairs with guanine (C-G). These paired, or *complementary,* bases fit together like two pieces of a puzzle.

    The order of the nucleotides in DNA is a code that carries information. The DNA code is read like a book. *Genes* are segments of DNA that relate to a certain trait. Each gene has a starting point and an ending point, with the DNA code being read in one direction. The bases A, T, C, and G form the alphabet of the code. The code stores information about which proteins the cells should build. The types of proteins your body makes help to determine your traits.

10 Apply Place boxes around the bases that pair with each other.

Adenine (A)

Thymine (T)

Cytosine (C)

Guanine (G)

11 Devise The bases are often referred to simply by their initials—A, T, C, and G. The phrase "all tigers can growl" may help you remember them. Think of another phrase that uses words starting with A, T, C, and G that could help you remember the bases. Write your phrase below.

_____

_____

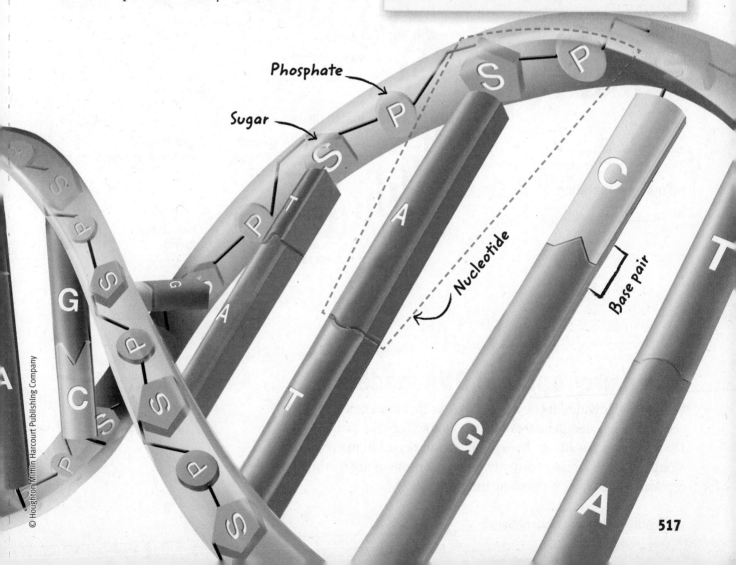

Phosphate

Sugar

Nucleotide

Base pair

How are copies of DNA made?

The cell is able to make copies of DNA molecules through a process known as **replication**. During replication, the two strands of DNA separate, almost like two threads in a string being unwound. The bases on each side of the molecule are used as a pattern for a new strand. As the bases on the original molecule are exposed, complementary nucleotides are added. For example, an exposed base containing adenine attaches to a nucleotide containing thymine. When replication is complete, there are two identical DNA molecules. Each new DNA molecule is made of one strand of old DNA and one strand of new DNA.

Visualize It!

12 Apply Fill in the blanks to complete the labels on this model of replicating DNA.

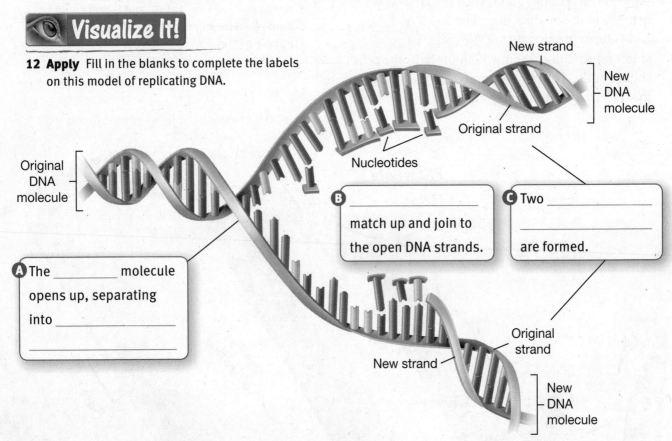

New strand

New DNA molecule

Original strand

Nucleotides

Original DNA molecule

B _____ match up and join to the open DNA strands.

C Two _____ _____ are formed.

A The _____ molecule opens up, separating into _____ _____

Original strand

New strand

New DNA molecule

When are copies of DNA made?

Before a cell divides, it copies the DNA so that each new daughter cell will have a complete set of instructions. Our cells can replicate DNA in just a few hours. How? Replication begins in many places along the DNA strand. So, many groups of proteins are working to replicate your DNA at the same time.

Mutation

What are mutations?

Changes in the number, type, or order of bases on a piece of DNA are known as **mutations**. Sometimes, a base is left out. This kind of change is known as a *deletion*. Or, an extra base might be added. This kind of change is an *insertion*. The most common mutation happens when one base replaces another. This kind of change is known as a *substitution*.

How do mutations happen? Given the large number of bases in an organism's DNA, it is not surprising that random errors can occur during replication. However, DNA can also be damaged by physical or chemical agents called *mutagens*. Ultraviolet light and the chemicals in cigarette smoke are examples of mutagens.

Cells make proteins that can fix errors in DNA. But sometimes a mistake isn't corrected, and it becomes part of the genetic code. Mutations to DNA may be beneficial, neutral, or harmful. A *genetic disorder* results from mutations that harm the normal function of a cell. Some of these disorders, such as Tay-Sachs disease and sickle-cell anemia, are *inherited*, or passed on from parent to offspring. Other genetic disorders result from mutations that occur during a person's lifetime. Most cancers fall into this category.

 **Visualize It!**

13 Apply Place a check mark in the box to indicate which type of mutation is being shown.

Original sequence

Ⓐ

☐ deletion ☐ insertion ☐ substitution

Ⓑ

☐ deletion ☐ insertion ☐ substitution

Ⓒ

☐ deletion ☐ insertion ☐ substitution

This snake has albinism, a condition in which the body cannot make the pigments that give color to the skin and eyes.

14 Explain Albinism is an inherited genetic disorder. Explain what is meant by "inherited genetic disorder."

_____

_____

_____

_____

ProteinFactory

What is the role of DNA and RNA in building proteins?

Imagine that you are baking cookies. You have a big cookbook that contains the recipe. If you take the book with you into the kitchen, you risk damaging the book and losing important instructions. You only need one page from the book, so you copy the recipe on a piece of paper and leave the cookbook on the shelf. This process is similar to the way that the cell uses DNA to build proteins. First, some of the information in the DNA is copied to a separate molecule called ribonucleic acid, or **RNA.** Then, the copy is used to build proteins. Not all the instructions are needed all the time. In eukaryotes, the DNA is protected inside the cell's nucleus.

Like DNA, RNA has a sugar-phosphate backbone and the bases adenine (A), guanine (G), and cytosine (C). But instead of thymine (T), RNA contains the base uracil (U). Also, the sugar found in RNA is different from the one in DNA. There are three types of RNA: messenger RNA, ribosomal RNA, and transfer RNA. Each type of RNA has a special role in making proteins.

Active Reading **15 Identify** As you read, number the sentences that describe the steps of transcription.

Transcription: The Information in DNA Is Copied to Messenger RNA

When a cell needs a set of instructions for making a protein, it first makes an RNA copy of the necessary section of DNA. This process is called *transcription*. Transcription involves DNA and messenger RNA (mRNA). Only individual genes are transcribed, not the whole DNA molecule. During transcription, DNA is used as a template to make a complementary strand of mRNA. The DNA opens up where the gene is located. Then RNA bases match up to complementary bases on the DNA template. When transcription is complete, the mRNA is released and the DNA molecule closes.

DNA

RNA

Protein

RNA uses the genetic information stored in DNA to build proteins.

mRNA

Cell nucleus

A During transcription, DNA is used as a template to make a complementary strand of mRNA. In eukaryotes, the mRNA then exits the nucleus.

Translation: The Information in Messenger RNA Is Used to Build Proteins

Once the mRNA has been made, it is fed through a protein assembly line within a ribosome. A **ribosome** is a cell organelle made of ribosomal RNA (rRNA) and protein. As mRNA passes through the ribosome, transfer RNA (tRNA) molecules deliver amino acids to the ribosome. Each group of three bases on the mRNA strand codes for one amino acid. So the genetic code determines the order in which amino acids are brought to the ribosome. The amino acids join together to form a protein. The process of making proteins from RNA is called *translation*.

B A ribosome attaches to an mRNA strand at the beginning of a gene.

tRNA

Amino acid

Ribosome

C A tRNA molecule enters the ribosome. Three bases on the tRNA match up to 3 complementary bases on the mRNA strand. The bases on the mRNA strand determine which tRNA and amino acid move into the ribosome.

Chain of amino acids

Chain of amino acids is released

D The tRNA transfers its amino acid to a growing chain. Then, the tRNA is released. The ribosome moves down the mRNA and the process repeats.

E Once the ribosome reaches the end of the gene, the chain of amino acids is released.

16 Apply Fill in the table below by placing check marks in the appropriate boxes and writing the product of transcription and translation.

Process	What molecules are involved?				What is the product?
Transcription	☐ DNA	☐ mRNA	☐ tRNA	☐ ribosome	
Translation	☐ DNA	☐ mRNA	☐ tRNA	☐ ribosome	

Visual Summary

To complete this summary, fill in the blanks with the correct word or phrase. Then use the key below to check your answers. You can use this page to review the main concepts of the lesson.

DNA Structure and Function

DNA has a double-helix shape and is made up of nucleotides.

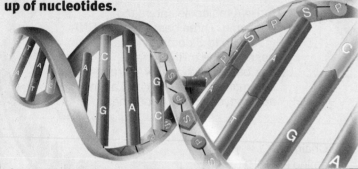

17 The four bases in DNA nucleotides are

_____

_____

_____

The cell can make copies of DNA.

18 DNA replication happens before cells _____

DNA can mutate.

19 Three types of DNA mutations are _____

_____

_____

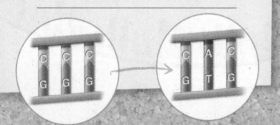

DNA and RNA are involved in making proteins.

20 The two processes involved in making proteins from the DNA code are

21 **Explain** How could a mutation in the DNA affect what proteins are made by the cell?

Lesson Review

Vocabulary
In your own words, define the following terms.

1 A(n) _____ of DNA consists of a sugar, a phosphate, and a nitrogen-containing base.

2 A(n) _____ is a change in the base sequence of a DNA molecule.

Key Concepts
Draw a line to connect the following scientists to their contributions to our understanding of DNA.

3 Erwin Chargaff

4 Rosalind Franklin and Maurice Wilkins

5 James Watson and Francis Crick

A took x-ray images of DNA molecule

B proposed a double-helix model of DNA

C found that the amount of adenine equals the amount of thymine and that the amount of guanine equals the amount of cytosine

6 Identify How does the structure of RNA differ from the structure of DNA?

_____

_____

_____

7 Identify When does DNA replication occur?

_____

_____

8 Describe Name the three types of RNA and list their roles in making proteins.

_____

_____

_____

_____

_____

_____

9 Identify What can cause DNA mutations?

_____

_____

_____

Critical Thinking
Use this diagram to answer the following questions.

10 Describe What is the sequence of bases on DNA strand *b*, from left to right?

_____

11 Apply This segment of DNA is transcribed to form a complementary strand of mRNA. The mRNA then undergoes translation. How many amino acids would the RNA code for?

_____

_____

12 Infer After many cell divisions, a segment of DNA has more base pairs than it originally did. Explain what has happened.

_____

_____

_____

13 Explain Why must DNA replicate?

_____

_____

_____

_____

_____

_____

Identifying Variables

Indiana Standards

NOS 8.8 Analyze data, using appropriate mathematical manipulation as required, and use it to identify patterns and make inferences based on these patterns.

When you are analyzing or designing a scientific experiment, it is important to identify the variables in the experiment. Usually, an experiment is designed to discover how changing one variable affects another variable. In a scientific investigation, the independent variable is the factor that is purposely changed. The dependent variable is the factor that changes in response to the independent variable.

Tutorial

Use the following strategies to help you identify the variables in an experiment.

Summary: We genetically modified corn plants to increase growth in low-light conditions.

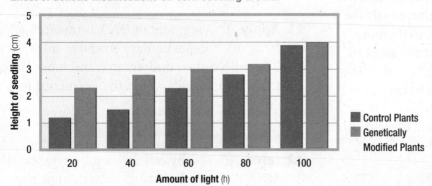

Effect of Genetic Modifications on Corn Seedling Growth

Height of seedling (cm) / Amount of light (h)

Control Plants
Genetically Modified Plants

Reading a Summary The published results of an experiment usually include a brief summary. You should be able to identify the variables from it. In the summary to the left, the independent variable is the DNA of the corn plants, and the dependent variable is the height of the plants.

Analyzing a Graph Making a graph can be a very effective way to show the relationship between variables. For a line graph, the independent variable is usually shown on the *x*-axis, or the horizontal axis. The dependent variable is usually shown on the *y*-axis, or the vertical axis.

Describing the Data When you read a graph, describing the information in complete sentences can help you to identify the variables. For example, you could write, "In the first 80 hours, the genetically modified corn plants grew much more quickly than the control plants grew. But by 100 hours, both kinds of plants were about the same height. This shows that the effect of the independent variable was greatest during the first 80 hours of plant growth."

Identifying the Effects of Variables Look closely at the graph. Notice that the genetically modified seedlings grew more quickly than the control seedlings, but the effects were greatest in the early part of the experiment. A variable's effect is not always constant throughout an experiment.

You Try It!

The passage below describes the process of gel electrophoresis. Use the description to answer the question that follows.

> During gel electrophoresis, DNA is broken into separate fragments. These fragments are added to a gel. When an electric current is applied to the gel, the fragments travel different distances through the gel. The size of the DNA fragments determines how far they travel. Smaller fragments travel farther than larger fragments do. Scientists can use these data to identify unknown samples of DNA.

1 Reading a Summary Identify the variables described in the passage.

_____

_____

The graph below shows the results of DNA analysis using gel electrophoresis. Look at the graph, and answer the questions that follow.

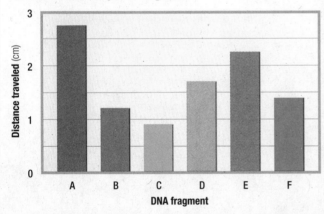

Distance Traveled by DNA Fragments

2 Analyzing a Graph Which variables are shown in the graph? Circle the axis that shows the dependent variable.

_____

_____

3 Analyzing the Data What is the relationship between the size of the DNA fragments and the distance they traveled? Circle the DNA fragment that is the smallest.

_____

_____

4 Applying Mathematics Calculate the average distance that the DNA fragments traveled. How much farther than the average distance did the smallest DNA fragment travel?

5 Applying Concepts Why is it important to limit the number of variables in an experiment?

_____

_____

_____

_____

Take It Home

With an adult, plan and conduct a simple experiment that includes an independent variable and a dependent variable. Record your results and graph your data if possible. Then share your results with the class.

Biotechnology

ESSENTIAL QUESTION

How does biotechnology impact our world?

By the end of this lesson, you should be able to explain how biotechnology impacts human life and the world around us.

Indiana Standards

8.3.10 Recognize and describe how new varieties of organisms have come about from selective breeding.

These glowing bands contain fragments of DNA that have been treated with a special chemical. This chemical glows under ultraviolet light, allowing scientists to see the DNA.

Engage Your Brain

1 Predict Fill in the blanks with the word or phrase you think correctly completes the following sentences.

A medical researcher might study DNA in order to learn _____

_____

_____

A crime scene investigator might study DNA in order to learn _____

_____

_____

2 Apply *GMO* stands for "genetically modified organism." Write a caption to accompany the following photo.

_____

_____

_____

Active Reading

3 Apply Use context clues to write your own definition for the words *inserted* and *technique.*

Example sentence
Using special technologies, a gene from one organism can be <u>inserted</u> into the DNA of another.

inserted:

_____

_____

Example sentence
Cloning is a <u>technique</u> in which the genetic information of an organism is copied.

technique:

_____

_____

Vocabulary Terms

- biotechnology
- artificial selection
- genetic engineering
- clone

4 Apply As you learn the definition of each vocabulary term in this lesson, create your own definition or sketch to help you remember the meaning of the term.

Bio**TECHNOLOGY**

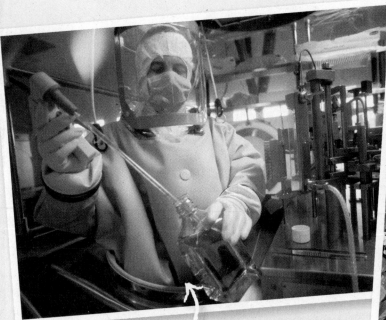

Protective clothing keeps this geneticist safe as he works with infectious particles.

This scientist works inside of a greenhouse. He breeds potato plants.

© Houghton Mifflin Harcourt Publishing Company • Image Credits: (l) ©Patrick Landmann/Photo Researchers, Inc.; (r) ©Scott Bauer/U.S. Department of Agriculture/Photo Researchers, Inc

What is biotechnology?

A forensic scientist makes copies of DNA from a crime scene. A botanist breeds flowers for their bright red blooms. A geneticist works to place a human gene into the DNA of bacteria. What do these processes have in common? They are all examples of biotechnology. **Biotechnology** is the use and application of living things and biological processes. In the past 40 years, new technologies have allowed scientists to directly change DNA. But biotechnology is not a new scientific field. For thousands of years, humans have been breeding plants and animals and using bacteria and yeast to ferment foods. These, too, are examples of biotechnology.

Active Reading **6 Identify** Name three examples of biotechnology.

_____

_____

_____

Different dog breeds are produced by artificial selection.

What are some applications of biotechnology?

Biotechnology processes fall into some broad categories. Artificial selection, genetic engineering, and cloning are some of the most common techniques.

Artificial Selection

For thousands of years, humans have been carefully selecting and breeding certain plants and animals that have desirable traits. Over many generations, horses have gotten faster, pigs have gotten leaner, and corn has become sweeter. **Artificial selection** is the process of selecting and breeding organisms that have certain desired traits. Artificial selection is also known as *selective breeding*.

Artificial selection can be successful as long as the desirable traits are controlled by genes. Animal and plant breeders select for alleles, which are different versions of a gene. The alleles being selected must already be present in the population. People do not change DNA during artificial selection. Instead, they cause certain alleles to become more common in a population. The different dog breeds are a good example of artificial selection. All dogs share a common ancestor, the wolf. However, thousands of years of selection by humans have produced dogs with a variety of characteristics.

Visualize It!

These vegetables have been developed through artificial selection. Their common ancestor is the mustard plant.

kale

broccoli

cabbage

cauliflower

Brussels sprouts

7 Infer Why might farmers use artificial selection to develop different types of vegetables?

_____

_____

_____

_____

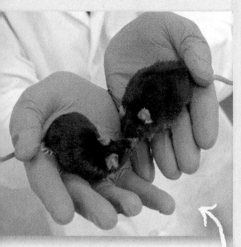

Scientists have disabled a gene in the mouse on the right. As a result, this mouse cannot control how much food it eats.

Genetic Engineering

Within the past 40 years, it has become possible to directly change the DNA of an organism. **Genetic engineering** is the process in which a piece of DNA is modified for use in research, medicine, agriculture, or industry. The DNA that is engineered often codes for a certain trait of interest. Scientists can isolate a segment of DNA, change it in some way, and return it to the organism. Or, scientists can take a segment of DNA from one species and transfer it to the DNA of an organism from another species.

Active Reading **8 Describe** For what purposes can genetic engineering be used?

_____

_____

_____

These genetically modified plant cells produce tiny, biodegradable plastic pellets. The pellets are then collected to make plastic products.

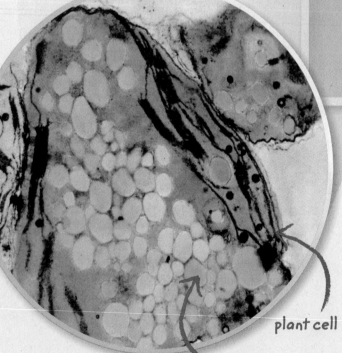

plant cell

plastic pellets

9 Infer Traditional plastics are made from petroleum, a nonrenewable resource. What benefit could plastic made by plants have over traditional plastic?

_____

_____

_____

_____

_____

_____

© Houghton Mifflin Harcourt Publishing Company • Image Credits: (tl) ©Penni Gladstone/San Francisco Chronicle/Corbis; (cr) ©Peter Yates/ Photo Researchers, Inc.; (bl) ©Dr. Chris Somerville/Photo Researchers, Inc.

Cloning

A **clone** is an organism, cell, or piece of genetic material that is genetically identical to the one from which it was derived. Cloning has been used to make copies of small traces of DNA found at crime scenes or on ancient artifacts. Also, cloning can be used to copy segments of DNA for genetic engineering.

In 1996, scientists cloned the DNA from one sheep's body cell to produce another sheep named Dolly. The ability to clone a sheep, which is a mammal, raised many concerns about the future uses of cloning, because humans are also mammals. It is important that people understand the science of genetics. Only then can we make informed decisions about how and when the technology should be used.

Dolly was cloned from a body cell of an adult sheep.

10 Apply Review each of the examples of biotechnology below. Then classify each as artificial selection, genetic engineering, or cloning.

	Scientists have introduced a gene to the DNA of these fish that causes the fish to glow.	☐ artificial selection ☐ genetic engineering ☐ cloning
	A scientist is gathering DNA from clothing found at a crime scene. Then many copies of the DNA sample will be made. This will allow the scientist to better study the DNA. Then the scientist might be able to confirm the identity of the person at the crime scene.	☐ artificial selection ☐ genetic engineering ☐ cloning
	Wild carrots have thin, white roots. Over time, carrot farmers have selected carrots that have thick, bright orange roots.	☐ artificial selection ☐ genetic engineering ☐ cloning
	Diabetes can be treated in some people with injections that contain the hormone insulin. The gene responsible for producing insulin in humans has been inserted into the DNA of bacteria. These bacteria then produce the human insulin that is used in the injection.	☐ artificial selection ☐ genetic engineering ☐ cloning

Feel the IMPACT!

How does biotechnology impact our world?

Scientists are aware that there are many ethical, legal, and social issues that arise from the ability to use and change living things. Biotechnology can impact both our society and our environment. We must decide how and when it is acceptable to use biotechnology. The examples that follow show some concerns that might be raised during a classroom debate about biotechnology.

11 Evaluate Read the first two examples of biotechnology and what students had to say about their effects on individuals, society, and the environment. Then complete Example 3 by filling in questions or possible effects of the technology.

Example 1

A Glowing Mosquito?

This is the larva of a genetically engineered mosquito. Its DNA includes a gene from a glowing jellyfish that causes the engineered mosquito to glow. Scientists hope to use this same technology to modify the mosquito's genome in other ways. For example, it is thought that the DNA of the mosquito could be changed so that the mosquito could not spread malaria.

Effects on Individuals and Society

"If the mosquito could be engineered so that it does not spread malaria, many lives could be saved."

Effects on Environment

"Mosquitoes are a food source for birds and fish. Are there health risks to animals that eat genetically modified mosquitoes?"

Think Outside the Book · Inquiry

12 Debate As a class, choose a current event that involves biotechnology. Then hold a debate to present the benefits and risks of this technology.

Example 2

Cloning the Gaur

The gaur is an endangered species. In 2001, a gaur was successfully cloned. The clone, named Noah, died of a bacterial infection 2 days after birth.

Effects on Individuals and Society

"How will we decide when it is appropriate to clone other types of organisms?"

Effects on Environment

"Cloning could help increase small populations of endangered species like the gaur and save them from extinction."

Example 3

Tough Plants!

Much of the corn and soybeans grown in the United States is genetically engineered. The plants have bacterial genes that make them more resistant to plant-eating insects.

Effects on Individuals and Society

Effects on Environment

Visual Summary

To complete this summary, circle the correct word or phrase. Then use the key below to check your answers. You can use this page to review the main concepts of the lesson.

Biotechnology

Biotechnology is the use of living things and biological processes.

13 Modern biotechnology techniques can change an organism's DNA / environment.

Artificial selection, genetic engineering, and cloning are three types of biotechnology.

14 The DNA of the mouse on the right has been modified through a technique called cloning / genetic engineering.

Biotechnology impacts individuals, society, and the environment.

15 Creating a clone / gene of an endangered species could impact the environment.

Answers: 13 DNA; 14 genetic engineering; 15 clone

16 **Compare** Both artificial selection and genetic engineering produce organisms that have traits that are different from the original organism. Explain how these two techniques differ.

Lesson Review

Vocabulary

In your own words, define the following terms.

1 biotechnology

_____

_____

_____

2 artificial selection

_____

_____

_____

3 clone

_____

_____

_____

Key Concepts

4 Identify Wheat has been bred by farmers for thousands of years to improve its ability to be ground into flour. This is an example of what kind of biotechnology?

A artificial selection

B genetic engineering

C cloning

D PCR

5 Identify Which of the following statements correctly describes why society must carefully consider the use of biotechnology?

A Biotechnology is a relatively new scientific field.

B Biotechnology can impact individuals and the environment.

C The methods of genetic engineering are not well understood.

D Artificial selection is an example of biotechnology.

Critical Thinking

Use this graph to answer the following questions.

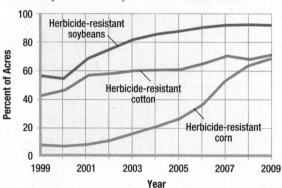

Genetically-modified Crops Grown in United States

Source: *USDA, 2009*

6 Analyze In 2003, what percentage of soybean crops in the United States were genetically engineered to be herbicide resistant?

_____

7 Analyze From 1999 to 2009, which genetically engineered crop had the greatest increase in acreage?

_____

_____

8 Synthesize Some salmon have been genetically engineered to grow more quickly. The salmon are raised in pens set in rivers or in the sea. Describe how these salmon might impact society and the environment.

_____

_____

_____

_____

_____

_____

_____

_____

_____

My Notes

Unit 8 **Summary**

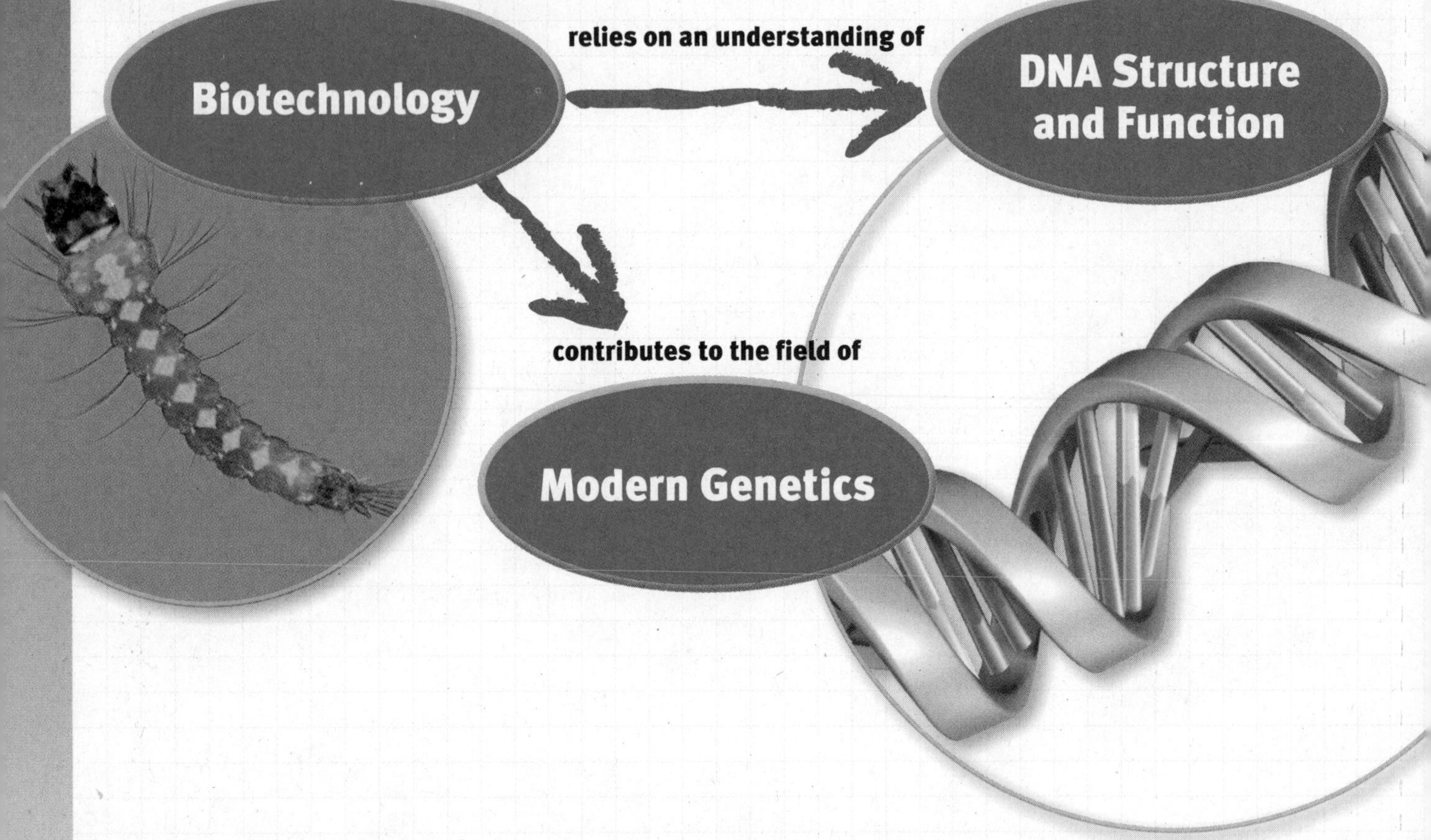

Biotechnology

relies on an understanding of

DNA Structure and Function

contributes to the field of

Modern Genetics

1 Interpret The Graphic Organizer above shows that biotechnology relies on an understanding of the structure and function of DNA. Explain.

_____

_____

_____

_____

_____

_____

_____

_____

2 Compare How are DNA replication and DNA cloning similar? How are they different?

_____

_____

_____

_____

3 Predict The variety of traits seen in house cats is due in part to artificial selection. Explain how mutations could contribute to the artificial selection of cats.

_____

_____

_____

_____

_____

![Indiana] ISTEP+ Review

Name _____

Multiple Choice

1 Dylan is listing the molecules that make up DNA. Which of these substances is a NUCLEOTIDE BASE in DNA?

   A. adenine

   B. phosphate

   C. sugar

   D. uracil

2 Rachel is analyzing a DNA sample to identify base pairs. Her results show that 40% of the sample is adenine. Which other base must also make up 40% of the sample?

   A. Cytosine makes up 40% of the sample.

   B. Guanine makes up 40% of the sample.

   C. Thymine makes up 40% of the sample.

   D. Uracil makes up 40% of the sample.

3 What process is illustrated in the diagram below?

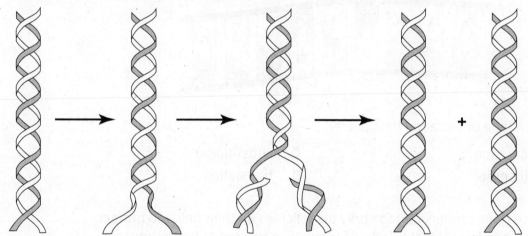

   A. the process of mutation

   B. the process of replication

   C. the process of transcription

   D. the process of translation

4 Sickle-cell anemia is a disease that is caused by a mutation in DNA.
Which of the following is a TRUE statement about sickle-cell anemia?

   A. It is never inherited from a parent.

   B. The mutation occurs during a person's lifetime.

   C. It is an infectious disease.

   D. It is a genetic disorder.

5 The diagram below shows an original sequence of DNA and then a
mutated sequence of DNA.

Original sequence

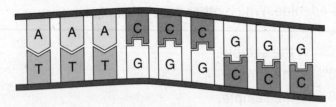

New sequence

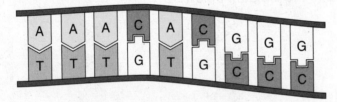

Which type of mutation took place?

   A. deletion

   B. insertion

   C. substitution

   D. translation

6 At one time, farmers had to spray insecticides on their fields to protect
their crops from insects. Today, farmers can buy seeds that produce
plants that are resistant to many insects. Which process contributed to
the development of these seeds?

   A. cloning

   B. natural selection

   C. selective breeding

   D. sexual reproduction

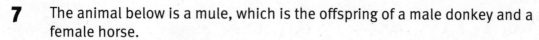

7 The animal below is a mule, which is the offspring of a male donkey and a female horse.

What kind of biotechnology is used to create mules?

A. cloning   **C.** genetic engineering

B. selective breeding   **D.** cell and tissue cultures

Constructed Response

8 The data in the table show some results of selective breeding.

Plant	Number of Flowers	Disease Resistance
A	131	Not disease-resistant
B	96	Disease-resistant
C	140	Disease-resistant
D	47	Not disease-resistant

Which two plants would you breed together if you wanted plants that produced the most flowers?

_____

Which two plants would you breed together if you wanted plants that were disease-resistant?

_____

Which plant is the BEST choice for including in a new garden? Explain your answer.

_____

_____

Extended Response

9   These shapes can be used to represent models of the hereditary material inside cells.

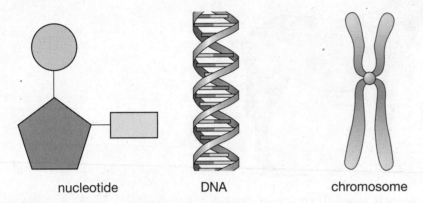

nucleotide   DNA   chromosome

What is the relationship between the shape on the left and the shape in the middle?

_____

_____

What is the relationship between the shape in the middle and the shape on the right?

_____

_____

What are parts within the cell called that relate to certain traits? Where would they be represented with respect to one of these models?

_____

Describe the process by which the shape in the middle copies the information to be sent to cells.

_____

_____

_____

The Design Process

Look at your surroundings and you will see examples of objects, systems, and techniques that were created through the design process. Objects such as buildings, clothing, cars, and cellular phones are all products that were designed to meet a need. Systems must be designed to make these products efficiently. Techniques, or methods for using a device, are also designed.

The design process involves a series of steps that lead to the development of a new object, system, or technique. The process diagram below shows the basic steps of the design process. As you can see, the design process, like scientific methods, often involves repeated steps that can be completed in different orders.

The design process always begins by clearly identifying the need or problem to be solved. As much information as possible is needed before imagining possible solutions. Planning involves choosing a solution and making a list of materials necessary to create the solution. Once the planning is complete, then the *prototype*, or working model, is made and tested. Finally, the prototype is presented for review, evaluated, and improved as needed.

Indiana Standards

As citizens of the constructed world, students will participate in the design process. Students will learn to use materials and tools safely and employ the basic principles of the engineering design process in order to find solutions to problems.

DP 8.1 Identify a need or problem to be solved.

DP 8.2 Brainstorm potential solutions.

DP 8.3 Document the design throughout the entire design process so that it can be replicated in a portfolio/notebook with drawings including labels.

DP 8.4 Select a solution to the need or problem.

DP 8.5 Select the most appropriate materials to develop a solution that will meet the need.

DP 8.6 Create the solution through a prototype.

DP 8.7 Test and evaluate how well the solution meets the goal.

DP 8.8 Evaluate and test the design using measurement.

DP 8.9 Present evidence using mathematical representations (graphs, data tables).

DP 8.10 Communicate the solution including evidence using mathematical representations (graphs, data tables), drawings or prototypes.

DP 8.11 Redesign to improve the solution based on how well the solution meets the need.

Process Diagram

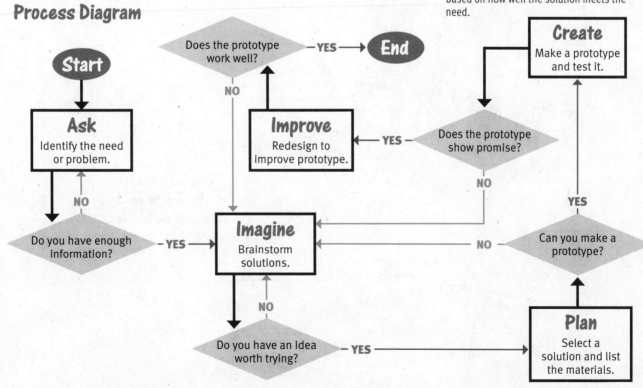

What are the steps of the design process?

While there is no single way to carry out the design process, it generally includes five basic steps. The process usually involves a team of people who are familiar with different aspects of the product design. For example, developers may explore and research a variety of possible solutions, while engineers build and test the prototype. Once the prototype is built, marketing and advertising experts might introduce the product to customers, who can provide feedback and evaluation. The product may be redesigned based on customer feedback or because of problems the developers and engineers may find during testing.

Identify a Problem

Often, new technology is designed to meet a specific need or to solve a problem. For example, an inventor might develop a wheelchair that can climb stairs to assist the disabled or a designer in the textile industry might develop flexible, lightweight, and breathable clothing to improve an athlete's performance. The goal for what the technology should achieve depends on the need or the problem to be solved.

Constraints, or restrictions, must also be considered. For example, a developer may be working with a limited amount of money or materials. There are social constraints as well. For example, an automobile must meet emissions standards so that air quality is protected.

1 Ask The chair below was designed to fold up. Why would a chair be designed to do this?

_____

_____

_____

_____

This chair was designed to fold up and use outdoors.

Brainstorm Solutions

Developers must conduct research to fully understand the goal and the constraints involved in designing a product. Research might involve reading about previous related solutions that succeeded or failed, or testing and experimenting with specific aspects of an existing or proposed design. Someone developing a new bottle for soft drinks, for example, might first test how consumers react to different bottle shapes. A geneticist would research the traits of a plant before trying to modify it genetically.

Once the problem and goal are well defined, the project developer explores possible solutions. He or she may invite others to *brainstorm* solutions, a process in which people suggest as many creative ideas as they can.

2 Imagine Cool Chairs, Inc. needs suggestions for a classroom desk chair that is portable and can store materials when in use. Brainstorm with a classmate and write down some potential solutions.

_____

_____

_____

_____

Select a Solution

The developers consider the advantages and disadvantages of each solution. Solutions may involve tradeoffs, where one advantage is given up in order to gain a different advantage. For example, one design might look more appealing but be a little harder to use than another design.

Engineers design and try out different versions of a technology or a solution to determine whether it solves the problem and meets the goals and constraints. An engineer designing a bridge, for example, must make sure the bridge can support a minimum weight so that it can be used safely. Once the engineer chooses a solution, he or she makes a list of the materials necessary to create a prototype.

3 Plan What might the materials list for the chair shown below include?

_____

_____

_____

_____

This chair changes shape and is fun to sit in.

This chair was designed for a barbershop. It moves up and down and turns around.

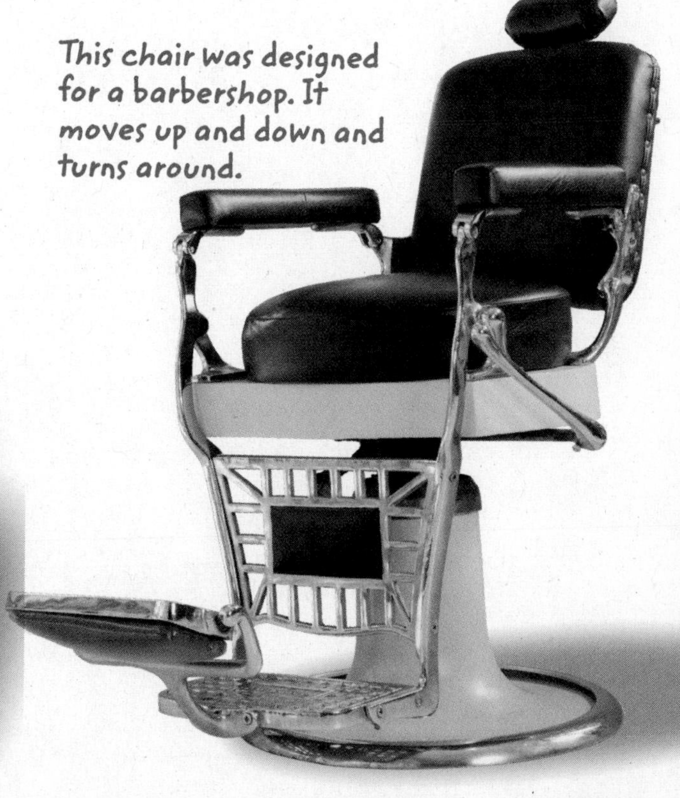

Create a Prototype

Once engineers decide on a particular solution and develop the plans, they build a prototype. The prototype should meet the goals and constraints identified earlier in the process. The procedures and the design stages for the prototype should be clearly documented so that the prototype can be replicated by someone not involved in the initial design process.

Developers often need to share their successes, failures, and reasoning with others. They may submit details of the design process to technical journals, so that others can build on their work. They may also work with marketing and advertising experts to explain and promote the product to customers or to inform the public through news releases and advertisements.

4 Create Draw a prototype of the classroom desk chair that you plan to submit to Cool Chairs, Inc. Be sure to provide labels if necessary.

Redesign to Improve

During the testing process, engineers may encounter unexpected problems with their design. For instance, a toy designer may discover that a small part on a new toy can break off, creating a choking hazard for young children. Developers troubleshoot, or find the sources of problems, and fix them. Often, troubleshooting involves redesigning parts of the technology.

5 Improve How might you redesign the chair below to make it more student-friendly?

☐ **Color** _____

_____

☐ **Materials** _____

_____

☐ _____

_____

☐ _____

_____

This chair has a unique design.

Documenting the Design Process

Some of the objects you use every day can be redesigned to be more efficient or be improved in some way. Perhaps a new system or technique can be designed to solve a particular problem. When you redesign an existing object or design a new one, follow the steps below to document your design process.

Identify a Problem

What is the goal that the solution must achieve?

_____

_____

_____

_____

What are the constraints?

_____

_____

_____

_____

Brainstorm Solutions

In a group, or on your own, write down on a separate sheet of paper as many creative ideas for a solution as you can. Consider every idea, even those that seem strange or unrealistic.

Select a Solution

Write down the solution you think will best address the need and meet the goal you identified earlier.

_____

_____

_____

Make a list of materials you will need to develop your prototype.

_____

_____

_____

_____

Create a Prototype

In the space below, describe the prototype. Your description may be a drawing or a flowchart. Provide labels or steps where necessary.

How will you test your prototype?

_____

_____

What data will you collect in order to evaluate the design of the prototype?

_____

_____

How will you organize your data and document your procedures so that the prototype can be replicated?

_____

_____

_____

Use the plan you have outlined above to create the prototype, test the prototype, organize the data, and communicate the results.

Redesign to Improve

How well did the solution meet the goal?

_____

_____

_____

What changes could be made to improve the design?

_____

_____

_____

Look It Up!

Reference Tables

Mineral Properties

Here are five steps to take in mineral identification:

1 Determine the color of the mineral. Is it light-colored, dark-colored, or a specific color?

2 Determine the luster of the mineral. Is it metallic or non-metallic?

3 Determine the color of any powder left by its streak.

4 Determine the hardness of your mineral. Is it soft, hard, or very hard? Using a glass plate, see if the mineral scratches it.

5 Determine whether your sample has cleavage or any special properties.

TERMS TO KNOW	DEFINITION
adamantine	a non-metallic luster like that of a diamond
cleavage	how a mineral breaks when subject to stress on a particular plane
luster	the state or quality of shining by reflecting light
streak	the color of a mineral when it is powdered
submetallic	between metallic and nonmetallic in luster
vitreous	glass-like type of luster

Silicate Minerals					
Mineral	**Color**	**Luster**	**Streak**	**Hardness**	**Cleavage and Special Properties**
Beryl	deep green, pink, white, bluish green, or yellow	vitreous	white	7.5–8	1 cleavage direction; some varieties fluoresce in ultraviolet light
Chlorite	green	vitreous to pearly	pale green	2–2.5	1 cleavage direction
Garnet	green, red, brown, black	vitreous	white	6.5–7.5	no cleavage
Hornblende	dark green, brown, or black	vitreous	none	5–6	2 cleavage directions
Muscovite	colorless, silvery white, or brown	vitreous or pearly	white	2–2.5	1 cleavage direction
Olivine	olive green, yellow	vitreous	white or none	6.5–7	no cleavage
Orthoclase	colorless, white, pink, or other colors	vitreous	white or none	6	2 cleavage directions
Plagioclase	colorless, white, yellow, pink, green	vitreous	white	6	2 cleavage directions
Quartz	colorless or white; any color when not pure	vitreous or waxy	white or none	7	no cleavage

Nonsilicate Minerals					
Mineral	**Color**	**Luster**	**Streak**	**Hardness**	**Cleavage and Special Properties**
Native Elements					
Copper	copper-red	metallic	copper-red	2.5–3	no cleavage
Diamond	pale yellow or colorless	adamantine	none	10	4 cleavage directions
Graphite	black to gray	submetallic	black	1–2	1 cleavage direction
Carbonates					
Aragonite	colorless, white, or pale yellow	vitreous	white	3.5–4	2 cleavage directions; reacts with hydrochloric acid
Calcite	colorless or white to tan	vitreous	white	3	3 cleavage directions; reacts with weak acid; double refraction
Halides					
Fluorite	light green, yellow, purple, bluish green, or other colors	vitreous	none	4	4 cleavage directions; some varieties fluoresce
Halite	white	vitreous	white	2.0–2.5	3 cleavage directions
Oxides					
Hematite	reddish brown to black	metallic to earthy	dark red to red-brown	5.6–6.5	no cleavage; magnetic when heated
Magnetite	iron-black	metallic	black	5.5–6.5	no cleavage; magnetic
Sulfates					
Anhydrite	colorless, bluish, or violet	vitreous to pearly	white	3–3.5	3 cleavage directions
Gypsum	white, pink, gray, or colorless	vitreous, pearly, or silky	white	2.0	3 cleavage directions
Sulfides					
Galena	lead-gray	metallic	lead-gray to black	2.5–2.8	3 cleavage directions
Pyrite	brassy yellow	metallic	greenish, brownish, or black	6–6.5	no cleavage

Reference Tables

Classification of Living Things

Domains and Kingdoms

All organisms belong to one of three domains: Domain Archaea, Domain Bacteria, or Domain Eukarya. Some of the groups within these domains are shown below. (Remember that genus names are italicized.)

Domain Archaea

The organisms in this domain are single-celled prokaryotes, many of which live in extreme environments.

Archaea		
Group	**Example**	**Characteristics**
Methanogens	*Methanococcus*	produce methane gas; can't live in oxygen
Thermophiles	*Sulpholobus*	require sulphur; can't live in oxygen
Halophiles	*Halococcus*	live in very salty environments; most can live in oxygen

Domain Bacteria

Organisms in this domain are single-celled prokaryotes and are found in almost every environment on Earth.

Bacteria		
Group	**Example**	**Characteristics**
Bacilli	*Escherichia*	rod shaped; some fix nitrogen; some cause disease
Cocci	*Streptococcus*	spherical shaped; cause diseases; can form spores
Spirilla	*Treponema*	spiral shaped; cause diseases, such as syphilis

Domain Eukarya

Organisms in this domain are single-celled or multicellular eukaryotes.

Kingdom Protista Many protists resemble fungi, plants, or animals, but are smaller and simpler in structure. Most are single-celled.

Protists		
Group	**Example**	**Characteristics**
Sarcodines	*Amoeba*	radiolarians; single-celled consumers
Ciliates	*Paramecium*	single-celled consumers
Flagellates	*Trypanosoma*	single-celled parasites
Sporozoans	*Plasmodium*	single-celled parasites
Euglenas	*Euglena*	single celled; photosynthesize
Diatoms	*Pinnularia*	most are single celled; photosynthesize
Dinoflagellates	*Gymnodinium*	single celled; some photosynthesize
Algae	*Volvox*	single celled or multicellular; photosynthesize
Slime molds	*Physarum*	single celled or multicellular; consumers or decomposers
Water molds	powdery mildew	single celled or multicellular; parasites or decomposers

Kingdom Fungi Most fungi are multicellular. Their cells have thick cell walls. Fungi absorb food from their environment.

Fungi		
Group	**Examples**	**Characteristics**
Threadlike fungi	bread mold	spherical; decomposers
Sac fungi	yeast; morels	saclike; parasites and decomposers
Club fungi	mushrooms; rusts; smuts	club shaped; parasites and decomposers
Lichens	British soldier	symbiotic with algae

Kingdom Plantae Plants are multicellular and have cell walls made of cellulose. Plants make their own food through photosynthesis. Plants are classified into divisions instead of phyla.

Plants		
Group	**Examples**	**Characteristics**
Bryophytes	mosses; liverworts	no vascular tissue; reproduce by spores
Club mosses	*Lycopodium;* ground pine	grow in wooded areas; reproduce by spores
Horsetails	rushes	grow in wetland areas; reproduce by spores
Ferns	spleenworts; sensitive fern	large leaves called fronds; reproduce by spores
Conifers	pines; spruces; firs	needlelike leaves; reproduce by seeds made in cones
Cycads	*Zamia*	slow-growing; reproduce by seeds made in large cones
Gnetophytes	*Welwitschia*	only three living families; reproduce by seeds
Ginkgoes	*Ginkgo*	only one living species; reproduce by seeds
Angiosperms	all flowering plants	reproduce by seeds made in flowers; fruit

Kingdom Animalia Animals are multicellular. Their cells do not have cell walls. Most animals have specialized tissues and complex organ systems. Animals get food by eating other organisms.

Animals		
Group	**Examples**	**Characteristics**
Sponges	glass sponges	no symmetry or segmentation; aquatic
Cnidarians	jellyfish; coral	radial symmetry; aquatic
Flatworms	planaria; tapeworms; flukes	bilateral symmetry; organ systems
Roundworms	*Trichina;* hookworms	bilateral symmetry; organ systems
Annelids	earthworms; leeches	bilateral symmetry; organ systems
Mollusks	snails; octopuses	bilateral symmetry; organ systems
Echinoderms	sea stars; sand dollars	radial symmetry; organ systems
Arthropods	insects; spiders; lobsters	bilateral symmetry; organ systems
Chordates	fish; amphibians; reptiles; birds; mammals	bilateral symmetry; complex organ systems

Reference Tables

Aquatic Ecosystems and Land Biomes

Aquatic Ecosystems

An ecosystem located in a body of water is called an *aquatic ecosystem*. Aquatic ecosystems are organized into freshwater ecosystems, wetlands, estuaries, and marine ecosystems.

Freshwater Ecosystem

Freshwater ecosystems are located in bodies of fresh water, such as lakes, ponds, and rivers.

Wetland

Wetlands are saturated by water for at least part of the year. Water-loving plants dominate wetlands.

Estuary

An estuary is an area where fresh water from a river mixes with salt water from an ocean.

Marine Ecosystem

Marine ecosystems, such as this coral reef, are found in the salty waters of the oceans.

Land Biomes

A *biome* is a large region characterized by a specific type of climate and certain types of plant and animal communities.

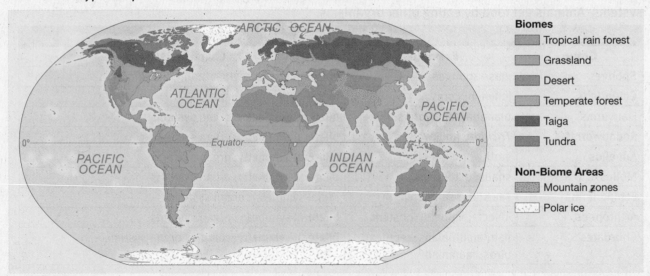

Biomes
- Tropical rain forest
- Grassland
- Desert
- Temperate forest
- Taiga
- Tundra

Non-Biome Areas
- Mountain zones
- Polar ice

Tropical

Tropical rain forest
- Warm temperatures and abundant rainfall occur all year.
- Vegetation includes lush thick forests.
- Animals that live within the thick cover of the upper-most branches of rain forest trees use loud vocalizations to defend their territory and attract mates.

Grassland

Tropical grassland
- Temperatures are warm throughout the year, with definite dry and rainy seasons.
- Vegetation includes tall grasses with scattered trees and shrubs.
- Hoofed animals, such as gazelles and other herbivores, are common in this biome.

Temperate grassland
- This biome is dry and warm during the summer; most precipitation falls as snow during the winter.
- Vegetation includes short or tall grasses, depending on the amount of precipitation.
- Many animals live underground to avoid the dry, windy conditions.

Desert

Desert
- This biome has a very dry climate.
- Plants, such as cacti, are either able to store water or have deep root systems.
- Many animals are nocternal; they limit their activies during the day to avoid exposure to the sun and heat.

Temperate

Temperate decidous forest
- Temperatures are hot in the summer and cold in the winter; precipitation is spaced evenly over the year.
- Deciduous trees lose their leaves in the winter.
- During the winter, animals must adjust to the cold temperatures and less cover to hide themselves from predators.

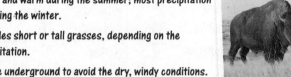

Temperate rain forest
- This biome has one long wet season and a relatively dry summer.
- Evergreen conifers, which keep their leaves (needles) year-round, dominate this biome.
- Some animal species remain active during the winter; others migrate to warmer climates or hibernate.

Taiga

Taiga
- This biome has long, cold winters and short, warm summers.
- Coniferous trees dominate this biome.
- Mammals have heavy fur coats to withstand the cold winters.

Tundra

Tundra
- Subzero temperatures are common during the long winter, and there is little precipitation.
- The ground is permanently frozen; only mosses and other low-lying plants survive.
- Animal diversity is low in this biome.

Reference Tables

Periodic Table of the Elements

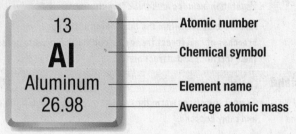

13	Atomic number
Al	Chemical symbol
Aluminum	Element name
26.98	Average atomic mass

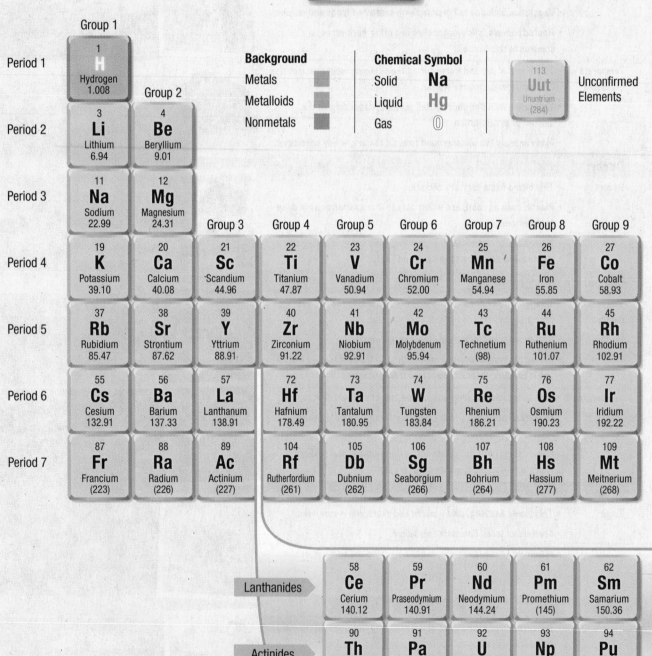

Background
Metals
Metalloids
Nonmetals

Chemical Symbol
Solid **Na**
Liquid **Hg**
Gas Ⓞ

113
Uut
Ununtrium
(284)

Unconfirmed Elements

Group 1

Period 1
1
H
Hydrogen
1.008

Group 2

Period 2
3
Li
Lithium
6.94

4
Be
Beryllium
9.01

Period 3
11
Na
Sodium
22.99

12
Mg
Magnesium
24.31

	Group 3	Group 4	Group 5	Group 6	Group 7	Group 8	Group 9

Period 4
19
K
Potassium
39.10

20
Ca
Calcium
40.08

21
Sc
Scandium
44.96

22
Ti
Titanium
47.87

23
V
Vanadium
50.94

24
Cr
Chromium
52.00

25
Mn
Manganese
54.94

26
Fe
Iron
55.85

27
Co
Cobalt
58.93

Period 5
37
Rb
Rubidium
85.47

38
Sr
Strontium
87.62

39
Y
Yttrium
88.91

40
Zr
Zirconium
91.22

41
Nb
Niobium
92.91

42
Mo
Molybdenum
95.94

43
Tc
Technetium
(98)

44
Ru
Ruthenium
101.07

45
Rh
Rhodium
102.91

Period 6
55
Cs
Cesium
132.91

56
Ba
Barium
137.33

57
La
Lanthanum
138.91

72
Hf
Hafnium
178.49

73
Ta
Tantalum
180.95

74
W
Tungsten
183.84

75
Re
Rhenium
186.21

76
Os
Osmium
190.23

77
Ir
Iridium
192.22

Period 7
87
Fr
Francium
(223)

88
Ra
Radium
(226)

89
Ac
Actinium
(227)

104
Rf
Rutherfordium
(261)

105
Db
Dubnium
(262)

106
Sg
Seaborgium
(266)

107
Bh
Bohrium
(264)

108
Hs
Hassium
(277)

109
Mt
Meitnerium
(268)

Lanthanides
58
Ce
Cerium
140.12

59
Pr
Praseodymium
140.91

60
Nd
Neodymium
144.24

61
Pm
Promethium
(145)

62
Sm
Samarium
150.36

Actinides
90
Th
Thorium
232.04

91
Pa
Protactinium
231.04

92
U
Uranium
238.03

93
Np
Neptunium
(237)

94
Pu
Plutonium
(244)

Group 18

2 **He** Helium 4.003

Group 13	Group 14	Group 15	Group 16	Group 17
5 **B** Boron 10.81	6 **C** Carbon 12.01	7 **N** Nitrogen 14.01	8 **O** Oxygen 16.00	9 **F** Fluorine 19.00	10 **Ne** Neon 20.18
13 **Al** Aluminum 26.98	14 **Si** Silicon 28.09	15 **P** Phosphorus 30.97	16 **S** Sulfur 32.07	17 **Cl** Chlorine 35.45	18 **Ar** Argon 39.95

Group 10	Group 11	Group 12

28 **Ni** Nickel 58.69	29 **Cu** Copper 63.55	30 **Zn** Zinc 65.41	31 **Ga** Gallium 69.72	32 **Ge** Germanium 72.64	33 **As** Arsenic 74.92	34 **Se** Selenium 78.96	35 **Br** Bromine 79.90	36 **Kr** Krypton 83.80
46 **Pd** Palladium 106.42	47 **Ag** Silver 107.87	48 **Cd** Cadmium 112.41	49 **In** Indium 114.82	50 **Sn** Tin 118.71	51 **Sb** Antimony 121.76	52 **Te** Tellurium 127.6	53 **I** Iodine 126.9	54 **Xe** Xenon 131.29
78 **Pt** Platinum 195.08	79 **Au** Gold 196.97	80 **Hg** Mercury 200.59	81 **Tl** Thallium 204.38	82 **Pb** Lead 207.2	83 **Bi** Bismuth 208.98	84 **Po** Polonium (209)	85 **At** Astatine (210)	86 **Rn** Radon (222)
110 **Ds** Darmstadtium (271)	111 **Rg** Roentgenium (272)	112 **Uub** Ununbium (285)	113 **Uut** Ununtrium (284)	114 **Uuq** Ununquadium (289)	115 **Uup** Ununpentium (288)	116 **Uuh** Ununhexium (292)		118 **Uuo** Ununoctium (294)

63 **Eu** Europium 151.96	64 **Gd** Gadolinium 157.25	65 **Tb** Terbium 158.93	66 **Dy** Dysprosium 162.5	67 **Ho** Holmium 164.93	68 **Er** Erbium 167.26	69 **Tm** Thulium 168.93	70 **Yb** Ytterbium 173.04	71 **Lu** Lutetium 174.97
95 **Am** Americium (243)	96 **Cm** Curium (247)	97 **Bk** Berkelium (247)	98 **Cf** Californium (251)	99 **Es** Einsteinium (252)	100 **Fm** Fermium (257)	101 **Md** Mendelevium (258)	102 **No** Nobelium (259)	103 **Lr** Lawrencium (262)

© Houghton Mifflin Harcourt Publishing Company

A How-To Manual for Active Reading

This book belongs to you, and you are invited to write in it. In fact, the book won't be complete until you do. Sometimes you'll answer a question or follow directions to mark up the text. Other times you'll write down your own thoughts. And when you're done reading and writing in the book, the book will be ready to help you review what you learned and prepare for tests.

Active Reading Annotations

Before you read, you'll often come upon an Active Reading prompt that asks you to underline certain words or number the steps in a process. Here's an example.

Active Reading

12 **Identify** In this paragraph, number the sequence of sentences that describe replication.

Marking the text this way is called **annotating,** and your marks are called **annotations.** Annotating the text can help you identify important concepts while you read.

There are other ways that you can annotate the text. You can draw an asterisk (*) by vocabulary terms, mark unfamiliar or confusing terms and information with a question mark (?), and mark main ideas with a <u>double underline</u>. And you can even invent your own marks to annotate the text!

Other Annotating Opportunities

Keep your pencil, pen, or highlighter nearby as you read, so you can make a note or highlight an important point at any time. Here are a few ideas to get you started.

- Notice the headings in red and blue. The blue headings are questions that point to the main idea of what you're reading. The red headings are answers to the questions in the blue ones. Together these headings outline the content of the lesson. After reading a lesson, you could write your own answers to the questions.

- Notice the bold-faced words that are highlighted in yellow. They are highlighted so that you can easily find them again on the page where they are defined. As you read or as you review, challenge yourself to write your own sentence using the bold-faced term.

- Make a note in the margin at any time. You might
  - Ask a "What if" question
  - Comment on what you read
  - Make a connection to something you read elsewhere
  - Make a logical conclusion from the text

Use your own language and abbreviations. Invent a code, such as using circles and boxes around words to remind you of their importance or relation to each other. Your annotations will help you remember your questions for class discussions, and when you go back to the lesson later, you may be able to fill in what you didn't understand the first time you read it. Like a scientist in the field or in a lab, you will be recording your questions and observations for analysis later.

Active Reading Questions

After you read, you'll often come upon Active Reading questions that ask you to think about what you've just read. You'll write your answer underneath the question. Here's an example.

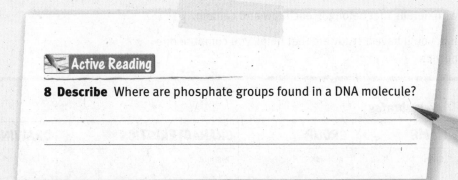

Active Reading

8 Describe Where are phosphate groups found in a DNA molecule?

_____

_____

This type of question helps you sum up what you've just read and pull out the most important ideas from the passage. In this case the question asks you to **describe** the structure of a DNA molecule that you have just read about. Other times you may be asked to do such things as **apply** a concept, **compare** two concepts, **summarize** a process, or **identify a cause-and-effect** relationship. You'll be strengthening those critical thinking skills that you'll use often in learning about science.

Reading and Study Skills

Using Graphic Organizers to Take Notes

Graphic organizers help you remember information as you read it for the first time and as you study it later. There are dozens of graphic organizers to choose from, so the first trick is to choose the one that's best suited to your purpose. Following are some graphic organizers to use for different purposes.

To remember lots of information	To relate a central idea to subordinate details	To describe a process	To make a comparison
• Arrange data in a Content Frame • Use Combination Notes to describe a concept in words and pictures	• Show relationships with a Mind Map or a Main Idea Web • Sum up relationships among many things with a Concept Map	• Use a Process Diagram to explain a procedure • Show a chain of events and results in a Cause-and-Effect Chart	• Compare two or more closely related things in a Venn Diagram

Content Frame

1 Make a four-column chart.

2 Fill the first column with categories (e.g., snail, ant, earthworm) and the first row with descriptive information (e.g., group, characteristic, appearance).

3 Fill the chart with details that belong in each row and column.

4 When you finish, you'll have a study aid that helps you compare one category to another.

Invertebrates

NAME	GROUP	CHARACTERISTICS	DRAWING
snail	mollusks	mangle	
ant	arthropods	six legs, exoskeleton	
earthworm	segmented worms	segmented body, circulatory and digestive systems	
heartworm	roundworms	digestive system	
sea star	echinoderms	spiny skin, tube feet	
jellyfish	cnidarians	stinging cells	

Combination Notes

1 Make a two-column chart.

2 Write descriptive words and definitions in the first column.

3 Draw a simple sketch that helps you remember the meaning of the term in the second column.

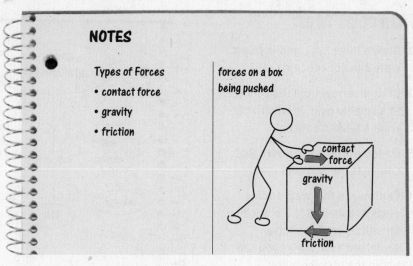

Mind Map

1 Draw an oval, and inside it write a topic to analyze.

2 Draw two or more arms extending from the oval. Each arm represents a main idea about the topic.

3 Draw lines from the arms on which to write details about each of the main ideas.

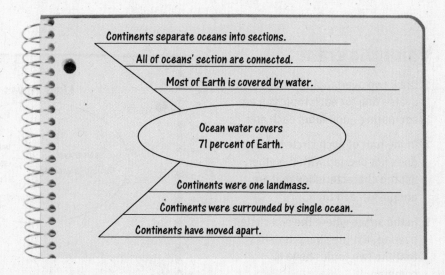

Main Idea Web

1 Make a box and write a concept you want to remember inside it.

2 Draw boxes around the central box, and label each one with a category of information about the concept (e.g., definition, formula, descriptive details)

3 Fill in the boxes with relevant details as you read.

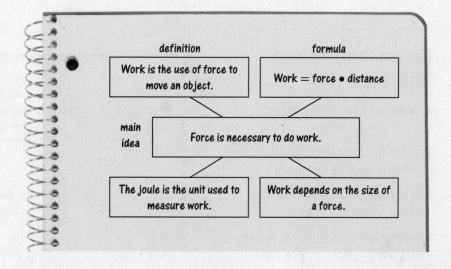

Reading and Study Skills

Concept Map

1 Draw a large oval, and inside it write a major concept.

2 Draw an arrow from the concept to a smaller oval, in which you write a related concept.

3 On the arrow, write a verb that connects the two concepts.

4 Continue in this way, adding ovals and arrows in a branching structure, until you have explained as much as you can about the main concept.

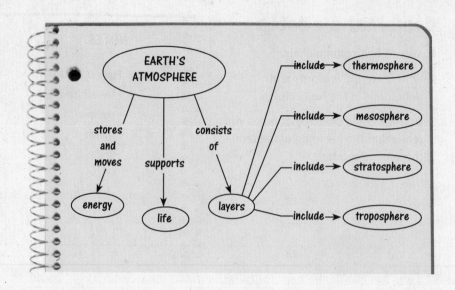

Venn Diagram

1 Draw two overlapping circles or ovals—one for each topic you are comparing—and label each one.

2 In the part of each circle that does not overlap with the other, list the characteristics that are unique to each topic.

3 In the space where the two circles overlap, list the characteristics that the two topics have in common.

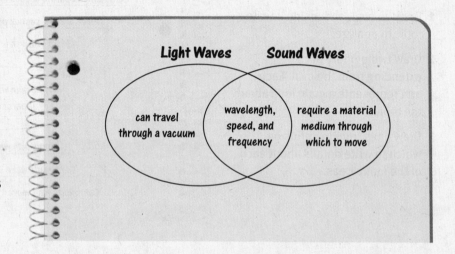

Cause-and-Effect Chart

1 Draw two boxes and connect them with an arrow.

2 In the first box, write the first event in a series (a cause).

3 In the second box, write a result of the cause (the effect).

4 Add more boxes when one event has many effects, or vice versa.

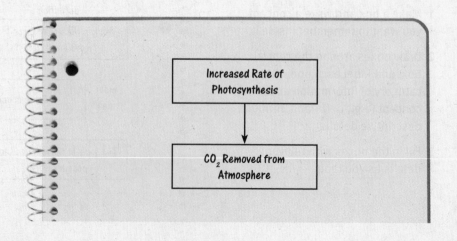

Process Diagram

A process can be a never-ending cycle. As you can see in this technology design process, engineers may backtrack and repeat steps, they may skip steps entirely, or they may repeat the entire process before a useable design is achieved.

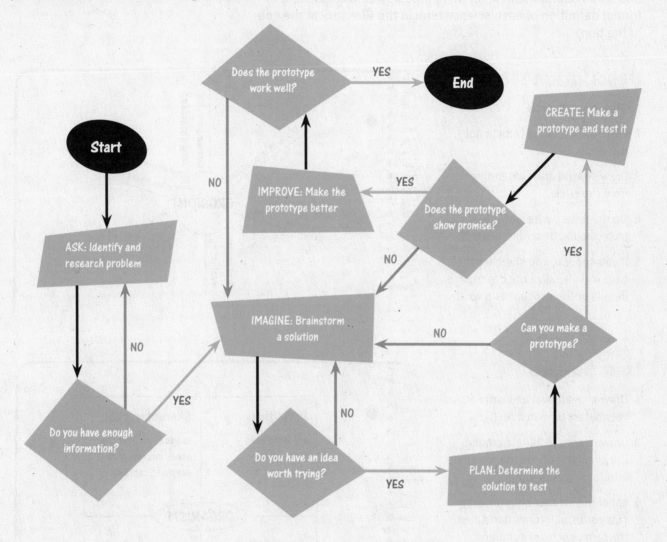

Reading and Study Skills

Using Vocabulary Strategies

Important science terms are highlighted where they are first defined in this book. One way to remember these terms is to take notes and make sketches when you come to them. Use the strategies on this page and the next for this purpose. You will also find a formal definition of each science term in the Glossary at the end of the book.

Description Wheel

1 Draw a small circle.

2 Write a vocabulary term inside the circle.

3 Draw several arms extending from the circle.

4 On the arms, write words and phrases that describe the term.

5 If you choose, add sketches that help you visualize the descriptive details or the concept as a whole.

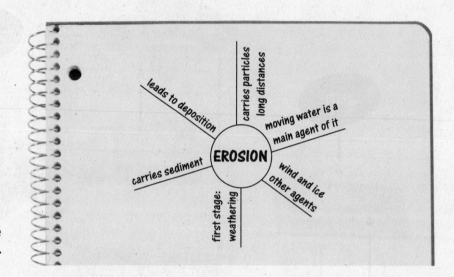

Four Square

1 Draw a small oval and write a vocabulary term inside it.

2 Draw a large rectangle around the oval, and divide the rectangle into four smaller squares.

3 Label the smaller squares with categories of information about the term, such as: definition, characteristics, examples, non-examples, appearance, and root words.

4 Fill the squares with descriptive words and drawings that will help you remember the overall meaning of the term and its essential details.

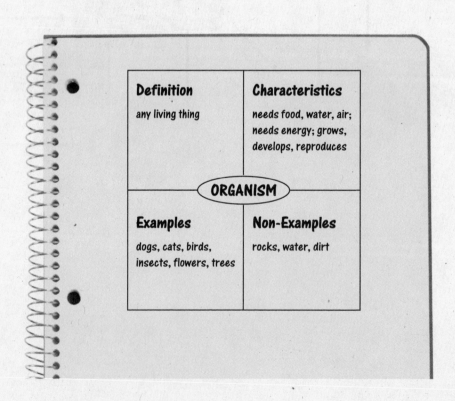

Frame Game

1 Draw a small rectangle, and write a vocabulary term inside it.

2 Draw a larger rectangle around the smaller one. Connect the corners of the larger rectangle to the corners of the smaller one, creating four spaces that frame the word.

3 In each of the four parts of the frame, draw or write details that help define the term. Consider including a definition, essential characteristics, an equation, examples, and a sentence using the term.

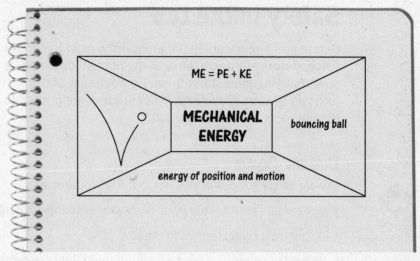

Magnet Word

1 Draw horseshoe magnet, and write a vocabulary term inside it.

2 Add lines that extend from the sides of the magnet.

3 Brainstorm words and phrases that come to mind when you think about the term.

4 On the lines, write the words and phrases that describe something essential about the term.

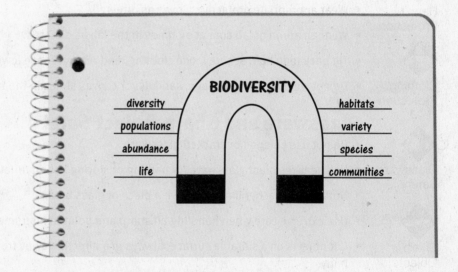

Word Triangle

1 Draw a triangle, and add lines to divide it into three parts.

2 Write a term and its definition in the bottom section of the triangle.

3 In the middle section, write a sentence in which the term is used correctly.

4 In the top section, draw a small picture to illustrate the term.

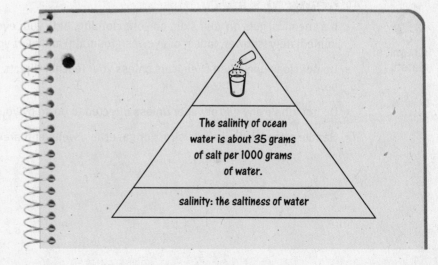

Science Skills

Safety in the Lab

Before you begin work in the laboratory, read these safety rules twice. Before starting a lab activity, read all directions and make sure that you understand them. Do not begin until your teacher has told you to start. If you or another student are injured in any way, tell your teacher immediately.

Dress Code

Eye Protection

- Wear safety goggles at all times in the lab as directed.

- If chemicals get into your eyes, flush your eyes immediately.

- Do not wear contact lenses in the lab.

- Do not look directly at the sun or any intense light source or laser.

Hand Protection

- Do not cut an object while holding the object in your hand.

- Wear appropriate protective gloves as directed.

Clothing Protection

- Wear an apron or lab coat at all times in the lab as directed.

- Tie back long hair, secure loose clothing, and remove loose jewelry.

- Do not wear open-toed shoes, sandals, or canvas shoes in the lab.

Glassware and Sharp Object Safety

Glassware Safety

- Do not use chipped or cracked glassware.

- Use heat-resistant glassware for heating or storing hot materials.

- Notify your teacher immediately if a piece of glass breaks.

Sharp Objects Safety

- Use extreme care when handling all sharp and pointed instruments.

- Cut objects on a suitable surface, always in a direction away from your body.

Chemical Safety

Chemical Safety

- If a chemical gets on your skin, on your clothing, or in your eyes, rinse it immediately (shower, faucet or eyewash fountain) and alert your teacher.

- Do not clean up spilled chemicals unless your teacher directs you to do so.

- Do not inhale any gas or vapor unless directed to do so by your teacher.

- Handle materials that emit vapors or gases in a well-ventilated area.

Electrical Safety

Electrical Safety

- Do not use equipment with frayed electrical cords or loose plugs.

- Do not use electrical equipment near water or when clothing or hands are wet.

- Hold the plug housing when you plug in or unplug equipment.

Heating and Fire Safety

Heating Safety

- Be aware of any source of flames, sparks, or heat (such as flames, heating coils, or hot plates) before working with any flammable substances.

- Know the location of lab fire extinguishers and fire-safety blankets.

- Know your school's fire-evacuation routes.

- If your clothing catches on fire, walk to the lab shower to put out the fire.

- Never leave a hot plate unattended while it is turned on or while it is cooling.

- Use tongs or appropriate insulated holders when handling heated objects.

- Allow all equipment to cool before storing it.

Wafting

Plant and Animal Safety

Plant Safety

Animal Safety

- Do not eat any part of a plant.

- Do not pick any wild plants unless your teacher instructs you to do so.

- Handle animals only as your teacher directs.

- Treat animals carefully and respectfully.

- Wash your hands thoroughly after handling any plant or animal.

Cleanup

Proper Waste Disposal

Hygienic Care

- Clean all work surfaces and protective equipment as directed by your teacher.

- Dispose of hazardous materials or sharp objects only as directed by your teacher.

- Keep your hands away from your face while you are working on any activity.

- Wash your hands thoroughly before you leave the lab or after any activity.

Science Skills

Designing an Experiment

An **experiment** is an organized procedure to study something under controlled conditions. Use the following steps of the scientific method when designing or conducting an experiment.

1 Identify a Research Problem

Every day you make **observations** by using your senses to gather information. Careful observations lead to good **questions,** and good questions can lead you to a purpose, or problem, for an experiment.

Imagine, for example, that you pass a pond every day on your way to school, and you notice green scum beginning to form on top of it. You wonder what it is and why it seems to be growing. You list your questions, and then you do a little preliminary research to find out what is already known.

You talk to others about your observations, learn that the scum is algae, and look for relvant information in books, journals, and online. You are especially interested in the data and conclusions from earlier experiments. Finally, you write the problem that you want to investigate. Your notes might look like these.

Area of Interest	Research Questions	Research Problem
Algae growth in lakes and ponds	• How do algae grow? • How do people measure algae? • What kind of fertilizer would affect the growth of algae? • Can fertilizer and algae be used safely in a lab? How?	How does fertilizer affect the presence of algae in a pond?

2 Make a Prediction

A **prediction** is a statement of what you expect will happen in your experiment. Before making a prediction, you need to decide in a general way what you will do in your procedure. You may state your prediction in an if-then format.

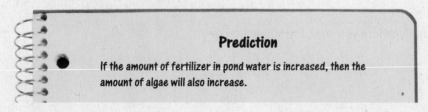

Prediction

If the amount of fertilizer in pond water is increased, then the amount of algae will also increase.

3 Form a Hypothesis

Many experiments are designed to test a hypothesis. A **hypothesis** is a tentative explanation for an expected result. You have predicted that additional fertilizer will cause additional algae growth in pond water; your hypothesis goes beyond your prediction to explain why fertilizer has that effect.

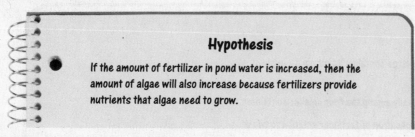

Hypothesis

If the amount of fertilizer in pond water is increased, then the amount of algae will also increase because fertilizers provide nutrients that algae need to grow.

4 Identify Variables to Test the Hypothesis

The next step is to design an experiment to test the hypothesis. The experiment may or may not support the hypothesis. Either way, the information that results from the experiment may be useful for future investigations.

Experimental Group and Control Group

An experiment to determine how two factors are related has a control group and an experimental group. The two groups are the same, except that the experimenter changes a single factor in the experimental group and does not change it in the control group.

Experimental Group: two containers of pond water with one drop of fertilizer solution added to each

Control Group: two containers of the same pond water sampled at the same time but with no fertilizer solution added

Variables and Constants

In a controlled experiment, a **variable** is any factor that can change. **Constants** are all of the variables that are kept the same in both the experimental group and the control group.

The **independent variable** is the factor that is manipulated or changed in order to test the effect of the change on another variable. The **dependent variable** is the factor that the experimenter measures to gather data about the effect.

Independent Variable	Dependent Variable	Constants
Amount of fertilizer in pond water	Amount of algae that grow	• Where and when the pond water is obtained • The type of container used • Light and temperature conditions where the water is stored

Science Skills

5 Write a Procedure

Write each step of your procedure. Start each step with a verb, or action word, and keep the steps short. Your procedure should be clear enough for someone else to use as instructions for repeating your experiment.

Procedure

1. Put on your gloves. Use the large container to obtain a sample of pond water.

2. Divide the water sample equally among the four smaller containers.

3. Use the eyedropper to add one drop of fertilizer solution to two of the containers.

4. Use the masking tape and the marker to label the containers with your initials, the date, and the identifiers "Jar 1 with Fertilizer," "Jar 2 with Fertilizer," "Jar 1 without Fertilizer," and "Jar 2 without Fertilizer."

5. Cover the containers with clear plastic wrap. Use the scissors to punch ten holes in each of the covers.

6. Place all four containers on a window ledge. Make sure that they all receive the same amount of light.

7. Observe the containers every day for one week.

8. Use the ruler to measure the diameter of the largest clump of algae in each container, and record your measurements daily.

6 Experiment and Collect Data

Once you have all of your materials and your procedure has been approved, you can begin to experiment and collect data. Record both quantitative data (measurements) and qualitative data (observations), as shown below.

Fertilizer and Algae Growth

Date and Time	Experimental Group		Control Group		Observations
	Jar 1 with Fertilizer (diameter of algae in mm)	Jar 2 with Fertilizer (diameter of algae in mm)	Jar 1 without Fertilizer (diameter of algae in mm)	Jar 2 without Fertilizer (diameter of algae in mm)	
5/3 4:00 P.M.	0	0	0	0	condensation in all containers
5/4 4:00 P.M.	0	3	0	0	tiny green blobs in jar 2 with fertilizer
5/5 4:15 P.M.	4	5	0	3	green blobs in jars 1 and 2 with fertilizer and jar 2 without fertilizer
5/6 4:00 P.M.	5	6	0	4	water light green in jar 2 with fertilizer
5/7 4:00 P.M.	8	10	0	6	water light green in jars 1 and 2 with fertilizer and jar 2 without fertilizer
5/8 3:30 P.M.	10	18	0	6	cover off jar 2 with fertilizer
5/9 3:30 P.M.	14	23	0	8	drew sketches of each container

Drawings of Samples Viewed Under Microscope on 5/9 at 100x

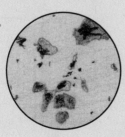

Jar 1 with Fertilizer

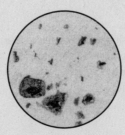

Jar 2 with Fertilizer

Jar 1 without Fertilizer

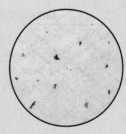

Jar 2 without Fertilizer

7 Analyze Data

After you have completed your experiments, made your observations, and collected your data, you must analyze all the information you have gathered. Tables, statistics, and graphs are often used in this step to organize and analyze the data.

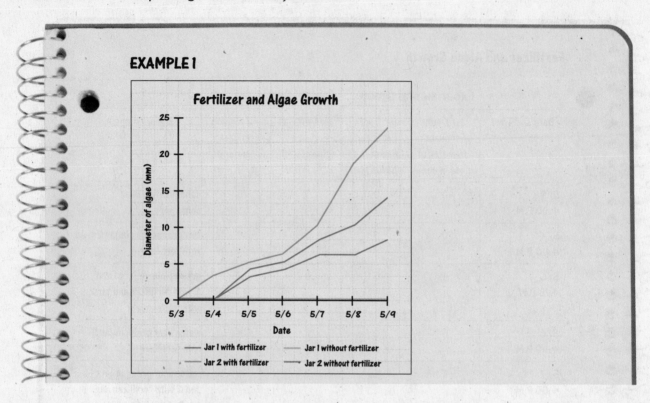

EXAMPLE 1

Fertilizer and Algae Growth

Diameter of algae (mm) vs. Date

- Jar 1 with fertilizer
- Jar 2 with fertilizer
- Jar 1 without fertilizer
- Jar 2 without fertilizer

8 Make Conclusions

To draw conclusions from your experiment, first write your results. Then compare your results with your hypothesis. Do your results support your hypothesis?

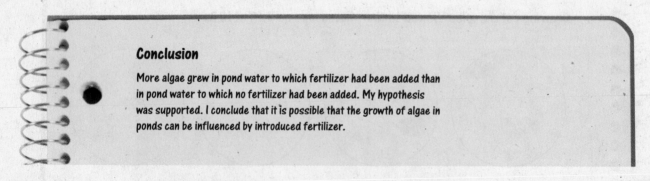

Conclusion

More algae grew in pond water to which fertilizer had been added than in pond water to which no fertilizer had been added. My hypothesis was supported. I conclude that it is possible that the growth of algae in ponds can be influenced by introduced fertilizer.

Using a Microscope

Scientists use microscopes to see very small objects that cannot easily be seen with the eye alone. A microscope magnifies the image of an object so that small details may be observed. A microscope that you may use can magnify an object 400 times—the object will appear 400 times larger than its actual size.

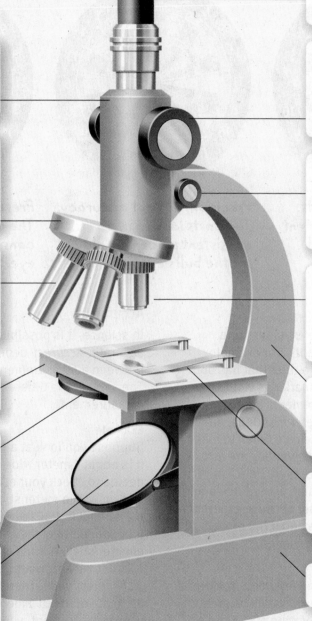

Body The body separates the lens in the eyepiece from the objective lenses below.

Nosepiece The nosepiece holds the objective lenses above the stage and rotates so that all lenses may be used.

High-Power Objective Lens This is the largest lens on the nosepiece. It magnifies an image approximately 40 times.

Stage The stage supports the object being viewed.

Diaphragm The diaphragm is used to adjust the amount of light passing through the slide and into an objective lens.

Mirror or Light Source Some microscopes use light that is reflected through the stage by a mirror. Other microscopes have their own light sources.

Eyepiece Objects are viewed through the eyepiece. The eyepiece contains a lens that commonly magnifies an image ten times.

Coarse Adjustment This knob is used to focus the image of an object when it is viewed through the low-power lens.

Fine Adjustment This knob is used to focus the image of an object when it is viewed through the high-power lens.

Low-Power Objective Lens This is the smallest lens on the nosepiece. It magnifies images about 10 times.

Arm The arm supports the body above the stage. Always carry a microscope by the arm and base.

Stage Clip The stage clip holds a slide in place on the stage.

Base The base supports the microscope.

Science Skills

Measuring Accurately

Precision and Accuracy

When you do a scientific investigation, it is important that your methods, observations, and data be both precise and accurate.

Low precision: The darts did not land in a consistent place on the dartboard.

Precision, but not accuracy: The darts landed in a consistent place, but did not hit the bull's eye.

Prescision and accuracy: The darts landed consistently on the bull's eye.

Precision

In science, *precision* is the exactness and consistency of measurements. For example, measurements made with a ruler that has both centimeter and milimeter markings would be more precise than measurements made with a ruler that has only centimeter markings. Another indicator of precision is the care taken to make sure that methods and observations are as exact and consistent as possible. Every time a particular experiment is done, the same procedure should be used. Precision is necessary because experiments are repeated several times and if the procedure changes, the results might change.

Example

Suppose you are measuring temperatures over a two-week period. Your precision will be greater if you measure each temperature at the same place, at the same time of day, and with the same thermometer than if you change any of these factors from one day to the next.

Accuracy

In science, it is possible to be precise but not accurate. *Accuracy* depends on the difference between a measurement and an actual value. The smaller the difference, the more accurate the measurement.

Example

Suppose you look at a stream and estimate that it is about 1 meter wide at a particular place. You decide to check your estimate by measuring the stream with a meter stick, and you determine that the stream is 1.32 meters wide. However, because it is difficult to measure the width of a stream with a meter stick, it turns out that your measurement was not very accurate. The stream is actually 1.14 meters wide. Therefore, even though your estimate of about 1 meter was less precise than your measurement, your estimate was actually more accurate.

Graduated Cylinders

How to Measure the Volume of a Liquid with a Graduated Cylinder

- Be sure that the graduated cylinder is on a flat surface so that your measurement will be accurate.

- When reading the scale on a graduated cylinder, be sure to have your eyes at the level of the surface of the liquid.

- The surface of the liquid will be curved in the graduated cylinder. Read the volume of the liquid at the bottom of the curve, or meniscus (muh-NIHS-kuhs).

- You can use a graduated cylinder to find the volume of a solid object by measuring the increase in a liquid's level after you add the object to the cylinder.

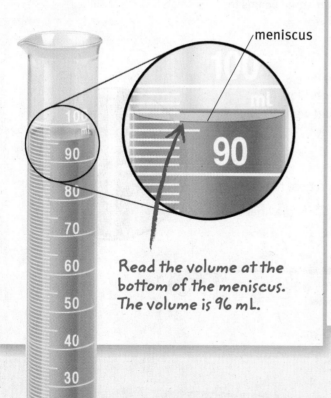

meniscus

Read the volume at the bottom of the meniscus. The volume is 96 mL.

Metric Rulers

How to Measure the Length of a Leaf with a Metric Ruler

1 Lay a ruler flat on top of the leaf so that the 1-centimeter mark lines up with one end. Make sure the ruler and the leaf do not move between the time you line them up and the time you take the measurement.

2 Look straight down on the ruler so that you can see exactly how the marks line up with the other end of the leaf.

3 Estimate the length by which the leaf extends beyond a marking. For example, the leaf below extends about halfway between the 4.2-centimeter and 4.3-centimeter marks, so the apparent measurement is about 4.25 centimeters.

4 Remember to subtract 1 centimeter from your apparent measurement, since you started at the 1-centimeter mark on the ruler and not at the end. The leaf is about 3.25 centimeters long (4.25 cm − 1 cm = 3.25 cm).

Triple Beam Balance

This balance has a pan and three beams with sliding masses, called riders. At one end of the beams is a pointer that indicates whether the mass on the pan is equal to the masses shown on the beams.

How to Measure the Mass of an Object

1 Make sure the balance is zeroed before measuring the mass of an object. The balance is zeroed if the pointer is at zero when nothing is on the pan and the riders are at their zero points. Use the adjustment knob at the base of the balance to zero it.

2 Place the object to be measured on the pan.

3 Move the riders one notch at a time away from the pan. Begin with the largest rider. If moving the largest rider one notch brings the pointer below zero, begin measuring the mass of the object with the next smaller rider.

4 Change the positions of the riders until they balance the mass on the pan and the pointer is at zero. Then add the readings from the three beams to determine the mass of the object.

300 g	position of largest rider
90 g	position of middle rider
+ 3 g	position of smallest rider
393 g	mass of beaker and water

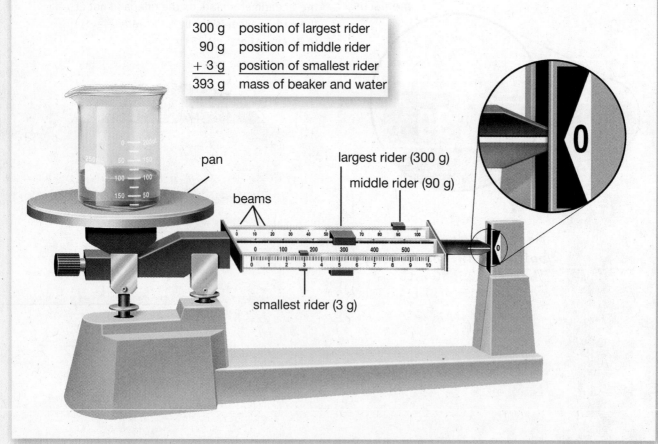

pan

beams

largest rider (300 g)

middle rider (90 g)

smallest rider (3 g)

Using the Metric System and SI Units

Scientists use International System (SI) units for measurements of distance, volume, mass, and temperature. The International System is based on powers of ten and the metric system of measurement.

Basic SI Units		
Quantity	**Name**	**Symbol**
length	meter	m
volume	liter	L
mass	gram	g
temperature	kelvin	K

SI Prefixes		
Prefix	**Symbol**	**Power of 10**
kilo-	k	1000
hecto-	h	100
deca-	da	10
deci-	d	0.1 or $\frac{1}{10}$
centi-	c	0.01 or $\frac{1}{100}$
milli-	m	0.001 or $\frac{1}{1000}$

Changing Metric Units

You can change from one unit to another in the metric system by multiplying or dividing by a power of 10.

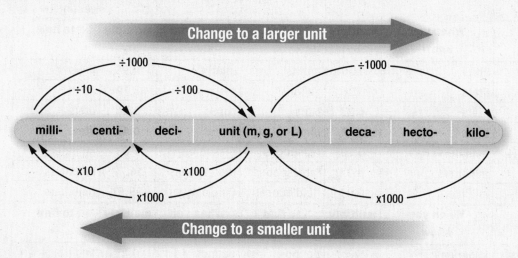

Example

Change 0.64 liters to milliliters.
1 Decide whether to multiply or divide.
2 Select the power of 10.

Change to a smaller unit by multiplying

mL ←——— x 1000 ——— L

0.64 x 1000 = 640.

ANSWER 0.64 L = 640 mL

Example

Change 23.6 grams to kilograms.
1 Decide whether to multiply or divide.
2 Select the power of 10.

Change to a larger unit by dividing

g ——— ÷ 1000 ——→ kg

26.3 ÷ 1000 = 0.0263

ANSWER 23.6 g = 0.0236 kg

Science Skills

Converting Between SI and U.S. Customary Units

Use the chart below when you need to convert between SI units and U.S. customary units.

SI Unit	From SI to U.S. Customary			From U.S. Customary to SI		
Length	**When you know**	**multiply by**	**to find**	**When you know**	**multiply by**	**to find**
kilometer (km) = 1000 m	kilometers	0.62	miles	miles	1.61	kilometers
meter (m) = 100 cm	meters	3.28	feet	feet	0.3048	meters
centimeter (cm) = 10 mm	centimeters	0.39	inches	inches	2.54	centimeters
millimeter (mm) = 0.1 cm	millimeters	0.04	inches	inches	25.4	millimeters
Area	**When you know**	**multiply by**	**to find**	**When you know**	**multiply by**	**to find**
square kilometer (km²)	square kilometers	0.39	square miles	square miles	2.59	square kilometers
square meter (m²)	square meters	1.2	square yards	square yards	0.84	square meters
square centimeter (cm²)	square centimeters	0.155	square inches	square inches	6.45	square centimeters
Volume	**When you know**	**multiply by**	**to find**	**When you know**	**multiply by**	**to find**
liter (L) = 1000 mL	liters	1.06	quarts	quarts	0.95	liters
	liters	0.26	gallons	gallons	3.79	liters
	liters	4.23	cups	cups	0.24	liters
	liters	2.12	pints	pints	0.47	liters
milliliter (mL) = 0.001 L	milliliters	0.20	teaspoons	teaspoons	4.93	milliliters
	milliliters	0.07	tablespoons	tablespoons	14.79	milliliters
	milliliters	0.03	fluid ounces	fluid ounces	29.57	milliliters
Mass	**When you know**	**multiply by**	**to find**	**When you know**	**multiply by**	**to find**
kilogram (kg) = 1000 g	kilograms	2.2	pounds	pounds	0.45	kilograms
gram (g) = 1000 mg	grams	0.035	ounces	ounces	28.35	grams

Temperature Conversions

Even though the kelvin is the SI base unit of temperature, the degree Celsius will be the unit you use most often in your science studies. The formulas below show the relationships between temperatures in degrees Fahrenheit (°F), degrees Celsius (°C), and kelvins (K).

$$°C = \frac{5}{9} \ (°F - 32) \qquad °F = \frac{9}{5} \ °C + 32 \qquad K = °C + 273$$

Examples of Temperature Conversions		
Condition	**Degrees Celsius**	**Degrees Fahrenheit**
Freezing point of water	32	0
Cool day	10	50
Mild day	20	68
Warm day	30	86
Normal body temperature	37	98.6
Very hot day	40	104
Boiling point of water	100	212

Math Refresher

Performing Calculations

Science requires an understanding of many math concepts. The following pages will help you review some important math skills.

Mean

The mean is the sum of all values in a data set divided by the total number of values in the data set. The mean is also called the *average*.

Example

Find the mean of the following set of numbers: 5, 4, 7, and 8.

Step 1   Find the sum.

           $5 + 4 + 7 + 8 = 24$

Step 1   Divide the sum by the number of numbers in your set. Because there are four numbers in this example, divide the sum by 4.

           $24 \div 4 = 6$

Answer The average, or mean, is 6.

Median

The median of a data set is the middle value when the values are written in numerical order. If a data set has an even number of values, the median is the mean of the two middle values.

Example

To find the median of a set of measurements, arrange the values in order from least to greatest. The median is the middle value.

      13 mm   14 mm   16 mm   21 mm   23 mm   25 mm

Answer The median is 16 mm.

Mode

The mode of a data set is the value that occurs most often.

Example

To find the mode of a set of measurements, arrange the values in order from least to greatest and determine the value that occurs most often.

        13 mm, 14 mm, 14 mm, 16 mm,
        21 mm, 23 mm, 25 mm

Answer The mode is 14 mm.

A data set can have more than one mode or no mode. For example, the following data set has modes of 2 mm and 4 mm:

      2 mm   2 mm   3 mm   4 mm   4 mm

The data set below has no mode, because no value occurs more often than any other.

      2 mm   3 mm   4 mm   5 mm

Math Refresher

Ratios

A **ratio** is a comparison between numbers, and it is usually written as a fraction.

Example

Find the ratio of thermometers to students if you have 36 thermometers and 48 students in your class.

Step 1 Write the ratio.

$$\frac{36 \text{ thermometers}}{48 \text{ students}}$$

Step 2 Simplify the fraction to its simplest form.

$$\frac{36}{48} = \frac{36 \div 12}{48 \div 12} \div 12 = \frac{3}{4}$$

The ratio of thermometers to students is 3 to 4 or 3:4.

Proportions

A **proportion** is an equation that states that two ratios are equal.

$$\frac{3}{1} = \frac{12}{4}$$

To solve a proportion, you can use cross-multiplication. If you know three of the quantities in a proportion, you can use cross-multiplication to find the fourth.

Example

Imagine that you are making a scale model of the solar system for your science project. The diameter of Jupiter is 11.2 times the diameter of the Earth. If you are using a plastic-foam ball that has a diameter of 2 cm to represent the Earth, what must the diameter of the ball representing Jupiter be?

$$\frac{11.2}{1} = \frac{x}{2 \text{ cm}}$$

Step 1 Cross-multiply.

$$\frac{11.2}{1} = \frac{x}{2}$$

$$11.2 \times 2 = x \times 1$$

Step 2 Multiply.

$$22.4 = x \times 1$$

$$x = 22.4 \text{ cm}$$

You will need to use a ball that has a diameter of 22.4 cm to represent Jupiter.

Rates

A **rate** is a ratio of two values expressed in different units. A unit rate is a rate with a denominator of 1 unit.

Example

A plant grew 6 centimeters in 2 days. The plant's rate of growth was $\frac{6 \text{ cm}}{2 \text{ days}}$. To describe the plant's growth in centimeters per day, write a unit rate.

Divide numerator and denominator by 2:

$$\frac{6 \text{ cm}}{2 \text{ days}} = \frac{6 \text{ cm} \div 2}{2 \text{ days} \div 2}$$

Simplify:

$$= \frac{3 \text{ cm}}{1 \text{ day}}$$

Answer The plant's rate of growth is 3 centimeters per day.

Percent

A **percent** is a ratio of a given number to 100. For example, 85% = 85/100. You can use percent to find part of a whole.

Example
What is 85% of 40?

Step 1 Rewrite the percent as a decimal by moving the decimal point two places to the left.

$$0.85$$

Step 2 Multiply the decimal by the number that you are calculating the percentage of.

$$0.85 \times 40 = 34$$

85% of 40 is 34.

Decimals

To **add** or **subtract decimals**, line up the digits vertically so that the decimal points line up. Then, add or subtract the columns from right to left. Carry or borrow numbers as necessary.

Example
Add the following numbers: 3.1415 and 2.96.

Step 1 Line up the digits vertically so that the decimal points line up.

$$\begin{array}{r} 3.1415 \\ + 2.96 \\ \hline \end{array}$$

Step 2 Add the columns from right to left, and carry when necessary.

$$\begin{array}{r} 3.1415 \\ + 2.96 \\ \hline 6.1015 \end{array}$$

The sum is 6.1015.

Fractions

A **fraction** is a ratio of two nonzero whole numbers.

Example
Your class has 24 plants. Your teacher instructs you to put 5 plants in a shady spot. What fraction of the plants in your class will you put in a shady spot?

Step 1 In the denominator, write the total number of parts in the whole.

$$\frac{?}{24}$$

Step 2 In the numerator, write the number of parts of the whole that are being considered.

$$\frac{6}{24}$$

So, $\frac{6}{24}$ of the plants will be in the shade.

Math Refresher

Simplifying Fractions

It is usually best to express a fraction in its simplest form. Expressing a fraction in its simplest form is called **simplifying a fraction**.

Example

Simplify the fraction $\frac{30}{45}$ to its simplest form.

Step 1 Find the largest whole number that will divide evenly into both the numerator and denominator. This number is called the greatest common factor (GCF).

Factors of the numerator 30:
1, 2, 3, 5, 6, 10, 15, 30

Factors of the denominator 45:
1, 3, 5, 9, 15, 45

Step 2 Divide both the numerator and the denominator by the GCF, which in this case is 15.

$$\frac{30}{45} = \frac{30 \div 15}{45 \div 15} = \frac{2}{3}$$

Thus, $\frac{30}{45}$ written in its simplest form is $\frac{2}{3}$.

Adding and Subtracting Fractions

To **add** or **subtract fractions** that have the same denominator, simply add or subtract the numerators.

Examples

$\frac{3}{5} + \frac{1}{5} = ?$ and $\frac{3}{4} - \frac{1}{4} = ?$

To **add** or **subtract fractions** that have **different denominators**, first find the least common denominator (LCD).

Step 1 Add or subtract the numerators.

$$\frac{3}{5} + \frac{1}{5} = \frac{4}{\ } \text{ and } \frac{3}{4} - \frac{1}{4} = \frac{2}{\ }$$

Step 2 Write the sum or difference over the denominator.

$$\frac{3}{5} + \frac{1}{5} = \frac{4}{5} \text{ and } \frac{3}{4} - \frac{1}{4} = \frac{2}{4}$$

Step 3 If necessary, write the fraction in its simplest form.

$\frac{4}{5}$ cannot be simplified, and $\frac{2}{4} = \frac{1}{2}$.

Examples

$\frac{1}{2} + \frac{1}{6} = ?$ and $\frac{3}{4} - \frac{2}{3} = ?$

Step 1 Write the equivalent fractions that have a common denominator.

$$\frac{3}{6} + \frac{1}{6} = ? \text{ and } \frac{9}{12} - \frac{8}{12} = ?$$

Step 2 Add or subtract the fractions.

$$\frac{3}{6} + \frac{1}{6} = \frac{4}{6} \text{ and } \frac{9}{12} - \frac{8}{12} = \frac{1}{12}$$

Step 3 If necessary, write the frction in its simplest form.

$\frac{4}{6} = \frac{2}{3}$, and $\frac{1}{12}$ cannot be simplifed.

Multiplying Fractions

To **multiply fractions**, multiply the numerators and the denominators together, and then simplify the fraction to its simplest form.

Example

$\frac{5}{9} \times \frac{7}{10} = ?$

Step 1 Multiply the numerators and denominators.

$$\frac{5}{9} \times \frac{7}{10} = \frac{5 \times 7}{9 \times 10} = \frac{35}{90}$$

Step 2 Simplify the fraction.

$$\frac{35}{90} = \frac{35 \div 5}{90 \div 5} = \frac{7}{18}$$

Dividing Fractions

To **divide fractions**, first rewrite the divisor (the number you divide by) upside down. This number is called the reciprocal of the divisor. Then multiply and simplify if necessary.

Example

$$\frac{5}{8} \div \frac{3}{2} = ?$$

Step 1 Rewrite the divisor as its reciprocal.

$$\frac{3}{2} \rightarrow \frac{2}{3}$$

Step 2 Multiply the fractions.

$$\frac{5}{8} \times \frac{2}{3} = \frac{5 \times 2}{8 \times 3} = \frac{10}{24}$$

Step 3 Simplify the fraction.

$$\frac{10}{24} = \frac{10 \div 2}{24 \div 2} = \frac{5}{12}$$

Using Significant Figures

The **significant figures** in a decimal are the digits that are warranted by the accuracy of a measuring device.

When you perform a calculation with measurements, the number of significant figures to include in the result depends in part on the number of significant figures in the measurements. When you multiply or divide measurements, your answer should have only as many significant figures as the measurement with the fewest significant figures.

Examples

Using a balance and a graduated cylinder filled with water, you determined that a marble has a mass of 8.0 grams and a volume of 3.5 cubic centimeters. To calculate the density of the marble, divide the mass by the volume.

Write the formula for density: $\text{Density} = \dfrac{mass}{volume}$

Substitute measurements: $= \dfrac{8.0\,g}{3.5\,cm^3}$

Use a calculator to divide: $\approx 2.285714286\ g/cm^3$

Answer Because the mass and the volume have two significant figures each, give the density to two significant figures. The marble has a density of 2.3 grams per cubic centimeter.

Using Scientific Notation

Scientific notation is a shorthand way to write very large or very small numbers. For example, 73,500,000,000,000,000,000,000 kg is the mass of the Moon. In scientific notation, it is 7.35×10^{22} kg. A value written as a number between 1 and 10, times a power of 10, is in scientific notation.

Examples

You can convert from standard form to scientific notation.

Standard Form	Scientific Notation
720,000	7.2×10^5
5 decimal places left	Exponent is 5.
0.000291	2.91×10^{-4}
4 decimal places right	Exponent is −4.

You can convert from scientific notation to standard form.

Scientific Notation	Standard Form
4.63×10^7	46,300,000
Exponent is 7.	7 decimal places right
1.08×10^{-6}	0.00000108
Exponent is −6.	6 decimal places left

Math Refresher

Making and Interpreting Graphs

Circle Graph

A circle graph, or pie chart, shows how each group of data relates to all of the data. Each part of the circle represents a category of the data. The entire circle represents all of the data. For example, a biologist studying a hardwood forest in Wisconsin found that there were five different types of trees. The data table at right summarizes the biologist's findings.

Wisconsin Hardwood Trees	
Type of tree	**Number found**
Oak	600
Maple	750
Beech	300
Birch	1,200
Hickory	150
Total	3,000

How to Make a Circle Graph

1 To make a circle graph of these data, first find the percentage of each type of tree. Divide the number of trees of each type by the total number of trees, and multiply by 100%.

$$\frac{600 \text{ oak}}{3,000 \text{ trees}} \times 100\% = 20\%$$

$$\frac{750 \text{ maple}}{3,000 \text{ trees}} \times 100\% = 25\%$$

$$\frac{300 \text{ beech}}{3,000 \text{ trees}} \times 100\% = 10\%$$

$$\frac{1,200 \text{ birch}}{3,000 \text{ trees}} \times 100\% = 40\%$$

$$\frac{150 \text{ hickory}}{3,000 \text{ trees}} \times 100\% = 5\%$$

2 Now, determine the size of the wedges that make up the graph. Multiply each percentage by 360°. Remember that a circle contains 360°.

$20\% \times 360° = 72°$ $25\% \times 360° = 90°$

$10\% \times 360° = 36°$ $40\% \times 360° = 144°$

$5\% \times 360° = 18°$

3 Check that the sum of the percentages is 100 and the sum of the degrees is 360.

$20\% + 25\% + 10\% + 40\% + 5\% = 100\%$

$72° + 90° + 36° + 144° + 18° = 360°$

4 Use a compass to draw a circle and mark the center of the circle.

5 Then, use a protractor to draw angles of 72°, 90°, 36°, 144°, and 18° in the circle.

6 Finally, label each part of the graph, and choose an appropriate title.

A Community of Wisconsin Hardwood Trees

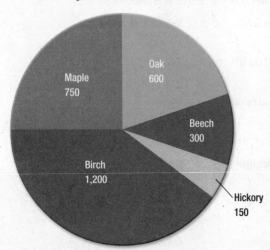

Line Graphs

Line graphs are most often used to demonstrate continuous change. For example, Mr. Smith's students analyzed the population records for their hometown, Appleton, between 1910 and 2010. Examine the data at right.

Because the year and the population change, they are the variables. The population is determined by, or dependent on, the year. Therefore, the population is called the **dependent variable,** and the year is called the **independent variable**. Each year and its population make a **data pair**. To prepare a line graph, you must first organize data pairs into a table like the one at right.

Population of Appleton, 1910–2010	
Year	**Population**
1910	1,800
1930	2,500
1950	3,200
1970	3,900
1990	4,600
2010	5,300

How to Make a Line Graph

1 Place the independent variable along the horizontal (*x*) axis. Place the dependent variable along the vertical (*y*) axis.

2 Label the *x*-axis "Year" and the *y*-axis "Population." Look at your greatest and least values for the population. For the *y*-axis, determine a scale that will provide enough space to show these values. You must use the same scale for the entire length of the axis. Next, find an appropriate scale for the *x*-axis.

3 Choose reasonable starting points for each axis.

4 Plot the data pairs as accurately as possible.

5 Choose a title that accurately represents the data.

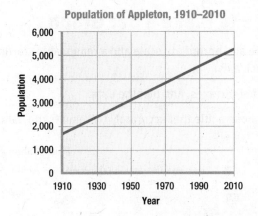

Population of Appleton, 1910–2010

How to Determine Slope

Slope is the ratio of the change in the *y*-value to the change in the x-value, or "rise over run."

1 Choose two points on the line graph. For example, the population of Appleton in 2010 was 5,300 people. Therefore, you can define point A as (2010, 5,300). In 1910, the population was 1,800 people. You can define point B as (1910, 1,800).

2 Find the change in the *y*-value.
(*y* at point A) − (*y* at point B) =
5,300 people − 1,800 people =
3,500 people

3 Find the change in the x-value.
(*x* at point A) − (*x* at point B) =
2010 − 1910 = 100 years

4 Calculate the slope of the graph by dividing the change in *y* by the change in *x*.

$$slope = \frac{change\ in\ y}{change\ in\ x}$$

$$slope = \frac{3,500\ people}{100\ years}$$

$$slope = 35\ people\ per\ year$$

In this example, the population in Appleton increased by a fixed amount each year. The graph of these data is a straight line. Therefore, the relationship is **linear**. When the graph of a set of data is not a straight line, the relationship is **nonlinear**.

Math Refresher

Bar Graphs

Bar graphs can be used to demonstrate change that is not continuous. These graphs can be used to indicate trends when the data cover a long period of time. A meteorologist gathered the precipitation data shown here for Summerville for April 1–15 and used a bar graph to represent the data.

	Precipitation in Summerville, April 1–15		
Date	Precipitation (cm)	Date	Precipitation (cm)
April 1	0.5	April 9	0.25
April 2	1.25	April 10	0.0
April 3	0.0	April 11	1.0
April 4	0.0	April 12	0.0
April 5	0.0	April 13	0.25
April 6	0.0	April 14	0.0
April 7	0.0	April 15	6.50
April 8	1.75		

How to Make a Bar Graph

1 Use an appropriate scale and a reasonable starting point for each axis.

2 Label the axes, and plot the data.

3 Choose a title that accurately represents the data.

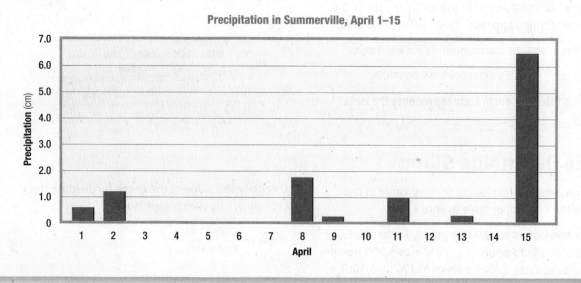

Precipitation in Summerville, April 1–15

Glossary

Pronunciation Key								
Sound	**Symbol**	**Example**	**Respelling**	**Sound**	**Symbol**	**Example**	**Respelling**
ă	a	pat	PAT	ŏ	ah	bottle	BAHT'l
ā	ay	pay	PAY	ō	oh	toe	TOH
âr	air	care	KAIR	ô	aw	caught	KAWT
ä	ah	father	FAH•ther	ôr	ohr	roar	ROHR
är	ar	argue	AR•gyoo	oi	oy	noisy	NOYZ•ee
ch	ch	chase	CHAYS	o͝o	u	book	BUK
ĕ	e	pet	PET	o͞o	oo	boot	BOOT
ĕ (at end of a syllable)	eh	settee lessee	seh•TEE leh•SEE	ou	ow	pound	POWND
ĕr	ehr	merry	MEHR•ee	s	s	center	SEN•ter
ē	ee	beach	BEECH	sh	sh	cache	CASH
g	g	gas	GAS	ŭ	uh	flood	FLUHD
ĭ	i	pit	PIT	ûr	er	bird	BERD
ĭ (at end of a syllable)	ih	guitar	gih•TAR	z	z	xylophone	ZY•luh•fohn
ī	y eye (only for a complete syllable)	pie island	PY EYE•luhnd	z	z	bags	BAGZ
				zh	zh	decision	dih•SIZH•uhn
				ə	uh	around broken focus	uh•ROWND BROH•kuhn FOH•kuhs
îr	ir	hear	HIR	ər	er	winner	WIN•er
j	j	germ	JERM	th	th	thin they	THIN THAY
k	k	kick	KIK				
ng	ng	thing	THING	w	w	one	WUHN
ngk	ngk	bank	BANGK	wh	hw	whether	HWETH•er

Glossary

A

accuracy (AK•yur•uh•see) a description of how close a measurement is to the true value of the quantity measured (R26)
exactitud término que describe qué tanto se aproxima una medida al valor verdadero de la cantidad medida

acid precipitation (AS•id prih•sip•ih•TAY•shun) precipitation, such as rain, sleet, or snow, that contains a high concentration of acids, often because of the pollution of the atmosphere (367)
precipitación ácida precipitación tal como lluvia, aguanieve o nieve, que contiene una alta concentración de ácidos debido a la contaminación de la atmósfera

adaptation a characteristic that improves an individual's ability to survive and reproduce in a particular environment (405)
adaptación una característica que mejora la capacidad de un individuo para sobrevivir y reproducirse en un determinado ambiente

air mass a large body of air throughout which temperature and moisture content are similar (266)
masa de aire un gran volumen de aire, cuya temperatura y cuyo contenido de humedad son similares en toda su extensión

air pollution the contamination of the atmosphere by the introduction of pollutants from human and natural sources (365)
contaminación del aire la contaminación de la atmósfera debido a la introducción de contaminantes provenientes de fuentes humanas y naturales

air pressure the measure of the force with which air molecules push on a surface (181, 258)
presión del aire la medida de la fuerza con la que las moléculas del aire empujan contra una superficie

air quality (AIR KWAHL•ih•tee) a measure of the pollutants in the air that is used to express how clean or polluted the air is (368)
calidad de aire una medida de los contaminantes presentes en el aire que se usa para expresar el nivel de pureza o contaminación del aire

allele (uh•LEELZ) one of the alternative forms of a gene that governs a characteristic, such as hair color (482)
alelo una de las formas alternativas de un gene que rige un carácter, como por ejemplo, el color del cabello

Animalia a kingdom made up of complex, multicellular organisms that lack cell walls, can usually move around, and quickly respond to their environment (430)
Animalia un reino formado por organismos pluricelulares complejos que no tienen pared celular, normalmente son capaces de moverse y reaccionan rápidamente a su ambiente

Archaea a domain made up of prokaryotes most of which are known to live in extreme environments that are distinguished from other prokaryotes by differences in their genetics and in the makeup of their cell wall (428)
Archaea un dominio compuesto por procariotes la mayoría de los cuales viven en ambientes extremos que se distinguen de otros procariotes por su genética y por la composición de su pared celular

artificial selection the human practice of breeding animals or plants that have certain desired traits (402, 529)
selección artificial la práctica humana de criar animales o cultivar plantas que tienen ciertos caracteres deseados

asexual reproduction (ay•SEHK•shoo•uhl ree•pruh•DUHK•shuhn) reproduction that does not involve the union of sex cells and in which one parent produces offspring that are genetically identical to the parent (470)
reproducción asexual reproducción que no involucra la unión de células sexuales, en la que un solo progenitor produce descendencia que es genéticamente igual al progenitor

atmosphere a mixture of gases that surrounds a planet, moon, or other celestial body (170, 180)
atmósfera una mezcla de gases que rodea un planeta, una luna, u otras cuerpos celestes

atom the smallest unit of an element that maintains the properties of that element (104, 121)
átomo la unidad más pequeña de un elemento que conserva las propiedades de ese elemento

atomic number the number of protons in the nucleus of an atom; the atomic number is the same for all atoms of an element (124)
número atómico el número de protones en el núcleo de un átomo; el número atómico es el mismo para todos los átomos de un elemento

average atomic mass the weighted average of the masses of all naturally occurring isotopes of an element (134)
masa atómica promedio el promedio ponderado de las masas de todos los isótopos de un elemento que se encuentran en la naturaleza

B

Bacteria a domain made up of prokaryotes that usually have a cell wall and that usually reproduce by cell division (428)
Bacteria un dominio compuesto por procariotes que por lo general tienen pared celular y se reproducen por división celular

biosphere the part of Earth where life exists; includes all of the living organisms on Earth (171)
biosfera la parte de la Tierra donde existe la vida; comprende todos los seres vivos de la Tierra

biotechnology (by•oh•tek•NAHL•uh•jee) the use and application of living things and biological processes (528)

biotecnología el uso y la aplicación de seres vivos y procesos biológicos

blizzard (BLIZ•erd) a severe weather condition that includes low temperatures, strong winds, blowing snow, and low visibility (309)

tormenta de nieve una condición climática severa que incluye temperaturas bajas, vientos fuertes, ventisca de nieve y visibilidad redu cida

C

cell cycle the life cycle of a cell (450)

ciclo celular el ciclo de vida de una célula

chemical bond an interaction that holds atoms or ions together (142)

enlace químico la fuerza de atracción que mantiene unidos a los átomos o iones

chemical change a change that occurs when one or more substances change into entirely new substances with different properties (94)

cambio químico un cambio que ocurre cuando una o más sustancias se transforman en sustancias totalmente nuevas con propiedades diferentes

chemical equation a representation of a chemical reaction that uses symbols to show the relationship between the reactants and the products (143)

ecuación química una representación de una reacción química que usa símbolos para mostrar la relación entre los reactivos y los productos

chemical formula a combination of chemical symbols and numbers to represent a substance (143)

fórmula química una combinación de símbolos químicos y números que se usan para representar una sustancia

chemical property a property of matter that describes a substance's ability to participate in chemical reactions (78)

propiedad química una propiedad de la materia que describe la capacidad de una sustancia de participar en reacciones químicas

chemical symbol a one-, two-, or three-letter abbreviation of the name of an element (134)

símbolo químico una abreviatura de una, dos o tres letras que corresponde al nombre de un elemento

chromosome (KROH•muh•sohmz) in a eukaryotic cell, one of the structures in the nucleus that are made up of DNA and protein; in a prokaryotic cell, the main ring of DNA (449)

cromosoma en una célula eucariótica, una de las estructuras del núcleo que está hecha de ADN y proteína; en una célula procariótica, el anillo principal de ADN

climate the weather conditions in an area over a long period of time (292)

clima las condiciones del tiempo en un área durante un largo período de tiempo

clone (KLOHN) an organism, cell, or piece of genetic material that is genetically identical to one from which it was derived (531)

clon un organismo, célula o fragmento de material genético que es genéticamente idéntico al organismo, célula o material genético del cual proviene

codominance (koh•DAHM•uh•nuhns) a condition in which two alleles are expressed such that the phenotype of a heterozygous individual is a combination of the phenotypes of the two homozygous parents (487)

codominancia una condición en la que dos alelos están expresados de modo que el fenotipo de un individuo heterocigoto es una combinación de los fenotipos de los dos padres homocigotos

compound a substance made up of atoms or ions of two or more different elements joined by chemical bonds (105)

compuesto una sustancia formada por átomos de dos o más elementos diferentes unidos por enlaces químicos

condensation (kahn•den•SAY•shuhn) the change of state from a gas to a liquid (245)

condensación el cambio de estado de gas a líquido

conduction (kun•DUHK•shuhn) the movement of matter due to differences in density that are caused by temperature variations; can result in the transfer of energy as heat (198)

conducción calor la transferencia de energía en forma de calor a través del contacto directo

conservation (kahn•sur•VAY•shuhn) the wise use of and preservation of natural resources (376)

conservación el uso inteligente y la preservación de los recursos naturales

convection (kun•VECK•shuhn) the movement of matter due to differences in density that are caused by temperature variations; can result in the transfer of energy as heat (196)

convección el movimiento de la materia debido a diferencias en la densidad que se producen por variaciones en la temperatura; puede resultar en la transferencia de energía en forma de calor

convection current (kuhn•VEK•shuhn) any movement of matter that results from differences in density; may be vertical, circular, or cyclical (223)

corriente de convección cualquier movimiento de la materia que se produce como resultado de diferencias en la densidad; puede ser vertical, circular o cíclico

Coriolis effect (kawr•ee•OH•lis ih•FEKT) the curving of the path of a moving object from an otherwise straight path due to Earth's rotation (205, 219)

efecto de Coriolis la desviación de la trayectoria recta que experimentan los objetos en movimiento debido a la rotación de la Tierra

cryosphere (KRY•oh•sfir) one of Earth's spheres where water is in solid form, including snow cover, floating ice, glaciers, ice caps, ice sheets, and frozen ground permafrost (169)
criosfera una de las esferas de la Tierra donde el agua se encuentra en estado sólido en forma de capas de nieve, hielos flotantes, glaciares, campos de hielo, capas de hielo continentales y porciones de suelo permanentemente congeladas permafrost

cytokinesis the division of the cytoplasm of a cell; cytokinesis follows the division of the cell's nucleus by mitosis or meiosis (451)
citocinesis la división del citoplasma de una célula; la citocinesis ocurre después de que el núcleo de la célula se divide por mitosis o meiosis

data (DAY•tuh) information gathered by observation or experimentation that can be used in calculating or reasoning (29)
datos la información recopilada por medio de la observación o experimentación que puede usarse para hacer cálculos o razonar

deep current a streamlike movement of ocean water far below the surface (222)
corriente profunda un movimiento del agua del océano que es similar a una corriente y ocurre debajo de la superficie

deforestation (dee•fohr•ih•STAY•shuhn) the removal of trees and other vegetation from an area (343)
deforestación la remoción de árboles y demás vegetación de un área

dependent variable (dih•PEN•duhnt VAIR•ee•uh•buhl) in a scientific investigation, the factor that changes as a result of manipulation of one or more independent variables (29, 42)
variable dependiente en una investigación científica, el factor que cambia como resultado de la manipulación de una o más variables independientes

desertification (dih•zer•tuh•fih•KAY•shuhn) the process by which human activities or climatic changes make areas more desertlike (343)
desertificación el proceso por el cual las actividades humanas o los cambios climáticos hacen que un área se vuelva más parecida a un desierto

dew point at constant pressure and water vapor content, the temperature at which the rate of condensation equals the rate of evaporation (255)
punto de rocío a presión y contenido de vapor de agua constantes, la temperatura a la que la tasa de condensación es igual a la tasa de evaporación

dichotomous key (di•KOT•uh•muhs KEE) an aid that is used to identify organisms and that consists of the answers to a series of questions (432)
clave dicotómica una ayuda para identificar organismos, que consiste en las respuestas a una serie de preguntas

DNA deoxyribonucleic acid, the material that contains the information that determines inherited characteristics (449, 514)
AND ácido desoxirribonucleico, el material que contiene la información que determina las características que se heredan

domain in a taxonomic system, one of the three broad groups that all living things fall into (428)
dominio en un sistema taxonómico, uno de los tres amplios grupos al que pertenecen todos los seres vivos

dominant (DAHM•uh•nuhnt) describes the allele that is fully expressed when carried by only one of a pair of homologous chromosomes (483)
dominante describe al alelo que contribuye al fenotipo de un individuo cuando una o dos copias del alelo están presentes en el genotipo de ese individuo

Earth system all of the nonliving things, living things, and processes that make up the planet Earth, including the solid Earth, the hydrosphere, the atmosphere, and the biosphere (166)
sistema terrestre todos los seres vivos y no vivos y los procesos que componen el planeta Tierra, incluidas la Tierra sólida, la hidrosfera, la atmósfera y la biosfera

electron a subatomic particle that has a negative charge (123)
electrón una partícula subatómica que tiene carga negativa

electron cloud a region around the nucleus of an atom where electrons are likely to be found (123)
nube de electrones una región que rodea al núcleo de un átomo en la cual es probable encontrar a los electrones

element a substance that cannot be separated or broken down into simpler substances by chemical means; all atoms of an element have the same atomic number (105)
elemento una sustancia que no se puede separar o descomponer en sustancias más simples por medio de métodos químicos; todos los átomos de un elemento tienen el mismo número atómico

elevation the height of an object above sea level (296)
elevación la altura de un objeto sobre el nivel del mar

empirical evidence (em•PIR•ih•kuhl EV•ih•duhns) the observations, measurements, and other types of data that people gather and test to support and evaluate scientific explanations (7)
evidencia empírica las observaciones, mediciones y demás tipos de datos que se recopilan y examinan para apoyar y evaluar explicaciones científicas

energy resource a natural resource that humans use to generate energy (333)
recurso energético un recurso natural que utilizan los humanos para generar energía

Eukarya in a modern taxonomic system, a domain made up of all eukaryotes; this domain aligns with the traditional kingdoms Protista, Fungi, Plantae, and Animalia (429)

Eukarya en un sistema taxonómico moderno, un dominio compuesto por todos los eucariotes; este dominio coincide con los reinos tradicionales Protista, Fungi, Plantae y Animalia

eutrophication (yoo•TRAWF•ih•kay•shuhn) an increase in the amount of nutrients, such as nitrates, in a marine or aquatic ecosystem (350)

eutrofización un aumento en la cantidad de nutrientes, tales como nitratos, en un ecosistema marino o acuático

evaporation the change of state from a liquid to a gas (244)

evaporación el cambio de estado de líquido a gas

evolution the process in which inherited characteristics within a population change over generations such that new species sometimes arise (400)

evolución el proceso por medio del cual las características heredadas dentro de una población cambian con el transcurso de las generaciones de manera tal que a veces surgen nuevas especies

experiment (ik•SPEHR•uh•muhnt) an organized procedure to study something under controlled conditions (28)

experimento un procedimiento organizado que se lleva a cabo bajo condiciones controladas para estudiar algo

extinction the death of every member of a species (407)

extinción la muerte de todos los miembros de una especie

F

fertilization (fer•tl•i•ZAY•shuhn) the union of a male and female gamete to form a zygote (472)

fecundación la unión de un gameto masculino y femenino para formar un cigoto

fossil the trace or remains of an organism that lived long ago, most commonly preserved in sedimentary rock (415)

fósil los indicios o los restos de un organismo que vivió hace mucho tiempo, comúnmente preservados en las rocas sedimentarias

fossil fuel a nonrenewable energy resource formed from the remains of organisms that lived long ago; examples include oil, coal, and natural gas (331)

combustible fósil un recurso energético no renovable formado a partir de los restos de organismos que vivieron hace mucho tiempo; algunos ejemplos incluyen el petróleo, el carbón y el gas natural

fossil record the history of life in the geologic past as indicated by the traces or remains of living things (415)

registro fósil la historia de la vida en el pasado geológico según la indican los rastros o restos de seres vivos

front the boundary between air masses of different densities and usually different temperatures (266)

frente el límite entre masas de aire de diferentes densidades y, normalmente, diferentes temperaturas

Fungi a kingdom made up of nongreen, eukaryotic organisms that reproduce by using spores, and get food by breaking down substances in their surroundings and absorbing the nutrients (430)

Hongos reino compuesto por organismos eucarióticos sin clorofila que se reproducen por medio de esporas y que, para alimentarse, descomponen sustancias del ambiente y absorben sus nutrientes

G

gene one set of instructions for an inherited trait (482)

gene un conjunto de instrucciones para un carácter heredado

genetic engineering a technology in which the genome of a living cell is modified for medical or industrial use (530)

ingeniería genética una tecnología en la que el genoma de una célula viva se modifica con fines médicos o industriales

genotype (JEEN•uh•typ) the entire genetic makeup of an organism; also the combination of genes for one or more specific traits (483)

genotipo la constitución genética completa de un organismo; también, la combinación de genes para uno o más caracteres específicos

genus (JEE•nuhs) the level of classification that comes after family and that contains similar species (426)

género el nivel de clasificación que viene después de la familia y que contiene especies similares

geosphere the mostly solid, rocky part of Earth; extends from the center of the core to the surface of the crust (167)

geosfera la capa de la Tierra que es principalmente sólida y rocosa; se extiende desde el centro del núcleo hasta la superficie de la corteza terrestre

global wind (GLOH•buhl WIND) the movement of air over Earth's surface in patterns that are worldwide (206)

viento global el movimiento del aire sobre la superficie terrestre según patrones globales

greenhouse effect the warming of the surface and lower atmosphere of Earth that occurs when water vapor, carbon dioxide, and other gases absorb and reradiate thermal energy (185, 364)

efecto invernadero el calentamiento de la superficie y de la parte más baja de la atmósfera, el cual se produce cuando el vapor de agua, el dióxido de carbono y otros gases absorben y vuelven a irradiar la energía térmica

group a vertical column of elements in the periodic table; elements in a group share chemical properties (136)

grupo una columna vertical de elementos de la tabla periódica; los elementos de un grupo comparten propiedades químicas

heat the energy transferred between objects that are at different temperatures (192)
calor la transferencia de energía entre objetos que están a temperaturas diferentes

heredity (huh•RED•ih•tee) the passing of genetic material from parent to offspring (480)
herencia la transmisión de material genético de padres a hijos

heterogeneous (het•uhr•uh•JEE•nee•uhs) describes something that does not have a uniform structure or composition throughout (112)
heterogéneo término que describe algo que no tiene una estructura o composición totalmente uniforme

homogeneous (hoh•muh•JEE•nee•uhs) describes something that has a uniform structure or composition throughout (112)
homogéneo término que describe a algo que tiene una estructura o composición global uniforme

homologous chromosome (huh•MAHL•uh•guhs KROH•muh•sohmz) chromosomes that have the same sequence of genes and the same structure (458)
cromosoma homólogo cromosomas con la misma secuencia de genes y la misma estructura

humidity the amount of water vapor in the air (255)
humedad cantidad de vapor de agua que hay en el aire

hurricane (HER•ih•kayn) a severe storm that develops over tropical oceans and whose strong winds of more than 119 km/h spiral in toward the intensely lowpressure storm center (280)
huracán una tormenta severa que se desarrolla sobre océanos tropicales, con vientos fuertes que soplan a más de 119 km/h y que se mueven en espiral hacia el centro de presión extremadamente baja de la tormenta

hydrosphere the portion of Earth that is water (168)
hidrosfera la porción de la Tierra que es agua

hypothesis (hy•PAHTH•eh•sys) a testable idea or explanation that leads to scientific investigation (28)
hipótesis una idea o explicación que conlleva a la investigación científica y que se puede probar

incomplete dominance (in•kuhm•PLEET DAHM•uh•nuhns) a condition in which two alleles are expressed such that the phenotype of a heterozygous individual is an intermediate of the phenotypes of the two homozygous parents (486)
dominancia incompleta una condición en la que dos alelos se expresan de modo que el fenotipo de un individuo heterocigoto es intermedio entre los fenotipos de sus dos padres homocigotos

independent variable (in•dih•PEN•duhnt VAIR•ee•uh•buhl) in a scientific investigation, the factor that is deliberately manipulated (42)
variable independiente en una investigación científica, el factor que se manipula deliberadamente

interphase (IN•ter•fayz) the period of the cell cycle during which activities such as cell growth and protein synthesis occur without visible signs of cell division (450)
interfase el período del ciclo celular durante el cual las actividades como el crecimiento celular y la síntesis de proteínas existen sin signos visibles de división celular

jet stream a narrow band of strong winds that blow in the upper troposphere (208, 271)
corriente en chorro un cinturón delgado de vientos fuertes que soplan en la parte superior de la troposfera

L

lake-effect snow (LAYK•uh•fekt SNOH) snow that is produced when cold, dry air moves over warmer lake water, picks up moisture, and deposits it as snow in a localized area on the lake shore (309)
nieve de efecto lago nieve que se produce cuando una masa de aire frío y seco avanza sobre el agua cálida de un lago, se carga de humedad y la deposita en forma de nieve en una zona determinada de la costa del lago

land degradation (LAND deg•ruh•DAY•shuhn) the process by which human activity and natural processes damage land to the point that it can no longer support the local ecosystem (342)
degradación del suelo el proceso por el cual la actividad humana y los procesos naturales dañan el suelo de modo que el ecosistema local no puede subsistir

latitude (LAHT•ih•tood) the angular distance north or south from the equator; expressed in degrees (294)
latitud la distancia angular hacia el norte o hacia el sur del ecuador; se expresa en grados

law of conservation of mass the law that states that mass cannot be created or destroyed in ordinary chemical and physical changes (98)
ley de la conservación de la masa la ley que establece que la masa no se crea ni se destruye por cambios químicos o físicos comunes

lightning an electric discharge that takes place between two oppositely charged surfaces, such as between a cloud and the ground, between two clouds, or between two parts of the same cloud (279)
relámpago una descarga eléctrica que ocurre entre dos superficies que tienen carga opuesta, como por ejemplo, entre una nube y el suelo, entre dos nubes o entres dos partes de la misma nube

local wind (LOH•kuhl WIND) the movement of air over short distances; occurs in specific areas as a result of certain geographical features (210)

viento local el movimiento del aire a través de distancias cortas; se produce en áreas específicas como resultado de ciertas características geográficas

mass number the sum of the numbers of protons and neutrons in the nucleus of an atom (125)

número de masa la suma de los números de protones y neutrones que hay en el núcleo de un átomo

material resource a natural resource that humans use to make objects or to consume as food and drink (332)

recurso material un recurso natural que utilizan los seres humanos para fabricar objetos o para consumir como alimento o bebida

meiosis (my•OH•sis) a process in cell division during which the number of chromosomes decreases to half the original number by two divisions of the nucleus, which results in the production of sex cells (gametes or spores) (459)

meiosis un proceso de división celular durante el cual el número de cromosomas disminuye a la mitad del número original por medio de dos divisiones del núcleo, lo cual resulta en la producción de células sexuales (gametos o esporas)

mesosphere (MEZ•uh•sfir) 1. the strong, lower part of the mantle between the asthenosphere and the outer core, 2. the layer of the atmosphere between the stratosphere and the thermosphere and in which temperature decreases as altitude increases (182)

mesosfera 1. la parte fuerte e inferior del manto que se encuentra entre la astenosfera y el núcleo externo, 2. la capa de la atmósfera que se encuentra entre la estratosfera y la termosfera, en la cual la temperatura disminuye al aumentar la altitud

metal an element that is shiny and that conducts heat and electricity well (135)

metal un elemento que es brillante y conduce bien el calor y la electricidad

metalloid an element that has properties of both metals and nonmetals (135)

metaloide un elemento que tiene propiedades tanto de metal como de no metal

mitosis (my•TOH•sis) in eukaryotic cells, a process of cell division that forms two new nuclei, each of which has the same number of chromosomes (451)

mitosis en las células eucarióticas, un proceso de división celular que forma dos núcleos nuevos, cada uno de los cuales posee el mismo número de cromosomas

mixture a combination of two or more substances that are not chemically combined (105)

mezcla una combinación de dos o más sustancias que no están combinadas químicamente

model a pattern, plan, representation, or description designed to show the structure or workings of an object, system, or concept (48)

modelo un diseño, plan, representación o descripción cuyo objetivo es mostrar la estructura o funcionamiento de un objeto, sistema o concepto

molecule (MAHL•ih•kyool) a group of atoms that are held together by chemical bonds; a molecule is the smallest unit of a substance that can exist by itself and retain all of the substance's chemical properties (142)

molécula un grupo de átomos unidos por enlaces químicos; una molécula es la unidad más pequeña de una sustancia que puede existir por sí misma y conservar todas las propiedades químicas de esa sustancia

mutation a change in the structure or amount of the genetic material of an organism (519)

mutación un cambio en la estructura o cantidad del material genético de un organismo

natural resource any natural material that is used by humans, such as water, petroleum, minerals, forests, and animals (330)

recurso natural cualquier material natural que es utilizado por los seres humanos, como agua, petróleo, minerales, bosques y animales

natural selection the process by which individuals that are better adapted to their environment survive and reproduce more successfully than less well adapted individuals do (404)

selección natural el proceso por medio del cual los individuos que están mejor adaptados a su ambiente sobreviven y se reproducen con más éxito que los individuos menos adaptados

neutron a subatomic particle that has no charge and that is located in the nucleus of an atom (122)

neutrón una partícula subatómica que no tiene carga y que está ubicada en el núcleo de un átomo

nonmetal an element that conducts heat and electricity poorly (135)

no metal un elemento que es mal conductor del calor y la electricidad

nonpoint-source pollution pollution that comes from many sources rather than from a single specific site; an example is pollution that reaches a body of water from streets and storm sewers (350)

contaminación no puntual contaminación que proviene de muchas fuentes, en lugar de provenir de un solo sitio específico; un ejemplo es la contaminación que llega a una masa de agua a partir de las calles y los drenajes

nonmetal an element that conducts heat and electricity poorly (135)

no metal un elemento que es mal conductor del calor y la electricidad

nonrenewable resource a resource that forms at a rate that is much slower than the rate at which the resource is consumed (331)

recurso no renovable un recurso que se forma a una tasa que es mucho más lenta que la tasa a la que se consume

nucleotide in a nucleic-acid chain, a subunit that consists of a sugar, a phosphate, and a nitrogenous base (517)

nucleótido en una cadena de ácidos nucleicos, una subunidad formada por un azúcar, un fosfato y una base nitrogenada

nucleus in physical science, an atom's central region, which is made up of protons and neutrons (122)

núcleo en ciencias físicas, la región central de un átomo, la cual está constituida por protones y neutrones

observation the process of obtaining information by using the senses; the information obtained by using the senses (28)

observación el proceso de obtener información por medio de los sentidos; la información que se obtiene al usar los sentidos

ocean current a movement of ocean water that follows a regular pattern (218)

corriente oceánica un movimiento del agua del océano que sigue un patrón regular

ozone layer the layer of the atmosphere at an altitude of 15 to 40 km in which ozone absorbs ultraviolet solar radiation (184)

capa de ozono la capa de la atmósfera ubicada a una altitud de 15 a 40 km, en la cual el ozono absorbe la radiación solar

particulate (per•TIK•yuh•lit) a tiny particle of solid that is suspended in air or water (365)

material particulado una pequeña partícula de material sólido que se encuentra suspendida en el aire o el agua

pedigree a diagram that shows the occurrence of a genetic trait in several generations of a family (498)

pedigrí un diagrama que muestra la incidencia de un carácter genético en varias generaciones de una familia

period in chemistry, a horizontal row of elements in the periodic table (137)

período en química, una hilera horizontal de elementos en la tabla periódica

periodic table an arrangement of the elements in order of their atomic numbers such that elements with similar properties fall in the same column, or group (131)

tabla periódica un arreglo de los elementos ordenados en función de su número atómico, de modo que los elementos que tienen propiedades similares se encuentran en la misma columna, o grupo

phenotype (FEEN•uh•typ) an organism's appearance or other detectable characteristic (483)

fenotipo la apariencia de un organismo u otra característica perceptible

physical change a change of matter from one form to another without a change in chemical properties (92)

cambio físico un cambio de materia de una forma a otra sin que ocurra un cambio en sus propiedades químicas

physical property a characteristic of a substance that does not involve a chemical change, such as density, color, or hardness (74)

propiedad física una característica de una sustancia que no implica un cambio químico, tal como la densidad, el color o la dureza

Plantae a kingdom made up of complex, multicellular organisms that are usually green, have cell walls made of cellulose, cannot move around, and use the sun's energy to make sugar by photosynthesis (430)

Plantae un reino formado por organismos pluricelulares complejos que normalmente son verdes, tienen una pared celular de celulosa, no tienen capacidad de movimiento y utilizan la energía del Sol para producir azúcar mediante la fotosíntesis

point-source pollution pollution that comes from a specific site (350)

contaminación puntual contaminación que proviene de un lugar específico

potable suitable for drinking (353)

potable que puede beberse

precipitation (pri•sip•i•TAY•shuhn) any form of water that falls to Earth's surface from the clouds; includes rain, snow, sleet, and hail (245, 256)

precipitación cualquier forma de agua que cae de las nubes a la superficie de la Tierra; incluye a la lluvia, nieve, aguanieve y granizo

precision (pree•SIZH•uhn) the exactness of a measurement (R26)

precisión la exactitud de una medición

probability the likelihood that a possible future event will occur in any given instance of the event (496)

probabilidad la probabilidad de que ocurra un posible suceso futuro en cualquier caso dado del suceso

product a substance that forms in a chemical reaction (143)

producto una sustancia que se forma en una reacción química

protista a kingdom of mostly one-celled eukaryotic organisms that are different from plants, animals, and fungi (430)
Protista un reino compuesto principalmente por organismos eucarióticos unicelulares diferentes de las plantas, los animales y los hongos

proton a subatomic particle that has a positive charge and that is located in the nucleus of an atom; the number of protons in the nucleus is the atomic number, which determines the identity of an element (122)
protón una partícula subatómica que tiene una carga positiva y que está ubicada en el núcleo de un átomo; el número de protones que hay en el núcleo es el número atómico, y éste determina la identidad del elemento

pseudoscience a process of investigation that in one or more ways resembles science but deviates from the scientific methods (12)
pseudociencia un proceso de investigación que tiene semejanzas con la actividad científica, pero no cumple con los métodos científicos

Punnett square a graphic used to predict the results of a genetic cross (494)
cuadro de Punnett una gráfica que se usa para predecir los resultados de una cruza genética

pure substance a sample of matter, either a single element or a single compound, that has definite chemical and physical properties (106)
sustancia pura una muestra de materia, ya sea un solo elemento o un solo compuesto, que tiene propiedades químicas y físicas definidas

R

radiation (ray•dee•AY•shuhn) the transfer of energy as electromagnetic waves (194)
radiación la transferencia de energía en forma de ondas electromagnéticas

ratio a comparison of two numbers using division (496)
razón comparacion de dos números mediante la división

reactant a substance that participates in a chemical reaction (143)
reactivo una sustancia o molécula que participa en una reacción química

recessive (rih•SES•iv) in genetics, describes an allele that is expressed only when no dominant allele is present in an individual (483)
recesivo en genética, término que describe un alelo que se expresa sólo cuando no hay un alelo dominante presente en el individuo

relative humidity the ratio of the amount of water vapor in the air to the amount of water vapor needed to reach saturation at a given temperature (255)
humedad relativa la proporción de la cantidad de vapor de agua que hay en el aire respecto a la cantidad de vapor de agua que se necesita para alcanzar la saturación a una temperatura dada

renewable resource a natural resource that can be replaced at the same rate at which the resource is consumed (331)
recurso renovable un recurso natural que puede reemplazarse a la misma tasa a la que se consume

replication the duplication of a DNA molecule (518)
replicación la duplicación de una molécula de AND

reservoir (REZ•uhr•vwohr) an artificial body of water that usually forms behind a dam (355)
represa una masa artificial de agua que normalmente se forma detrás de una presa

ribosome a cell organelle composed of RNA and protein; the site of protein synthesis (521)
ribosoma un organelo celular compuesto de ARN y proteína; el sitio donde ocurre la síntesis de proteínas

RNA ribonucleic acid, a molecule that is present in all living cells and that plays a role in protein production (520)
ARN ácido ribonucleico, una molécula que está presente en todas las células vivas y que juega un papel en la producción de proteínas

S

science the knowledge obtained by observing natural events and conditions in order to discover facts and formulate laws or principles that can be verified or tested (6)
ciencia el conocimiento que se obtiene por medio de la observación natural de acontecimientos y condiciones con el fin de descubrir hechos y formular leyes o principios que puedan ser verificados o probados

sexual reproduction (SEHK•shoo•uhl ree•pruh•DUHK•shuhn) reproduction in which the sex cells from two parents unite to produce offspring that share traits from both parents (472)
reproducción sexual reproducción en la que se unen las células sexuales de los dos progenitores para producir descendencia que comparte caracteres de ambos progenitores

smog (SMAHG) air pollution that forms when ozone and vehicle exhaust react with sunlight (366)
esmog contaminación del aire que se produce cuando el ozono y sustancias químicas como los gases de los escapes de los vehículos reaccionan con la luz solar

species (SPEE•seez) a group of organisms that are closely related and can mate to produce fertile offspring (426)

especie un grupo de organismos que tienen un parentesco cercano y que pueden aparearse para producir descendencia fértil

stewardship (stoo•urd•SHIP) behavior that leads to the protection, conservation, and reclamation of natural resources (377)

gestión ambiental responsable comportamiento que hace posible la protección, la conservación y el rescate de los recursos naturales

storm surge a local rise in sea level near the shore that is caused by strong winds from a storm, such as those from a hurricane (281)

marea de tempestad un levantamiento local del nivel del mar cerca de la costa, el cual es resultado de los fuertes vientos de una tormenta, como por ejemplo, los vientos de un huracán

stratosphere the layer of the atmosphere that lies between the troposphere and the mesosphere and in which temperature increases as altitude increases; contains the ozone layer (182)

estratosfera la capa de la atmósfera que se encuentra entre la troposfera y la mesosfera y en la cual la temperatura aumenta al aumentar la altitud; contiene la capa de ozono

sublimation the process in which a solid changes directly into a gas (244)

sublimación el proceso por medio del cual un sólido se transforma directamente en un gas

surface current a horizontal movement of ocean water that is caused by wind and that occurs at or near the ocean's surface (218, 299)

corriente superficial un movimiento horizontal del agua del océano que es producido por el viento y que ocurre en la superficie del océano o cerca de ella

temperature (TEM•per•uh•chur) a measure of how hot or cold something is; specifically, a measure of the average kinetic energy of the particles in an object (190)

temperatura una medida de qué tan caliente o frío está algo; específicamente, una medida de la energía cinética promedio de las partículas de un objeto

thermal energy the total kinetic energy of a substance's atoms (190)

energía térmica la energía cinética de los átomos de una sustancia

thermal expansion an increase in the size of a substance in response to an increase in the temperature of the substance (191)

expansión térmica un aumento en el tamaño de una sustancia en respuesta a un aumento en la temperatura de la sustancia

thermal pollution a temperature increase in a body of water that is caused by human activity and that has a harmful effect on water quality and on the ability of that body of water to support life (350)

contaminación térmica un aumento en la temperatura de una masa de agua, producido por las actividades humanas y que tiene un efecto dañino en la calidad del agua y en la capacidad de esa masa de agua para permitir que se desarrolle la vida

thermosphere the uppermost layer of the atmosphere, in which temperature increases as altitude increases (182)

termosfera la capa más alta de la atmósfera, en la cual la temperatura aumenta a medida que la altitud aumenta

thunder the sound caused by the rapid expansion of air along an electrical strike (279)

trueno el sonido producido por la expansión rápida del aire a lo largo de una descarga eléctrica

thunderstorm a usually brief, heavy storm that consists of rain, strong winds, lightning, and thunder (278)

tormenta eléctrica una tormenta fuerte y normalmente breve que consiste en lluvia, vientos fuertes, relámpagos y truenos

topography (tuh•POG•ruh•fee) the size and shape of the land surface features of a region, including its relief (296)

topografía el tamaño y la forma de las características de una superficie de terreno, incluyendo su relieve

tornado a destructive, rotating column of air that has very high wind speeds and that may be visible as a funnelshaped cloud (282)

tornado una columna destructiva de aire en rotación cuyos vientos se mueven a velocidades muy altas y que puede verse como una nube con forma de embudo

transpiration the process by which plants release water vapor into the air through stomata; also the release of water vapor into the air by other organisms (244)

transpiración el proceso por medio del cual las plantas liberan vapor de agua al aire por medio de los estomas; también, la liberación de vapor de agua al aire por otros organismos

troposphere the lowest layer of the atmosphere, in which temperature drops at a constant rate as altitude increases; the part of the atmosphere where weather conditions exist (182)

troposfera la capa inferior de la atmósfera, en la que la temperatura disminuye a una tasa constante a medida que la altitud aumenta; la parte de la atmósfera donde se dan las condiciones del tiempo

upwelling the movement of deep, cold, and nutrient-rich water to the surface (224)

surgencia el movimiento de las aguas profundas, frías y ricas en nutrientes hacia la superficie

urbanization (er•buh•nih•ZAY•shuhn) the growth of urban areas caused by people moving into cities (339, 348)

urbanización el crecimiento de las áreas urbanas producido por el desplazamiento de personas hacia las ciudades

valence electron an electron that is found in the outermost shell of an atom and that determines the atom's chemical properties (147)

electrón de valencia un electrón que se encuentra en el orbtial más externo de un átomo y que determina las propiedades químicas del átomo

variation (vair•ee•AY•shuhn) the occurrence of hereditary or nonhereditary differences between different individuals of a population (404)

variabilidad la incidencia de diferencias hereditarias o no hereditarias entre distintos individuos de una población

visibility The distance at which a given standard object can be seen and identified with the unaided eye (259)

visibilidad la distancia a la que un objeto dado es perceptible e identificable para el ojo humano

water cycle the continuous movement of water between the atmosphere, the land, the oceans, and living things (242)

ciclo del agua el movimiento continuo del agua entre la atmósfera, la tierra, los océanos y los seres vivos

water pollution (WAW•ter puh•LOO•shuhn) waste matter or other material that is introduced into water and that is harmful to organisms that live in, drink, or are exposed to the water (350)

contaminación del agua material de desecho u otro material que se introduce en el agua y que daña a los organismos que viven en el agua, la beben o están expuestos a ella

weather the short-term state of the atmosphere, including temperature, humidity, precipitation, wind, and visibility (254, 292)

tiempo el estado de la atmósfera a corto plazo que incluye la temperatura, la humedad, la precipitación, el viento y la visibilidad

wind the movement of air caused by differences in air pressure (204, 258)

viento el movimiento de aire producido por diferencias en la presión barométrica

Index

Page numbers for definitions are printed in **boldface** type.
Page numbers for illustrations, photographs, maps, and
charts are printed in *italics*.

accuracy, 181, 215, R26
acid, 109
acid precipitation, 367, 350
acid rain, 350. *See also* **acid
    precipitation.**
acquired trait, 403, 408, 485
Active Reading, lesson opener pages,
    5, 17, 27, 41, 53, 73, 91, 119,
    129, 141, 165, 179, 189, 203,
    217, 241, 253, 263, 277, 291,
    307, 329, 337, 347, 363, 375,
    399, 413, 423, 447, 457, 469,
    479, 493, 513, 527
    instruction, R10–R11
adaptation
    as principle of natural selection,
        405–406, *405*
    survival and, 407
adenine (A), 517, 520
agricultural land, 339
agronomist, 361
AIDS, 58
air mass, 266–268
air pollution, *362,* 365
    health and, *369*
    ozone layer affected by, 371
    reducing, 384–385
air pressure, 181, **258**
air quality, 368
    affecting health, 369
    measure of, 368–369
Air Quality Index (AQI), 368
albinism, 518–519
allele, 482–484, 486–487, 495–498,
    521
    as represented in Punnett squares,
        494-497
almanac, 304
aluminum, *77, 108,* 134
Alvarez, Luis, 20
Alvarez, Walter, 20
Alvin, 176
amber fossil, 414
Ambulocetus natans, 418
amino acid, 417, 521
anaphase, *452, 453, 460–461*
ancestor species, 406
anemometer, 258
Animalia, kingdom, 430
antigen, on red blood cells, 487
annotations, R10–R11
Apollo 11, 57
AQI (Air Quality Index), 368
aqueduct, 355
Aquatic Ecosystems and Land Biomes,
    R6–R7

aquifer, 349, 356
Aral sea, 357
Archaea, (domain), 428, R4
Archaeopteryx, **23**
arctic fox, *485*
Aristotle, 120
artificial eutrophication, 350. *See also*
    eutrophication.
artificial selection, 402, **529**
asexual reproduction, 470–471,
    474–475
    advantages of, 474–475
    binary fission, 471, **471,** *471*
    budding, 471, **471,** *471*
    offspring, 470
    parent, 470
    spores, 471, **471,** *471*
    vegetative reproduction, 471
atmosphere, *166,* **170,** 173, 178–187,
    178, **180,** 244, 332, **364**
    composition of, *170, 180,* 330
    concentration of CFC in, *373*
    human impact on, 362–372
    importance of, 364
    importance on Indiana climate,
        309–314
    layers of, 182–183, *183*
    **as mixture of gas and small
        particles,** 180
    **pressure and temperature change
        in,** 181
    protecting life on earth, 184–185
    water in, 245
    water moving into, *250*
    weather, 254, 260
    wind in, 202–213
atmospheric scientist, 305
atom, 104, *105,* 106–107, 119, *120–
    121,* **121,** 122–124, *125,* 126,
    142, 143, *144–150*
atomic number, 124, 131–132, 134,
    137
    average atomic mass, 134, 132
    energy levels of, 147–149
    mass number, 125
    modeling, *120–123, 146–147, 150*
    parts of, *122–123*
atomic theory, 120–121
average atomic mass, 132, **134**

Bacteria (domain), 428, R4
bacteria, 428
    reproduction, *471*
    use in bioengineering, 531
bacterial population, growth of, *477*

balancing equation, 144
baking soda, 79, 99, 109
bar graph, 44
barometer, 258
base, 109
base pair, DNA, *517,* 520
binary fission, 471, **471,** *471*
biochemical, 109
biological pollution, 350, *351*
biology. *See* **life science.**
bioluminescence, *140*
biosphere, *166,* **171**
biotechnology, 528
    applications, 529–531
    artificial selection, 529
    cloning, 531
    genetic engineering, 530
    impact on environment and society,
        532–533
bird, *32–33*
    theory for, 23
bismuth, 130
"black blizzards," 341
blizzard, 309
blood type, 487
Bohr, Niels, 146
Bohr model, 146–150
branching diagram, 431
bromine, 130
budding, 471, *471*

calculations, performing, R31–R35
    decimals, R33
    fractions, R33–R35
    mean, median, mode, R31
    percentage, R33
    proportions, R32
    rates, R32
    ratios, R32
    scientific notation, R35
    significant figures, R35
camouflage, *398*
canal. *See* **aqueduct.**
carbohydrate, 109
carbon dioxide molecule, 143
carrier, 498. *See also* **trait.**
Carson, Rachel, 10
cast fossil, 415
cattle, *492*
cell cycle, 450
    cytokinesis, 447, **451**
    interphase, 450
    mitosis, 451
cell division, 448
    genetic material in, 449

Dorudon, *418*
Do the Math, 83, 144–145, 170, 244,
    311, 313, 378, 496, 497
double helix, 516
down syndrome, 463
drought, 341
ductility, 135
Dust Bowl, 341

E

Earth, 240, 328
    changes in climate, 370, 403
    solar energy, 294
    spheres, interaction of, 172–173
Earth science, 6
Earth system, 166
    atmosphere, **170**
    biosphere, **171**
    cryosphere, **169**
    geosphere, **167**
    hydrosphere, **168**
    interactions among Earth's spheres,
        172-173
economics and science, 59
egg cell, *456,* **472,** *472*
electrical conductivity, 76
electrical thermometer, 254
electromagnetic radiation, 194
electromagnetic wave, 194–195
electron cloud, 123, 126, *146*
electron, 122, 123, 136–137, 139,
    146–150
    energy levels, 147–149
    valence, 136–137, **147,** 148–150
element, 104, **105,** 106–108, 121,
    124–125, 130–138
    classification, 108, 135
    Periodic Table of the Elements, 131,
        132–135, 136–*138,* R8–R9
elevation, 296
    influence on temperature, 297
embryology, 417
empirical evidence, 7–8
energy
    chemical changes and, 97
    conservation of, 384
    temperature and, 190
    transfer, 192, 223
energy levels, 147–149
energy resource, 333
Engage Your Brain, lesson opener
    pages, 5, 17, 27, 41, 53, 73, 91,
        103, 119, 129, 141, 165, 179,
        189, 203, 217, 241, 253, 263,
        277, 291, 307, 329, 337, 347,
        363, 375, 399, 413, 423, 447,
        457, 469, 479, 493, 513, 527
engineering
    design process, *543,* 543–546
    environmental, 177, 361
    properties of materials, 86–89
    genetic, **530**–533
environment
    effect of supplying water on, 356
    influencing traits, 485

    populations adapting to, 404–407
    species change in response to, 406
environmental engineering technician,
    177, 361
Environmental Protection Agency
    (EPA), 55, 353, 368, 385
erosion, 342
Eukarya
    domain, **429,** R4–R5
    kingdoms within, 430
eukaryote, 429, 430
eutrophication, 350, *351*
evaporation, 243–**244,** *243, 248,* 264
evolution, 400
    by natural selection, 404-407
    Darwin's observations, 400-401
    evidence supporting, 414–419
    ideas influencing Darwin, 402-403
experiment, 19, **28,** 27–31, 34–35, 51,
    410, 524
    conducting, R22–R24
    designing, R20 –R24
experimental group, R21
extinction, 407–408, 533
    caused by environmental changes,
        407
    of dinosaurs, 20–21

F

family
    in periodic table, 132, 136
    level of classification, *431*
fertilization, 472, *472*
fiber analysis, 81
fieldwork, 19
finches, 33, 400–401
flammability, 78–79
flash flood, 308
flocculation, 353
flooding, 277, 284, 288
    in Indiana, 308
flood safety rules, 284
flu. *See* **influenza.**
fly, *70*
Focus on Engineering, Materials Matter,
    86–89
Forde, Evan B., 176, *176*
forensic science, 81, 510–511
fossil, *411, 412,* **415**
    amber, *414*
    cast, *414–415*
    change over time, 415
    formation of, 414–415
    sedimentary rocks and, 415
    transitional, **415,** *415*
fossil evidence, 21, 418, *418*
fossil fuel, 201, **331,** 333, 338, 365,
    367, 370, 384–385
fossil record, 415
Franklin, Rosalind, 515
freezing, *243*
fresh water, 348–349
    factors threatening quality of,
        350–351
    system, 354

front, 266–267
    cold, 267, *267*
    stationary, 267, *267*
    warm, 267, *267*
Fungi, kingdom, 430, 430

G

Galápagos Islands, *400–401*
Galileo, 34
gamete. *See* **sex cell**
gas.
    pollutants, 365
gaur, cloned, *533*
gel electrophoresis, 525
genes, 482, *482,* **517**
    traits determined by, 483–484
genetic diversity, 404, 499
genetic disorder, 484, 519
genetic engineering, 530–534
genetic variation as principle of natural
    selection, 404, *405*
genotype, 483
genus, 426, *428*
geology. *See* **Earth science.**
geosphere, *166,* **167**
geothermal energy, 385
glacier, 246–247
global wind, 206–208, *207,* 220, *221,*
    295
    doldrums, 206–207, *206*
    as factor affecting surface current,
        218, 220
    horse latitudes, 206, **207,** *207*
    patterns affecting local weather,
        270, *270*
    polar easterlies, 206, **206**
    trade winds, 206, **206**
    westerlies, 206, **206**
globe, as model, 48
glow worm, *140*
glowing mosquito, 532
gold, *69,* 74–75, 82, *83–84, 129*
Goldsworthy, Andy, 117
Grand Canyon, 403
    as barrier for species, 425
graph, 43–47, *46–47, 50, 187,* 524
    bar, 44, R38
    circle, 44, R36
    line, R37
    linear, 46
    making and interpreting, R36
    conducting, R22–R24
    designing, R20 –R24
    nonlinear, 47
    scatter plot, 43
    slope, R37
    trend, 46
graphic organizer, using, R12–15
graphite, 135
Great Lakes, 55, 312
greenhouse gas, 185, **364**
greenhouse effect, 185, *185,* **364**
ground-level ozone, 366
groundwater, 349, 354

law of conservation of mass, 98–100, 144–145
levels of classification, 427
Levene, Phoebus, 514
life science, 6
    scientific methods in, 33
lightning, *276*, **279**, *279*, 284–285
linear graph, 46
linear relationship, 46, **46**, *46*
Linnaeus, Carolus, 426–427, *426*
lipid, 109
lithium, *147*, *150*
litmus paper, 109
living things, classification of, 424
    chemical characteristics, 425
    physical characteristics, 425
living things, naming, 426
local winds, **210**–211, 295
    land breeze, 210
    mountain breeze, 211
    sea breeze, 210
    valley breeze, 210
Look It Up! Reference Section, R1–R38
low-pressure system, **268**–269, *268*
luster, *77*
Lyell, Charles, 403

magnetism, 77
malleability, 77, 135
Malthus, Thomas, 403
map, as model, 48–49
mass, 75, 80, 100
    average atomic, 132, **134**
    conservation of, **98**–100, 144–145
    of an electron, 123
    of a neutron, 122
    of a proton, 122
mass number, **125**
material resource, **332**, *332*
Math Refresher, R31–R38
matter, 113, 247
    chemical changes of, **94**–100, 107, 142–145, 150
    chemical properties of, **78**–79
    physical changes of, **92**–93, 98–100
    physical properties of, **74**–77
mantle, 167, *167*
measurement, 42, 253
    of air pressure, **258**
    of humidity, **255**
    of precipitation, **256**
    of temperature, 254
    of visibility, **259**
    of water quality, *352*
    of wind, **258**
measuring, R26–R27
    graduated cylinder, R27
    metric ruler, R27
    triple beam balance, R28
Mediterranean climate, 300
meiosis, 456, **459**, *460*, 464, 472
    comparison with mitosis, 462, *462*
    meiosis I, 460–461

meiosis II, 461
melting, **243**, *243*
melting point, 77
Mendel, Gregor, 480–481, 488, 494
Mendeleev, Dmitri, 131
mercury, 130
mesosphere, **182**
messenger RNA (mRNA), 520–521
metalloid, 108, **135**
metal, *77*, 108, **135**
metaphase, *452*, 453, *460*, *461*
meteor, 20–21
meteorology, 304
metric system, using, R29–R30
Mexico, Yucatan peninsula, 20, *21*
microbial load, *352*
microscope, 19. *See also* science tools.
    compound light, R25
    using, R25
Miescher, Friedrich, 514
minerals
    nonsilicate, R3
    properties table, R2–R3
    silicate, R2
mitosis, 451, *451*, 454, 464, **471**
    anaphase, *452*–453
    in asexual reproduction, 471
    metaphase, *452*–453
    comparison with meiosis, 462
    prophase, *452*–453
    telophase, *452*–453
mixture, 104–**105**, *110–111*, 114
    colloid, 112
    heterogeneous, **112**
    homogeneous, **112**
    separation of, 111, 114
    solution, 112
    suspension, 112
model, 32, **48**–49, 370, 453
    atom, 120–123, 146–147, 150
molecule, 49, 106, **142**, 181, 258
    DNA, 514–520
    RNA, 521
    water, 105, 107, *114*, 222, 226, 255
monsoon, 272
Montoya, Angel, *360*
moon, 57
Moseley, Henry, 131
mountain breeze, *211*
Mount Kilimanjaro, 297
Mount St. Helens, volcano, *8*
multiple births, 467
mutagen, **519**
mutation, **513**, **519**

National Weather Service, 308
natural areas, **339**
natural resource, 328–334, 330, **330**
    categorize, 331
    energy resource, 333, **333**, *333*
    fossil fuel, **331**
    material resource, 332, **332**, *332*
    nonrenewable resource, 331, **331**
    recycling of, 382

renewable resource, 331, **331**
    use, 332–333
natural selection, **404**–405, *404–405*
    adaptation, **405**–406, 405
    genetic variation, **404**, *405*
    overproduction, 404, *405*
    principles of, *405*
neon, 137
neutron, **122**
nonlinear graph, 47
nonlinear relationship, **47**, *47*
nonmetal, 108, **135**
nonpoint-source pollution, **350**
nonrenewable resource, **331**
note taking, R12–15
no-till farming, 383
nucleic acid, 109, 514
nucleotide, **517**, *517–518*, 522
nucleus (of atom), **122**, *122–123*, 124–126
nutrition depletion, 343

observation, 28–29
ocean circulation, 246
ocean current, 216–229, 218, **218**, 242, 246, **299**
    characteristics of, 227, 273
    and climate, 302
    cool, 247, 273
    energy transport and, 227
    impact on climate, 299
    influencing weather, 272–273
    matter transport and, 227
    transport, 226
    warm, 273
    water movement in, 169, 246
offspring, 402–404, 408, 448, 458, **470**, 472, 474–476, 481–482, 486, 490, 494, 496
    characteristics of Guinea pig, *491*
    identical, 448
    organisms passing traits to, 402
    passage of genes from parents to, 482
    predictions about traits of, 496, *500*
organic compound, 109
organism, *348*, 417
    identification, 432
    relation, 418–419
overproduction, as principle of natural selection, 404, *405*
oxygen, *105*, 145, 364
ozone, 366
"ozone hole," 184
ozone layer, **184**, 366
    affected by air pollution, 371
ozone molecule, 182

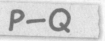

Pakicetus, *418*
paramecium, *448*
parent, **470**, 481–483, 494–495, 498